Placing Children in Special Education: A Strategy for Equity

Kirby A. Heller, Wayne H. Holtzman, and Samuel Messick, *Editors*

Panel on Selection and Placement of Students in Programs for the Mentally Retarded

Committee on Child Development Research and Public Policy

Commission on Behavioral and Social Sciences and Education

National Research Council

NATIONAL ACADEMY PRESS
Washington, D.C.   1982

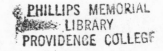

NOTICE: The project that is the subject of this report was approved by the Governing Board of the National Research Council, whose members are drawn from the Councils of the National Academy of Sciences, the National Academy of Engineering, and the Institute of Medicine. The members of the committee responsible for the report were chosen for their special competences and with regard for appropriate balance.

This report has been reviewed by a group other than the authors according to procedures approved by a Report Review Committee consisting of members of the National Academy of Sciences, the National Academy of Engineering, and the Institute of Medicine.

The National Research Council was established by the National Academy of Sciences in 1916 to associate the broad community of science and technology with the Academy's purposes of furthering knowledge and of advising the federal government. The Council operates in accordance with general policies determined by the Academy under the authority of its congressional charter of 1863, which establishes the Academy as a private, nonprofit, self-governing membership corporation. The Council has become the principal operating agency of both the National Academy of Sciences and the National Academy of Engineering in the conduct of their services to the government, the public, and the scientific and engineering communities. It is administered jointly by both Academies and the Institute of Medicine. The National Academy of Engineering and the Institute of Medicine were established in 1964 and 1970, respectively, under the charter of the National Academy of Sciences.

This project was supported by a contract from the Office for Civil Rights of the U.S. Department of Education. The contents do not necessarily reflect the views or policies of the agency.

Library of Congress Cataloging in Publication Data

National Research Council (U.S.). Panel on
  Selection and Placement of Students in
  Programs for the Mentally Retarded.
  Placing children in special education.

    1. Mentally handicapped children—Education—Congresses. 2. Students, Rating of—Congresses. 3. Educational tests and measurements—Congresses.
I. Heller, Kirby A. II. Holtzman, Wayne H. III. Messick, Samuel. IV. National Research Council (U.S.). Committee on Child Development Research and Public Policy. V. National Research Council (U.S.). Commission on Behavioral and Social Sciences and Education. VI. Title. [DNLM: 1. Education of mentally retarded. 2. Educational measurement. LC 4602 P698]
LC4602.N35 1982   371.92′8   82-3635
ISBN 0-309-03247-4   AACR2

Available from

NATIONAL ACADEMY PRESS
2101 Constitution Avenue, N.W.
Washington, D.C. 20418

Printed in the United States of America

PANEL ON SELECTION AND PLACEMENT OF STUDENTS IN PROGRAMS FOR THE MENTALLY RETARDED

WAYNE H. HOLTZMAN (*Chair*), Hogg Foundation for Mental Health, University of Texas, Austin

SAMUEL MESSICK (*Vice Chair*), Educational Testing Service, Princeton, N.J.

DONALD N. BERSOFF, Ennis, Friedman, Bersoff, and Ewing and University of Maryland School of Law

IAN CANINO, Department of Pediatric Psychiatry, Columbia Presbyterian Medical Center, New York

C. KEITH CONNERS, Department of Psychiatry, Children's Hospital, Washington, D.C.

ALONZO A. CRIM, Superintendent, Atlanta Public Schools

JAMES J. GALLAGHER, Frank Porter Graham Child Development Center, University of North Carolina

THOMAS H. GILHOOL, Public Interest Law Center of Philadelphia

ASA GRANT HILLIARD, College of Education, Georgia State University

REGINALD B. JONES, Department of Education and Department of Afro-American Studies, University of California, Berkeley

JANE R. MERCER, Department of Sociology, University of California, Riverside

JOHN U. OGBU, Department of Anthropology, University of California, Berkeley

AMADO M. PADILLA, Department of Psychology, University of California, Los Angeles

LAUREN B. RESNICK, Learning Research and Development Center, University of Pittsburgh

ROBERT J. SERFLING, Department of Mathematical Sciences, The Johns Hopkins University

KIRBY A. HELLER, Study Director
JEFFREY R. TRAVERS, Senior Consultant
JEREMY D. FINN, Senior Research Associate
SUZANNE S. MAGNETTI, Research Associate
WILLIAM E. BICKEL, Consultant
ANN M. DAVIS, Administrative Secretary

COMMITTEE ON CHILD DEVELOPMENT RESEARCH AND PUBLIC POLICY

v

Contents

Preface

For the past 12 years, national surveys by the Office for Civil Rights (OCR) of the U.S. Department of Education have revealed an overrepresentation of minority children and males in special education programs for mentally retarded students. The 1978 survey, for example, indicated that across the nation black children constituted 38 percent of the students in classes for educable mentally retarded students, although black students constitute only about 16 percent of all elementary and secondary students. Charged with ensuring the compliance of local school districts with prohibitions of discrimination against minority students, OCR turned to the National Research Council for help in understanding the nature of this disproportion and in formulating sound policies for carrying out its mandate.

The Panel on Selection and Placement of Students in Programs for the Mentally Retarded was established in 1979 under the auspices of the Committee on Child Development Research and Public Policy of the National Research Council. The panel's mission was twofold: (1) to determine the factors that account for disproportionate representation of minority students and males in special education programs, especially programs for mentally retarded students and (2) to identify placement criteria or practices that do not affect minority students and males disproportionately. The task confronting the panel required balance, objectivity, and dispassion in an area marked by emotion and controversy in the courts, in the schools, and in society at large.

Comprised of 15 individuals representing a wide range of viewpoints, the panel included some members closely identified with the specific issue of disproportion in special education and some who were known for their expertise in related fields—education of the handicapped, testing, and school administration. Most of the panel members, however, were selected because they were not closely allied with the questions at issue or current debates. These members represented such fields as law, psychiatry, statistics, and clinical psychology. All have changed their views in some way during the course of the panel's work. All agree on the panel's primary message and recommendations.

We began our work by commissioning several preliminary studies, a series of background papers, and an extensive analysis of recent survey data from the OCR. Additional papers provided a basis for debating the major questions and issues involved in the disproportion of minorities and males in classes for mentally retarded students.

From the outset we recognized the difficulties facing us, but, perhaps naively, we did not recognize how difficult they would prove to be. To understand why minority students, and to a lesser extent males, are disproportionately represented in programs for educable mentally retarded children, we felt obliged to examine a wide range of topics—the role of IQ testing; the appropriateness of placing special education students in regular classes; the meaning, causes, and proper assessment of mental retardation in schools; and racial discrimination in educational practices. Each of these obviously demands a report of its own. Each of these disturbed us, divided us, and many times distracted us from our original mandate.

Our ultimate message is a strikingly simple one. The purpose of the entire process—from referral for assessment to eventual placement in special education—is to improve instruction for children. The focus on educational benefits for children became our unifying theme, cutting across disciplinary boundaries and sharply divergent points of view.

With this goal in mind we recast many of the original questions that had been asked. Our initial question "What are the causes of disproportionate representation of minorities and males in special education" became *"Why* is disproportionate representation of minorities and males a problem?" This change in focus altered both the assumptions on which our work was based and the goals toward which we strived. Our reformulated question is premised on the belief that disproportion per se is not a problem; unequal numbers do not by themselves constitute an inequity. Instead, disproportion signals that certain underlying conditions may be problematic, and the task becomes one of identifying these conditions. The reformulated question also changed the outcomes of our study. Rather than suggest procedures that eliminate or reduce disproportion, we recommend practices that directly redress the inequitable conditions underlying it.

Two key issues are at the heart of the debate about disproportion. First, disproportion is a problem when children are invalidly assessed for placement in programs for educable mentally retarded children. Second, disproportion is a problem when children receive low-quality instruction. This problem may arise in the regular classroom, where opportunities for academic success may be restricted, or in the special education classroom, where a child's educational progress may falter due to lowered or inappropriate expectations and goals.

These two themes—the validity of assessment and the quality of instruction—are the subject of this report. Valid assessment, in our view, is marked by its relevance to and usefulness for instruction. These criteria move the debate away from the traditional questions raised by IQ testing to concern with the educational implications of assessment. This narrowing of the purpose of assessment is accompanied by a broadening of its focus. To understand a child's learning problems, one must assess not only intellectual functioning and other aspects of the individual outside the intellectual domain but also the contribution of the child's educational environment to his or her performance in school. Individual failures in school must be understood within this broadened context. Valid assessment of the learning environment is as critical as valid assessment of the individual.

Our views about labeling children and determining the setting in which special education services are best provided were similarly guided by an emphasis on their relevance for instruction. Again, arguments that have traditionally dominated the field—e.g., those for and against "mainstreaming"—were viewed as less critical than evidence for and against the utility of certain instructional practices for helping children with academic difficulties.

This report is primarily concerned with racial and ethnic disproportion; less attention has been paid to sex disproportion. Much of the scientific literature we reviewed as well as the public debates concerning disproportion in special education have neglected the phenomenon of sex disproportion or subordinated it to the more visible and controversial issue of racial and ethnic disproportion. Although we did not examine sex disproportion in isolation or in detail, the recommendations of this report are as equally valid for males as they are for minority children. More important, the analysis we offer applies to all children who have been invalidly assessed or have become the victims of poor instruction, regardless of their racial or ethnic identification or sex.

Our recommendations are consistent with current law and educational theory and best practice. Some critics will no doubt point out that what we recommend is already taking place and that our suggestions are not relevant to current practices, at least as they exist in some school districts. Others may consider the recommendations idealistic and perhaps farfetched. The recommendations are offered in the spirit of adhering faithfully to principles of sound educational practice. We hope they will be useful in guiding practice. We know they will stimulate debate. If such debate is moved onto a new and productive level of discourse that eventually moves children into better educational settings, we will consider the report successful.

This volume comprises two parts. The first is the panel's report and represents the consensus of the panel members. The second is a series of background papers that were prepared by staff and consultants to inform the panel, to aid its deliberations, and to provide comprehensive reviews of literature that support the conclusions of the report. While each paper represents the views of its author, all papers were carefully reviewed by the panel and relevant outside experts.

Although the report closely follows the work of the panel as a group, at some point it becomes necessary for individuals to transform panel discussions and agreement into a written document. Chapter 1 was principally drafted by Samuel Messick, Kirby A. Heller, and Jeremy D. Finn. Chapter 2 was drafted by Kirby A. Heller and Suzanne S. Magnetti. The preparation of Chapters 3 and 4 was guided by subgroups of the panel: Jeffrey R. Travers drafted Chapter 3 primarily in consultation with Donald N. Bersoff, C. Keith Conners, Reginald B. Jones, Jane R. Mercer, and Samuel Messick. Lauren B. Resnick drafted Chapter 4 primarily in consultation with James J. Gallagher and Asa Grant Hilliard. Chapter 5 was drafted by Kirby A. Heller, Samuel Messick, Jeffrey R. Travers, and Jeremy D. Finn.

The final consensus and report endorsed by this diverse, hard-working panel would not have been achieved without the able assistance of Kirby A. Heller, study director, and her colleagues, Jeremy D. Finn and Suzanne S. Magnetti. Special thanks also go to Jeffrey R. Travers, who helped the panel in the initial stages of its work as study director and continued to work closely with the panel as a consultant and writer. The major contributions of Kirby A. Heller, Jeremy D. Finn, Suzanne S. Magnetti, and Jeffrey R. Travers, and special consultants William E. Bickel and Jack P. Shonkoff, are also evident in the background papers they wrote for this volume. Dorothy Gilford prepared important background materials and helped with the analysis of the survey data. Christine L. McShane edited the report and prepared it for publication. Ann M.

Davis, administrative secretary, typed the many drafts of this report and helped with the countless administrative details that were essential to the panel's functioning.

While at the OCR, Rebecca Fitch helped launch the project, and she maintained her interest throughout. In the Commission on Behavioral and Social Sciences and Education, David A. Goslin, executive director, gave support and encouragement when they were crucial for maintaining the enthusiastic involvement of panel members. Discussions with members of the parent Committee on Child Development Research and Public Policy stimulated and guided the panel throughout the course of its work. The committee's executive officer, Cheryl D. Hayes, was a source of invaluable advice to the panel and its staff. The report was critically reviewed at various stages in its development by a number of specialists too numerous to mention by name but nonetheless of great value to the panel.

Finally, my personal thanks go to my fellow panel members, especially the vice chair, Samuel Messick, for their unfailing support and willingness to close ranks around a central theme and set of recommendations despite divergent viewpoints.

WAYNE H. HOLTZMAN, *Chair*
Panel on Selection and Placement of Students
in Programs for the Mentally Retarded

REPORT
OF THE
PANEL

1

Introduction:
Disproportion in Special Education

The overrepresentation of minorities in special education classes is a pressing and volatile issue, not only because of society's continuing concern with equality of opportunity and equity of treatment but also because of an increasing number of legal statutes and judicial precedents that have broadened entitlement to needed educational services. Unequal representation in special education is not a new phenomenon. What is at issue is whether it constitutes an inequity, either new or long-standing. The controversies that surrounded the earliest programs for children considered unable to profit from regular instruction still dominate the field of special education today: Is there a harmful and enduring stigma associated with placement in special education classes? Is the quality of education in special classes adequate? Can special education students ever return to the regular classroom? Are the methods of assessment and assignment fair and unbiased?

Recent legislation attempts to ensure that the benefits of special education programs are available to all who need them. Both Section 504 of the Rehabilitation Act of 1973 and the Education for All Handicapped Children Act of 1975 (P.L. 94-142) require the formal identification of children with handicapping conditions and the provision of appropriate educational services. At the same time, the equal protection clause of the Fourteenth Amendment and Title VI of the Civil Rights Act of 1964 prohibit the classification of persons in such a way that disproportionate harm—including the harm of separateness—accrues to members of a group identified by race, color, or national origin. The Office for Civil

Rights (OCR), having enforcement responsibilities under Title VI and Section 504, routinely examines disproportion in special education and other programs by means of a biannual survey of the nation's school and school district enrollments. An immediate and primary concern of OCR, revealed by the survey data, is a persistent disproportion of minority children and males in classes for educable mentally retarded (EMR) students. The Panel on Selection and Placement of Students in Programs for the Mentally Retarded was established to aid OCR in identifying factors that account for this disproportion and in developing procedures for remedying the imbalance.

The panel analyzed the data gathered by OCR through its Elementary and Secondary School Survey to document the nature and extent of disproportion in special education classes. The analysis accomplished three purposes: (1) it verified that the relative disproportions cited by OCR do indeed exist, documenting in the process the magnitude and distribution of minority-white and sex differences in EMR rates; (2) it identified geographic trends in racial and sex imbalances in EMR programs; and (3) it provided an examination of possible correlates of disproportion (e.g., the size and racial composition of a school district, the overall prevalance of EMR classifications in a district, and the desegregation status of a district) as well as an appraisal of minority-white and sex differences for special education programs other than EMR and for individual racial or ethnic categories. By disaggregating the survey data to the district level, this analysis provided a detailed picture of the disproportion by race or ethnicity, by sex, and by special education classification. The next section of this chapter provides a summary of the results of the panel's statistical investigation; a detailed examination of these analyses is presented in the paper by Finn in this volume.

Having confirmed that EMR disproportion is a nationwide phenomenon and that there are clear geographic and demographic conditions under which it occurs to a greater extent, the panel considered a long list of possible "causes." These include characteristics of the legal and administrative systems within which special education programs operate, characteristics of the instruction and of the instructional setting, characteristics of the students themselves as well as possible biases in their assessments, characteristics of the students' homes and family environments, and the broader historical and cultural contexts in which they are embedded.

It seemed likely that if we could identify the probable causes of disproportion, we could then determine effective solutions. However, the panel recognized that disproportion is very probably determined by multiple interacting factors that are inextricably confounded in any concrete instance. To focus on identifying causes, especially with the hopes of correcting or eliminating them to directly reduce disproportion, was deemed insufficient and unfruitful. Furthermore, to continue to focus on factors associated with disproportionate placement rates unduly emphasizes statistical differences that are simply symptomatic of other, more significant issues. Altering placement rates and reducing disproportion in EMR programs may remedy one set of problems—e.g., the immediate problem of racial imbalance—but it does not attend to the fundamental educational problems that underlie student placement in programs for mentally retarded students. Rather than continuing to explore plausible explanations or underlying causes, the panel focused on recurring dimensions of the problem, common to a variety of causes, that cut through the issues in potentially powerful ways.

Accordingly, we recast the issue of existing disproportionality by asking *why* the overrepresentation of minorities in EMR programs is perceived as a problem. The controversy has typically centered on two assumptions. First, it is claimed that assessment procedures may lead to inappropriate placement and services for certain children, especially blacks, who are not really "mentally retarded." This debate has traditionally focused on the use of IQ scores to place children in EMR programs. The second assumption, directly related to the first, concerns perceptions of the EMR programs themselves. EMR classes are often perceived as programs offering few valid educational services, channeling students into tracks that impede their return to regular programs while isolating them from their regular classroom peers. These negative views of the services offered in EMR classes are in marked contrast to the more positive perceptions of other programs designed to provide special services. For example, the significant overrepresentation of minorities in Title I programs has not been contested in major court cases, presumably because such children are perceived as obtaining effective remedial services designed to help them achieve the levels attained by their regular classroom peers.

From this perspective, the key issue is not disproportionality per se but rather the validity of referral and assessment procedures and the quality of instruction received, whether in the regular classroom or in special education settings. If needed and effective educational services are provided in the least restrictive environment to students validly targeted, then any resulting inequality in minority representation in those programs would not constitute an inequity. Emphasizing the validity of referral and assessment procedures and the quality of special education programs and outcomes is consistent with legal tenets since all four major laws stipulating entitlements to special education services focus on consequences, either in terms of harm to be avoided or in the types and quality of services to be provided.

THE EXTENT OF EMR DISPROPORTION
IN AMERICAN PUBLIC SCHOOLS

The panel sought to describe the magnitude of disproportion in EMR programs by race or ethnicity and by sex. The survey data collected biannually by OCR were used for this purpose. Although inferences concerning the processes that lead to disproportion and the appropriateness or validity of special education placements cannot be drawn from these data, they do illuminate important differences in placement rates and the context in which these differences arise. Most striking in the description is the extreme variability in the magnitude of disproportion; these differences are attributable to ethnic group membership, to geographic region, to specific demographic characteristics of districts, and to handicapping condition.

The 1978 OCR survey sampled 6,040 school districts including 54,082 schools, about one third of the districts in the nation.[1] Questionnaires were sent to all district offices and to each school, requesting counts of the total number of students enrolled, the number enrolled in special education programs, and additional global characteristics of the student population. All student counts were classified by racial or ethnic identity,[2] and some were also classified by sex. Both sex and race classifications were required (but not sex-by-race cross classifications) for students in special education programs for educable mentally retarded, trainable mentally retarded, seriously emotionally disturbed, specific learning-disabled, and

---

[1]Details of the sampling design for 1978 are given in U.S. Department of Health, Education, and Welfare (1978a,b). The survey depends for its accuracy on an adequate count and report from numerous school districts and thus may be subject to some unknown degree of error. (This issue is discussed further in the paper by Finn in this volume.)

[2]According to the general instructions for the fall 1978 school survey (Form OS/CR 102), the following racial or ethnic categories are identified:

American Indian or Alaskan native: A person having origins in any of the original peoples of North America and who maintains cultural identification through tribal affiliation or community recognition.

Asian or Pacific Islander: A person having origins in any of the original peoples of the Far East, Southeast Asia, the Pacific Islands, or the Indian subcontinent. This area includes, for example, China, India, Japan, Korea, the Philippine Islands, and Samoa.

Hispanic: A person of Mexican, Puerto Rican, Cuban, Central or South American, or other Spanish culture or origin—regardless of race.

Black, not of Hispanic origin: A person having origins in any of the black racial groups of Africa.

White, not of Hispanic origin: A person having origins in any of the original peoples of Europe, North Africa, or the Middle East.

speech-impaired children, as defined by the Office of Special Education and adapted by OCR.[3]

For purposes of correlating the degree of disproportion with other school-related characteristics, a sensitive "log-odds index" of disproportion was calculated for each special education category.[4] The index is positive whenever the odds of minorities being assigned to a special program is higher than the odds for whites; it is zero if the odds for minorities

---

[3]According to the general instructions to the fall 1978 school survey, the following special programs are identified:

Educable mentally retarded (or handicapped)—a condition of mental retardation which includes pupils who are educable in the academic, social, and occupational areas even though moderate supervision may be necessary.

Trainable mentally retarded (or handicapped)—a condition of mental retardation which includes pupils who are capable of only very limited meaningful achievement in the traditional basic academic skills but who are capable of profiting from programs of training in self-care and simple job or vocational skills.

Seriously emotionally disturbed—a condition exhibiting one or more of the following characteristics over a long period of time and to a marked degree, which adversely affects educational performance: an inability to learn which cannot be explained by intellectual, sensory, or health factors; an inability to build or maintain satisfactory interpersonal relationships with peers and teachers; inappropriate types of behavior or feelings under normal circumstances; a general pervasive mood of unhappiness or depression; or a tendency to develop physical symptoms or fears associated with personal or school problems. The term includes children who are schizophrenic or autistic. The term does not include children who are socially maladjusted, unless it is determined that they are seriously emotionally disturbed.

Specific learning disability—a disorder in one or more of the basic psychological processes involved in understanding or in using language, spoken or written, which may manifest itself in an imperfect ability to listen, think, speak, read, write, spell, or to do mathematical calculations. The term includes such conditions as perceptual handicaps, brain injury, minimal brain dysfunction, dyslexia, and developmental aphasia. The term does not include children who have learning problems which are primarily the result of visual, hearing, or motor handicaps; of mental retardation; or of environmental, cultural, or economic disadvantage.

Speech-impaired—a communication disorder, such as stuttering, impaired articulation, a language impairment, or a voice impairment, which adversely affects a child's educational performance.

[4]The basic element in the log-odds index is the "odds" of being assigned to a particular special education category. For example, the odds of a minority student being assigned to an EMR class is the percentage of minority students classified as EMR divided by the percentage of minorities who are not in special programs. From Table 1, this is 2.54/92.60, or 0.027. The odds of a white student being classified as EMR is 1.06/94.12, or 0.011. The disproportion index is the ratio of these two odds, scaled by a natural logarithm transformation; that is, $\ln(0.027/0.011) = 0.89$. The *unscaled* odds ratio ranges from zero to infinity; values greater than unity indicate that the EMR odds for minorities is higher than those for

and whites is equal; and it is negative if the odds of minorities being assigned to special education classes is lower than the odds for whites. The log-odds index is a linear contrast of the logarithms of the two odds and has a distribution in the population of school districts that closely approximates the normal; thus, it is particularly appropriate for analysis by normal-theory methods, e.g., Pearson correlations or analysis of variance. Unfortunately, the index is not simple to interpret since it is unbounded, i.e., it can vary from $-\infty$ to $+\infty$, depending on the magnitude of the disproportion. For interpretive purposes, however, the log-odds index can be transformed to a measure of association, Yule's Q-statistic, which, like a correlation, is limited to values between -1 and $+1$.[5] For EMR programs, the association of race or ethnicity (minority versus nonminority) with placement (EMR versus none) is approximately $+.42$.

Although of some general interest, national aggregate indexes do not provide adequate means to describe the pattern of disproportional enrollment in special education classes. Disaggregation is particularly important since students are placed in special education programs on a district-by-district basis; hence, a wide range of placement rates and racial disproportions may be found among districts operating within the same state guidelines. The OCR survey provides data from which placement rates and the disproportion index may be calculated for each school district. State summary statistics can be obtained by averaging the log-odds measure across districts of similar size, with dispersion measures (e.g., the range or standard deviation) providing an indicator of variability within the larger unit. Such disaggregation prevents results for large districts from obscuring those for smaller districts. Moreover, districts with no students in a particular special education program are eliminated from the respective analyses and thus do not distort summary statistics. The 1978 OCR sample included 4,917 districts with both minority and white students enrolled in EMR programs; these districts provide the data base for statistical analyses of EMR disproportion.

Nationwide percentages of students in each of the five special education

---

whites, while values less than unity indicate that the EMR odds for minorities is lower than those for whites. The logarithmic transformation creates an index that is symmetric around zero, ranging from $-\infty$ to $+\infty$. Furthermore, the log-odds ratio is equivalent to the difference between the logarithms of the two odds—i.e., $\ln(0.027/0.011) = \ln(0.027) - \ln(0.001)$—and the transformation to a logarithmic scale produces linear contrasts. For further information, see Bishop et al., 1975.

[5]The relationship is given by $Q = (a - 1)/(a + 1)$, where $a = e^x$ and x is the log-odds index.

program areas, as estimated from the survey data, are given in Table 1[6]; more refined breakdowns are presented in Tables 2 through 5.

Despite the fact that a race or ethnicity EMR disproportion appears from Table 1 to be a national phenomenon—the average percentage of minority students in EMR classes exceeds the average percentage of whites in every state except four[7]—massive regional variation in minority representation is evident in the survey data (see the paper by Finn in this volume for a breakdown by state). The average disproportion in southern states (Table 2) is consistently and notably high. Among districts in the South, the median disproportion index is 1.50, which corresponds to an association (Q) of .63. Although substantially lower than in the South, relatively high minority disproportion also pervades the data for the states bordering the South; the median log-odds disproportion value is 0.66, corresponding to a Q value of .32. Minority disproportion does not appear as a general problem in the Northeast or the Midwest, where the corresponding measure of association in each region is .03. Minority disproportion in the West is also relatively low; the association (Q) of race or ethnicity with EMR placement is .17.

Dramatic differences in minimum and maximum percentages of minorities assigned to EMR classes are also evident in summary regional data (Table 3). Again, the South exhibits the highest minimum and maximum average EMR placement rates for minority students of any geographic region—up to an average of 9.09 percent of minorities enrolled in EMR classes in Alabama. The northeastern and midwestern states show a lower range for minority placement than does the South. At the low extreme, the range of placements for minorities in the West is similar to the relatively homogeneous range for whites throughout the country. In addition, there is a regional tendency for larger disproportions to occur in areas in which the total proportion of children in EMR classes is high. This effect also operates at both the state and district levels. The data indicate that, in general, smaller degrees of disproportion occur in districts, states, and regions that have smaller proportions of students in EMR programs.

The average level of racial disproportion in EMR programs is smallest for districts with 1,000–3,000 students. It is somewhat higher for districts with fewer than 1,000 students, higher for districts in the 3,000–10,000 student range, and highest for districts with more than 30,000 students.

[6]The figures in Table 1 are based on projections to state and national totals obtained by weighting each district in the sample by the inverse of its sampling probability. Details of the procedure are given in the 1976 survey *Final File Documentation* (U.S. Department of Health, Education, and Welfare, 1978a).

[7]The exceptions, New Hampshire, Vermont, West Virginia, and Iowa, have very small percentages of minority students.

10

TABLE 1 Nationwide Special Education Placements, by Sex and by Race or Ethnicity

Classification	Race or Ethnicity				Sex			
	Percentage		Log Odds (Minority-White)	Q	Percentage		Log-Odds (Male-Female)	Q
	Minority	White			Male	Female		
Educable mentally retarded (EMR)	2.54	1.06	0.89	.42	1.65	1.19	0.37	.18
Trainable mentally retarded (TMR)	0.33	0.19	0.55	.27	0.25	0.20	0.26	.13
Seriously emotionally disturbed (SED)	0.42	0.29	0.37	.18	0.48	0.16	1.14	.52
Specific learning disabilities (SLD)	2.29	2.30	0.01	.01	3.22	1.33	0.92	.43
Speech-impaired (SI)	1.82	2.02	−0.09	−.04	2.40	1.53	0.48	.24
None of above	92.60	94.12			92.00	95.59		

NOTE: Weighted projections to national totals, from *State, Regional, and National Summaries of Data from the 1978 Civil Rights Survey of Elementary and Secondary Schools*, prepared for OCR by Killalea Associates, Inc., April 1980.

TABLE 2   Regional Summary of EMR Disproportion

Region	Number of States[a]	Race or Ethnicity		Sex	
		Median Log-Odds	Q	Median Log-Odds	Q
Northeast	9	0.06	.03	0.30	.15
Border	6	0.66	.32	0.50	.24
South	11	1.50	.63	0.51	.25
Midwest	11	0.055	.03	0.38	.19
West	12	0.34	.17	0.35	.17

[a]Hawaii and the District of Columbia, each with only one school district, are not included.

The relation of disproportion to the percentage of minority students in a district is not the same for smaller and larger districts. In districts of all sizes, there is an increase from small or nonexistent average disproportion to moderate disproportion as minority enrollment increases from 0 to 50 percent. In medium and large districts, as the minority enrollment increases from 50 to 90 percent or more, racial disproportion in EMR programs decreases to close to zero. Among small districts, by contrast, those with 50 percent minority enrollment or greater have still larger disproportions (see Figure 1 in the paper by Finn in this volume). These may involve a significant number of children at a statewide or regional level.

Nationwide placement percentages are presented in Table 4 for five specific racial or ethnic groups in each of the five types of special education programs. As is to be expected, since blacks represent approximately two

TABLE 3   Minimum and Maximum Average EMR Percentages, by Region

Region	Number of States[a]	Minority		White	
		Minimum	Maximum	Minimum	Maximum
Northeast	4	1.83	3.35	0.71	1.60
Border	4	2.54	5.20	0.70	2.41
South	11	3.60	9.09	0.84	2.23
Midwest	5	1.57	5.42	1.07	2.46
West	7	0.85	2.51	0.59	1.17

[a]For 31 states with more than 10 percent minority enrollment each.

TABLE 4 Nationwide Special Education Placements for Specific Racial/Ethnic Groups

	American Indian or Alaskan Native	Asian or Pacific Island	Hispanic	Black	White	All Students
Percentage of student population	0.79	1.42	6.75	15.72	75.32	100.00
Percentage in special education programs:						
Educable mentally retarded (EMR)	1.73	0.37	0.98	3.46	1.07	1.43
Trainable mentally retarded (TMR)	0.23	0.15	0.24	0.39	0.19	0.23
Seriously emotionally disturbed (SED)	0.33	0.10	0.29	0.50	0.29	0.32
Specific learning disabilities (SLD)	3.49	1.27	2.58	2.23	2.32	2.31
Speech-impaired (SI)	1.87	1.85	1.78	1.87	2.04	1.99

TABLE 5 Distribution of EMR Disproportion for Hispanic Students

Size Category	Number of Districts	Mean	Standard Deviation	Minimum		Maximum	
				Log-Odds	Q	Log-Odds	Q
Fewer than 1,000 students	124	1.08	1.71	−4.30	−.97	7.41	.99+
1,000 to 2,999 students	242	0.66	0.99	−2.13	−.79	7.67	.99+
3,000 to 9,999 students	232	0.47	0.85	−2.11	−.78	6.94	.99+
10,000 or more students	167	0.35	0.63	−3.35	−.93	2.17	.80
All districts	765	0.64	1.12	−4.30	−.97	7.67	.99+

thirds of the minority enrollment in the country's public schools, the pattern of black enrollment in each of the special program areas closely parallels that for the total minority population, as shown in Table 1.

Each of the other minority groups identified in the survey is characterized by some idiosyncratic discrepancies from the total minority group results. For example, students of Asian or Pacific Island origin are typically assigned to special education programs at rates that are considerably below those for whites. In small districts in several western states, however, positive disproportions are found that might reflect a relatively high incidence of recent immigrations. Verification of this hypothesis was not possible from the survey data. Although there is a tendency for American Indian or Alaskan native students to be assigned more frequently than white students to EMR programs, the OCR survey may not provide an adequate data base for evaluating the extent of disproportion, since relatively large numbers of American Indians are enrolled in schools or programs outside those sampled by OCR.

Despite the fact that the nationwide summary statistics indicate that the proportion of Hispanic pupils[8] enrolled in EMR classes is slightly below that for whites (Table 4), the reverse situation is true in 26 of 31 states reporting 10 percent or more total minority enrollment. To explore this apparent inconsistency, a subsample of school districts was selected in which Hispanic students comprise at least 5 percent of the total enrollment with at least 50 Hispanic students enrolled (see Table 5). Of the 4,917 districts in the survey data, 765 met these criteria. For this subsample, the average EMR disproportion is positive for each of the school district size intervals presented in Table 5. The striking aspect of the data in Table 5, however, is the broad range of log-odds indexes within each category of district size—from large negative disproportions (many fewer Hispanics than whites) to large positive disproportions (many more Hispanics than whites). Unlike disproportion for all minorities combined or for blacks in particular, the small Hispanic-white difference for the nation as a whole is an average of many sizable positive and negative disproportions. Correlates of this phenomenon, including the districts' racial composition and the availability of bilingual education, are discussed in the paper by Finn in this volume.

[8]The March 1980 Current Population Survey published by the U.S. Bureau of the Census estimates that 59.9 percent of the Hispanic population is of Mexican origin, 13.8 percent Puerto Rican, 6.3 percent Cuban, 7.7 percent Central and South American, and 12.3 percent of "other Spanish origin." While there may be noteworthy differences among these groups in school performance or factors affecting performance, research on educational programs frequently does not make such distinctions, and the OCR survey instruments obtain only total Hispanic counts. Furthermore, the subgroups are not geographically distinct; the census reveals that sizable Hispanic populations in most states include two or more of these subgroups.

Unlike disproportion by race or ethnicity, the overrepresentation of males in EMR programs is relatively uniform across geographic regions (Table 2). As a consequence of this relative uniformity in the sex disproportion, this summary has little distinctive information to impart about the demography of male-female placement in special education classes. Nonetheless, it must be kept in mind that the problems we address concerning minorities apply to males as well.

POTENTIAL CAUSES OF DISPROPORTION IN EMR PROGRAMS

Although the magnitude of the minority-white and male-female disproportion in EMR placements rates and the systematic variation in EMR disproportionality as a function of geographic region and demographic characteristics can be clearly documented, the factors that account for this disproportion are less easily analyzed. The multiplicity of potential causes of disproportionate placement rates may be categorized for purposes of a brief overview under six main rubrics:

1. Legal and administrative requirements
2. Characteristics of students
3. Quality of the instruction received
4. Possible biases in the assessment process
5. Characteristics of the home and family environment
6. Broader historical and cultural contexts

Each of these potential causes is described below.

Legal and Administrative Requirements

Federal, state, and local legal and administrative requirements establish a network of incentives and constraints within which special education programs operate. Definitions of particular diagnostic categories, policies adopted that establish a particular referral and evaluation system, and policies concerning the funding of special education programs affect which children are referred for special education, how they are evaluated and placed, and the types of services that are available in special education programs. Some of these factors may contribute to disproportionate placement of minorities in EMR programs. For example, funding schemes that directly tie the number of dollars made available to a special education program to the number of children in that program may encourage overcounting, and minority children may be more likely to be eligible and therefore placed in expanded special education programs. The legal and regulatory structure for the identification, assessment, and placement of students in special education programs and the fiscal factors that may influence these programs are discussed in more detail in Chapter 2 and in the paper by Magnetti in this volume on potential fiscal incentives.

CHARACTERISTICS OF STUDENTS

A variety of causes for disproportionate placement have been proposed that focus directly on the characteristics of students. Students may experience difficulty in school because of undiagnosed or untreated medical and physical problems (see the paper by Shonkoff in this volume); because of difficulties in information processing, comprehension, reasoning, or judgment; because of emotional or motivational disturbances, such as hyperactivity or anxiety, that disrupt or block effective learning; and because of the absence of adaptive skills and behaviors that are needed in school, etc. Learning deficiencies in the early grades may persist in later years and become barriers to future achievement.

QUALITY OF THE INSTRUCTION RECEIVED

An almost uniform feature of the selection process for EMR placement is that it begins with an observation of weak academic performance. Poor performance may be accompanied by other behaviors, such as disruptive classroom behavior, but referral for EMR placement seldom occurs in the absence of weak academic performance (see the paper by Bickel in this volume). To the extent that a greater proportion of minority children score below accepted norms on achievement measures used in particular schools, they will be overrepresented in the pool of "potential" special education children.

While academic failure is often attributed to characteristics of the learners, current achievement also reflects the opportunities available to learn in school. If such opportunities have been lacking or if the quality of instruction offered varies across subgroups of the school-age population, then school failure and subsequent EMR referral and placement may represent a lack of exposure to quality instruction for disadvantaged or minority children.

POSSIBLE BIASES IN THE ASSESSMENT PROCESS

The measures employed in classification procedures for EMR placement may not yield valid assessments of the cognitive skills of particular minority or disadvantaged groups. Much of the controversy regarding assessment has centered on mental ability tests from which IQ scores are derived. Frequently referred to as "IQ tests," these instruments play a primary role in the determination of eligibility for placement in EMR programs (see the paper by Bickel in this volume). Critics charge that such tests underestimate the skills of minority children—that the items do not tap the same underlying construct for minority groups as for white middle-class children, that particular items are insensitive to minority cultures, that differences exist in the predictive validity of the test for different groups. Furthermore, the test-taking situation may artificially depress the scores of minority children compared with those of whites. This position argues that there is a fundamental mismatch between the language and culture reflected in IQ tests and those of various minority groups. Any such mismatch could cause inferior performance on IQ tests by minorities, which in turn has profound implications for later educational experiences, including an increased likelihood of EMR placement. These issues are discussed in detail in Chapter 3 and in the paper by Travers in this volume.

In addition, it is possible that features of the placement process may contribute to overrepresentation of minorities in EMR programs. For example, minority students with academic problems may be referred for evaluation more often than other children experiencing similar academic difficulties. An analysis of the placement process and its contribution to minority overrepresentation in EMR programs is presented in the paper by Bickel in this volume.

CHARACTERISTICS OF THE HOME AND FAMILY ENVIRONMENT

Well-established relationships between parents' socioeconomic status and children's school performance have led to the investigation of variations in home environments and child-rearing styles as possible causes of low achievement among minority and disadvantaged children. Proposed differences in home environments include the extent to which motivational support is provided for cognitive achievement and the extent to which parents and others encourage verbal development and provide appropriate verbal models. Families may also differ dramatically in the degree to which children are encouraged or required to practice the use of complex systems of verbal symbols; the lack of such practice may be related both to the underdevelopment of cognitive skills and to an increased likelihood of EMR placement.

BROADER HISTORICAL AND CULTURAL CONTEXTS

As noted above, many of the proposed causes of disproportionate EMR placement are attributed to the student directly; so it is not surprising that to date, studies of mental retardation have generally emphasized characteristics of the individual. The problem of disproportion can also be viewed in a broader sociocultural context—not just the sociocultural influences on individual students of their familial and street cultures but a pervasive collective influence of minority status within a dominant majority culture. Discontinuities arise from the child's experiences as mediated by the family and home environment, especially when children from various subgroups are confronted with the curriculum and value structures of the public schools. Discontinuities may also arise from the collective historical confrontation and conflict between minority cultures and the dominant culture. This perspective emphasizes the importance of coping mechanisms and survival strategies that have developed in response to the long-term denial of equal opportunity, status, and rewards for minorities. From this analysis, possible societal causes of problems involving the educability of minority children may be identified that in turn contribute to disproportionate EMR placement rates.

DISPROPORTION: PROBLEMATIC OR SYMPTOMATIC?

The panel agreed that disproportion undoubtedly reflects all of these causes—singly and in combination—in some school districts some of the time. It became apparent, however, that even if the multiplex causes of EMR disproportion could be identified and disentangled, it is unlikely that remedies could be easily or effectively implemented. Furthermore, an analysis that relies on eliminating the causes of disproportion presupposes that effective solutions will result in a lack of disproportion in EMR programs. The assumption that effective practices are necessarily ones that reduce disproportion has led individual school districts, and in some cases entire states, to attempt simplistic solutions to the problem of disproportion, e.g., by eliminating part or all of the EMR program, by combining EMR classes with a program that has fewer nonminorities enrolled so that the overall racial enrollments are more balanced (see Table 4), or by prohibiting the use of IQ tests for EMR placement.

Approaches such as these may be misdirected. Each is likely to result in increased disproportion elsewhere in the educational system—in placement in other special education programs, in over-age grade placements, in disciplinary actions and dropout rates, or perhaps in the number of high school students who cannot read or perform simple numerical tasks proficiently or meet minimum competency standards at graduation. More significantly, such simplistic solutions fail to focus on the needs of the children or on the services that should be provided.

Rather than inquiring about the causes of disproportion and how to remedy the problem of disproportion in special education and in EMR classes in particular, a different and more constructive perspective is to ask: Under what circumstances does disproportion constitute a problem? While remedies to disproportion per se are based on an assumption that the disproportions in themselves constitute an inequity, the educational and social conditions under which such an assumption is true should be examined explicitly. Three aspects of the regular and special education programs and placement procedures are most salient in this regard: Disproportion is a problem (1) if children are invalidly placed in programs for mentally retarded students; (2) if they are unduly exposed to the likelihood of such placement by virtue of having received poor-quality regular instruction; or (3) if the quality and academic relevance of the special instruction programs block students' educational progress, including decreasing the likelihood of their return to the regular classroom.

Disproportion is a problem if children are invalidly placed in programs for mentally retarded students. If children are systematically assigned to EMR classes when other settings or programs would be more beneficial, then the assessment system for special education is of questionable validity, either for students in general or for particular subgroups that are overidentified. On the other hand, if the assessment system results in disproportion for particular subgroups, the assessments may still be successfully defended if their educational utility and relevance can be demonstrated. If not, the procedures should be changed to improve their validity and to lead more directly to appropriate and demonstrably effective educational practices. From this perspective, the panel's primary concern is with the validity of the assessment system and its implications for educational practice rather than with the resulting adverse disproportion as such.

The validity of assessment practices for placement in EMR programs is inextricably tied to the meaning of the category itself. Educable mental retardation is at least in part a function of the social and educational demands on an individual. The category resists precise definition, allowing a wide variety of measurement practices to be employed in the schools. While federal regulations implementing P.L. 94-142 define mental retardation as "significantly subaverage general intellectual functioning existing concurrently with deficits in adaptive behavior and manifested during the developmental period which adversely affects a child's educational performance," the translation of these guidelines into assessment practices is neither direct nor uniform. Thus the category EMR is operationalized in different ways at different times in different areas. For example, adaptive behavior ratings—sometimes focusing on achievement-related behaviors and other times not—play a variety of roles in special education assessment. In addition, IQ cutoff scores vary from district to district, and different cutoff scores may result in different proportions of students being classified as EMR; a regular student in one district may be classified as mentally retarded in another. At the same time, the resulting category of EMR children is far from homogeneous. To the extent that the use of the label initiates a process of individual diagnosis, planning, and treatment, the lack of homogeneity of the category is not troublesome. The use of the EMR label becomes problematic, however, when it is presumed to imply common instructional interventions for children with a wide variety of educational needs or when it leads to inappropriate expectations for the performance of certain children within this diagnostic category.

Moreover, the measures used to classify students as mentally retarded may not discriminate among groups of children who require or can profit from different educational settings or programs and hence may not be valid measures for the placements that result. Individually administered IQ tests are a major instrument used in the ultimate classification of referred students. The fact that IQ scores predict a variety of school achievements makes such tests appealing, and their high reliability gives the user confidence in the results. However, the predictive power of the IQ does not necessarily make it a good measure of mental processes; different processes may underlie the same IQ scores for different groups of children, and different types of remediation may be necessary in cases of poor performance. For example, it has frequently been argued that levels of motivation and effort of minority students are systematically different from those of white students. Similarly, language factors undoubtedly affect performance more for some groups than others. IQ tests administered entirely in English to students for whom English is a second language are an extreme case in point. Because of these and a host of other factors, there is no direct way to infer the source of a child's difficulty from incorrectly answered test items, nor does a test score or a profile of subscores provide the kinds of information needed to design an individualized curriculum for a child in academic difficulty.

Furthermore, despite the mandates of federal laws and regulations, imprecision and looseness in the referral, assessment, and placement systems cannot prevent discretion and personal bias from affecting placement decisions. After all, referral rests largely in the hands of the classroom teacher. If the teacher is distracted by the higher activity level of boys or feels uncomfortable in the presence of minority students, then those groups may be more likely to be referred for possible special placement. Similarly, the choice of assessment instruments and their interpretation remain largely in the domain of the school psychologist. Local discretion at many points in the placement process thus allows a wide range of factors, some of which may be extraneous, to affect placement decisions.

Disproportion is a problem if children are unduly exposed to the likeli-

hood of EMR placement by being in schools or classes with poor-quality regular instruction. Students are referred for special education assessment primarily after they have experienced academic failure. However, children whose regular classroom instruction is poor may experience failure at a higher rate than they would if the quality of instruction were better. Since assessment instruments typically measure the outcomes of learning rather than learning processes, there is a danger that the child who has not learned because of poor instruction will be judged unable to learn from any instruction.

The unequal distribution of quality instruction in large urban centers with high minority enrollments, compared with that in higher-income suburban areas, has long been a point of contention and debate. The well-established differences in the outcomes of schooling as a function of socioeconomic and racial or ethnic variation (see, for example, Coleman et al., 1966; Education Commission of the States, 1974) raise significant questions about the quality of instruction in schools serving children from low-income areas. This issue, in turn, has significant implications for the numbers of children who require special education services. Would fewer minority students be classified as mentally retarded if they were exposed to the highest quality instructional practices?

Disproportion is a problem if the quality and academic relevance of instruction in special classes block students' educational progress, including decreasing the likelihood of their return to the regular classroom. There has been much debate over the advantages and disadvantages of separate classes for children diagnosed as EMR. Proponents point to the advantages of smaller classes and more individualized instruction for EMR students. Critics argue that expectations for children classified as EMR are low and that behaviors in the classroom are adversely affected by these expectations. In addition, they charge that the EMR curriculum—based on the assumption that educable mental retardation is a permanent and unremediable disability—is not designed to help students learn the skills necessary to return to a regular instructional setting. Indeed, early concepts of mental retardation were explicit on this issue; Doll (1941) included both "constitutional origin" and "essentially incurable" among the necessary components of the definition of mental deficiency. However, early beliefs that intelligence is predetermined and fixed by genetic endowment have been replaced by the understanding that intelligence is not fixed at birth, that it can be modified through environmental manipulation, and that it partially reflects learned skills and behaviors (Hunt, 1961; Kirk, 1958). Similarly, current professional definitions and views of mental retardation emphasize observed levels of functioning and behavior rather than permanent and unalterable biological conditions inherent in the individual.

Thus, a reasonable goal for many EMR students, children who are considered only mildly mentally retarded, and especially those in the elementary school grades, may be to reenter the regular instructional program following the provision of effective remedial services.

The question as to what constitutes quality instruction for students in special programs is complex, both because there is a variety of outcomes to consider (including the positive and negative effects on the special group, the positive and negative effects on the regular students, and the consequences for the regular-classroom teacher) and because EMR programs frequently serve children with a wide mix of functional needs (including diverse combinations of cognitive disabilities and adaptive behavior problems). Research on the efficacy of EMR classes has generally focused on the effects of particular settings—regular classes versus separate special education classes—rather than on the characteristics of effective instruction. Given that children in EMR programs have functional educational needs that are pressing and real, improved educational practices depend on an appropriate match between instruction and each child's individual needs.

A significant question also arises as to the mechanism by which special instruction may best be provided. In particular, to what extent must children be classified and labeled according to a generic class of deficiencies in order to receive special education services? Diagnostic categories such as EMR may be more an administrative convenience than an educational necessity, allowing schools to count the number of children in this and other special programs in accord with federal requirements. If categorical labels are required for administrative purposes, they could be chosen to reflect the educational services provided, thereby emphasizing the responsibilities of school systems rather than the failings of the child.

A LOOK AHEAD

The statistical phenomenon of different percentages of minority and white students in programs for mentally retarded students has a number of political, scientific, and philosophical dimensions. While the sources of disproportion are legion, the more basic issues are educational. Disproportion in EMR classes may be indicative of a significant inequity if children are invalidly placed in such programs, if poor instruction in the regular classroom increases the likelihood that certain children more than others will be referred or placed in EMR classes, or if EMR classes do not provide instruction commensurate with the functional needs of the individual. Thus, by focusing on the conditions under which the inequality of placement proportions signals inequity of treatment, two major educational issues are highlighted: (1) the validity of referral, assessment, and placement procedures and (2) the quality of instruction received, whether in the regular classroom or in special education settings. These two critical issues are explored in detail in this report.

Refocusing attention on the questions of validity and quality—i.e., the valid assessment of students' functional needs and the provision of high-quality, effective instruction—has consequences affecting research and practice for students in special education and regular programs alike. If this new focus leads to the formulation of effective instructional programs for individuals in the least restrictive environment, then the statistical issue of disproportion—by race or ethnicity or by sex—ceases to be a problem.

2
Placement in Special Education: Historical Developments and Current Procedures

In the United States, definitions of educable mental retardation and methods of recognizing its existence are closely tied to social expectations inherent in our education system. In contrast to the often obvious manifestations of severe mental deficiency, educable mental retardation is not as easily identifiable. In fact, the category itself did not exist until the advent of compulsory education at the turn of the century and the adoption of intelligence tests as a simple method of tagging deficient performance. Even today it is not recognized by many cultures in less-developed areas of the world and is identified at widely varying rates among industrialized countries.

To understand the concepts and issues concerning the identification and education of educable mentally retarded (EMR) children, we first describe characteristics of children identified as mildly or educably mentally retarded. We then review the historical origins of special education in America. Within the historical context, the central role of the standardized intelligence test for identification and placement of mentally retarded students receives special note. The development of a nationally supported system of special education set the stage for a rising debate over disproportionate representation of black students and, to a lesser extent, Hispanic students in classes for EMR children. This controversy has resulted in recent court decisions and federal and state legislation dealing with placement procedures and the rights of handicapped children.

We turn then to a detailed examination of current procedures for special education placement. According to the regulations of Section 504 of the Rehabilitation Act and P.L. 94-142, a child can be placed in an EMR program only after various stages in the process of referral, assessment, and placement have been completed. The relation of each step in the process to the eventual receipt of the EMR label is discussed, with special attention to those factors that mediate the placement of minority students.

WHO ARE THE CHILDREN CLASSIFIED AS EMR?

Defining and describing the population of EMR children is fraught with difficulties because of the inherently social nature of such identification. A child is considered to be educably mentally retarded only after he or she has proceeded through the steps of referral, evaluation, and placement in the classificatory systems used by schools. He or she may receive the label not only on the basis of identified subnormal functioning but also as a consequence of administrative factors operating within schools.

Formal definitions of mental retardation reflect the changing social perceptions of those who are considered members of this group. Although several classification systems for mental retardation exist in this country, the one that is most commonly used by schools—and adopted, with only slight modification by P.L. 94-142—is that of the American Association on Mental Deficiency (AAMD). The AAMD defines mental retardation as "significantly subaverage general intellectual functioning existing concurrently with deficits in adaptive behavior and manifested during the developmental period" (Grossman, 1977:5).[1] The term "significantly subaverage" refers to an upper limit of two standard deviations below the mean score for measured intelligence. The highest category of mental retardation is "mild," equivalent to the education category EMR, and covers those whose IQ scores are between 55 and 70. This definition differs from the previous AAMD definition of mental retardation (1959), which included the category "borderline retardation," which had IQ score limits from one to two standard deviations below the mean. With this change in definition, many children previously considered mentally retarded, although mildly so, were transferred to the normal population.

Not only has the definition of mental retardation changed, but the boundaries that define eligibility for placement in programs for mentally retarded students in public schools also vary among states and districts. For example, a child with an IQ of 75 may be considered EMR in one state, while the same child would not be eligible for such a placement in another state.

---

[1]A new edition of the AAMD's *Manual on Terminology and Classification in Mental Retardation* is expected to be published in 1982. It will incorporate modest revisions to the current AAMD definition of mental retardation.

Estimates of the prevalence of mental retardation lack precision because of the absence of a clear categorical definition. For example, when IQ scores alone are used as evidence of mental retardation,[2] an arbitrary cutoff of two standard deviations below the mean IQ of 100 would be an IQ of 70, and the prevalence of all degrees of mental retardation would be 2.28 percent. Studies that examined intelligence alone derived figures close to this percentage (Birch et al., 1970; Mercer, 1973; Rutter et al., 1970). The introduction of additional criteria to the definition, such as adaptive behavior measures (Mercer, 1973; Tarjan et al., 1973) or the use of such selective screening mechanisms as nominations by school staff (Birch et al., 1970), reduce the percentage of children identified as mentally retarded to between 1.0 and 1.3 percent. The total percentage of students in EMR classes in 1978 was closer to these values;[3] it is estimated from the OCR school survey to be 1.4 percent.

SOME DESCRIPTIVE INFORMATION ABOUT THE EMR POPULATION[4]

Different definitions of mental retardation yield discrepant prevalence rates, and the methods used in a particular study to define mental retardation determine which children are included in the category. There is, nonetheless, some consistency in the characteristics of individuals currently classified as educable or mildly mentally retarded within our school systems.

Age

One of the most consistent findings is the marked drop in prevalence rates of mild mental retardation with age. In a variety of social contexts and regardless of the specific definition employed, the number of children identified as mentally retarded reaches a maximum in the elementary and junior high school years and drops precipitously thereafter (Lapouse and Weitzner, 1970). About two-thirds of the individuals diagnosed as mildly mentally retarded may disappear into the normal population during late adolescence, losing the label once they leave school (Tarjan et al., 1973). Since schools have always been the principal identifier of mildly mentally

[2]Theoretically and legally, an IQ test score alone does not define mental retardation. Low IQ scores may suggest intellectual subnormality, but mental retardation is expressed by both low IQ and low adaptive behavior scores. Much research, however, defines mentally retarded populations on the basis of IQ scores alone.
[3]The vast majority of children considered mentally retarded fall within the mild range (see the paper by Shonkoff in this volume).
[4]Much of the information in this section is based on the paper by Shonkoff in this volume.

retarded children, and their single most salient characteristic is their failure to meet the academic standards demanded by schools, these results are not surprising.

Sex

Boys outnumber girls in EMR classes by a ratio of 7:5. One would expect some sex differences since boys on the average show a greater degree of biological vulnerability (e.g., a higher rate of spontaneous abortions and neonatal deaths, a greater susceptibility to infectious diseases) than do girls. Yet the evidence from epidemiological studies is inconsistent with respect to sex differences in the prevalence of mild mental retardation. Rutter et al. (1970) reported in a British study that, although there is general agreement that severe mental retardation is somewhat more common in boys than in girls, the sex distribution for mild mental retardation as defined by IQ scores is fairly equal. Data from the Collaborative Perinatal Project of the National Institute of Neurological and Communicative Disorders and Stroke (unpublished data from S. H. Broman) revealed that for whites, girls have a slightly higher rate of mild mental retardation (defined as a score of 50–69 on the WISC-R at age 7) than do boys (1.29 percent versus 1.03 percent) and that for blacks, boys have a higher rate than do girls (4.99 percent versus 4.24 percent). The greater tendency of boys to have reading problems and to exhibit disruptive behavior may in large part account for the greater proportion of boys than girls in special education classes.

The panel was able to gather only limited data on EMR placements categorized by sex and race. The OCR does not collect sex-by-race cross tabulations, and other sources offer little information about sex-by-race placements. Where such data are available, however, they consistently indicate that the male-female ratio is larger among black children than white children.

Socioeconomic Status, Ethnicity, and Sociocultural Factors

However defined, the prevalence of mild mental retardation is correlated with the socioeconomic status of the family and the neighborhood in which a child lives (the lower the status, the higher the rate). As we have seen, mild mental retardation is also correlated with ethnicity; minority children have higher rates. The correlation of mild mental retardation with these factors is especially pronounced when IQ test scores alone are used as the diagnostic criterion (Lemkau et al., 1941, 1942; Mercer, 1973; Reschly and Jipson, 1976).

A recent analysis of data on more than 35,000 seven-year-olds from the Collaborative Perinatal Project (Broman et al., 1975) investigated the relationship of race (black, white) and socioeconomic status (bottom 25 percent, middle 50 percent, top 25 percent) to the prevalence of mild mental retardation as defined by IQ scores. Among white children, the rates ranged from 3.3 percent for the bottom socioeconomic quartile, to 1.3 percent for the middle group, to 0.3 percent for the upper quartile. Rates for black children were 7.7 percent for the lower group, 3.6 percent for the middle group, and 1.2 percent for the upper group. The Collaborative Perinatal Project data also show that sociocultural factors, such as family structure and amount of formal schooling of parents, are related to mental retardation rates, even within particular ethnic groups (Broman et al., 1975).

Biosocial Characteristics

In contrast to most of the people who are characterized as more seriously mentally retarded, the frequency of observable abnormal medical conditions is negligible in most mildly mentally retarded persons. However, the lack of recognized specific relationships between biological factors and mental retardation cannot be taken as evidence that biological elements are not important. Biologically based insults to the brain can affect a child throughout the developmental period and can result in impaired intellectual functioning later. Many of these biological factors, such as intra-uterine viruses, malnutrition, and lead intoxication, are more frequently observed among poor and minority populations. (For a more extensive treatment of biological factors affecting intellectual performance, see the paper by Shonkoff in this volume.) While no empirical evidence has yet been uncovered that causally links such factors to the disproportions found in EMR programs, it is conceivable that future research might reveal such causative relationships.[5]

HISTORICAL DEVELOPMENTS IN SPECIAL EDUCATION

ORIGINS OF SPECIAL EDUCATION

The controversies that surround special education classes—concern over the stigma associated with placement in a special class, questions about

---

[5]For cross-cultural variations in the meaning of biological factors in development, see Werner (1979) and Stewart (1981).

the quality of education in separate classes, and the likelihood of returning from special programs to a regular class—have dominated discussions
of special education practices since their inception. Many of these controversies are rooted in the origins of special classes. Separate classes for
those who could not function adequately in the regular academic program
permitted the adjustment of instruction to a level considered appropriate
for these children. In so doing, poor, immigrant, and minority children were
often segregated from those in regular classes. In particular, labeling a
student "mentally retarded" allowed the school system to classify and separate children on the basis of their intellectual functioning and performance.

Before the introduction of special programs in public schools, the care
and education of mentally retarded individuals were undertaken privately
by families or in institutions. During the 19th century, mental retardation
was considered a physiological condition, caused by the lack of social order and stability that were associated with urbanization and industrialization. Institutions for the feeble-minded helped the inmates acquire the
necessary habits and values that would lead to eventual adjustment to the
changing environment (Leinhardt et al., in press).

Although administrators of these institutions had hoped to work with
those mentally retarded children who were most likely to benefit from
training, large numbers of the more severe cases were institutionalized
and care became almost entirely custodial rather than therapeutic. Thus,
by the end of the 19th century, those who did not require custodial care
were not being treated in institutions (Lazarson, 1975).

Excluded from residential institutions, large numbers of mentally retarded children fell under the purview of another institution—the public
schools. Two changes in the nature of public schooling, firmly entrenched
by the beginning of the 20th century, caused this shift of responsibility for
the care of mentally retarded individuals: the enforcement of compulsory
attendance laws and an age-graded system of group instruction. Compulsory attendance meant that children who formerly would have dropped
out of school or who had never enrolled were now attending in large numbers. An age-graded system altered views of individual differences, influencing the expectations of educators concerning children's performance.
Children who could not meet these standards were considered to have
some disability (Levine, 1976).

For a variety of reasons that were typically not differentiated (e.g., ill-
ness, truancy, language problems), a large percentage of children were
overage for their grade, perceived as unable to profit from regular instruction, and unlikely to move through the normal grade sequence. In the early
20th century, it was children of various immigrant groups, notably south-

ern Italians, who were failing in school, scoring lower on IQ tests, and overrepresented in special education programs.[6]

The differential achievement of various groups was a subject of research and led to general hypotheses about the causes of mental retardation. Two competing theories about the causes of these group differences have remained at the center of current arguments concerning overrepresentation in special classes: (1) group differences are innate and are unlikely to change through educational intervention and (2) group differences are attributable to environmental factors.

Justifications for special classes were economic, educational, and societal. Of primary importance was the removal of the mentally deficient child from the regular classroom because he or she impeded the progress of the normal child and occupied an inordinate amount of the teacher's time. However, the segregated child was schooled under conditions deemed beneficial: He or she was instructed in a smaller class, was given more effective teaching geared to an appropriate level, and was freed from demoralizing comparisons with more competent peers. Although these smaller special classes increased costs, they saved the schools the expenses associated with children repeating the same grades. Long-range savings also were envisioned, since mentally retarded children receiving vocational education in the schools might obtain self-supporting jobs and thus not become burdens on society (Sarason and Doris, 1979).

INTELLIGENCE TESTING FOR PLACEMENT OF MENTALLY RETARDED STUDENTS

The origins of the IQ test are well known. At the turn of the century, Alfred Binet was asked by the French minister of education to develop a means of identifying those children in public schools who could not meet the demands imposed by the regular classroom and who needed special programs. The purpose of Binet's test was, therefore, to provide guidance for educational planning; it was not, in Binet's view, a measure of innate potential or fixed capacity.

The Binet-Simon scales were quickly adapted for use both in Europe and the United States. Although the establishment of special classes preceded the use of IQ tests in American public schools, the two soon became closely linked. The scientific development of intelligence testing

---

[6]Because black students were at that time largely excluded from the schools operated for native and foreign white students, their overrepresentation in special education was not yet recognized as a significant issue (Sarason and Doris, 1979).

provided a rationale for the labeling and separation of mentally retarded children.

National standardization of the Stanford-Binet intelligence test in 1916 influenced conceptions of intelligence for generations to come. A child's mental age was defined on a normative basis using samples of children at selected ages for standardizing a large number of short tests or items comprising the final version of the instrument. Dividing the mental age by the chronological age and multiplying the ratio by 100 yielded the intelligence quotient—the IQ. Subnormality was identified with IQs below 70, embracing about 3 percent of the total population.[7]

Large-scale IQ testing highlighted the number of subnormal children in the public schools, leading to public pressure for the control and regulation of socially deviant children. Intelligence testing was quickly adopted by the education system as an objective, expedient, and efficient method of identifying children deemed unsuitable for advanced academic studies as well as those children thought to have the greatest potential for rapid advancement (Lazarson, 1975).

The increased use of IQ tests contributed to the expansion of the special education system, especially in urban schools. In 1914, 10,890 children were counted as enrolled in special classes for the mentally subnormal; in 1922, this figure had increased to 23,252. Only 10 years later, the count was an astounding 75,099 (Leinhardt et al., in press; Sarason and Doris, 1979). By then, the AAMD had succeeded in refining the traditional classification system to include a milder type of feeble-mindedness, the "moron," which was defined in terms of mental age. Thousands of individuals previously unrecognized were now categorized and labeled as mentally retarded because their IQ scores fell below 70. While the more severely retarded—the "imbecile" and the "idiot"—could be identified without the assistance of an IQ score, intelligence testing led to the definition and acceptance of a new category.

Intelligence tests met the needs of an education system that valued efficiency, categorization, prediction, science, and the careful use of limited resources based on scientifically accepted procedures. Empirical studies of intelligence provided scientific evidence on a number of critical issues that were the focus of public attention. Such studies bolstered the belief that low intelligence was a cause of social deviance and legitimized the practice of differential treatment for different groups. These early studies of IQ tests were viewed as supporting the idea that intelligence was largely

[7]More current scoring practices derive an IQ measure as a composite of multiple subtests usually scaled to have a mean of 100 and a standard deviation of 15 (or 16) in a large normative sample.

inherited and unmodifiable and that it predicted (or even caused) later school achievement as well as future adaptation to social and occupational demands (Lazarson, 1975; Levine, 1976; Sarason and Doris, 1979).

Even in their heyday between the two world wars, IQ tests did not receive untempered acclaim. Many questioned the assumptions underlying the tests and criticized the consequences of large-scale application of intelligence testing, including placement in special classes. But most of the challenges raised by critics of the tests were largely overlooked. Intelligence tests were accepted by the public schools as efficient sorters of individuals with different abilities and different future roles in society.

DEVELOPMENTS IN THE SPECIAL EDUCATION SYSTEM

The emerging special education system was influenced by other forces in the later decades of the 20th century. The number of children entering special education programs rose dramatically. States began the process of defining new categories of and treatments for mentally handicapped children, based on the model of physical handicaps. The courts became increasingly involved in the conflicts surrounding placement, treatment, and outcome in special education. In response to these forces, federal support for special education programs grew rapidly.

After World War II, the baby boom flooded the schools with children. The number of children requiring special attention grew even faster as medical technology enabled more children with debilitating health problems to survive than ever before. In addition, as a result of school desegregation and large migrations of Hispanic populations, schools were faced with serving a more diverse group of children. The growing concern of parents over the type of education provided to their children by public schools was a powerful force for upgrading and maintaining quality services, not only in the regular school program but also in special programs for the handicapped. Advocacy groups assumed an increasingly important role in this period, although their themes varied. Parent and advocacy groups for the handicapped, dominated primarily by the middle class, were demanding an expansion of the scope of special education and an increase in the quality of services provided by the public schools for handicapped children. Groups representing blacks and other minorities were pressing not for separate special education services but for an expanded integration of the public school systems.[8]

---

[8]These two themes persisted in later years. Actions brought by middle- and upper-income white parents have almost exclusively dominated the appeals process that is guaranteed by

State after state instituted funding provisions to support programs for special students. State definitions of handicaps and methods of funding special services were adjusted in recognition of the increased number of children needing these services and the expanding variety of settings in which they could be provided. At the federal level, the years 1957–1966 saw the creation and initial development of national special education programs for which the political presence and influence of parent groups was at least partially responsible (Reynolds and Birch, 1977).

There was also a growing recognition of a group of children, distinct from the mentally retarded population, who had specific learning and perceptual problems. Rooted initially in neuropsychological research on people who had experienced traumatic brain damage, the term "specific learning disability" gained widespread public recognition when promoted by parent advocacy organizations. The category of learning disabled (LD) was defined to encompass children who exhibited a markedly uneven development of mental abilities compared with mentally retarded children, who demonstrated a more general deficiency. Typical would be the LD child who had severe problems learning to read (dyslexia) or doing simple arithmetic but who was otherwise normal in measured intelligence. Originally, LD children were considered members of a relatively small and well-defined population; however, as schools began to use the term "learning disabled" to identify larger numbers of children, the lines that separated EMR from LD groups were frequently difficult to discern (Grossman, 1977).

Parents and education researchers alike began to raise questions about the quality of special education classes and even the validity of the special education system itself. In part a reflection of broader social concerns such as the civil rights movement, much of the public debate centered on the appropriateness of placing poor and minority children in special classes for mildly mentally retarded students (Dunn, 1968). The overrepresentation of poor and minority children in special education classes was apparent as the system grew. At the same time there was increasing concern about the educational value of placement of handicapped children in separate classes. Studies comparing the efficacy of regular versus separate class placements, although of generally poor quality, highlighted the failure of special classes to improve the educational functioning of mildly mentally handicapped children. In the subsequent years, these two themes—

P.L. 94-142, by demanding more specialized and expensive treatments than are offered by public schools. Minority groups have been more concerned about the overrepresentation of minority children in special programs and the segregative aspects of these programs.

discrimination in placement and the questionable quality of instruction—dominated most discussions of special education.

DISPROPORTIONATE PLACEMENT OF MINORITIES AND COURT DECISIONS

Most of the arguments raised for or against certain special education practices were not new, but with the rising concern for civil rights, these debates were increasingly shifted to the courts.

The basis for claims against the segregation of minority children in special classes lies in the Supreme Court's decision in *Brown* v. *Board of Education* (1954) that school segregation was a violation of constitutional guarantees. As a result of that decision, public schools were required to treat children equally, regardless of race.

Previously segregated white school districts, faced with including large numbers of minority students in their schools, often implemented practices designed to exclude blacks and other minorities. One device to screen out minority students, which relied heavily on intelligence tests, may have been special education, especially classes for mildly mentally retarded students. For example, the repeal of the law in California excluding Mexican-Americans from white schools coincided with the legislative creation of programs for EMR students (Mercer and Richardson, 1975). A disproportionately high enrollment of minority students in the new EMR programs accompanied their increased enrollment in the state's public schools.

The debate over disproportionate special class placements first questioned why those children were considered to be in need of special services. As the use of standardized intelligence tests became universal, they were increasingly blamed as the mechanism of identification and placement. Minority children, their advocates argued, were disproportionately over-represented in special classes, especially classes for EMR children, because the tests used to place them failed to properly measure their mental ability.

Other charges were raised against the use of intelligence tests: that they are biased against poor minority children because of differences in culture, language, values, experience, or method of administration and therefore are not appropriate measures by which to evaluate minority students. In 1969 the Association of Black Psychologists called for a moratorium on the use of mental ability tests standardized on white populations as the basis for placing black children in special education classes (Williams, 1972). In *Diana* v. *State Board of Education* (1970), the use of standardized intelligence tests for placement of Mexican-American children in EMR classes was challenged on the grounds that the tests had been standardized only on majority-group children and thus were culturally biased against minorities. As a result of this kind of litigation, states began to reconsider testing and evaluation procedures. The state of California, after *Diana*, suggested that districts test children in the language they were most familiar with and that they use multiple measures for evaluating children suspected of being mentally handicapped (Bersoff, in press).

In 1972 a group of black children in EMR classes in the San Francisco school system sued the district and the state, again challenging the use of standardized intelligence tests as a placement tool for minority children. As in *Diana*, it was claimed that the children's minority group—blacks— was overrepresented in EMR classes. An attempt was made to prove that a reason for that overrepresentation was misclassification. By 1975, as a result of this ligitation (*Larry P.* v. *Riles*, 1972, 1974), California had removed the controversial IQ tests from the list of approved instruments for evaluation and placement of children in EMR classes.

The *Larry P.* case became the focus of national attention. Between 1972, when the original complaint was filed, and 1979, when the decision was issued (*Larry P.* v. *Riles*, 1979), federal and state laws governing special education had changed considerably, and the relationship between racial and minority segregation and special education placement had become a subject of increasing national debate.

The 1979 decision on the merits in *Larry P.* looked at the phenomenon of minority overrepresentation in EMR classes in terms of the appropriateness of the selection criteria and the outcome of placement in an EMR class. The decision noted that black children were substantially overrepresented in EMR classes compared with the total black enrollment in California schools. Even as total enrollment in EMR classes declined over the years, the overrepresentation of blacks in EMR classes remained relatively constant. The history of EMR classes in California, wrote the judge, indicated that such classes were not primarily intended to help slow learners acquire the skills necessary to return to a regular program of instruction. Instead, EMR classes emphasized training to improve social adjustment and economic usefulness, rather than acquisition of academic skills and proficiencies. Thus, the judge decided that separate classes for EMR students were "dead-ends"; the children in these classes fall further and further behind children in regular programs and generally remain in separate classes until the end of their school career. As a result, there was a considerable disadvantage to being placed in the separate classes of an EMR program, especially for those children who might have had a better chance to learn in other programs.

Court cases in other parts of the country also raised the problem of minority overrepresentation in special classes. In most of these cases the methods used to evaluate and place children suspected of being handicapped were the focus of keen attention. Sometimes the entire system of identification, evaluation, and placement was questioned as, for example, in *Mattie T. v. Holliday*, in which black children and advocacy groups protested much of Mississippi's special education system. In other cases a particular evaluation method was challenged. For example, in Chicago, a group of minority students challenged the use of standardized intelligence tests to place black children in EMR classes, but the result of this litigation was significantly different from the decision in *Larry P.* Like the plaintiffs in *Larry P.*, the black children in *Parents in Action for Special Education v. Hannon* (1980) claimed that blacks were substantially overrepresented in EMR classes as a result of the school system's use of what they considered to be culturally biased IQ tests. They demonstrated that some black children in those classes were of normal intelligence but had other learning problems that resulted in school failure. The court ruled that the tests were not unfair to minorities and that, when used with other assessment criteria as statutorily mandated, they did not discriminate against minority children.[9]

The outcome of this litigation has been a relatively intense scrutiny of the proper use of intelligence testing and an expanding search for new methods of assessment.

MAINSTREAMING IN REGULAR CLASSES

While the schools were confronting the relationship of segregation and special education placement, there was a growing realization that many of the legal and constitutional questions raised by minorities through the civil rights movement were also applicable to handicapped people. Integration of handicapped students into regular classes was seen by some educators as a way to avoid some of the purported ills of special education—stigmatizing labels, dead-end curricula, and isolation (Dunn, 1968).

In *Pennsylvania Association for Retarded Citizens* [PARC] v. *Pennsylvania* (1971, 1972) this "mainstreaming" movement for handicapped children gained legal endorsement. In that case, plaintiffs argued that mentally retarded children in state institutions were excluded from public schools without due process. The court in *PARC* required that education placement decisions for these children be made in light of the principle that placement in regular public school programs is preferable to any

---

[9]Subsequent voluntary action by the Chicago school board has discontinued the use of standardized intelligence tests for special education placements.

other type of placement. It was stated that all handicapped children should be moved into the mainstream of regular classes to the extent permitted by their handicaps. In a related decision, the right of all handicapped children to a free public education regardless of handicap or financial resources of the school district was supported by another court (*Mills* v. *Board of Education*, 1972).

Controversy over the concept of mainstreaming has continued. Many educators believe that mainstreaming was forced on them by judicial decisions and political pressure, and they doubt the wisdom of such policy (Sarason and Doris, 1979). Resistance to mainstreaming is based on several arguments: (1) that the training of regular classroom teachers lags far behind the special demands that handicapped children place on them, to the detriment of all students; (2) that handicapped children are not accepted by many of their peers; (3) that such children may receive less special attention and service as a result of their placement in regular classes; and (4) that their presence takes needed teacher attention from normal students.

FEDERAL LEGISLATION AND THE RIGHTS OF THE HANDICAPPED

The rights of all handicapped persons were advanced appreciably when Congress passed the Rehabilitation Act of 1973. Section 504 of this act generally prohibits discrimination against "... otherwise qualified handicapped individuals ... under any program or activity receiving federal financial assistance." The final regulations implementing this legislation were published in 1977, requiring that a free, appropriate, public education must be given to every handicapped child. Specific requirements are stated for the evaluation and placement process to prevent misclassification, unnecessary labeling, and inappropriate placement. In addition, the regulations of Section 504 require that placement follows the principle of education in the least restrictive environment.

In 1975, Congress passed the Education for All Handicapped Children Act (P.L. 94-142), which provides both funding and detailed requirements for education programs for handicapped children.[10] The purpose of the law was to ensure that handicapped children receive an education appropriate to their specific needs through the public school system. The act and its implementing regulations focus on the following six aspects of placement for EMR children:

---

[10]Federal funding of special education programs amounts to not more than 15 percent of the costs of special education. The remainder is provided by state and local governments (Hartman, 1980).

1. Mental retardation is defined in terms of intellectual functioning, adaptive behavior, and school performance.

2. State and local education agencies are required to develop procedures to ensure that all children who are handicapped and in need of special education and related services are identified, located, and evaluated.

3. The education agencies must establish specific procedural safeguards to protect the handicapped child's right to a free appropriate education. These regulations guarantee parents the right to review pertinent educational records; to obtain an independent evaluation of the child; to receive written notice before a public agency initiates the placement process, including a full explanation of procedural safeguards available to the parent; and to demand a hearing before an impartial officer if the placement is challenged.

4. The regulations require a full evaluation of a child's educational needs prior to any placement decision or action. The tests used must be validated for their intended use, given in the child's native language, and administered by trained personnel. Assessments must go beyond "single intelligence quotients" to include measures of "specific areas of educational need," and no single procedure may be used as the sole criterion for placing a child. The assessment must be made by a multidisciplinary team, and the child must be assessed in all areas related to the suspected disability. The regulations further stipulate that the multiple data sources to be used in decision making include aptitude and achievement tests, teacher recommendations, physical condition, social or cultural background, and adaptive behavior. Reevaluations must be made at least every three years.

5. A written individual education plan (IEP) must be developed before a child is placed and must be updated annually. The IEP must contain information on the child's current performance, annual and short-term goals, specific services to be provided, and objective criteria to be used in evaluating progress.

6. Children must be placed in the least restrictive environment compatible with their handicap. Education agencies are required to provide a continuum of alternative placements (e.g., regular classes, special classes and schools, home instruction, etc.). Placements are to be close to the child's home and, if possible, in the school the child would normally attend. Placement must be based on the IEP developed for the child.

There has been some question recently whether the Education for All Handicapped Children Act will maintain its current form. The Reagan administration's proposed Elementary and Secondary Education Consolidation Act of 1981 would have replaced categorical funding under P.L. 94-142 with block grants that would give broad discretion in the use of funds to local education agencies, would have left substantially monitoring and enforcement activities to the states, and would have repealed the substantive provisions of the statute. However, the proposed legislation was not passed, and P.L. 94-142 was not included in the education block grants, and it remains an independent, categorically funded program. The regulations implementing the new law, however, are currently under review, and the future of those provisions is uncertain.

CURRENT PROCEDURES IN EDUCATIONAL PLACEMENT[11]

A DESCRIPTION OF THE PLACEMENT PROCESS

The intricate system of checks and balances mandated by Section 504 and P.L. 94-142 and their implementing regulations, the emphasis on decision making by multidisciplinary teams, the requirements of multiple tests and other assessment procedures, and the thrust toward placement in the least restrictive environment appear quite compatible in spirit with models of the placement process proposed by various educators (e.g., Jones, 1979; Oakland, 1977). However, the degree of implementation of the law varies considerably among districts. In some cases, districts have accommodated their special education system to legal requirements; in others, little change is apparent. Although research has assessed the degree to which schools comply with the law, it has yet to demonstrate that adherence to required policies leads to effective educational practices.

Children enter the placement process in·one of two ways. Many are referred in response to "child find" campaigns conducted by states and school districts, largely initiated under the impetus of P.L. 94-142. Children may be referred by parents, teachers, doctors, counselors, social workers, or others. Most children are referred by their teachers because of repeatedly poor academic performance or poor social adjustment. Teachers have always been the single main source of referrals (Birman, 1979; Blaschke, 1979; Stearns et al., 1979; U.S. Department of Health, Education, and Welfare, 1979c), although others, such as school principals and social workers, appear to be assuming a larger role since the implementation of P.L. 94-142. IQ test scores, although significant in a later stage of the process, are not used as an initial screening device.

Once children are referred, they must be evaluated in order to determine their special educational needs. P.L. 94-142 and the Section 504

---

[11]The information in this section is based on the paper by Bickel in this volume.

regulations are explicit and detailed in their prescriptions regarding evaluation procedures, who will be involved, and the types of data to be considered. Several studies have shown that states and school districts are gradually bringing their policies and practices into line with the law and its implementing regulations. For example, a longitudinal study of the implementation of P.L. 94-142 in 22 sites (Stearns et al., 1979) revealed a shift from assessment by a psychologist using a single intelligence test to procedures involving a wider variety of instruments and specialists, in which an attempt is made to tailor the assessment battery to the child's apparent skills and deficiencies.

In spite of these improvements, the altered procedures may not be operating as intended. A few individuals, usually school administrators or psychologists, tend to dominate the placement meetings in which decisions are made, and parents and teachers play a relatively passive role (Association of State Directors of Education, 1980; Thouvenelle and Hebbeler, 1978). Occasionally, school personnel meet in advance to iron out disagreements and present a united front to parents (Poland et al., 1979; Thouvenelle and Hebbeler, 1978). Although a variety of data are collected on each student, members of the team still rely heavily on IQ scores and achievement measures as a basis for labeling a child as mentally retarded (Poland et al., 1979; Thouvenelle and Hebbeler, 1978).

Once a child has been evaluated as belonging to the EMR category, decisions must be made concerning his or her placement and method of instruction. Under the P.L. 94-142 regulations, an IEP must be devised to meet the child's particular needs. Placement in regular or special classes, full- or part-time, is determined by the requirements spelled out in the IEP.

States have made considerable progress in adopting policies to ensure that IEPs are in fact written (U.S. Department of Health, Education, and Welfare, 1979b). Several implementation studies suggest, however, that despite conformity to the letter of the law the intent of the federal regulations is often not met in practice. Writing IEPs is a time-consuming task, provoking resistance by some teachers and administrators that leads to shortcuts. Often, a single brief meeting is held to classify the child, to settle on a placement, and to write a plan. Plans are often written prior to the meeting with little or no parental involvement. The content of IEPs often falls short of the ideal envisioned in the federal regulations; important details are omitted, goals are ambiguous, and the procedures for evaluating achievement of goals are not specified. The plans themselves may be *pro forma* and may not be followed in fact (Alper, 1978; Blaschke, 1979; Marver and David, 1978; Schenk and Levy, 1979; U.S. Department of Health, Education, and Welfare, 1979c). Most important, the type of placement recommended and the nature of the IEP often are determined by the types of classes and resources available, not by the needs of the child (Stearns et al., 1979).

FACTORS INFLUENCING THE PLACEMENT PROCESS

One salient, consistent finding of research on the implementation of P.L. 94-142 is the extreme variability in practice from district to district and from state to state. Several factors can be identified at the state, district, and school levels that encourage this diversification of practice. One such cause of diversity, mentioned previously, is that the definition of educable mental retardation varies among states (see, for example, U.S. General Accounting Office, 1981). States differ primarily in their choice of IQ cut-off scores—whether such scores are specified and what they are—and requirements concerning measures of adaptive behavior.

Policies regarding the dispensation of funds for special education also may influence the placement process. At a very basic level, the amount of money a school district can spend is a limiting factor influencing the quality and coverage of its special education programs. The availability of resources has a pervasive effect on referrals, evaluation, and placements. Referral rates are highest where services are plentiful. Rates of referral for specific types of problems tend to mirror the particular programs available. The amount of resources allocated to other programs, such as compensatory education classes, also may affect EMR referrals and subsequent placements, although such factors have not been specifically documented.

The financing formulas that states use to transfer funds to local school districts influence various aspects of the placement process. Fiscal policies may influence a district's decisions concerning other factors that affect the placement of children—the numbers of children classified as mentally (and physically) handicapped, the types of handicaps identified, the placement of children in mainstreamed settings, the quality and type of programs and services provided, and the size of classes. The incentives created by one such financing formula, the child-based formula, illustrate this point. States using child-based funding formulas reimburse local jurisdictions for each child identified as handicapped; the more children so identified, the more state money received. In general, such formulas may provide a strong incentive to identify previously unserved children, at least in some categories. For those jurisdictions in which certain categories (usually the more severely handicapped) are reimbursed more generously than others, the incentive would be to classify more children in those categories. In other versions of this formula, in which reimbursement is constant across categories, the incentive would be to classify more children as mildly mentally handicapped, since services for these problems are less costly per child than services for the severely handicapped. Child-based formulas provide an apparent incentive to increase class sizes and case loads as a means of maximizing reimbursement while minimizing costs to the local jurisdiction. Mainstreaming would also be encouraged, since full reimbursement may be provided despite less costly services.

A final factor that may affect the placement process is the discretion exercised by various participants in the system (see, for example, U.S. General Accounting Office, 1981). Even finely detailed regulations cannot eliminate the power of individuals to shape the system. Disproportionate representation of minorites in EMR classes could well arise from racial discrimination on the part of individual decision makers in the placement process, a possibility that could only be checked by monitoring a district on a case-by-case basis.

The Effects of the Placement Process on Minority Students

In what ways does the placement process affect minority and white students differentially? Minority children might conceivably have experiences that vary from those of white students in any or all of the steps in the placement process. They might be referred for evaluation more often than whites for both academic and behavior problems. Once referred, they might have a higher likelihood of being classified as EMR. Once labeled as EMR, they might be more likely than white children to end up in special programs or separate classes, rather than in regular classrooms. The bewildering variety of patterns suggests that conflicting claims about the effects of the placement process on minority students cannot be resolved easily. Nevertheless, on the basis of research to date, some procedural factors that may affect the proportions of minorities enrolled in EMR programs can be highlighted.

Does the level of disproportion at the referral stage mirror the patterns found in actual enrollments in EMR programs, or are they higher, as some have suggested? Only limited data are available on this issue. The scattered evidence that documents the generally higher disproportion in referral rates cannot be easily generalized across districts because of the great variability in enrollment patterns and practices across the nation.

A commonly held perception is that teachers more often refer black children because of disciplinary problems. Only one report was noted that investigated this hypothesis. A study of 355 students referred for psychological services in an urban school system found that more minority children were referred, but the proportions of white and minority students referred for academic as opposed to disciplinary problems did not differ (Tomlinson et al., 1977).

Most of the attention in the controversies surrounding minority students and EMR placements has been directed to the evaluation process (see Chapter 3 for a discussion of the controversy over IQ testing). A number of studies have considered the kind of information that is most influential in EMR placement decisions and the importance assigned to various assessment measures by the decision makers. Using a variety of techniques, such as simulation of assessment decisions and interviews with participants in placement decisions, these studies have shown that academic achievement, as measured by standardized tests or as reported by the teacher, and IQ scores are consistently among the most important considerations, especially for school psychologists (Berk et al., 1981; Matuszek and Oakland, 1979; Thurlow and Ysseldyke, 1980; Ysseldyke et al., 1979).

Special education placement decisions other than those involving EMR classes use additional types of information; for example, decisions concerned with emotional disturbance rely heavily on the teacher's report of the child's social behavior in the classroom. Placement decisions concerning emotional disturbance or specific learning disabilities tend to be inconsistent—independent experts disagree as to the proper classification of a given child. EMR decisions are among the most consistent of all, in part because of heavy reliance on clear-cut indicators such as IQ (Petersen and Hart, 1978).

The balance that is struck between IQ and other measures is likely to have significant consequences for the proportion of minority children placed in EMR classes, since minority children consistently score lower on standardized tests of ability than do white children. For blacks the typical estimate of average IQ across the nation is 85, about one standard deviation below the white mean of 100. The difference has stark consequences at the upper and lower ends of the distribution. If the cutoff point for the EMR category is set at 70 (a fairly typical criterion), two standard deviations below the white mean and one standard deviation below the black mean, then 2.3 percent of the white population will fall into the subnormal category, compared with 15.9 percent of the black population. If IQ tests were given to all children and IQ scores were applied mechanically as the sole criterion for EMR placement, the resulting minority overrepresentation would be almost 8 to 1. Actual figures for EMR placement as reported in OCR's survey data are 1.1 percent for whites and 3.7 percent for blacks, a disproportion of 3.4 to 1.

Two conclusions follow inescapably from these considerations. First, the use of IQ scores as placement criteria will tend to maintain a disproportionate representation of minority children in EMR classes. IQ testing may not be the cause of disproportion; conceivably it might even reduce the high disproportion evident in teacher referrals, as Lambert (1981) has argued. IQ testing will certainly protect some children from EMR placement—children with IQs above the EMR cutoff who have been re-ferred as candidates for EMR placement. Nevertheless, given the almost 8 to 1 difference in the proportion of blacks and whites falling in the rele-vant IQ range, as long as IQ scores play a role in decision making, some disproportion will undoubtedly remain in EMR placements.

The second conclusion follows from the discrepancy between actual EMR placement rates and the rates that would theoretically prevail if IQ alone was the placement criterion. Elements other than testing, which are part of the chain of referral, evaluation, and placement, must also be operating to reduce both the overall proportions of children placed in EMR classes and the disproportion between minority children and whites.

As already noted, federal law and regulations require evaluations to in-clude several kinds of information in addition to IQ test scores. Available research suggests that the use of such information, particularly informa-tion on adaptive behavior outside school, dramatically reduces the propor-tion of all children placed in EMR classes, although there is a greater reduction for minority students (Fischer, 1977; Reschly, 1979).

Additional information often available in the child's placement dossier may include the child's race, socioeconomic status, family situation, and classroom deportment. Does knowledge of a child's race by the school psy-chologist bias his or her decision about classification of a child as EMR? Research on this question is not consistent; some studies indicate that black children are more often labeled as EMR than are white children, even when profiles are identical for the two groups (e.g., Pickholtz, 1977); some show the reverse pattern (e.g., Amira, et al., 1977); and others find no relation at all between race and psychologists' decisions (Berk et al., 1981).

In the final step of the process of referral, evaluation, and placement, there is no evidence that minority children are affected differentially. The few studies available do not indicate that placement decisions and IEPs result in the segregation of minority students. Few EMR students are as-signed to a placement that blocks *all* contact with the mainstream (Thou-venelle and Hebbeler, 1978).[12] While the data are limited, available in-

---

[12] Contradictory evidence is provided by MacMillan and Borthwick (1980), who note that the EMR category in California now includes children who are more seriously disabled than previous populations of EMR children. Most of the EMR children in their sample did not receive instruction in integrated settings.

formation suggests that minority students are either assigned to special classes at the same rate as are whites (Ashurst and Meyers, 1973; Matuszek and Oakland, 1979) or are placed in less restrictive settings than are white students (Tomlinson et al., 1977).

One element of the placement process that has not been considered is the role of parent involvement and parental rights to due process. P.L. 94-142 regulations guarantee parents access to full information, prior approval of evaluation activities, participation in placement decisions and the writing of IEPs, and the right to appeal unsatisfactory decisions and to demand independent evaluation of the child. In theory, minority parents might make use of this right to appeal, contesting EMR placement decisions. Appeals could become a significant factor offsetting disproportion arising in referral or evaluation. In actual practice, however, due process hearings have rarely been used by minority parents for this purpose. The appeals process has been used almost exclusively by middle- and upper-income white parents who often request more specialized and expensive treatment—e.g., private school placement—than education agencies are prepared to provide.

3
Assessment:
Issues and Methods

Most discussions of assessment in the context of special education placement for mildly mentally retarded students focus on proper classification and the avoidance of misclassification. These issues have been treated extensively by other panels and professional organizations (e.g., Hobbs, 1975). This panel was convened because of public concern about the possible misclassification of minority students and about the violations of civil rights that such misclassification might entail. As we argued in Chapter 1, however, issues of classification or valid assessment surrounding the educable mentally retarded (EMR) category are inextricably linked to issues of instruction. One major reason why misclassification is a policy concern is that it may lead to inappropriate educational treatments. Consequently, we focus our discussion of assessment instruments and procedures on their educational relevance and utility—their usefulness in identifying students who need and can profit from special forms of instruction or intervention[1] and their usefulness as guides to the type of instruction or intervention that is needed.

Assessment procedures and instruments may have many functions, of

---

[1] Although our discussion concentrates primarily on the direct contribution of assessment to classroom instruction, we recognize that other forms of intervention may be appropriate and necessary for some children before any program of classroom instruction can be effective. For example, the correction of defective vision or hearing, medical treatment, or even psychotherapy or family intervention might be needed before a child can function successfully in the classroom.

which guiding intervention is only one. They might be used to diagnose abnormal or debilitating organic conditions, to predict future academic performance, or in theory even to infer the underlying capacity to learn. Each of these functions would imply different assumptions about the nature of the instrument being used and about the entity being measured. Each would raise different scientific controversies. Each could contribute to intervention; for example, diagnosis could point to treatment, although there might be some conditions that can be diagnosed but not treated. The discussion below subordinates these other functions to that of facilitating effective educational intervention. For example, much of the debate surrounding IQ tests has to do with their use in inferring learning potential. Although we sketch the broad outlines of this debate, we base our conclusions about IQ tests primarily on their utility, or lack of utility, in helping educators select and design instructional programs.

Our decision to focus on the educational utility of various assessment devices and procedures, rather than on their role in classification and misclassification, is based primarily on the fact that we are analyzing assessment in an educational context, in which it is a means to the end of improving instruction. Two additional considerations reinforce our decision. First, as shown in Chapter 2, definitions of EMR originated with a particular instrument—the IQ test—and have shifted over time. Data on the prevalence of EMR are confounded with the assessment practices and instruments used in different states and localities (see Chapter 2 and the paper by Shonkoff in this volume). It is difficult to discuss cogently the contribution of different assessment practices to classification and misclassification in the face of this confusion and circularity. Furthermore, it would be fruitless to cover the same ground as the far more extensive discussions of classification mentioned above.

Many scientific controversies about the validity of assessment techniques, notably the IQ test, are unresolved. To attempt to take sides on these issues would require a detailed, technical discussion that probably would neither settle the issues nor lead to useful recommendations for educational policy and practice.[2] Decisions about policy and practice cannot await the final resolution of scientific debates. By focusing on educational utility, we hope to provide a framework for approaching these decisions despite the ambiguities in current understanding.

This chapter has two major sections. The first section, the bulk of the chapter, reviews salient issues surrounding the instruments that comprise

[2]For a comprehensive discussion of the issues involved in ability testing generally, see the report of the National Research Council's Committee on Ability Testing (Wigdor and Garner, 1982).

a comprehensive battery for assessing a child who has proved unable to learn normally in the classroom. The section covers IQ tests and other measures of intellectual functioning, biomedical measures, and measures of adaptive behavior—the child's ability to meet normal expectations appropriate to age and setting, with regard to self-help skills, independence, impulse control, cooperation, and the like. The second section describes an ideal assessment process in which the comprehensive assessment would be embedded. The process takes place in two phases. The first phase, prior to any attempt to find problems or deficiencies in the child, is a systematic investigation of the learning environment and the instruction the child receives. The purpose of this phase, which is almost nonexistent in current practice, is to be certain that the child cannot perform adequately in a well-designed instructional setting. Only after deficiencies in the environment have been ruled out, by showing that the child fails to learn under several reasonable programs of instruction, is it legitimate to expose the child to the risks of stigma and misclassification that are inherent in any individual assessment process. The second phase is the comprehensive individual assessment itself, which it is hoped would be applied to significantly fewer children than are affected under the current referral and placement system.

COMPREHENSIVE INDIVIDUAL ASSESSMENT

The purpose of comprehensive assessment is to locate the source of the child's difficulties in learning in the classroom. In many ways a comprehensive assessment represents an attempt to test, at the individual level, some of the hypotheses about the causes of deficient classroom functioning that were discussed in Chapter 1. The causes may lie in physical malfunctions, emotional disturbances, deficient social skills (either specific to the school or encompassing the home as well), lack of relevant academic preparation, lack of more general cognitive skills, or a basic limitation in intellectual capacity. The causes may also lie in broader sociocultural factors of the kind discussed in Chapter 1, such as value systems antithetical to that of the school. Such factors may be manifested in the child's behavior in the classroom or during test situations and, to some degree, in measures of adaptive behavior.

As noted in Chapter 2, broad-based assessment is required under P.L. 94-142, its implementing regulations, and the regulations implementing Section 504. The regulations require, among other provisions, that assessments go beyond "a single general intelligence quotient" to include measures of "specific areas of educational need." They prohibit the use of any single procedure as the sole criterion for placing a child. They require that tests be selected in a manner designed to reflect a child's aptitude and achievement, rather than "the child's impaired sensory, manual or speaking skills." Further, the regulations for P.L. 94-142 require that a child be assessed in "all areas related to the suspected disability." In practice, as seen in Chapter 2, compliance with the law is far from complete. Whether or not other measures are administered, IQ and achievement tests tend to dominate EMR placement decisions (see Chapter 2 and the paper by Bickel in this volume).

We therefore begin this section with an examination of the major controversies surrounding IQ tests—arguing, however, that their relevance for educational practice is limited. The section also discusses attempts to develop better measures of intellectual functioning, whether by improving the IQ test or by developing supplementary or substitute measures. The section then surveys biomedical measures and measures of adaptive behavior. Both types of measure lie outside the intellectual domain, as it is usually defined; they are essential, however, to understanding the child's classroom performance and more general capabilities and limitations as well as to designing appropriate interventions.

IQ TESTING: CONTROVERSIES, IMPLICATIONS, AND ALTERNATIVES[3]

Of all the elements in the assessment process, standardized tests of "intelligence" have been the most controversial. They have been the subject of protracted litigation, as discussed in Chapter 2. They have been the focus of acrimonious debate in the academic community.

Three related questions are at the heart of the debate as it is usually conducted: Are IQ scores[4] determined primarily by genes or by the environment? Are IQ scores valid measures of academic ability? Are IQ tests culturally biased? These questions, though central to virtually all discussions of IQ testing, do not neatly divide proponents and opponents of testing in the schools. There is considerable diversity of opinion within both camps, and there has been little attempt to spell out the practical implications of these scientific controversies.

---

[3]Much of the information in this section is based on the paper by Travers in this volume.

[4]We recognize that leaders in the field of educational assessment have long recommended against the use of single IQ scores and have urged the use of multiple instruments and careful consideration of performance profiles across subscales within tests for assessing an individual's mental abilities. Our focus on summary scores and use of the term "IQ test" rather than "test of mental abilities" or the like arises because of data cited in Chapter 2 and elsewhere in this report that show that summary scores are often accorded predominant weight in placement decisions. While the extent of this practice is uncertain, it is an important source of the controversy surrounding the use of such tests in educational placements.

Our discussion of the three issues bears primarily on widely used, individually administered IQ tests, notably the Stanford-Binet and the revised Wechsler Intelligence Scale for Children (WISC-R). Special issues raised by group ability testing and by the use of various substitutes for the major IQ tests are not discussed.

The Nature-Nurture Issue

Of all the questions surrounding IQ testing, the nature-nurture issue is the one most bitterly debated, although, as we argue below, it has little relevance for education policy or practice. In recent years the controversy has centered on the relative contributions of heredity and environment to the 15-point average difference usually found between the IQ scores of blacks and whites. Most of the existing scientific evidence bears on the contribution of genotypic variation to *individual* differences in measured (phenotypic) IQ *within* ethnic groups. For example, Arthur Jensen's controversial article (1969) examined correlations among IQs of persons in various biological kinship relationships and concluded that about 80 percent of the variation in IQ is genetically determined. Others (e.g., Jencks et al., 1972) have arrived at substantially lower estimates of heritability; however, a fairly recent review (Loehlin et al., 1975) offers a figure close to Jensen's for the heritability of individual differences in IQ within European and American Caucasian populations. The reviewers found less consistent evidence for American black populations; heritability is substantial for these populations but perhaps somewhat lower than for whites.

Numerous critics have attacked the assumptions, methods, and data that led Jensen to his high estimate of the heritability of IQ. Among the many factors cited by the critics are the confounding of genes and environments, restriction in the range of environments studied, and the inappropriateness of the statistical techniques borrowed from population genetics that were used to estimate heritability.

The most controversial aspect of Jensen's work was his speculation that the average IQ difference *between* races in the United States is due partly to genetic factors. His critics have stressed that group differences in distributions of a trait can be due mostly or entirely to the environment, even if the heritability of the trait within groups is high. Loehlin et al. addressed the issue of between-group differences, primarily by examining studies relating IQ distributions to indices of racial mixture, such as blood types, skin color, and direct genealogical information. They concluded that the data "are consistent with either moderate hereditarian or environmentalist interpretations" but perhaps "more easily accommodated in an environmentalist framework (p. 238)." A similar statement could be made regarding other data, which show that the IQ gap between black and white children is inversely related to the black child's exposure to white, middle-class culture and schooling. These include studies of black families who migrated from the rural South to the urban North, studies of black children adopted by white parents, studies of the effects of early intervention programs, and studies of sociocultural variations *within* black and white populations.

In short, scientific controversy continues to exist with respect to the issue of heredity versus environment. Virtually everyone involved in the controversy agrees that both genetic and experiential factors influence IQ; what is at issue is the degree of influence and the mechanisms involved. The controversy has been carried into the courts, and several major judicial decisions on testing have reflected the judges' convictions that IQ tests fail to measure native intelligence (Bersoff, 1979). Yet on closer examination, we feel that the ultimate, substantive, scientific outcome of the controversy is less important for education policy and practice than it may appear, in particular for policies affecting placement of students in EMR classes.

There is a widespread assumption outside the field of special education that mental retardation is by definition an innate incapability to learn. (This belief is clearly reflected in the *Larry P.* decision; see also E. Smith, 1980.) It follows from this assumption that IQ must measure innate capacity if it is to be a legitimate index of mental retardation. These views are not shared, however, by medical and educational professionals concerned with mental retardation (see Goodman, 1977, for a forceful exposition of this point). Mental retardation is currently defined as a deficit in functioning and adaptive behavior, which may be due to a wide variety of factors, experiential as well as organic. This purely functional definition is motivated by the fact that, within the limits of current knowledge, there are no differences in prognosis or indicated educational "treatment" that distinguish organically caused deficits from experientially caused deficits. That is, children at the same level of functional ability have about the same expected level of future performance and can be taught most effectively in about the same ways, regardless of whether their deficits have a known organic cause, such as Down's syndrome (see Chapter 4 for further discussion of educational treatment). If education practice is independent of etiology in these clear-cut cases, it is hard to see why practice should be affected by the heritability of IQ.

It is important to recognize that a wide range of academic performance can be achieved by children with any given IQ. Even if differences in academic ability or achievement are in large part genetically caused, proper instruction can do a great deal to ensure that children develop to their fullest potential. For example, children with Down's syndrome reportedly make significant gains under certain programs of instruction (Hayden and Haring, 1977). Although a teacher, administrator, or policy maker of the hereditarian persuasion might be pessimistic about the likelihood of change in underlying intellectual ability, this pessimism would be no justification for failing to provide conditions that allow each child to learn as much as possible. Decisions about curricula and teaching methods to be used with children at different levels of IQ or initial academic performance as well as decisions about whether to teach these children separately or together can and should be based on the demonstrated pedagogical effectiveness of the various approaches, not on preconceptions about the causes of initial differences in performance.

Finally, one's position on the nature-nurture question gives little or no guidance as to the degree of ethnic imbalance in special education placement that one should be willing to tolerate. As long as there are special programs for children who lack traditional academic skills, environmentalists and hereditarians alike would expect minority children to be overrepresented in such programs, at least for the immediate future.

If children are indeed being stigmatized or denied educational opportunity because of presumed native incapacity, such practices represent an inappropriate and unjustified use of IQ scores. The practices should be discontinued, but their discontinuation does not depend on proof that IQ has low heritability.

The Issue of Test Validity

Are IQ tests valid measures of "intelligence" or academic ability? Though often equated or confused with the nature-nurture issue, the issue of validity is in fact a separate one. Many psychologists think of intelligence as an ability (or set of abilities) to absorb complex information and grasp and manipulate abstract concepts—an ability that is developed through the interaction of genetic endowment and experience. In this view, intelligence is not native capacity, but it is much more than knowledge of answers to the specific questions on the Stanford-Binet or the WISC-R. Almost all children could be taught to answer the specific questions correctly. The question is how to interpret their performance in the absence of instruction related directly to the test items.

The validity question thus posed has two parts: the first asks whether the skills measured by IQ tests are specific or general; the second asks whether the entity or entities measured by the tests can legitimately be interpreted as "developed ability."

There was a long debate in psychometrics over whether IQ tests measure "general intelligence" or differentiated abilities—verbal ability, perceptual ability, quantitative ability, etc. Contemporary opinion holds that they measure both; there is variation shared by all items, and there are also clusters of items that are particularly closely related. The overriding conclusion, however, is that some variation *is* shared within clusters and across the whole test. The rather disparate items on different IQ tests seem to be measuring the same thing or a small number of things—not a miscellaneous collection of isolated facts and skills. This conclusion is consistent with the interpretation that tests measure underlying abilities, which are manifested in the mastery of specific skills and knowledge. It is equally consistent with the interpretation that the common factor arising from shared variation across different tests and items is really the degree of exposure to middle-class culture and schooling.

There is no general resolution to this interpretive issue. All performance depends on both specific learning and broader abilities. For example, a child's performance on verbal analogies ("Tables are made of wood; windows are made of _____") depends on acquired vocabulary and familiarity with the named objects as well as a more general ability to perceive relationships. The relative contributions of ability and specific experience are not fixed properties of the item or test but depend on the ranges of ability and experience in the population tested. For example, English-speaking American children of elementary school age would presumably be familiar with the words in the above example, and their performance would probably be determined largely by their ability to perceive relationships. However, if children from non-English-speaking families or from cultures without windows and tables were tested, variations in familiarity with the vocabulary items would contribute significantly to performance. Claims about the validity and meaning of test scores, then, are always population-specific.

Rather than addressing the interpretive issue directly, most proponents of testing in the schools place their faith in the empirical phenomenon of predictive validity. Many studies have shown that IQ scores correlate with later school grades and scores on standardized achievement tests (see the paper by Travers in this volume). These validity coefficients (correlations) clearly do not settle the interpretive question. They are consistent with the hypothesis that IQ tests measure general academic ability, which is later manifested in scholastic performance. But, again, they also can be interpreted as showing merely that IQ tests, achievement tests, and teacher-made tests all sample the same domain of acquired skills. The question of importance, once again, is how these conflicting interpretations bear on education policy or practice.

Critics of testing have argued vehemently that tests are invalid as measures of children's general ability and are therefore unfair devices to use for placement. However, few critics have attempted to spell out why tests would be fair if they did measure ability or why they are unfair if they measure only acquired skills. Defenders of testing have justified the use of tests on grounds of predictive validity, apparently believing that they are fair even if they measure primarily acquired skills. Yet few defenders have spelled out their criteria of fairness either. The argument is not really about the degree to which IQ tests measure ability versus acquired skills but about the legitimacy of using a test that mixes the two as a basis for educational programming and placement.

As Messick (1980) points out, when we begin to ask about the legitimacy of a particular use of a test, we must consider more than just what the test measures (validity, in traditional psychometric terms). We must also ask about the consequences of the intended use. In the context of educational decision making it is not enough to know that IQ tests predict future classroom performance, nor would it be enough even to know that they measure general ability. It is necessary to ask whether IQ tests provide information that leads to more effective instruction than would otherwise be possible. Specifically, is it the case that children whose IQs fall in the EMR range require or profit from special forms of instruction or special classroom settings? In the language of contemporary education research, is there an "aptitude-treatment interaction" (Cronbach and Snow, 1977) such that different instructional methods are effective for children with low IQs? An affirmative answer to these questions would constitute a good reason to use IQ scores in programming and placement decisions. (Of course, there might also be other offsetting considerations.) If the answers are negative—and we argue in Chapter 4 that they probably are—then the IQ has limited usefulness[5] in educational decision making, and debates about the meaning of IQ scores are of secondary interest from practical and policy standpoints.

The Issue of Racial and Cultural Bias

Do IQ tests misrepresent the skills or abilities of minority children and those from low-income families? Are tests merely the bearers of bad news

---

[5]This is not necessarily an argument that IQ testing should be abandoned entirely. There is at least one use on which professionals with very different interpretations of IQ scores agree: If a child who is failing in school proves to have an IQ in the normal range, this finding would point to the need for further diagnostic work, e.g., a search for physical disabilities, emotional difficulties, or the like. The argument in the text applies to the use of IQ cutoffs at the low end of the scale in deciding on educational programs and placements.

about genuine differences in educational potential or academic functioning, or are they the creators of false differences? To address these questions it is necessary to clarify some points of definition that have caused confusion and miscommunication between specialists in psychological measurement, on one hand, and educators, policy makers, and the public, on the other.

For many persons outside the field of psychometrics, tests are "biased" if group differences in test scores can plausibly be attributed to average differences in environmental advantage enjoyed by children from different ethnic or socioeconomic groups. From this perspective a test can be biased even if it captures genuine differences in knowledge, skill, or developed ability between groups. In effect, bias, cultural causation, and unfairness become equivalent concepts from this point of view: It seems unfair to categorize children or allocate educational opportunities on the basis of performance differences that are culturally caused, and it seems proper to characterize the instruments that effectuate this unfair categorization as biased.

For specialists in psychological measurement, questions of bias, fairness, and cultural causation are separate. From the specialist's perspective, bias is purely a measurement issue: If a test shows the same internal structure and the same pattern of correlations with other variables across cultural groups, the test is held to be unbiased, even if different groups have different performance profiles due to differential opportunity and experience. Given this conception of bias, it is not inconsistent to argue that the use of a particular test for a particular purpose may be unfair even if the test is, in the technical sense, unbiased.

Three potential sources of bias have received the lion's share of attention in the psychometric literature to date: (1) differences in performance induced by culturally sensitive features of the test situation, such as the race or dialect of the tester; (2) differences across cultural groups in the difficulty of particular items or in other internal features of the pattern of responses generated by test items; and (3) differences in the predictive validity of tests for different groups.

Bias in the Test Situation   Aspects of the test situation, aside from the child's actual skill or ability, that might influence test scores include familiarity with the particular test or type of test (coaching and practice); the race and sex of the tester; the language style or dialect of the tester; the tester's expectations about the child's performance; distortions in scoring; time pressure or lack thereof; and attitudinal factors such as test anxiety, achievement motivation, self-esteem, and countercultural motives to avoid conspicuously good performance.

Cases have been cited in the courts of minority children whose IQs were low when tested by a school psychologist but increased dramatically when the children were retested by persons of the same ethnic group under non-threatening conditions. Most published research, however, finds little evidence that situational factors affect minority children differentially (Jensen, 1980: Chapter 12). Some situational factors have significant overall effects on test scores but show no interactions with ethnicity. For example, coaching and practice together can boost an individual's IQ score by about nine points, if the individual is retested after a fairly short time interval with a test that is similar to the one used for practice. Blacks and whites profit almost equally from coaching and practice. Thus, the reported data suggest that familiarization with tests cannot eliminate much of the IQ difference between the races. Not all of the other situational factors have significant overall effects on test scores, and none is as large as the effects of coaching and practice. More important, in no case is there a large interaction between a situational factor and ethnicity.

Item Bias One approach to the analysis of item bias, which might be called "editorial," is to analyze the face content of items on logical or semantic grounds or on the basis of apparent or presumed connections to particular subcultural milieux. Judge John F. Grady's recent decision in *Parents in Action on Special Education* v. *Hannon* (1980) provides a dramatic and socially significant illustration of this approach. Setting aside a variety of statistical and empirical arguments for and against the use of tests in placing black children in EMR classes, the judge chose instead to examine test items individually and to decide in each case whether the item appeared, *a priori*, to present special difficulties for black children. This "item analysis" led the judge to accept all but a few items on the Stanford-Binet and WISC-R and to uphold the use of these tests for educational placement by the Chicago schools. Others have drawn diametrically opposed conclusions from similar editorial item analyses.

One obvious flaw in this approach is that it places bias in the eye of the "editor," and different editors disagree. More important is the fact that judgments about item content (even if there is agreement) are neither necessary nor sufficient to prove that particular items discriminate against minority children, in the sense of lowering their test scores. An apparently innocent item can be disproportionately difficult for minority children compared with whites, while an item that is problematic on its face can be equally difficult for all groups.

A more systematic and empirical approach to item bias is to examine the proportions of minorities and whites who get each item correct; when an item deviates markedly from the overall profile for any group, that item is assumed to confer an unacceptable advantage or disadvantage for one group or the other and is deemed to be biased in this precise and limited sense. Related psychometric approaches to assessing item bias focus on item-scale correlations and the factor loadings of items. If correlations or loadings for particular items differ conspicuously for minorities and whites, those items are suspect on the grounds that they do not appear to measure the same construct for different groups. None of these psychometric approaches has produced data suggesting that item bias is a major factor causing ethnic differences in test scores. Profiles of item difficulty are similar across ethnic groups (Sandoval, 1979), and factor structures show only minor differences (Reschly, 1978). If there is bias in IQ tests, it is pervasive and not linked to a few offending items.

Differential Prediction   Because the IQ test's primary claim to validity rests on prediction of future academic performance, differential prediction for different ethnic groups could potentially represent important evidence of bias. For example, if IQ tests measure academic ability more accurately for whites than for blacks, IQ might correlate more highly with measures of future school success for whites than for blacks. Or if IQ systematically underestimates the academic abilities of blacks relative to whites, blacks might do better academically than their IQ scores would suggest. Thus, investigations of differential predictive validity involve two questions: whether the margin of error in prediction is the same for different ethnic groups, and whether given test scores predict the same level of success for members of different ethnic groups.

Surprisingly few studies have used appropriate statistical techniques (regression analyses) to investigate these issues for elementary and secondary school children. Most studies present only correlations. As indicated earlier, correlations between IQ scores and scores on standardized achievement tests are generally high. Reported correlations are often .7 or higher for minority children (Sattler, 1974) as well as for whites. Correlations with grades are less consistent. Correlations reported for black children range as high as .6–.7 (Sattler, 1974). One large study, which was influential in the *Larry P.* decision, found correlations of only .27 for Anglo students and .12–.18 for black and Hispanic students (Goldman and Hartig, 1976). This study, however, has been criticized on methodological grounds having mainly to do with the limitations of grades as criterion variables (e.g., by Messé et al., 1979).

Three studies present full regression information (Farr et al., 1971; Mercer, 1979; Reschly and Sabers, 1979). The Farr et al. and Reschly studies produced complex patterns of results, varying with the ages of the children involved, and on balance indicated only minor differences in prediction for whites, blacks, and, in the Reschly study, Hispanics. When patterns did differ, they often (not always) indicated "overprediction" for blacks and "underprediction" for whites. That is, black children did less well in school and on achievement tests than their IQ scores predicted, whereas whites did better. The Mercer analysis, based on data drawn from a sample overlapping with that of Goldman and Hartig, was unique in finding poor overall prediction, worse prediction for blacks and Hispanics than for whites, and underprediction of grades for minority children with IQs below the mid-70s—the range likely to be found among children being evaluated for placement in EMR classes. Mercer's findings suggest that, if the same cutoff scores were used to place children of all ethnic groups in EMR classes, minority children in those classes would be more academically able than their white counterparts. Mercer points out, however, that her findings may be limited by technical factors (e.g., range restriction within the minority samples). In addition, some of the methodological problems raised in connection with Goldman and Hartig's data may also apply to Mercer's analysis, although Mercer has pointed out that essentially the same results are obtained when a semantic differential rating of student competence by teachers is used as the criterion variable rather than grade point average.

Conclusion   In short, the technical studies of bias surveyed in the foregoing paragraphs indicate at most a relatively modest amount of distortion in the test scores of minority children. There is limited evidence for bias in aspects of the test situation external to the test itself. There is little evidence that bias lodges in particular test items, but this fact does not preclude the possibility of generalized bias across all items. Some evidence suggestive of predictive bias at the low end of the IQ scale is reported in the Mercer study. On balance, however, it appears that bias in the technical measurement sense contributes little to explaining ethnic differences in IQ and achievement.

It is important to recognize the limitations of this conclusion. These analyses of "cultural" bias are typically not informed by the participation or perspectives of academic specialists, such as comparative linguists and cultural anthropologists, who work with cultural data. Psychometric analyses may have neglected important sources or mechanisms of bias. Typical psychometric analyses use racial, language, or national designations as if they were equivalent to cultural categories, resulting in conceptual confusion and neglect of potentially important cultural differences within racial, language, or national groups.

In addition, psychometric investigations of bias do not address many concerns of other social scientists, educators, and policy makers regarding bias, as they use the term. For example, investigations of predictive bias ignore the problem of bias in the criteria: If school grades and/or achievement test scores understate the academic performance of minority students—as tests allegedly underestimate their abilities—it would be of no consequence, from a moral or policy standpoint, to find that prediction was perfect. Also, as noted at the beginning of this section, outside the field of psychological measurement, bias is often defined as the contribution of sociocultural factors that raise or lower the IQ scores of one group relative to another. Everyone, even the firmest believer in the genetic determination of IQ, admits that there is some cultural contribution, just as there is a cultural contribution to school success. Most important, even if there were no psychometric biases in IQ tests, questions raised earlier about the educational value of the tests would remain unanswered. Knowing that tests predict equally well for all cultural groups, or measure the same constructs for all groups, would not tell us whether instruction should differ as a function of IQ scores.

Alternative Measures of Intellectual Functioning

Standard IQ tests such as the WISC-R and the Stanford-Binet are not the only available means of measuring cognitive functioning. There have been a number of attempts to modify IQ tests, primarily with the intent of reducing or eliminating presumed cultural bias. There have also been several attempts to devise new measures, based on different assumptions about the nature and development of intelligence.

Among the approaches that have been tried in order to accommodate existing IQ tests to cultural differences are translation into other languages, altering procedures for administering and scoring tests, modifying items, and developing group-specific norms. Some of these changes have come about because of judicial or policy decisions. For example, in the case of *Diana* v. *State Board of Education*, which challenged the administration in English of the Stanford-Binet to Spanish-speaking children, the California Department of Education agreed to a consent decree requiring bilingual testing, the elimination of "unfair" verbal items, and the development of a revised test reflecting Mexican-American culture and norms on a Mexican-American population (Bersoff, 1979).

In light of what was said earlier about the modest contribution (at most) of item bias and variations in test procedure to ethnic differences in IQ scores, it is not surprising that item deletions and procedural changes have failed to reduce the discrepancy to any significant extent. (These approaches have not been tried and studied extensively, however.)

One modification that is likely to make a difference is translation. The one source of bias that survived even Jensen's critical scrutiny (1980: Chapter 12) is the use of English-language tests with children of limited English-speaking ability. There appears to be no doubt that such children are at an unfair disadvantage. Translation, however, introduces a problem of "norming," i.e., of constructing appropriate group standards for judging the individual child's IQ. There is no guarantee that items will retain their levels of difficulty, even when accurately translated. New norms are needed, but these norms will necessarily be specific to the cultural group for whom the test is translated. Translation is thus directly related to what is perhaps the most direct and radical approach to correcting the alleged cultural bias of IQ tests: constructing separate norms for each subcultural group.

The logic of culture-specific norms is straightforward: If subcultural groups have qualitatively different "experience pools," leading to differences in average performance, the fairest comparison for any child would seem to be with members of his or her own group, not society at large. The difficulty with this approach is equally obvious: Since the different experience pools do not equip children equally well to function in a school system and society dominated by the white middle class, numerically equal scores based on separate norms may no longer entail equivalent predictions about educational success. Proponents and critics of group norms are sharply split on the question of whether this reduction in predictive power invalidates group-specific norms.

Another alternative to traditional IQ testing is provided by new measures based on Piaget's influential theory of cognitive development, which holds that intelligence undergoes a series of qualitative changes from infancy to adolescence, each marked by a reorganization of the child's system of logic and understanding of natural phenomena. There is some evidence that this sequence occurs cross-culturally, although there are cultural variations in the rate of progress and the specific skills and knowledge that the child exhibits at each stage. Several investigators (e.g., Pinard and Laurendeau, 1964; Goldschmid and Bentler, 1968; Uzgiris and Hunt, 1975) have arranged Piagetian tasks in sequential order and collected age norms for performance, thus constructing scales by which an individual's level of development can be specified, both in terms of Piagetian theory and relative to others. These scales have proved to be extremely strong on traditional psychometric grounds of test-retest reliability and inter-item homogeneity. They also correlate highly with standard IQ tests (e.g., Kohlberg, 1968) and exhibit marked black-white differences in performance (Tuddenham, 1970), although there is one report that differences between Anglos and Hispanics are reduced (DeAvila and Havassy, 1974). Although the Piagetian tests have the virtue of a sophisticated theoretical rationale and a firm grounding in developmental research, their practical effects are likely to differ relatively little from those of standard IQ tests, with the possible important exception of use with Hispanic populations.

Another example is provided by attempts to construct culture-free and culture-fair tests. To use acquired skills and knowledge as a measure of intellectual capacity requires, among other assumptions, an assumption of roughly equal motivation and access to relevant experience throughout the tested population—an assumption that has repeatedly been challenged. In response, some investigators have attempted to build tests from items for which the assumption seems at least approximately tenable. The resulting tests typically include items heavily weighted toward perceptual or psychomotor performance and avoid verbal items. A few well-known examples include (1) the Ravens Matrices, in which respondents are shown a sequence of geometrical designs that exhibit a well-defined progression; the respondent's task is to identify the regularities in the sequence and predict the next pattern, choosing it from among several possibilities; (2) the Porteus Maze Test, which requires respondents to trace paths through a series of 28 mazes of increasing difficulty; and (3) the Goodenough-Harris Drawing Test, which requires the respondent to draw a man, a woman, and himself or herself; responses are scored to reflect developmental differences in depiction of body proportions, attachment of limbs and head, and inclusion of certain details of facial features, hands, and clothing. Developmental norms and conversions to IQ are available for all of the cited instruments. The verdict of many years of research on these and kindred tests is fairly clear and generally accepted: They have failed to yield the desired effect of substantially reducing or eliminating cultural differences in performance (Anastasi, 1976).

A final example is provided by new tests involving direct measures of learning. Almost 50 years ago, L. S. Vygotsky suggested that if one wants to measure children's ability to learn one should not test what they already know but rather put them in a situation in which there is something to learn and watch how they behave. Recently, Budoff (1968) and Feuerstein et al. (1979) devised approaches to testing that follow Vygotsky's long-ignored suggestion. Feuerstein's work is particularly relevant in the present context because he has tested many children and adolescents who would be labeled EMR by conventional test criteria. Feuerstein's Learning Potential Assessment Device (LPAD) is directly linked to remedial teaching. Children are tested on a wide variety of conceptual tasks involving analogies, seriation, logical classification, and the like. They are exposed to a highly structured instructional process involving explicit verbal explanation (mediation) and practice and feedback in a one-to-one interaction with a trained teacher. Children are then retested on the original tasks and on a set of related tasks designed to show how well newly learned concepts are generalized to similar problems. The measure of the child's potential is not his or her initial performance but the degree of progress made in response to instruction. More data on the validity of this approach and in particular its transference to other learning situations are needed.

Conclusions

The IQ test remains the most widely used, most influential (in terms of its effect on placement decisions), and most controversial of current measures. Much of the controversy centers on the adequacy of the tests as measures of innate capacity or learning potential, but this has little bearing on their adequacy as measures of developed cognitive abilities. We have also found reason to doubt that scientific resolution of the nature-nurture issue, even if it were possible, would dictate or justify different educational treatment of children with IQs in the EMR range. We have found little evidence for test bias, in the technical sense of the term, but we recognize that this null conclusion does not address many concerns about bias as the term is used in public discussion. The IQ test's claim to validity rests heavily on its predictive power. We find that prediction alone, however, is insufficient evidence of the test's educational utility. What is needed is evidence that children with scores in the EMR range will learn more effectively in a special program or placement. As argued in more detail in Chapter 4, we doubt that such evidence exists. Although we are not prepared, as a panel, to advocate discontinuation of IQ testing, we feel that the burden of justification lies with its proponents to show that in particular cases the tests have been used in a manner that contributes to the effectiveness of instruction for the children in question.

Attempts to modify or replace the IQ as a measure of intellectual functioning have in some cases clearly failed and in other cases remain promising but unproven. Thus, while we advocate further pursuit of the promising approaches, we cannot at present endorse any particular technique as a substitute or supplement to the IQ.

INDIVIDUAL MEASURES OUTSIDE THE INTELLECTUAL DOMAIN

Even if all the conceptual and technical problems involved in measuring intellectual functioning could be solved, the resulting instrument or instruments would constitute only a part of a fully adequate assessment battery. Many aspects of individual competence lie outside the intellectual domain, and these must be examined before an appropriate educational program and placement can be determined. In addition, a child's behavioral functioning must be understood in relation to the state of his or her physical development, nutrition, and physiological functioning; physical abnormalities and malfunctions, some of them correctable, may underlie apparent intellectual deficits and maladaptive behavior patterns.

The importance of both types of measures has been widely recognized. Virtually all authoritative discussions of educational assessment recommend inclusion of measures of adaptive behavior and biomedical screening devices. The following two sections examine some general characteristics of major existing measures and discuss salient issues surrounding their use in educational programming and placement. Although we concur with the widely accepted view that biomedical measures and measures of adaptive behavior deserve a place in a comprehensive assessment battery, we also believe that the use of such measures should be guided and evaluated by the same standards that we have applied to cognitive measures, i.e., their contribution to identifying functional needs and pointing toward effective interventions.

Biomedical Measures

The general purpose of biomedical assessment is to determine whether the child is an intact organism. In the context of a comprehensive assessment for EMR placement, biomedical measures have two more specific purposes: to ascertain whether the child's inability to learn in ordinary classes is due to sensory, motor, or other physical impairment and, whenever possible, to guide the selection of remedial approaches.

It is important to distinguish among the three different roles that physical factors may play with respect to categorization of a child as mentally retarded. First, peripheral physical disabilities may impair an otherwise normal child's performance in class and on measures of intellectual functioning, such as IQ tests. For example, poor vision, poor hearing, psychomotor malfunctions, or hunger could have these effects. Detection of such conditions is obviously essential to prevent misclassification and often points to effective interventions.

Second, neurological conditions or endocrine malfunctions may create specific deficits in intellectual functioning (such as language disorders or dyslexia) or distortions of behavior. In the classroom, the cognitive or behavioral symptoms may be indistinguishable from similar behaviors with different causes; however, appropriate biomedical probes may identify the causes and in some cases point to corrective steps.

Third, physical trauma or deprivation, particularly in the earliest stages of life, may create global deficits of functioning. Some of these deficits may have neurological or other physical correlates in the school-age child; others may not. Shonkoff (in this volume) reviews a variety of genetic, prenatal, perinatal, and postnatal conditions that have among their sequelae global impairment of intellectual functioning. Many of these conditions, such as maternal malnutrition or lead intoxication, can be prevented; others, such as phenolkytonuria (PKU), can be significantly ameliorated if detected early. In most cases, however, the damage cannot be corrected by known physical treatments when the child has reached school age. Remediation in these cases must address the symptom; that is, it must take the form of an educational program designed to meet the needs of an impaired learner. Within the limits of current knowledge there appear to be no differences between the educational treatments that work best for children who have global learning difficulties due to physical causes and those that work for other children with global deficits. Future research may lead to medical or educational interventions addressing physically based, global learning problems; if so, identification of long-term physical causes will become a major function of biomedical assessment in educational contexts. For now, however, its primary functions are the detection of physical impairments in mentally normal children and the detection of neuropsychological conditions that impair intellectual functioning but are distinct from mental retardation as it is usually conceived.

Another distinction is also important to understanding our view of biomedical assessment. Certain assessment procedures can be performed at relatively low costs; they give a preliminary indication of where a child's problem may lie. Other procedures are more extensive and require the services of highly trained professionals and are, therefore, costly. Screening procedures of the first kind are appropriate to use with all children who have been referred for learning problems. Detailed diagnostic procedures of the second kind are appropriate for use in a small number of carefully targeted cases.

Screening procedures are exemplified by the biomedical portion of Mercer's System of Multicultural Pluralistic Assessment (SOMPA) (Mercer and Lewis, 1978), a battery of instruments designed for use in comprehensive educational assessment. SOMPA includes six biomedical measures: the Snellen test of visual acuity, a measure of auditory acuity, weight standardized by height, a set of physical dexterity tasks, a health history inventory, and the Bender Visual Motor Gestalt Test (a test that requires the child to copy a set of figures, which is regarded as indicative of perceptual maturity and neurological impairment). None of these measures is sufficient in itself to precisely pinpoint a disability or to specify the necessary remediation. Each is capable, however, of identifying a general area of disability, within which more precise measures can be taken. In some cases the screening measures may point to widely prevalent problems, for which more refined diagnosis and remediation are routine; detection of common visual problems is an obvious example. In other cases the measures may point to areas of disability for which further diagnostic work may be extensive and for which remediation may or may not be available.

When a preliminary screening indicates the possible existence of neurological problems, a variety of specialized cognitive, sensory, and motor tests come into play. Interpretation of the results, which requires the services of a specialist in neuropsychology, rests on a large body of data accumulated mainly during the last 15 years (Hecaen and Albert, 1978; Lezak, 1976; Reitan and Davison, 1974). Unlike traditional ability and intelligence testing, neuropsychological analysis depends on at least four different uses of testing results: the level of function, pathognomonic signs, patterns, and disparities between the left and right sides of the body.

Investigations of individuals whose IQs fall in the mildly mentally retarded range (Matthews, 1974) have shown that their performance is sometimes strongly suggestive of localized lesions in the brain. Initially, in the classroom, poor performance may appear to be global in nature, whereas on closer investigation it may be seen as part of a picture resulting from selective damage to the nervous system. For example, a child may demonstrate low verbal ability, which is itself due to a lateralized damage to the speech centers of the brain. Other tests, such as comparison of performances from the two sides of the body, may reveal that the lateralized damage appears in other areas besides speech and language.

Some performances on tests are pathognomonic; that is, in this context, diagnostic of cerebral damage. For example, a partial hemiplegia may be revealed by unusual discrepancies between finger tapping of the left and right hands. Or abnormalities of the sensory pathways may be revealed by failures of recognition in tactual performance tests.

The application of neuropsychological analysis is by no means straightforward for young children and those whose verbal skills are impaired (Boll, 1974). Nevertheless, a thorough examination of neuropsychological integrity, based on knowledge of the structural features of the brain, can lead to the detection of specific genetic, traumatic, or pathophysiological conditions (Benton, 1974).

Adaptive Behavior Scales

As noted earlier, the AAMD as well as the federal government and many states define mental retardation as "significantly subaverage general intellectual functioning, *existing concurrently with deficits in adaptive be-*

havior, and manifested during the developmental period" (Grossman, 1977:5, emphasis added.) The AAMD goes on to define adaptive behavior as "the effectiveness or degree to which the individual meets the standards of personal independence and social responsibility expected of his age or cultural group" (Grossman, 1977:11). This broad definition is consistent with numerous more specific definitions that have been proposed by theoreticians and researchers (Coulter and Morrow, 1978, Chapter 1).

Because the definition is so broad, it has given rise to a large number of instruments (at least 132, according to a review cited in Meyers et al., 1979) that stress different aspects of adaptation and have different metric properties. However, as Meyers et al. point out, most of these instruments share certain general characteristics that sharply distinguish them from intelligence tests: (1) they focus on behavior rather than thought processes; (2) they focus on common or typical behavior rather than on "potential"; that is, they are descriptive rather than necessarily implying the existence of underlying traits or capacities; and (3) they are based on reports of informants, usually parents or teachers, rather than on direct observation of a child's performance.

Most of these instruments have been designed specifically for use with mentally retarded people and are particularly appropriate for differentiating levels of functioning in individuals who are clearly below the normal range. However, a few are designed for use in the public school population and are intended to help discriminate "EMR" from "normal" children. Our discussion is particularly concerned with the latter instruments, of which the most widely used are the AAMD Adaptive Behavior Scale-Public School Version (ABS) (Lambert et al., 1975) and the Adaptive Behavior Inventory for Children (ABIC) (Mercer and Lewis, 1978; Mercer, 1979). The two instruments have much in common, both in content and purpose, yet they also exhibit some important differences. Together they illustrate most of the major issues involved in the use of adaptive behavior scales in the schools.

The AAMD public school scale, which was derived from an earlier AAMD scale designed for mentally retarded people (Nihira et al., 1969), has two parts. The first contains 10 competence domains, each with one or more subscales: independent functioning (eating, toileting, etc.), physical development, economic activity (budgeting and shopping), language development, numbers and time, vocational activity, self-direction (initiative, perseverance, use of leisure time), and responsibility and socialization (cooperation, considerateness, interaction with others). The second part contains 12 domains of maladaptive behavior: violence and destruction, antisocial behavior, rebellion, untrustworthiness, withdrawal, stereotyped behavior and odd mannerisms, inappropriate manners, unacceptable vocalizations, unacceptable or eccentric habits, hyperactivity, psychological disturbance, and use of medication. The school version of the ABS is normally completed by a teacher, although at least one study has shown a high degree of agreement between parents and teachers in describing children's behavior with the ABS (Cole, 1976). The ABS school version has been standardized on a sample of 2,600 children, including normal children and children identified as EMR, trainable mentally retarded, and educationally handicapped. The standardization sample included a wide range of socioeconomic levels and ethnic backgrounds.

The ABIC is part of SOMPA, a comprehensive system for assessment of children from diverse cultural groups. This instrument includes 242 items, each referring to a specific practical or social skill or behavior. For example, can the child take a message on the telephone? Does the child cross the street with the traffic light? Does the child visit friends outside the neighborhood? Questions are answered by the child's mother or mother substitute. Most of the items are age graded, over the elementary school range from five to eleven; gradings are based on data from an extensive pretest and from the norm sample (described below). Items are organized into six competence areas or subscales—family, community, peer relations, nonacademic school roles, earner-consumer, and self-maintenance. Scores are normalized within each subscale and calibrated to yield a mean of 50 points and a standard deviation of 15. Subscale scores are averaged to yield an overall score. The instrument has been standardized on a sample of almost 2,100, including equal numbers of black, Hispanic, and white children, spanning a range of socioeconomic levels.

It is apparent that there is considerable overlap between the ABS and ABIC (and other adaptive behavior scales) in the types of behavior covered. There are differences as well. The ABS is completed by the teacher and focuses on adaptive behavior within the school. It contains items with intellectual content of the sort found in IQ tests. In contrast, the ABIC is completed by the mother and concentrates more exclusively on practical skills and social behavior exhibited outside the school. It is not surprising, therefore, that some of the ABS subscales (numbers and time, economic activity, and language development) correlate about .6 with IQ, whereas other scales show modest correlations, generally below .2 (Lambert, 1978). The ABIC subscales show uniformly low correlations with the WISC-R (Mercer, 1979). As Meyers et al. (1979) note, there is a wide range of variation in correlations with IQ among adaptive behavior scales generally, depending on, among other factors, item content and the populations sampled.

Another important characteristic of the ABIC is that subscale scores and overall scores have almost identical distributions among black, white, and Hispanic children (Mercer, 1979). There is some evidence that ethnicity does not affect scores on the ABS *within* EMR and regular classes (Lambert, 1978). However, since ethnic proportions probably differed between EMR and regular classes in the ABS norm sample, distributions of ABS scores may have differed for the ethnic groups overall.

What are the implications of these characteristics of adaptive behavior scales for use in educational decision making? First, it is evident that adaptive behavior scores are not redundant with IQ. The ABIC and most subscales of the ABS yield information about domains of competence that are distinct from the cluster of abilities tapped by IQ tests. One implication of this fact is that adaptive behavior measures cannot simply be substituted for IQ as measures of general competence. A more important implication is that the use of adaptive behavior measures in assigning children to EMR classes—a practice that is mandatory given existing theoretical and legal definitions of mental retardation—will reduce the numbers of children assigned to such classes relative to the numbers that would be assigned on the basis of IQ alone. (This is so because many children with low IQs have adequate adaptive behavior scores.) As we saw in Chapter 2, this outcome has been observed in practice.

The latter implication raises the important question of how children with low IQs but high adaptive behavior scores will fare in regular classes. The answer depends in part on how well those classes are designed to match the pace of instruction to each child's individual needs—an issue to which we return in Chapter 4. It also depends on how much the social and practical skills measured by adaptive behavior scales contribute to school success.

A second potential set of implications concerns the effects of adaptive behavior scales on ethnic disproportions in special education. Some have expressed the hope that the use of adaptive behavior measures will reduce the disproportionate representation of minorities in EMR classes. Logically, there is no necessity for such an outcome. As Coulter and Morrow (1978) point out, the use of one measure (adaptive behavior) that shows no ethnic differences does not affect the ethnic differences in another measure (IQ). If IQ and an ethnically neutral adaptive behavior measure, such as the ABIC, were jointly used to place children, the IQ could in effect control the ethnic composition of the group ultimately assigned to EMR classes, depending on the decision rules used to combine the measures. However there is some evidence, cited in Chapter 2, that the use of adaptive behavior measures does in fact decrease ethnic disproportion in EMR placement.

A final set of implications concerns the utility of adaptive behavior data in designing programs of instruction. As Coulter and Morrow (1978) point out, the distinction between using adaptive behavior measures as classificatory devices and using them as guides for programming is a critical one. Different measures may be appropriate for the two purposes. To date, the use of adaptive behavior measures in programming has been confined mainly to individuals whose deficiencies in functioning place them well below the EMR range. Measures geared to mildly mentally retarded populations have been used primarily for classification. It is easy to envision possible instructional applications of adaptive behavior scales in pinpointing areas of relative strength to be built on and areas of particular weakness to be remedied. Some areas needing remediation might be skills that are appropriate parts of the regular curriculum, e.g., telling time, mastering numbers, learning to handle money. Others might be the modification of practical skills, such as dressing and hygiene, which would not be part of the curriculum for most children but might well be included in a program for mentally retarded children. Still others might be the modification of maladaptive social behaviors that interfere with learning of any kind, e.g., destructiveness or withdrawal. However, these potentially promising applications remain largely unexplored.

COMPREHENSIVE ASSESSMENT IN CONTEXT: A TWO-PHASE PROCESS

Throughout our discussion of the elements of comprehensive individual assessment, we argue repeatedly that assessment should be linked to instruction—that it should discriminate among children who can profit from different modes of instruction or who require different forms of intervention before conventional instruction can work. This section suggests an even more fundamental link between assessment and instruction.

The section is premised on the belief that what seem to be individual failures are often failures of the educational system. Children may do poorly in class because they have not been taught or managed appropriately—and this may be disproportionately true of minority children. If this belief is correct, no assessment of the causes of learning failure would be complete without a systematic examination of the teaching and learning environment.

Moreover, there are good reasons to examine the learning environment before subjecting a child to a comprehensive individual assessment of the kind described above. Merely to be singled out as a learning failure and evaluated for placement in a category such as EMR may be distressing to a child and the child's parents and may affect the subsequent behavior of teachers and peers toward the child. And even with the most comprehensive and conscientious of assessments, there is some risk that the child will be misclassified. Given these risks of emotional damage, stigma, and misclassification, protection of the child's rights and interests would seem to require that possible deficiencies of the learning situation be examined and ruled out before comprehensive assessment begins.

We conclude that an ideal assessment process would take place in two phases, beginning with an assessment of the learning environment and proceeding to a comprehensive assessment of the individual child only after it has been established that he or she fails to learn in a variety of classroom settings under a variety of well-conceived instructional strategies.[5]

Our conclusion is very much in the spirit of P.L. 94-142 and the regulations implementing Section 504 and P.L. 94-142, which stipulate that students be placed in special education programs only when "the education of the person in the regular environment with the use of supplementary aids and services cannot be achieved satisfactorily" (34 CFR 104.34(a); see also 20 USC 1412 (5)(B), 34 CFR 300.550).[6] The main thrust of this provision has obviously been toward mainstreaming children already diagnosed as handicapped. However, a neglected implication of the provision is that there must be a systematic attempt to determine whether satisfactory progress can be achieved in a regular class. In the case of children who, under present circumstances, would be referred for possible placement in EMR classes, we suggest that there is much to be gained by making this determination without waiting until the label is assigned.

There are no universally established procedures for conducting the kind of two-phase assessment that we envision, nor is there a fully developed, widely used technology for conducting an assessment of the instructional environment. It is, therefore, incumbent on us to suggest the broad outlines of a procedure and to point to some directions that development of technology might take.

What kinds of information might be included in an ideal phase-one assessment? First, there should be some evidence that schools are using curricula known to be effective for the student populations they serve. Such

[5]One exception to the principle that environmental assessment should precede individual assessment is the case of biomedical screening for high-prevalence problems, such as vision defects. As suggested earlier, such screening is not stigmatizing and is appropriate for children who have not experienced classroom failure as well as for those who have.

[6]After the split of the U.S. Department of Education from the U.S. Department of Health, Education, and Welfare, the Code of Federal Regulations was revised to transfer the education regulations from the Public Welfare Title (Title 45) to an independent title for education (Title 34). The citations of regulations for Section 504 and P.L. 94-142 in this report are to their new location in the Code of Federal Regulations.

evidence might be provided by publishers or independent researchers or—better yet—by the district's own data. It is important that the data show not only that the curriculum is effective for students in general but also that it is effective for the various ethnic, linguistic, and socioeconomic groups actually served by the school or district in question. Standardized achievement tests or criterion-referenced performance tests (see below) might serve as assessment devices.

Second, there should be evidence that the teacher has implemented the curriculum effectively for the student in question. Such evidence might include documentation that other children in the class are performing adequately and that the child in question has been adequately exposed to the curriculum, i.e., has not missed many lessons due to absence, disciplinary exclusions from class, etc. Such evidence might also include observational data collected by a school psychologist, educational consultant, or resource teacher, showing that the child's teacher is providing adequate classroom management and appropriate instruction in accord with the curriculum; that he or she is attending to the child in question and providing appropriate direction, feedback, and reinforcement; and that the child is participating adequately in the instructional process. Observational data could also be used to detect and document problems of management and/or misbehavior that interfere with the effectiveness of the curriculum, e.g., lack of attention, disruption of class, and the like.

Third, there should be objective evidence that the child has not learned what was taught. Again, standardized norm-referenced tests or criterion-referenced tests keyed to the curriculum itself might be used for this purpose. Assessment of the child's progress should, however, be frequent enough so that problems are detected early and so that the child is not allowed to spend weeks in the classroom, falling further and further behind, without the teacher noticing.

Finally and most important, there should be evidence that, when early problems were detected, systematic efforts were made to locate the source of the difficulty and to take corrective measures. Again, school psychologists or specially trained educators could play a role, acting as consultants to the teacher in suggesting remedial approaches. Under some circumstances it might be appropriate to change teachers or curricula, in an attempt to find a better match to the child's needs. Results of such attempts at improvements should be documented, and only after reasonable efforts have been exhausted should the child be referred formally for assessment.

What kinds of instruments are needed to support this two-phase assessment process? Some possible answers have already been suggested. Standardized achievement tests can play a role in evaluating strong and weak points in the curriculum as a whole; assuming that sufficiently reliable tests are selected, they can also be used to assess the performance of individual children. The growing literature on "effective schools" suggests that these uses of standardized tests are among the distinguishing characteristics of schools that are particularly effective in teaching minority children from low-income families (see Chapter 4).

A developing technology that may have promise is criterion-referenced testing. Criterion-referenced tests are used to measure mastery of specific domains of subject matter. A child's performance is judged against some absolute standard; a typical measure might be the number of arithmetic problems of a specific sort that the child can solve. The child's performance is not scaled against that of other children, nor is the test used to draw inferences about broad intellectual abilities. Many informal, teacher-made tests are in effect criterion referenced, as are many of the tests included in packaged curricula and teachers' manuals accompanying standard textbooks. Recently, there have been advances in thinking about the design of such tests (e.g., Martuza, 1977; Harris et al., 1974), and improvements in their psychometric properties may be in the offing. Such tests are of interest in the context of this report because of their close link to instruction. They can be used at the beginning of an instructional sequence to determine whether the child has the prerequisite skills needed to profit from the instruction, and they can be used at the end of a sequence to determine whether the child has absorbed the material or needs further work to achieve mastery. Thus, they can potentially be used to evaluate the outcomes of the systematic variations in instruction that are part of a phase-one assessment.

Another technology that has some promise is systematic observation in the classroom. Systems for analyzing and recording behavior in the classroom have a long history in educational research (Medley and Mitzel, 1963). Most of the instruments used are too costly, time-consuming, and demanding in terms of observer training to be practical for use in self-evaluation by schools. However, there have been recent suggestions that suitably simplified and focused instruments may be useful as diagnostic devices and guides for the remediation of specific behavior problems (e.g., Alessi, 1980; Baker and Tyne, 1980). Observations have also been used by researchers to measure the implementation of curricula (Stallings, 1977) and time devoted to academic activities (Rosenshine and Berliner, 1978). Again, simplified observation systems may be useful for similar purposes in assessing the quality of learning environments.

None of the above suggestions about procedures and instrumentation is novel. All have been tried, in varying combinations, in different school districts. A few large districts have gone far in implementing systematic procedures of instruction and closely linked assessment; some of these districts have reported dramatic improvements in students' basic academic skills (Carnine et al., 1981; Monteiro, 1981) and, by implication, a decline in the rate of learning failures. These reports encourage us to believe that the suggestions above are both feasible to implement and potentially effective. The two-phase assessment process clearly entails new costs—the costs of training and maintaining staff to conduct evaluations of the learning environment. The process also entails financial savings, by reducing the number of children referred for costly, comprehensive assessments and possibly also the number who must be maintained in costly special classroom settings.

SUMMARY AND CONCLUSIONS

The discussion in this chapter follows from the premise that the main purpose of assessment in education is to improve instruction and learning. Children are or should be assessed in order to identify strengths and weaknesses that necessitate specific forms of remediation or educational practice. Remediation may take the form of intervention outside the school, such as medical treatment or family intervention. We believe, however, that a significant portion of children who experience difficulties in the classroom can be treated effectively through improved instruction.

These basic assumptions lead to a perspective on assessment and its contribution to ethnic and sex disproportions in EMR classes that is different from the one with which the study began. A concern with disproportion per se dictates a focus on bias in assessment instruments and a search for instruments that will reduce disproportion. A concern with instructional utility leads to a search for assessment procedures and instruments that will aid in selecting or designing effective programs for all children. We believe that better assessment and a closer link between assessment and instruction will in fact reduce disproportion, because minority children have disproportionately been the victims of poor instruction. We also believe that the problem should be attacked at its roots, which lie in the presumption that learning problems must imply deficiencies in the child and in consequent inattention to the role of education itself in creating and ameliorating these problems.

This viewpoint has led us to urge a greatly increased emphasis on systematic educational intervention *before* a child is referred for individual assessment. When poor instruction has been ruled out as a cause of learning failure, it becomes appropriate to look for problems within the child or in the child's environment outside the school, again with an eye toward problems that can be corrected; this is the purpose of individual assessment.

We believe, and have cited evidence to support our belief, that an assessment procedure like the one we outlined will significantly reduce the proportion of children whose failure to learn must be attributed to global intellectual deficits. The question remains whether it is necessary or useful to apply the label EMR to this residual group or to separate them from other children for instructional purposes. The answer, in our view, must hinge on another question: Do these children require and can they profit from modes of instruction that are different from those that work best with other children who have experienced learning difficulties? We turn to this question in the next chapter.

4

Effective Instruction for Mildly Mentally Retarded Children

In Chapter 1 we argued that the quality of instruction in special education programs is one of three key factors that determine whether disproportion should be considered problematic. Chapter 3 presented our view that the justification for assessment procedures derives from their contribution to effective teaching and learning. Thus, instruction for mildly mentally retarded children—both the quality offered and the setting in which it is best provided—are at the fore of the panel's concerns and recommendations.

This chapter begins by attempting to specify the characteristics of effective education for mildly mentally retarded children. With these characteristics in mind we are able to address two core policy questions: (1) Are separate classes for mildly mentally retarded children needed, or can such children be as well or better served in the regular classroom? (2) Does the mentally retarded label as used in current practice specify unique instructional programs, warranting a separate categorical grouping of children, or would a more general designation be just as useful in delivering educational services?

Our question then becomes: What is effective education for mildly mentally retarded students? The apparent simplicity of this question is illusory, and the difficulty of arriving at a simple answer is in great measure

The panel would like to thank Gaea Leinhardt, *who helped gather evidence and who consulted extensively with us during the preparation of this chapter.*

a function of the difficulty of deciding who is and who is not mildly mentally retarded. At the very heart of the demand for special education is the assumption that all children do not prosper under identical educational programs. The aim of the enterprise, the reason for elaborate assessment and placement procedures, is to match children and treatments so that each child is treated optimally. By definition, then, what is good or effective instruction is supposed to depend on the kind of children involved. This means that programs can only be evaluated with respect to a *properly identified* class of children. If an instructional program is not successful in a given case, it might not be a poor program but rather a misapplication to a given child or group of children.

Some of the difficulties that we address here emerge from attempts to transform educational practices that were originally based on clinical practice for a highly select population into a special education program for a much wider range of students that must accommodate the bureaucratic constraints of the public school. In the area of mental retardation, as in other areas of special education such as learning disabilities, many accepted principles of instruction have been based on careful observation and a tutorial type of instruction with highly atypical children. While this knowledge was being applied within the public school environment, changes were taking place in the identified population of exceptional children and in the educational practices that were functional within that setting (Cruickshank, 1967; Dunn, 1973). For example, clinical populations often include more severely handicapped individuals, while schools enroll children with mild or moderate handicapping conditions; clinical settings are usually able to provide individual tutorial instruction, while financial and organizational factors restrict schools to small-group instruction or separate special classes; clinicians often identify unique diagnostic problems of individuals, while schools tend to recognize more general problems of poor performance.

It was not the original intention of special educators that all children with school problems or minor difficulties in adjustment or coping be eligible for special education services. In recent years, however, public support for special education has been expanded to include a significant number of children with school problems or behavioral difficulties. Legal requirements and fiscal incentives have moved educators to identify and place more and more students in special education programs (U.S. Department of Health, Education, and Welfare, 1979a). As mentioned previously, the jury is still out as to the most effective placement for these students.

As we noted in Chapter 2, the variation and changes in the definition of educable mental retardation complicate the task of deciding what is effective education for mildly mentally retarded children, since it is unclear who should be classified as mentally retarded. The research on which we are able to draw has generally accepted the classifications made by school districts and sought statistically significant effects for groups of children with the mildly mentally retarded label. But these groups have usually been more heterogeneous than the common label implies. Since effective instruction for a given child is likely to depend more on his or her actual characteristics as a learner than on the classification as mentally retarded, the reliance on institutional labels to characterize children necessarily limits the kinds of conclusions that can be drawn from this research.

A further limitation in the use of existing research concerns historical changes in labeling practices in the schools. There has been a sharp decrease in the number of students classified as educable mentally retarded (EMR) in the past several years, with a concomitant increase in the number of children labeled as learning disabled (U.S. Department of Education, 1980). Children who are currently in the EMR category, especially those in self-contained classrooms, may therefore be more disabled than their counterparts of previous years. Research on this older cohort may not be generalizable to the current group of EMR children.

Special education for mildly mentally retarded children has grown from the widespread observation that children with generally low mental ability fare poorly in regular school programs. It is generally assumed that such children lack abilities, such as the ability to abstract or to transfer knowledge, that are assumed in regular instruction. These children are therefore expected to profit from an adapted curriculum and teaching procedures that make fewer assumptions of concept mastery; provide more explicit and more numerous examples through concrete experiences; allow more active participation in "hands-on" experiences by students; provide structure into which learners can insert specific information; and include specific efforts to build improved social cooperation skills, self-esteem, and work habits (Goldstein, 1974, 1975).

To accomplish these goals it is assumed that specially trained teachers and/or support staffs are required. Yet these special services can, at least in theory, be provided under a number of different institutional arrangements, including (1) the separate class structure, in which children are assigned to a special EMR class conducted by a specially trained teacher who provides a unique curriculum for the children for a full school day; (2) the resource room structure, in which the basic assignment of the child is to a regular class, but the child is removed for special instruction by a specially trained teacher for a portion of the school day; and (3) the teacher/consultant model, in which a specialist advises the regular teacher on special tasks and lessons that can aid the exceptional child, but all instruction is given in the regular classroom. We consider instruction under all of these arrangements as we attempt to define effective instruction for mildly mentally retarded students.

EVIDENCE ON EFFECTIVE INSTRUCTION FOR MILDLY MENTALLY RETARDED CHILDREN

Despite several decades of research it remains difficult to gather definitive evidence on the nature of effective instruction for mildly mentally retarded children. In addition to problems created by shifting definitions of the EMR population, there are reasons for the lack of evidence that lie deep in the prevailing tradition of educational research, a tradition in which research on mental retardation has quite naturally shared. Much of this research has set out to test whether some new program is better than "standard" practice. Groups of children in the new and the standard programs are compared on some outcome measures, but the programs themselves are not analyzed, nor is the actual functioning of children within them assessed. The result is a "black box" evaluation, comparing outcomes of differently labeled treatments without attempting to determine what features of the programs or treatments are responsible for the observed outcomes. Indeed, it is characteristic of most of these studies that only the most global descriptions of the educational treatments are offered. Typically, we are able to learn of class size and something about the age and perhaps IQ distributions of the children in the classes. Little detail is offered concerning the actual curricula being used, nor are there usually observations of how children interact with teachers, other children, or the curriculum materials.[1]

Other methodological limitations in the bulk of the research on instruction for mentally retarded children must also be noted. The most important are a failure to randomize treatment and control groups, so that subsequent comparisons of the effects of treatment can assume equality of initial status, and a tendency to rely on statistical significance between treatments even when differences are too small to reflect important differences in educational outcomes. Like other education research, research on mental retardation has also suffered from a lack of appropriate outcome measures. In most instances, those domains have been measured that

---

[1]This lack of attention to curricula partially reflects the fact that few systematically developed curricula have been available to teachers of EMR classes, forcing them to modify curricula themselves or to develop their own. It was not until the late 1960s that the Office of Education invested in curriculum development for mildly mentally retarded students, and then only to a limited extent.

could be measured easily. This means that IQ and achievement scores are most often available, whereas changes in personality, behavior, or social processes, which are more difficult to define and measure, are neglected.

With these limitations in mind we turn to a consideration of the research on effective instruction for mildly mentally retarded children. We consider first the pervading question of setting—do mildly mentally retarded children fare best in separate classes, or do they do better when allowed to remain in regular classrooms? We then examine the specific features of instruction that appear to be helpful for EMR children. This "feature analysis" allows us to raise in a new light the question of whether separate labels for different categories of special students are useful in providing appropriate education for these children.

THE QUESTION OF SETTING

Until very recently, research on effective education for mentally retarded students generally addressed the question of the kind of administrative setting in which mentally retarded children would fare best. At stake in most studies was the practice of creating separate classes for children identified as mildly mentally retarded. From the 1930s to about 1970, most studies shared an initial hypothesis favoring such separate classes—a hypothesis dictated by the widely shared belief that mentally retarded children needed both smaller classes and a distinctively different curriculum emphasis from that for "normal" children. A respectable number of studies accumulated data comparing the performance of mildly mentally retarded children in self-contained classes with the performance of such children in regular classes. Several summaries of this literature (Kaufman and Alberto, 1976; MacMillan and Meyers, 1979; MacMillan et al., 1974) indicate that no clear judgment about the two settings for instruction can be made on the basis of this research. With respect to academic performance (usually measured by standardized achievement tests), there is a slight favoring of regular class placement (e.g., Bennett, 1932; Cassidy and Stanton, 1959; Mullen and Itkin, 1961), but many studies showed no reliable differences between the two placements (e.g., Blatt, 1958; Goldstein et al., 1965).

Beginning in the early 1970s, professional and public opinion came to favor less segregation of the handicapped. The shift in opinion was probably fueled only in small part by the disappointing performance of children in separate special classrooms. A more powerful impetus appears to have been the growing press for fuller participation of all kinds of "minority" groups—including the handicapped—in the mainstream of public and social life. Whatever the impetus, the increasing interest in "mainstreaming" of the handicapped led to a new round of studies, testing the hypothesis that mildly mentally retarded children would prosper if they spent all or some of their school time with their "normal" peers. These mainstreamed students were not, however, to be left in ordinary classrooms to fare as they might. Instead they were to be identified as mentally retarded, and special services were to be provided either by the regular teacher supported by a specialist or by a specialist teacher with whom the mentally retarded child spent part of the day. The separate classroom for mentally retarded children now became the "standard" practice on which mainstreaming was to improve.

As in the earlier round of research, findings concerning the academic effects of mainstreaming have been contradictory (Corman and Gottlieb, 1978; Heller, in this volume; Jones et al., 1978). There is no clear favoring of either separate classes or full-time mainstreaming; each showed more favorable effects in some studies and less favorable effects in others. The resource room, a special instructional environment to which children are assigned for a part of the day, spending the remainder in the regular classroom, often—but not always—shows favorable effects in comparison with separate classes and full-time placement in regular classes. But children sometimes do best in regular classrooms in which their own teachers are assisted in providing special instruction. There is some evidence that children with initially higher IQs do better in regular classrooms and that those with lower IQs fare best in separate classrooms. However, even this common sense conclusion cannot be asserted with confidence on the basis of the research to date.

Our discussion thus far, like much of the research literature, has focused heavily on academic outcomes. As noted above, however, many studies have included one or more measures of social adjustment or self-concept. On the measures used, especially those assessing children's judgments of themselves, children in self-contained classrooms tended to rate themselves somewhat better than did children who remained in regular classrooms (see the review by Heller in this volume). Children in self-contained classrooms displayed more positive self-concepts. In more recent work that compares mainstream with separate class treatment, the results are more contradictory. In both bodies of research, there are major design problems that further confound any effort to decide what the real effects are. These include the problem of instrumentation—there is little unanimity in the field as to what a good self-concept is or how to measure it—and the problem of finding appropriately matched groups for the various treatments. Often, the mainstreamed children were those who, in the judgment of various professionals, were more competent and were believed to be better able to function in the regular classroom. This makes comparisons, particularly on measures of social adjustment and self-concept, virtually impossible; techniques of covariance may be difficult to apply because the measures do not meet necessary scaling assumptions. Finally, most of the research available that is relevant to this question is, like the research on achievement outcomes, a "black box" with respect to the actual treatment involved.

FEATURES OF EFFECTIVE INSTRUCTION

The most obvious conclusions from these kinds of inconclusive findings over several decades of research is that the instructional setting per se does not matter, that mildly mentally retarded children can do equally well—or equally poorly—in both kinds of settings. Yet this finding may mask some very real and important regularity in effects on children. Perhaps there are features of the educational treatment received by mentally retarded children that do systematically affect outcomes but that are not uniquely associated with any particular setting for instruction. Perhaps those studies that show a benefit for one setting or another were comparing programs with some specific features that are responsible for the effects. Reported as a comparison between self-contained and regular class or mainstreamed settings, we learn nothing from these studies about what these features might be.

Fortunately, a few recent studies offer descriptions of the educational process that are detailed enough to permit us to address the question of which features of instruction seem to be beneficial for mildly mentally retarded children. While the number of such studies is not large, there is substantial consistency in what has been found to be effective instructional practice for children with the mildly mentally retarded label.

Academic Outcomes

Several studies have documented academic gains for EMR children through the use of individualized "behavioral" methods of instruction (Bradfield et al., 1973; Haring and Krug, 1975; Jenkins and Mayhall, 1976; Knight et al., 1981). In the instructional programs studied, work assignments were given on a daily basis so that the teacher rather than the child determined the pace of work; a mastery learning approach was used in which detailed records and charts of progress (usually based on tests directly covering the curriculum content) were kept for each child; systematic reinforcement was used, and significant amounts of one-to-one instruction, sometimes by peer tutors, were offered. In general, these procedures resulted in larger amounts of time spent on academic work and in a heavy overlap between what was taught and what was tested in the instruments used to assess academic progress.

Although the practices described in these studies did not create academic stars of EMR-labeled children, clear learning benefits were achieved. It is striking that the settings in which these treatments were carried out varied from the self-contained EMR classrooms (Haring and Krug, 1975) to resource rooms (Jenkins and Mayhall, 1976) to regular classrooms (Bradfield et al., 1973; Knight et al., 1981). This fact, although based on a small number of studies, offers striking confirmation of the conclusion reached by Corman and Gottlieb (1978:257): "As a whole, these studies [of effectiveness] suggest that particular instructional techniques may be of greater relevance to improved achievement than the fact that these techniques are used in one of many possible integrated settings." A striking characteristic of the list of features associated with effective academic skill instruction for mildly mentally retarded students is its similarity to the features identified for other categories of children in academic difficulty and, indeed, for the school population as a whole. In the "effective schools" research (e.g., Brookover and Lezotte, 1979; Venezky and Winfield, 1979; Weber, 1971) features of school organization that are associated with good academic performance among poor and minority children include an emphasis on the direct teaching of basic skills and the frequent assessment of progress. Both are also features of effective instruction for mildly mentally retarded populations.

A number of large-scale studies (e.g., the Beginning Teacher Evaluation Study [Fisher et al., 1978], the Follow Through Evaluation [Stebbins et al., 1977], and the Instructional Dimensions Study [Cooley and Leinhardt, 1980]) identify features of classroom organization and process that are associated with good academic performance in schools with high proportions of children receiving compensatory education (i.e., poor and minority children). These studies, all conducted in large numbers of classrooms, took advantage of naturally occurring variations in instruction, rather than attempting to use control groups, random assignments, and other characteristics of experimental designs that can only be approximated in real school settings. They converge on a set of descriptors of "direct instruction" (see Rosenshine and Berliner, 1978) that include high content overlap between learning activities and criterion (test) tasks, built-in formal assessment techniques, increased time on academic tasks, teacher pacing, and the use of motivating management systems (i.e., some form of contingent reward).

Social Outcomes

As we indicated earlier, the rationale for special education for mildly mentally retarded students includes, even stresses, the social goals and outcomes that should be part of an educational plan for such children. The theory has been that mentally retarded children require special social environments for two different but related reasons: (1) they tend to interact poorly with "normal" children, to experience rejection, and, in part as a result, to develop weaker self-concepts and (2) they lack certain specific social and adaptive skills and require special training in these that is not necessary for other children.

A line of research that avoids the "black box" problem in that it is directly concerned with techniques for training social skills has been recently reviewed by Gresham (1981). Gresham summarizes a large number of studies that examined training techniques derived from social learning theory. The focus in these training efforts was on various aspects of social behavior as actually observed in the classroom and on social acceptance by peers (using peer sociometric ratings and teacher ratings), with little attention to the less easily definable construct of self-concept. Many of the training techniques studied have been viewed as suitable or necessary only for the severely disabled or sometimes the institutionalized mentally retarded population. For this reason a large portion of the research has been conducted in separate classes rather than in mainstream settings as well as with populations not directly relevant to this panel's concern. A large segment of the research on what are termed social skills has really been directed at increasing "classroom appropriate" behavior (staying in one's seat, attending to the assigned task, not talking out, etc.) or at minimizing disruptive behavior, rather than at building social interaction skills or enhancing peer acceptance.

Research dealing with mildly handicapped populations (including but not usually limited to EMR children) suggests that techniques such as arranging game playing to include the handicapped child and having peers initiate social interaction can increase interaction and peer acceptance (Aloia et al., 1978; Ballard et al., 1977). More direct teaching of social skills—for example, by providing competent models, rewarding the models, having children rehearse the social skills, and providing feedback—has been shown in a few studies to build certain social skills (e.g., Bondy and Erickson, 1976; Cooke and Apolloni, 1976). There is little evidence, however, for the generalization and maintenance of these skills beyond the training setting. Furthermore, while a considerable body of research points toward the general effectiveness of behavioral and social learning methods, there is a paucity of demonstrations of effectiveness in actual classrooms for mildly mentally retarded children.

A few comprehensive intervention programs for mildly mentally retarded students have focused on social skills. Perhaps the best known is Goldstein's Social Learning Curriculum (Goldstein, 1974, 1975). The principal focus of the curriculum is on the promotion of socially adaptive behavior, accomplished by teaching children to think critically and to act independently. The teacher transmits content through a special inductive teaching methodology (ITM), which aims to induce systematic and self-conscious problem-solving behavior. Although extensive field testing has been undertaken—the Social Learning Curriculum has been introduced in approximately 300 classes in 29 states—much of the work conducted during the field testing focused on testing the theoretical assumptions underlying the curriculum, developing new units, and revising others, and no summative evaluation data were collected.

In general there does not seem to be as clear a set of conclusions to draw about the effective teaching of social skills and the promotion of social acceptance of mildly mentally retarded children as there is for academic development.

Cognitive Process Skills

There is a line of instructional research on mentally retarded children that has been increasingly prominent in recent years and that may have important practical applications in the future. This is research on the direct training of those cognitive abilities that are thought to underlie the mentally retarded person's difficulties in learning under ordinary school conditions. The first phase of research on process deficits in mentally retarded students largely served to identify specific processing skills that were weak in children with low IQs. Prominent among such skills were rehearsal and other techniques of memorizing that were shown to be spontaneously used by normal children but not by mentally retarded learners. Several investigators showed that mentally retarded individuals could be trained to use various mnemonic techniques. However, in study after study it was found that the newly acquired learning skill was applied only to the specific task for which it had been trained, that there was little or no generalization and thus no general improvement in the cognitive functioning of the trained individuals (e.g., Brown and Barclay, 1976; Butterfield et al., 1973; Engle and Nagle, 1979; Turnure et al., 1976). More recently, a few studies showing some generalization and maintenance of learning skills of various kinds have begun to accumulate (Belmont et al., 1980; Brown, 1978; Chipman et al., in press; Segal et al., in press), and there is new optimism in some quarters about the potential for actually improving the cognitive functioning of mentally retarded learners.

Most of the studies clearly showing the acquisition of learning skills have been conducted with small samples under laboratory-like conditions rather than under normal school conditions. However, several programs currently being tested and refined in school settings have strong learning-skill/problem-solving orientations. These include the Instrumental Enrichment Program (Feuerstein et al., 1980) and other programs that teach inductive problem-solving skills to mentally retarded learners (e.g., I. L. Smith, 1980). A shared feature of the instruction in these programs is their focus on teaching children to monitor their own thinking and to plan strategies for learning and remembering as well as to solve social problems. All the programs rely heavily on social interaction between the student and a highly skilled, specially trained teacher. Discussion and analysis of problems and learning tasks seem to be required but are difficult to arrange in a self-study mode and seem to require the grouping of children according to their need for learning skill instruction. As research continues and as more extensive field data on these programs become available, learning skill procedures may emerge as a supplement or alternative to individual mastery-oriented direct teaching of academic skills.

CONCLUSIONS

INSTRUCTIONAL SETTING

What conclusions can be drawn from the research literature concerning the appropriate setting and instructional processes for mildly mentally retarded students? On the whole we are forced to conclude that administrative setting, in and of itself, does not determine whether an educational program is effective or appropriate. Rather it is the things that go on in that setting that matter. In principle, any setting can serve as an appropriate educational environment for mentally retarded children if certain principles of instruction are observed. Many observers agree that because of the belief that mentally retarded children cannot learn well, less is often demanded of them than might be. In classes for mentally retarded students there is little "cognitive press" (Leinhardt and Pallay, 1981) and often a sharply reduced curriculum, so that children in these classes are deprived of the opportunity to learn standard academic skills. There is no intrinsic reason why the cognitive press of a separate class for mentally retarded children cannot be increased. Nevertheless, a classroom of children bearing the label mentally retarded does not typically seem to evoke high expectations and, therefore, the academic demand on them may be reduced (Fine, 1967; Heintz, 1974; Meyen and Hieronymous, 1970; Salvia et al., 1973).

Unless this tendency can be overcome, it argues not only for reduced use of separate classes but also for reduced use of the label mentally retarded, since it seems likely that the tendency to lower cognitive demands would be applied to individual children as well as to groups. But there may be other reasons for lack of cognitive press than lowered expectations. If, in a class of children—even a small class—all children require a great deal of teacher attention in order to stay "on task" and thus make reasonable cognitive gains, it may be difficult or impossible to set high standards for the rate of progress through a curriculum. This argues for either heterogeneous class grouping, in which only a few children need substantial and frequent attention, or a tutorial-like setting, in which a single child at a time can be attended to. The regular classroom provides a heterogeneous setting, but there is some evidence that, except in certain specially designed individualized settings, the great heterogeneity coupled with the larger class size—often double that of the special classroom— makes it difficult for the special child to receive adequate attention.

Some kind of identification of the child is required if he or she is to receive the special attention needed. A practical solution in some cases seems to lie in the resource room, a special teaching/learning laboratory to which the child identified as in need of special help is assigned for a limited period each day, in which instruction is given on a one-to-one basis or in very small groups, and adequate monitoring and rewarding by the teacher (or paraprofessional or peer tutor) is possible. However, to be assigned to this resource room, some kind of identification procedure is needed. Thus it appears that—except perhaps in specially designed mainstream classrooms—a complete absence of labeling would also imply an absence of the kind of special instructional treatment needed by the child.

Categorical Labeling

Some form of identification of children is likely to be required if they are to receive the kind of special education services that they need and to which the law entitles them. The identification of children in need of special services does not necessarily imply that distinct categories of handicaps need to be specified or that special education services should be delivered according to the categorical label that a child carries. Current special education practice as well as much theory divides children with academic difficulties into several categories, the most important of which are the mentally retarded and the learning-disabled (LD) categories. To what extent does the evidence on effective instruction support this practice? That is, do EMR and LD children profit from distinctly different instructional treatments, or do the same features of effective instruction apply to both groups?

An extensive body of theory discriminates LD children from mildly mentally retarded children (Cruickshank et al., 1961; Lerner, 1976;

Strauss and Lehtinen, 1947). While the mentally retarded group is seen as being generally low in all aspects of mental functioning as well as having difficulties in social adaptation, LD children are expected to show uneven profiles of abilities (being strong in some areas and weak in others) and to have IQ scores higher than those of EMR children. Further, social skills are not identified as a major weakness in this category of children. The uneven profile of a LD child points, according to the theory, to an instructional program that is specifically adaptive to particular areas of strength and weakness. A dominant instructional model for LD children involves differential diagnosis and prescriptive teaching aimed at weaknesses in such areas as psycholinguistic skills, perceptual skills, motor skills, and the like. The underlying theory is that, through correction of these cognitive skill deficits, the child's ability to learn school subjects will improve.

A wide variety of programs designed to implement this instructional theory has been developed. It is difficult, however, to assemble strong evidence for the effectiveness of these programs in improving academic skills. While some of the identified cognitive subskills have been shown to be amenable to improvement through instruction (e.g., Kavale, 1981), there is little evidence to date that such training transfers to academic skills such as reading or mathematics or that teaching methods that adapt to skill deficits by making use of strong cognitive skills are more effective (Arter and Jenkins, 1981). A small but respectable body of evidence is available suggesting that direct instruction in academic subjects is effective for LD children (Bateman, 1979; Leinhardt and Pallay, 1981). The key features of this direct instruction are shared with those identified as effective for mildly mentally retarded children.

On the basis of documented effective practice in schools to date, it appears that basically the same kind of instructional processes may be needed for LD children as for mildly mentally retarded children. It should be noted that there is at least one other large group of children with academic difficulties who do not acquire special education labels but who nevertheless receive special instructional services in their schools. These are the children who by reason of low family income and poor performance on achievement tests are assigned to various compensatory education programs—usually in particular academic subjects for a part of each school day. The accumulating evidence about these children also suggests that the same features of direct, externally paced, and formally monitored instruction in academic content that have been noted for mentally retarded children produce the best learning results (Leinhardt et al., in press).

If these three theoretically distinct groups of children seem to prosper best under the same kind of instruction, there is good reason for calling into question the traditional system of categorical labeling within special education. At the very least, the burden of proof now seems to lie with those who would defend the traditional divisions within special education.

SUMMARY AND SOME CAUTIONS

The current evidence on instruction for mildly mentally retarded students seems to offer some clear directions for policy and for classroom practice. First, we can find little empirical justification for categorical labeling that discriminates mildly mentally retarded children from other children with academic difficulties, such as LD children or children receiving compensatory education.[2] Second, while there are fewer well-documented studies with clear results than we might wish, the weight of the evidence clearly points to a group of instructional practices that seem to benefit all of these types of children. Intense direct instructional methods, described earlier in this chapter, seem to be applicable in a variety of settings, from the separate special classroom to the mainstream classroom, and they are not different in spirit from the methods that appear to have been generally effective in schools that serve children with poor prognoses for academic success.

This similarity in the features of instructional treatments offers some hope that some proportion of the children now recognized as in need of special education might be reduced through the provision of more effective regular instruction, especially in schools with high minority representations. Of course, there is nothing in the evidence to date to suggest that an important subset of children who need more intensive attention, and thus more resources than the ordinary classroom is able to provide, will not continue to exist. Providing adequate services to these children will probably require some kind of identification and hence labeling. The labels need not categorize the children but can instead describe the types of special intensive instruction they need.

The question of appropriate setting for instruction appears to be one of administrative manageability rather than one of instructional theory. In keeping with the general public sentiment favoring a minimum of social separation between different segments of the population, there should probably be some favoring of mainstream classroom or resource-room ar-

[2]As we have noted, this statement refers explicitly to mildly mentally retarded children. Recent practice, responding in part to legal challenges to EMR placement for minority children, has in some states and local areas tended to reserve the EMR label for children who show very serious and sustained learning difficulties. The available research, by contrast, is based on a much more heterogeneous group of children that includes many with only mild dysfunctions.

rangements over separate classes. This does not mean, however, that children in need of intensive help should simply be put back in the regular classroom without recognized special status and without appropriate assistance for the classroom teacher. In planning instruction for the special child, primary attention should be directed to the specific features of the instructional treatments that have been identified as fostering academic progress in children with initial poor performance.

Although these broad conclusions seem to be well supported by the evidence at hand, we believe it is important to point to some cautions that must be kept in mind in formulating a policy that may well have far-reaching and long-lasting effects on the kinds of educational opportunities and services offered to children. The caveats that should be kept in mind are discussed below.

Masking Individual Differences

At the beginning of this chapter we indicated that most research on instruction for mildly mentally retarded students has proceeded as if the children with the EMR label were homogeneous with respect to cognitive capabilities and instructional needs. One possible effect of such research, which treats heterogeneous groups of children as if each had the same needs and capabilities—and of examining only the group effects of instruction—is that so much error variance is produced that potentially real differences in program characteristics that benefit children are statistically masked. This may be part of the reason for the preponderance of findings of no difference in the instructional effectiveness literature. If the definitions of mild mental retardation and learning disability were to be made tighter in future research—so that only individuals who were clearly those hypothesized to benefit most from a particular treatment were included in an evaluation—we might begin to obtain a clearer picture of effects. Such a trend in research findings would surely temper the conclusion that there is little basis for distinguishing between mildly mentally retarded children and others with academic difficulties.

On the other hand, in the course of further specification of who is to be considered an EMR or an LD child, it is to be expected that potentially important changes in the current definitions of mild mental retardation and learning disability would be suggested. Thus, there is little likelihood that such research would end up supporting current categorical labeling practice, although it might provide confirmation of some of the theoretical distinctions that experts in special education now offer. In any event, what seems crucial is that any policy of decategorization adopted in response to the current scientific evidence should not be constructed so as to actively prohibit the kinds of research on differential instruction that would be required to arrive at relevant distinctions among children with academic difficulties.

UNKNOWN EFFECTS ON OTHER CHILDREN

Integrating more special education students into regular programs may affect the achievement of the "normal" students. The limited data that are available on the effects of mainstreaming on children in regular programs suffer from the same problems that apply to the literature we reviewed on the effects of instructional setting on EMR children (see Heller in this volume for a review of the existing data on this topic). More critical from our standpoint are the effects of instructional processes that appear to benefit low-achieving children on students in the average or higher ranges. Along with research that identifies specific features of effective instruction for the special child should be an equally direct look at the effects of these features on other students in the classroom as well. Research in two related areas—the effects of grouping by ability or "tracking" and aptitude-treatment interactions—may shed some light on this issue. For reviews of the literature on those areas, see Calfee and Brown (1979), Cronbach and Snow (1977), and Esposito (1973).

BEHAVIORAL BIAS IN RESEARCH

Behaviorally oriented, direct instruction approaches have clearly emerged as the direction of effective practice in research to date, although there are reasons to remain open to changes in the weight of evidence in the longer run. First, for a variety of reasons rooted in both scientific and social value systems of the past two decades or so, behaviorally oriented researchers have focused more on academic skills and on clear outcome measurement and reporting than have other groups of researchers concerned with the same broad issues. For this reason, their work has had clearer, better documented results than some potentially competing or supplementary approaches. For example, the direct instruction approach as it has been used and documented to date favors a step-by-step, practice-oriented approach to education.

Approaches other than direct instruction have been less well analyzed and documented at the present time; nevertheless, they may also be effective. For example, several programs (e.g., SEED, Renee Fuller's reading program for mentally retarded children) that claim strong results rely less on step-by-step methods and more on the general reasoning skills of students. Strong evidence—other than the claims of those involved and of occasional observers—for the effectiveness of these programs with mildly mentally retarded students is not available at this time. Nevertheless, these programs and others like them deserve careful investigation. The results of such investigations may lead to clearer specification of when and for whom behavioral step-by-step methods are needed and when other approaches—which may have important "fringe benefits" in the kind of general adaptive capacities that they promote—may be preferred. Similarly, the cognitive-process training programs discussed earlier in this chapter also suggest an alternative or supplement to direct step-by-step instruction in academic skills. Again, no strong evaluative evidence is currently available concerning these approaches. However, it is important that they continue to be investigated and that practical policy be formulated in a way that remains open to the implementation of the findings that emerge.

EVALUATION CRITERIA

As we have noted, the research evidence on which conclusions concerning effective education are based relies heavily on a particular set of outcome criteria. These can be characterized as oriented to "basic skills": the central basis for deciding what features constitute effective instruction has been their contribution to improved performance on mathematics and reading tests of various kinds. Neither social outcomes nor other kinds of learning—e.g., the acquisition of knowledge relevant to functioning in a job or using various community resources—has received an equivalent amount of attention. Similarly, certain characteristics of individuals formerly educated in EMR programs, such as their employment, earnings, family lives, etc., may be sensitive indicators of the effectiveness of EMR programs yet remain at this time largely uncharted.

A focus on basic academic skills as a criterion is appropriate for a population whose major reason for referral to special education is academic difficulty. This is particularly true for younger children—perhaps ages 8 through 12 or 13—when there is reason to hope that with intensive instructional efforts the child can return to a regular classroom program with a competent level of basic skill performance. For children who continue to have difficulty in acquiring basic skills, other educational goals and curricula, especially those related to specific vocational and social adaptive skills, take on increasing importance. It may well be the case that a differentiated set of outcomes for older mildly mentally retarded children will prescribe somewhat more education in separate classes than is necessary for younger children who have recently been identified as having academic problems. The vast majority of the research that we reviewed has been conducted on children younger than age 12 or 13. The appropriate instruction of and placement for special education students at the secondary level is a largely undiscussed issue without firm research underpinnings.

CONCLUSION

For all of these reasons the panel believes it is essential that a clear distinction be made between recommendations for current "normal" practice and those for investigation that may eventually lead to changed views of "best" practice. While the educator facing the practical challenge of offering immediate educational services to children will do well to incorporate the features of direct instruction that have been outlined here, the total educational system must continue to be open to efforts to determine still better procedures, even if these point toward complex revisions in current practice. Thus, we do not recommend any single structure for the organization of special education. Rather we endorse a policy that allows for new approaches side by side with vigorous application of our best current knowledge about effective instruction.

5

New Approaches to Assessment and Instruction

The panel began its work by investigating the causes of existing minority and sex disproportions in special education programs and by studying solutions to the problem of disproportion. We came to view this approach as too narrow a perspective on the issue of disproportion and thus considered *why* disproportion is a problem. We view the disproportionate placement of minorities and males in programs for educable mentally retarded (EMR) children as problematic only under certain circumstances. Harm accrues to those children who have been invalidly referred and assessed for special education placement and to those who have received instruction of inferior quality. All children are potential victims of these conditions; however, minority children, particularly those in the southern and border states, and to a lesser extent males, face a greater chance of being placed in EMR programs, and the potential consequences of the EMR classification unduly affect these groups of children.

This perspective on disproportion has significant implications for any attempts to resolve the equity issues associated with disproportionate placement. Overrepresentation of minorities and males does not constitute an inequity if the students have been validly assessed and are receiving high-quality, educationally relevant services. Simplistic solutions that lead only to the reduction of racial or ethnic or sex disproportion are misdirected. The focus should be on fundamental educational problems underlying EMR placement—on the valid assessment of educational needs and on the provision of appropriate, high-quality services.

The panel's major recommendations emphasize improvements in assessment procedures and the provision of services rather than remedies that would directly eliminate disproportion in placement rates. To achieve these dual goals, we recommend adherence to six principles (see below) that ask participants at each major step in the placement process to demonstrate the educational utility and relevance of their actions before referring, placing, and maintaining children in special programs. Although these principles are consistent with current law and educational theory, to a large extent they are not followed in practice, nor do they underlie current systems of assessment, classification, and instruction.

Faithful adherence to these principles would have far-reaching effects on the organization of both the regular education and the special education systems. Two potential outcomes are of special significance. First, the current categorization system, which includes a class of children labeled EMR, would gradually evolve into a system that emphasizes the functional educational needs of children experiencing learning difficulties. Second, the use of global IQ scores would be deemphasized in favor of techniques that link assessment more directly to the provision of educational services.

The abolition of either IQ tests or EMR classes is not in itself a solution to the problems of educational failure or inequitable treatment of minority children. On the contrary, ethnic differences in IQ distributions and disproportionate representation of minority students in EMR programs are symptoms of deeper failings in the education and social systems—failings that will not be ameliorated by mere relabeling. Nevertheless, prevailing practices in the use of tests for assessment and the labeling and placement of EMR children obscure the importance of matching educational needs and services.

In this chapter the panel makes two sets of recommendations. Our major recommendations consist of six principles of responsibility that must be adhered to in order to ensure valid referral, assessment, and placement and high-quality programs of instruction. First, we list the six principles, then examine each individually, giving attention to problems of implementation, to suggested research that would facilitate implementation, and to intended as well as unintended effects. Whenever possible, the recommendations include suggestions for demonstration programs and the evaluation of natural experiments that seem to embody the principles that we consider critical. The second set of recommendations, addressed to the Office for Civil Rights (OCR), is specifically framed to aid OCR in its data collection and monitoring efforts.

Fundamental change in the special education system will take time, and procedures must evolve in response to practical experience that we believe should guide change in the system. For this reason we stress broad principles

rather than detailed administrative prescriptions. Although we have focused on the participants in the placement and instructional processes—
notably teachers and administrators—the responsibility for bringing about
these changes must be shared by all concerned with educating children:
parents, school boards, state education agencies, and the federal government. To ask for major institutional change and to ask public institutions to
support such change is to ask a great deal. Yet even in a time of increasing
financial stringency, we believe that these recommendations make sense.
No untried technology nor radically new functions are being proposed for
schools. All the recommendations are based on practices that have already
been implemented in some school districts. All are consistent with current
law and regulations. These existing practices are the basis of our detailed
recommendations for research—recommendations that are designed to
derive maximum guidance from demonstration programs and natural experiments that are already under way.

MAJOR RECOMMENDATIONS: PRINCIPLES OF RESPONSIBILITY

Each of the six principles listed below asks participants in the placement
and educational process to demonstrate that an individual child needs
special education services. Each also stipulates that improved educational
outcomes should be the final criterion on which to judge all decisions.

1. It is the responsibility of teachers in the regular classroom to engage
in multiple educational interventions and to note the effects of such interventions on a child experiencing academic failure before referring the
child for special education assessment. It is the responsibility of school
boards and administrators to ensure that needed alternative instructional
resources are available.

2. It is the responsibility of assessment specialists to demonstrate that
the measures employed validly assess the functional needs of the individual child for which there are potentially effective interventions.

3. It is the responsibility of the placement team that labels and places a
child in a special program to demonstrate that any differential label used
is related to a distinctive prescription for educational practices and that
these practices are likely to lead to improved outcomes not achievable in
the regular classroom.

4. It is the responsibility of the special education and evaluation staff to
demonstrate systematically that high-quality, effective special instruction
is being provided and that the goals of the special education program
could not be achieved as effectively within the regular classroom.

5. It is the responsibility of the special education staff to demonstrate,

on at least an annual basis, that a child should remain in the special education class. A child should be retained in the special education class only after it has been demonstrated that he or she cannot meet specified educational objectives and that all efforts have been made to achieve these objectives.

6. It is the responsibility of administrators at the district, state, and national levels to monitor on a regular basis the pattern of special education placements, the rates for particular groups of children or particular schools and districts, and the types of instructional services offered to affirm that appropriate procedures are being followed or to redress inequities found in the system.

ALTERNATIVE STRATEGIES WITHIN THE REGULAR CLASSROOM

1. *It is the responsibility of teachers in the regular classroom to engage in multiple educational interventions and to note the effects of such interventions on a child experiencing academic failure before referring the child for special education assessment. It is the responsibility of school boards and administrators to ensure that needed alternative instructional resources are available.*

As it becomes apparent that a child is experiencing academic failure and after consultation with parents, the classroom teacher should use all available regular program resources—remedial specialists, special education staff expertise, school psychologists, resource rooms, compensatory education programs, bilingual programs, and so forth—to identify and implement promising alternative instructional strategies in an attempt to reverse the pattern of failure. All avenues within the regular program should be pursued. If and only if a variety of alternative instructional interventions fail should there be a formal referral for special education assessment as required by the Section 504 regulations and the Education for All Handicapped Children Act of 1975.

A discussion of the rationale underlying this recommendation is found in Chapter 3. The contribution of the teaching/learning environment to the child's observed difficulties in the classroom must be systematically explored before the child receives a comprehensive individual assessment for special education placement. This approach shifts attention from presumed deficiencies in the child to possible contributors in the child's educational environment. The child who has been unable to learn under certain conditions of instruction in the regular program should not be judged as unable to learn under any conditions of regular instruction until a variety of such strategies has been attempted and demonstrated to be unsuccessful.

This perspective is consistent with P.L. 94-142, which requires that "special classes, separate schooling or other removal of handicapped children from the regular educational environment occur only when the nature or severity of the handicap is such that education in regular classes with the use of supplementary aids and services cannot be achieved satisfactorily ..." (20 USC 1412(5)(B)), and is consistent with the regulations implementing Section 504, which state that "a recipient shall place a handicapped person in the regular educational environment operated by the recipient unless it is demonstrated by the recipient that the education of the person in the regular environment with the use of supplementary aids and services cannot be achieved satisfactorily" (34 CFR 104.34(a)). While these provisions apply to children who have already been assessed and labeled, the approach is equally appropriate for the child who has not yet been labeled as mentally handicapped (see Chapter 3).

Implications for Implementation

A number of school districts have implemented, with some reported success, programs to facilitate the strategy of alternative instructional practices within the regular program. For example, in one district, school psychologists have been trained by special education experts at the local university to serve as educational consultants to teachers who have asked for assistance in the formulation of alternative instructional techniques for certain children. As a result, a majority of the children who previously would have been referred for special education first receive what is called a referral for observation and consultation, which triggers the intervention of the school psychologist/educational consultant. After interviews with the teacher, observations in the classroom, and the administration of criterion-referenced tests, the educational consultant works with the teacher in designing alternative approaches to instruction following behaviorally oriented, direct instruction theories. Only after these instructional approaches have failed to solve the initial problems is a referral for special education placement filed (Alessi and Leys, 1981).

A major consequence of this approach should be a reduction in the number of children referred for special education placement. In the district described above, approximately 80 percent of the children referred for observation and consultation were not later referred for special education placement.

This principle is not meant simply to shift liability from the child to the classroom teacher. Teachers, often working in overcrowded classrooms with insufficient materials, need a variety of levels of support to properly implement the recommended strategy. School boards and administrators must provide resources to enable teachers to work with children of varying abilities. These may include preservice and in-service training programs, appropriate materials, and access to and assistance from expert consultants. In turn, these educational consultants—e.g., school psychologists or resource teachers—must learn to develop individualized educational options and to train regular-classroom teachers in the use of these techniques.

This principle implies additional costs, such as those of retraining personnel, as well as potentially burdensome paperwork for those who are asked to document the use of alternative strategies in the classroom. These expenditures may be counterbalanced, however, by corresponding savings at later points in the placement and instructional process. Fewer students will probably require a formal comprehensive assessment or costly special programs if this recommendation is carried out. In the district cited above, for example, the average referral for observation and consultation required 5 to 10 hours; the average referral for special education placement required 16 to 20 hours. In addition, as noted above, a vast majority of the children referred for observation and consultation were not later referred for special education placement.

Suggested Research

On Alternative Strategies Within the Regular Classroom   Guidelines are needed to assist classroom teachers and educational consultants in the selection of appropriate interventions likely to succeed with individual children. To provide such assistance, we recommend the development of a taxonomy of alternate instructional strategies. Such a taxonomy would draw on the large body of existing research on instructional strategies for low-achieving pupils and on existing taxonomies of educational objectives and methods. Research is needed to determine reasonable expectations about the length of time a given strategy should be pursued before initiating another intervention and before referring for special education.

On the Evaluation of Natural Experiments   We recommend the investigation of existing districtwide programs in which alternative instructional strategies are being systematically implemented within the regular classroom for children experiencing academic failure. Monitoring of these programs should focus on such considerations as the administrative support systems needed to facilitate program implementation, the staff training required for implementation, the effects of the program on the functioning of the regular classroom (including major constraints imposed on the teacher's time and effects on other students) as well as the effects on targeted children who continue to experience failure after intervention and whose referral for special education assessment may be delayed. In addition, special attention should be paid to the incentives created by funding patterns that will facilitate implementation of this recommendation. The state of Louisiana recently revised its special education regulations and guidelines to promote the use of alternative resources within the regular program; this may prove to be an interesting candidate for a case study once the state's revised regulations are implemented.

In monitoring those sites that have implemented this "prereferral" phase of the assessment process, it would also be possible to investigate the extent to which improvement in the quality of regular instruction decreases total EMR placement in general and disproportionate placement rates by ethnicity and sex in particular. In addition to the data sources already cited, such a program could build on "effective schools" research (see Chapter 4) to determine whether schools serving minority and low-income students at or above grade level also have EMR placement rates that are lower than expected. Once identified, these effective schools might well serve as demonstration projects.

On the Assessment of Learning Environments   This recommendation implies that a child cannot be referred for special education until there is evidence that he or she has been exposed to effective instruction. Appropriate and valid assessments of instructional environments are essential, both to discover strengths and weaknesses in classroom processes and to identify alternative strategies that may prove beneficial. Research is needed on the development of measurement systems that describe the major dimensions of learning environments. These should include, at a minimum, demonstration of the effectiveness of curricula for the particular student populations served and the degree to which the curricula are actually used in the classroom.

Valid Assessment

2. *It is the responsibility of assessment specialists to demonstrate that the measures employed validly assess the functional needs of the individual child for which there are potentially effective interventions.*

If the alternative instructional interventions described in the preceding recommendation are not effective, the child should be referred for a comprehensive special education assessment. The primary justification for the use of any assessment technique during this process is, in our view, its contribution to educational practice. From this perspective a valid assessment must display two characteristics. First, measurement instruments should assess a child's functional needs and should thereby be evaluated on the basis of their relevance to education decisions. Functional needs may be categories of academically relevant skills (e.g., reading, mathematics), cognitive-process skills (e.g., generalization, self-monitoring), adaptive and motivational skills (e.g., impulse control, social skills), or physical problems that hamper learning (e.g., defective vision or hearing). Second, functional needs should be identified only if there exist potentially effective interventions. Thus, assessments can be judged in terms of their utility in moving the child toward appropriate educational goals.

Assessment techniques in general need not always identify functional characteristics of the individual that can be corrected through intervention. As noted in Chapter 3, for example, there are diseases that can be diagnosed but not treated. Furthermore, we do not mean to discourage research on new instructional practices with selected populations that may, in the future, ameliorate children's educational performance. However, we urge that the assessment procedures employed by school systems focus on individual characteristics that are relevant to classroom performance and susceptible to remediation. Such a focus would concentrate attention on the responsibilities of the school rather than on the shortcomings of the child, and it may help prevent diagnosis from becoming an excuse for inaction.

While potential interventions may be broad and may encompass actions beyond the school environs, we anticipate that each will also include an instructional component. For example, certain interventions may be as straightforward as providing a child with eyeglasses or improving his or her attendance; however, these remedies in isolation will not compensate for the instruction missed while the child could not see adequately or did not attend class.

The regulations implementing Section 504 and P.L. 94-142 require that evaluation and assessment materials be "... validated for the specific purpose for which they are used ..." (34 CFR 104.35(b)(1), 34 CFR 300.532(a)). Both the Section 504 regulations and those for P.L. 94-142 give additional guidance about the type of instruments to be used and the purpose of the assessment process. "Tests and other evaluation materials include those tailored to assess specific areas of educational need and not merely those which are designed to provide a single general intelligence quotient" (34 CFR 104.35(b)(2), 34 CFR 300.532 (3)(b)). The clear meaning of these requirements establishes a dual function for assessment procedures: measurement of the functional needs of the child and guidance for instructional interventions. The panel strongly endorses such provisions.

Implications for Implementation

The focus on assessments that stress functional needs disarms the controversy over the use of IQ test scores in special education placement procedures. As discussed in Chapter 3, the controversy focuses on the adequacy of IQ tests as measures of children's innate capacity to learn. A focus on functional needs makes it unnecessary to know whether the causes of poor performance are organic or experiential. The issue becomes one of whether children who perform poorly in class and on IQ tests will benefit from special types of instruction.

The principle of educational utility suggests a number of measures that could be included in an assessment. While the technology for this type of assessment is relatively undeveloped compared with that for IQ tests, a number of instruments currently in use or under development may potentially meet our criterion. For example, the increasing availability of instructionally related diagnostic tests that are tied to programs of remediation link assessments directly to instruction. Observing children's responses to intense instruction as an indication of their ability to learn and to generalize may also provide a promising alternative to current assessment techniques.

Changing established assessment practices and ingrained associations between IQ scores and the definitions of educable mental retardation would require both a change in attitudes toward the purposes and goals of assessment and the dissemination of information concerning instruments that would accomplish these goals. The retraining of school psychologists is, thus, central to successful implementation of this recommendation.

Several districts throughout the country have successfully abandoned IQ testing in special education placement. Some, for example, have relied on criterion-referenced testing to develop instructional objectives. For example, since 1970, districts in Vermont participating in the Vermont Consulting Teacher Program have trained teachers to conduct continuous, detailed measurements of a child's attainment of minimum objectives. These assessments identify those needing special services and are the basis for prescribing an educational program for such a child within the regular classroom. The state of California, too, has banned the use of IQ tests for placement in EMR programs and is promoting the development and use of alternative methods of evaluation. These and other approaches to special education assessment suggest that it is administratively feasible to use measures that appear to meet the criterion of educational utility.

Suggested Research

On the Identification and Development of Measurement Instruments That Validly Assess Functional Needs   A program of research should be undertaken to identify and/or develop instruments that assess those functional needs of the child for which there are potential prescriptions for intervention. This program must be coordinated with and complementary to the suggested development of a taxonomy of alternative instruction, as suggested above. The usefulness of instruments such as criterion-referenced tests and so-called measures of learning potential, such as those suggested by the work of M. Budoff and R. Feuerstein, also warrant additional investigation.

On Current Practices Providing an Alternative to IQ Tests We recommend a program of research on the effects of the court-mandated ban on the use of IQ test results for EMR placement in California and the similar ban in Chicago. Individual studies should address such questions as: What are the pitfalls associated with abandoning the IQ test? What are the assessment procedures being used to replace the IQ test? What are the implications of the ban on using IQ tests for training programs required for school psychologists and other special education personnel? What are the costs of needed training programs? What costs are associated with the revised assessment procedures? What are the effects on rates of disproportion in special education categories and on overall prevalence rates?

On Current Practices That Incorporate Broader Measures of Individual Functioning As indicated in Chapter 3, comprehensive assessment of functional needs must go beyond the intellectual domain to incorporate measures of adaptive behavior and organismic functioning. We recommend study of school districts and demonstration programs in which adaptive behavior measures are being used widely and systematically, in order to assess their effects on the children who remain in special education as well as those who are excluded on the basis of their adaptive behavior test scores. Such studies could include a documentation of the educational experiences—both academic and social—of those children whose adaptive behavior test scores disqualify them from special education placement. In addition, questions remain concerning the current and potential utility of information from adaptive behavior instruments for educational programming and their effects on the numbers of children placed in special classes and on racial and ethnic disproportions in those classes. Demonstration programs that incorporate medical screening as an integral part of the special education placement system should be studied. These demonstration programs should be established in low-income areas, where the prevalence of health-related learning problems is the highest. Medical screening should focus on those conditions that are likely to be amenable to educational interventions.

Classification and the Provision of Needed Services

3. *It is the responsibility of the placement team that labels and places a child in a special program to demonstrate that any differential label used*

is related to a distinctive prescription for educational practices and that
these practices are likely to lead to improved outcomes not achievable in
the regular classroom.

In order to warrant the continued use of any generic labels in special
education placement, the benefits of labeling must clearly outweigh a
range of potential costs. Ever since the establishment of the earliest programs, the extent of possible harm and enduring stigma associated with
labeling and placement in special education classes has remained a major
controversial issue. While a classification system based on functional
needs rather than global categories of deficiencies may mitigate problems
of potential stigma and inappropriately low expectations, problems associated with current systems of classification will not disappear merely if
new labels are substituted for old.

Resolution seems to lie in the answer to a key procedural question: To
what extent must children be classified and labeled in terms of *deficien-*
cies or *handicaps* in order to receive needed educational services? This
question does not deny the necessity of labeling and classification; both
state and federal funding is dependent on official identification of specific
individuals. Recognizing the need for such identification, we recommend
two criteria to guide decisions concerning labeling and placement. First,
differential labels should be linked to distinctive educational practices.
Only with evidence that children who receive a common label require instruction or interventions that are different from those needed by other
children—whether labeled or not—can the labeling be justified. Second,
the justification for a classification system must depend on its usefulness
in providing *effective* educational services. Since the negative connotations of labels often increase as the separateness of a program from the
regular classroom increases, it is imperative that the separation of children from their peers be justified by evidence demonstrating that a
separate program does indeed provide a better educational environment
for the child.

The placement of handicapped children in the least restrictive appropriate environment is a central part of P.L. 94-142, its regulations, and
the regulations implementing Section 504 of the Rehabilitation Act of
1973. The regulations of P.L. 94-142 also require placement based on the
child's educational needs as expressed in the individual education plan.
The panel endorses these requirements.

The evidence described in Chapter 4 indicates that similar instructional
processes appear to be effective with EMR, learning-disabled, and compensatory education populations. At the present time, therefore, we find
no educational justification for the current categorization system that
separates these three groups in the schools. If categorical labels remain

necessary for the provision of services, they should reflect the types of instruction, resources, and services that are necessary to meet children's functional needs.

Implications for Implementation

The difficulties inherent in reorganizing traditional classification systems should not be minimized. Institutional furniture should not be reshuffled, nor should the present system be dismantled without evidence that alternative approaches are likely to be effective. Thus, we suggest careful study of new and recommended practices through demonstration programs, natural experiments, and the like.

As noted in Chapter 4, the prevalence of the EMR label is sharply decreasing, often leaving an EMR population that more closely resembles the more severely retarded populations of the past. The problem remains, however, of defining the services delivered to the expanded groups of children now labeled learning disabled or such categories as educationally handicapped, learning handicapped, etc.

We are optimistic that our recommendations are harmonious with emerging trends in special education. Innovative reorganizations in special education programs, including attempts to modify classification procedures, have been undertaken or are being implemented in various states and districts. For example, the state of Massachusetts pioneered a noncategorical special education system that abandoned diagnostic labels in favor of programs structured around the amount of time a child spends outside the regular classroom receiving special services. The state of California also is in the process of reorganizing its special education system. The new code downplays specific diagnostic distinctions among children who are not severely handicapped but who experience learning difficulties. State reporting requirements are based on the type of instructional services required by the child and how these services are provided rather than on categorical labels.

Districts that participate in the Vermont Consulting Teacher Program are attempting to identify children for special education on the basis of functional needs. No one receives a formal label; instead, services are delivered to children not mastering the instructional objectives established for a particular grade level. The Vermont Department of Education has certified a new staff role within special education: the consulting teacher. After a teacher has referred a child for special education and obtained parental permission for an assessment to be conducted, the consulting teacher, together with the regular classroom teacher, administers criterion-referenced tests to measure the child's level of achievement in the areas that were identified as problematic. If the child's performance is below the minimum criterion established, the consulting teacher and classroom teacher develop an individual education plan that includes specific instructional objectives, the teaching and learning procedures that will lead to the attainment of the objectives, and a system to monitor daily progress. The plan is evaluated biweekly and altered if the child is not progressing satisfactorily (Christie et al., 1972; Hewett and Forness, 1977).

Experiences with this model in Vermont have been positive, perhaps because of support—both financial and moral—at all levels of the education system. Preliminary reports indicate that the cost of the consulting teacher approach is approximately $200 less per child per school year than special education services by resource teachers or in a special class (Fox et al., 1973). While the use of this model should not be promoted to the exclusion of all others, the instructional responsiveness and cost-effectiveness of this program are indeed encouraging.

Suggested Research

On Implications of Labeling Children on the Basis of Patterns of Functional Needs It has been argued that instructional approaches that have been found to be effective with children in compensatory or remedial groups within the regular school program appear to be similar in kind to effective special education instructional practices. Revisions of traditional classification systems that reflect our recommendations may blur existing distinctions between services provided under different funding sponsorships and different administrative systems. Demonstration programs are needed to evaluate the possible effects of new classification systems based on functional needs. Such programs should investigate the use of alternative funding practices to support the revised classification system, mechanisms for monitoring the racial and sex distributions of the children receiving additional services, the support systems needed within the regular program, and the costs associated with such programs. In addition, the effects on children and teachers should be studied, including the implications of revised classification systems for the individual children who are labeled, for interaction among children in various categories, for their peers in the regular classroom, for the regular-classroom teachers, and for the special education teachers.

On the Impact of Revised Classification Systems At least three major statewide reorganizations of special education programs have been or are being implemented—in Massachusetts, Vermont, and California. Each presents a different approach to the issue of classification and thereby provides unique opportunities for research on the implications of a variety of labeling or classification systems, supplementing the research suggested above on demonstration programs.

On the Effectiveness of Alternative Instructional Approaches Research to date indicates that behaviorally oriented, direct approaches seem most effective for EMR and other children experiencing learning difficulties. However, for reasons noted in Chapter 4, this behavioral bias in research may in part be due to the focus of the behaviorists on clear outcome measurement and on the documentation of results, which are less likely to be emphasized by researchers using other approaches. Other promising lines of research that appear less frequently in the literature include the training of cognitive processing skills and efforts to boost motivation and adjustment as a means to improving functioning in school. In addition, there is some evidence—mainly of a practical "lore" kind—that several programs and even entire schools (see Chapter 4) have improved children's academic achievement; these programs need careful investigation to expand our base of effective instructional practices.

EVALUATION OF THE QUALITY AND EFFECTIVENESS OF SPECIAL EDUCATION

4. *It is the responsibility of special education and evaluation staff to demonstrate systematically that high-quality, effective special instruction is being provided and that the goals of the special education program could not be achieved as effectively within the regular classroom.*

The foregoing recommendations should produce significant reductions in the use of categorical labels and separate classes and in the numbers of children requiring special instruction outside the expanded scope of normal classroom practice envisioned in our first recommendation. Nevertheless, some children will continue to require special programs, and in some cases the provision of such instruction may require separate placement. If special programs and/or placements are required, it is incumbent upon the responsible individuals within the school system to demonstrate that the particular mode of instruction is appropriate and effective for the children in question and that it could not be provided in other, less restrictive settings.

This recommendation goes beyond the second and third in that it requires demonstrating not only that the system of categorization and placement is valid in general and is rationally linked to variations in instruction but also that the needed instruction is actually being provided and is working. This responsibility entails monitoring both the instruction provided in special classes and student progress in those classes, relative to the regular classroom. This is consistent with, but goes beyond, P.L. 94-142 and its implementing regulations, under which state educational plans must require districts to adopt "promising educational practices and materials" (20 USC 1413(a)(3)(B)) and to disseminate these to teachers (34 CFR 300 380(c)).

For some students, special programs or classes may be needed to teach the same academic skills taught in ordinary classes; the means differ, but the ends are the same. For other students, special programs may be needed to teach skills or behaviors that are not ordinarily taught but that are prerequisites to successful academic performance. For example, special programs might be needed for children who have limited attention spans or who exhibit disruptive behavior not controllable by ordinary classroom management techniques. Both the means and immediate ends differ from those of ordinary classrooms, but the ultimate goal of improving academic performance is the same. For a much smaller group of severely disabled students, even the ultimate goals of special programs may not be commensurate with those of ordinary classes. Children who lack rudimentary self-help skills, for example, cannot realistically be expected to reach a goal of academic performance in the normal range. (These children correspond more nearly to the current trainable mentally retarded category than to the EMR category; for this group, diagnosis and special placement are not so controversial.)

For all children placed in special programs, especially those for whom regular placement is a realistic possibility, special placement must be continually justified. School personnel responsible for monitoring special programs, including teachers and perhaps also independent evaluators such as school psychologists or educational consultants, should be able to show that the instruction provided in special programs is significantly different from that ordinarily provided, that it embodies practices known to be effective for the problems or disabilities in question, and that it leads to more rapid progress in overcoming specific problems and improving academic performance than would occur in the regular classroom.

Implications for Implementation

To carry out the necessary monitoring requires two technologies, both of which have already been mentioned. Monitoring requires a system for describing learning environments and behaviors in the classroom and a method of assessing academic progress. As noted in Chapter 3, systematic observations of the behaviors of teachers and students provide a promising means of documenting effective classroom processes. While considerably more development is needed, such approaches seem to provide a natural way of comparing the practices of teachers in special programs both with the practices of regular classroom teachers and with ideal practices prescribed for dealing with particular problems or disabilities. Systematic observations also offer a way of documenting maladaptive student behavior (e.g., inattention or disruptiveness) and of measuring progress in dealing with problems in both regular and special classes. Several methods are available for assessing academic progress. One is the use of standardized achievement tests. Another is the use of tests targeted on specific areas of achievement. The latter technology is less developed than the former, but it is more readily linked to a particular program of instruction.

The major barriers to implementation are administrative, not technological. Other than the few school systems that have established experimental programs closely paralleling our recommendations, systematic monitoring of instruction is extremely rare, and the monitoring of student progress is not as extensive, frequent, or as closely tied to instruction as we suggest. Periodic achievement testing is common and is often used as a basis for placement, but the use of achievement scores to develop instructional plans for individual students is much less common. Systematic use of criterion-referenced tests as a means for monitoring student progress and guiding instruction is rare. Schools are not currently organized to keep relevant records and to feed back information to classroom teachers in a manner designed to shape their strategies for dealing with individual students.

Suggested Research

On Measurement Technologies   Research is needed on the design and psychometric properties of classroom observation instruments and criterion-referenced tests. In both cases there is a substantial foundation on which to build. As indicated in Chapter 3, elaborate observation instruments have been developed for basic research purposes. Further development of simpler, more focused instruments is needed to meet the practical needs of school psychologists and educational consultants charged with the periodic monitoring of student and teacher behaviors. Criterion-referenced tests have been developed in connection with various "direct instruction" curricula, and recently there have been several attempts to expand their theoretical and technical underpinnings. More of the latter work is needed, in conjunction with efforts to disseminate the technology in a form useful for practitioners.

On Administrative Practices   Studies of demonstration programs and natural experiments already under way should focus not only on the validity and effectiveness of assessment and intervention techniques, as already suggested, but also on the costs and administrative changes entailed by the information needs of such systems. Any recommendation that implies recordkeeping that goes beyond current practice runs the risk of imposing burdensome and ultimately unproductive paperwork on teachers and administrators already burdened by such requirements. It is therefore imperative to discover, through studies of successful practices, the most efficient ways of gathering information and feeding it back to classroom teachers and teaching consultants. The growing use by schools of microcomputers for instructional planning and the collection of data on the performance of individual students suggests a feasible and cost-effective solution to the management problems implied by this recommendation. It may also be possible to identify current practices that are inefficient or unnecessary and thus to recommend compensating reductions in paperwork.

RETENTION IN THE SPECIAL EDUCATION CLASSROOM

5. *It is the responsibility of the special education staff to demonstrate, on at least an annual basis, that a child should remain in the special education class. A child should be retained in the special education class only after it has been demonstrated that he or she cannot meet specified educational objectives and that all efforts have been made to achieve these objectives.*

Although no systematic data are collected on the number of EMR students who exit the special education system each year, it is commonly believed that once placed in EMR programs, there is little chance of returning to the regular classroom. Because these programs are not often considered remedial (as opposed to compensatory education programs such as Title I), it is frequently assumed that children placed in these programs will always need the supports associated with a more restricted environment, such as a modified curriculum or a smaller class size (Algozzine et al., 1979).

This recommendation is an extension of the previous one. It applies to the child who requires special education services after it has been demonstrated that he or she does not rightly belong in the regular program with supplementary instruction. This recommendation is premised on the belief that there is a group of children, albeit a reduced one, who require instruction in a self-contained special education program. Nevertheless, such children should not remain in special programs through inertia or default; their status should be contingent on informed decisions based on a continuous assessment of their progress in the special program.

We therefore recommend the formulation of specific objectives or "exit criteria" for all children who are placed in special education classes. Once a child has attained these objectives, he or she should return to the regular classroom or the next least restrictive environment. In addition, the initial placement in special education should be limited to one year. If the child has not met the objectives at the end of the school year, the special education staff must demonstrate that all efforts were put forth to help the child meet the assigned objectives and to prepare him or her to return to the regular classroom. If these criteria cannot be met, if the child fails to meet the program's goals because of inadequate implementation of instructional strategies, the child should not be retained in the special program but should return to the regular classroom.

Implications for Implementation

A serious obstacle to the implementation of this recommendation is the difficulty of establishing criteria that can be used to judge whether a child is ready to leave a special class. While there are relatively clear-cut indicators that are currently used to flag a child as EMR (e.g., low IQ scores, low scores on adaptive behavior measures; see Chapter 2), there are fewer consistent or salient criteria that signal that a child is ready to return to the regular class.

P.L. 94-142 requires that the individual education plan of special education students include annual and short-term goals, including criteria for determining whether short-term instuctional objectives have been met. These presumably could serve as exit criteria, yet research indicates that these goals are infrequently specified in practice and, when included, do not appear to serve that purpose (see the paper by Bickel in this volume for a review of this research).

To determine whether children should return to the regular classroom or to the next least restrictive environment, continuous assessment is critical. This does not necessarily require the full assessment that preceded the child's entrance into special education; it should focus instead on the attainment of measurable objectives and should be monitored by regular and special education teachers alike. While this may entail additional costs, it also results in financial savings, since fewer children will remain in the costly self-contained programs.

Louisiana's new regulations incorporate a variation of the principle we advocate. The individual education plan review process requires, at a minimum, a return to the next least restrictive setting unless the reviewers can justify why the child's placement should not be changed. Special education funds in Louisiana follow a child for one year after decertification.

Suggested Research

On Retention Guidelines   Because specifying exit criteria is not common practice, demonstration programs should be established that attempt to specify the conditions under which a child should lose his or her special education status. The establishment of such criteria obviously will match instructional objectives. While this may be relatively clear-cut in mastery learning approaches that emphasize the acquisition of a specified skill sequence, it may be less so in nonbehavioral programs. Research is needed on the specification of such criteria. In addition, methods of easing the transition from a special program to the regular classroom need to be identified. This should include a study of funding practices that will assist both the child and the teacher during the period of transition and reintegration. Finally, the progress of those children who move from special education to the regular classroom should be monitored.

On Children Who Require Ongoing Services   Not all children who have been placed in separate programs will improve significantly, even under the best of instructional strategies, so that they can reenter regular programs. Intensive study of this group of children is necessary. How much progress can be expected under ideal conditions? How might these children be identified so that they can receive appropriate services as quickly as possible? At what point in their development should social and vocational skills be introduced into the educational program?

Examination of the Patterns of Special Education Placement

6. *It is the responsibility of administrators at the district, state, and national levels to monitor on a regular basis the pattern of special education placements, the rates for particular groups of children or particular schools and districts, and the types of instructional services offered to affirm that appropriate procedures are being followed or to redress inequities found in the system.*

The panel recognizes that changes in practice such as those recommended here are difficult to implement and sustain. Even within a set of well-intended and well-defined guidelines, local practices vary dramatically, especially as the compositions of school populations and instructional staffs change over time. For these reasons and to ensure that valid assessment and intructional opportunities continue to be afforded to students with learning difficulties, it is important to monitor the special education system of referral, assessment, and instruction and to periodically investigate those situations that appear problematic.

Implications for Implementation

At a global level, annual or biannual monitoring can be accomplished by a review of the number of children receiving each type of special education service offered by a school district. These data should be gathered so that it is possible to determine the extent to which each type of service is utilized (i.e., the amount of time students receive for each form of special instruction) and so that comparisons can be made by student race or ethnicity and by sex. Such reports could be examined both for populations that receive particular services disproportionately and also for schools, subdistricts, and districts that make exceptionally high or low use of particular services or that have patterns of service delivery very different from those found elsewhere. Schools should be encouraged to report special education services according to the classification system actually in use.

Administrators at all three levels should review these data on a regular basis. At the state and district levels, two other functions in addition to data collection are necessary: analysis and feedback. When the statistical data reveal patterns that warrant further examination, state and local personnel should have in place a means for conducting an in-depth analysis of the extent to which valid assessments have been conducted and appropriate educational interventions have been provided for special students.

Each of the first five principles of responsibility we recommend can be recast in the form of a question and addressed by administrators. Were alternative educational interventions attempted before referral was made? Were they sufficiently distinct interventions? Were the measures employed in the assessment of children's functional needs valid for the special services now being received by them? Is there evidence that the programs are effective? Is it clear that different programs have demonstrably distinctive instructional features and that they produce outcomes that are less likely to occur in the regular classroom? Is there evidence that children who remain in special classes for more than a year could not function in the regular classroom at the end of a year? Are exit criteria specified clearly for each child and have attempts to work toward those objectives been documented?

To the extent that valid procedures have not been followed, local and state administrators should establish a means for providing feedback and support to the instructional staff. This may involve both suggestions for immediate changes with regard to particular groups of students and suggestions for changes in general procedures; the latter may include conducting in-service training or workshops or providing materials that document valid assessment procedures and instructional approaches. These responsibilities are completely consistent with Section 1413(a) of P.L. 94-142, which requires that states provide a system of personnel development as well as the means for disseminating and adopting "promising educational practices and materials."

The focus of the recommended system of monitoring, analysis, and feedback is on actual educational practice. While it may be infeasible for federal agencies such as OCR to evaluate the validity of such practices, their compliance activities should include reviews of the documentation required by recommendations 1 through 5 to determine whether the disproportionate placement of minorities and males is accompanied by valid assessment practices and effective instruction. In addition, administrators at the federal level can aid state and district personnel by preparing, disseminating, and updating documents that describe valid assessment technologies and effective instructional approaches for children with learning problems.

DISCUSSION

The panel's major recommendations emphasize improvements in special education referral, assessment, and placement procedures and instructional practices rather than direct mechanisms for the elimination of disproportionate special education placement rates. Because of the broad scope of recommended changes, with their concomitant complexities and unintended as well as intended consequences, research and demonstration programs are emphasized as a necessarily careful route to program implementation.

The unique possibilities for research involving natural experiments have been highlighted to take advantage of changes in special education programs that are under way at the district and state levels. These "cases" do not necessarily represent model programs that we wish to see implemented nationwide; in many instances their effectiveness has not yet been demonstrated. The panel does not endorse any specific program. The programs cited do serve as examples of the commitment of several districts and states to modifying and improving their special education systems. These cases may be particularly useful in isolating problems and suggesting remedies before they are implemented on a broader scale.

The proposed recommendations require participants in the process—teachers, assessment specialists, placement teams, administrators—to demonstrate and to document that they have fulfilled certain responsibilities. The question rightly can be asked: To whom are each of these participants responsible? Ultimately, the responsibility is to the children who are referred, assessed, and placed in special education.

On a more pragmatic level, responsibility entails monitoring and accountability both through self-analysis and feedback and through reviews by outside individuals and agencies. While the district must implement the recommended practices, the state departments of education must assume a central role in establishing and monitoring the special education policies to be followed by the local education agencies. Such policies include definitions of special education categories, required assessment procedures, and staff training and certification. We urge state departments of education to examine their policies in light of the six principles of responsibility recommended in this chapter.

Many of the changes intended by the recommendations would evolve gradually; others could be implemented in a relatively short time. Initial research efforts could include compilations and syntheses of current knowledge in the areas described, such as diagnostic tests that are linked to remediation programs, observational systems of learning environments, and alternative instructional practices that can be used within the regular program. These state-of-the-art documents would not only facilitate the design of additional needed research but could also encourage districts to adapt available practices to their own needs and to explore alternative strategies that go beyond the current knowledge base.

The panel's recommendations raise significant questions concerning the financing of needed services. As indicated earlier, the recommendations entail some shifting of special education funds from comprehensive assessment and remedial programs to preventive intervention in the regular classroom. This shift entails reconsideration of funding formulas based on head counts of children in various categories of disability. Recommending appropriate levels of special education funding and formulas for allocating funds are tasks far beyond the scope of this panel's work. Recommendations likely to have cost implications and research likely to be helpful in making funding decisions have been highlighted. We caution against two misinterpretations of our recommendations: (1) they provide no rationale for cutting funds for special education and (2) they should not be construed as a plea for more money for special education. The panel's recommendations are concerned solely with the principles on which placement decisions should be based; their cost implications remain to be worked out.

Finally, the panel is well aware that its recommendations place a heavy burden of responsibility on the schools. This is intentional. The burden is essentially one of educating all children, and it is one that educators and schools as institutions have already accepted. Our intention has not been to add to that burden or to denigrate teachers, schools, or special education. We have argued instead that educators and educational institutions, under pressure from many outside sources, have become distracted from this central responsibility. Concerns about assessment procedures, ethnic disproportion in special education, and related issues are important but ancillary. In the largest sense, the goal of our recommendations is to refocus the attention of educators, policy makers, and the public on the traditional goal of the schools: providing the best possible education for all children.

RECOMMENDATIONS FOR OCR'S DATA COLLECTION AND MONITORING

OCR's School and District Surveys, intended primarily for targeting and monitoring purposes, have proven to be an invaluable source of research data for this panel. Although many additional questions can be suggested that would enhance the utility of the data for research purposes, the panel recognizes that the time and effort required to respond to the survey questionnaires could easily become prohibitive. Therefore the recommendations for additional questionnaire items that follow are limited to those that are necessary accompaniments to the implementation of the recommendations discussed above.

THE OCR SURVEYS

The Questionnaires

Under the guidelines proposed by the panel, revised methods of reporting participation in special education programs and of targeting districts for investigation of possible civil rights violations would be required. The panel recommends that OCR, in consultation with educators formulating alternative assessment and service delivery methods, undertake a review of the data that will be required to identify districts in which some or all protected groups of students (those covered by civil rights laws) are "isolated" in separate special programs. While the panel is not prepared to undertake this task in any depth, it offers the following suggestions and recommendations for consideration in modifying the survey instruments.

The OCR survey questionnaire currently solicits information on the amount of time students spend in special education classes, categorized as "less than 10 hours per week, 10 hours or more per week but less than full-time, or full-time." There is some ambiguity in the way this item may be interpreted: It may imply the amount of time a student is considered to be classified in a special category such as EMR, the amount of time he or she receives special instruction, whether in the regular class or in a separate setting, or the amount of time the child is removed from the regular classroom.

An alternate way to document the extent of participation in special programs—either under the current categorical approach or under a service delivery orientation—would be through clarification and expansion of the time question. To identify the types of special programs in which students participate, this item could be restructured in terms of distinct instructional settings. For example, the amount of time a child receives instruction from an aide or tutor in the regular classroom, the amount of time a child participates in a resource room, or the amount of time a child is taught in a self-contained room with a class of special education students could be recorded. With little algebraic manipulation, these responses could be compiled either to the percentage of *students* (or students of any racial or ethnic group) who are spending more than x percent (e.g., 25 percent, 50 percent, 75 percent) of their instructional time outside the regular classroom or to the percentage of *instructional time* spent by one or all racial or ethnic groups in resource rooms, in separate classes, and so on.

As a second alternative, the question(s) could be structured in such a way that the resource rooms or separate special classrooms become the focus, and the numbers of children participating in instruction in those rooms could be recorded. This would make it possible to identify racially isolated classes more directly. However, if such an approach is taken, the question(s) should be worded in such a way as to determine the *amount of time* children spend in the separate classroom as well.

The appropriate composite index(es) (i.e., the "trigger") to be used for targeting purposes must be devised before the final format of questionnaire/item(s) can be specified. If classroom teachers make every effort to instruct children with learning problems in the regular classroom, the use of resource rooms or separate classrooms would probably diminish. An unusually large use of these separate facilities by a school or district might indicate that the degree of separation for a protected group of children or for all racial groups alike is too great. Thus, the overall extent of the use of special facilities may supplement measures of racial or sex disproportion in identifying districts in need of further investigation.

Level of Aggregation

Analyses of OCR survey data should be based on placement rates calculated separately for each racial or ethnic group (i.e., the number of group *x* in a special program divided by the number of group *x* in attendance). These rates could be compared with those of white students, nonminority students, or among themselves. However, only with separate rates for each group can patterns of disproportion be seen clearly for smaller minority populations (i.e., any group except blacks). Furthermore, in districts with two or more substantial minority populations, failure to disaggregate by race or ethnicity can easily produce misleading district appearances (e.g., a high overrepresentation of one minority and large underrepresentation of the other will average out to produce overall summary statistics indicating no disproportion. Current OCR targeting practices give some consideration to separate minority populations. This recommendation is particularly important for those examining the distribution of disproportion for a single racial or ethnic group and for those conducting secondary analyses of the survey data.

Many large school districts (e.g., New York City and Dallas) are organized into subdistricts, and these often mirror important demographic characteristics of the neighborhoods (e.g., racial composition, income, family size). The number of children attending school in the subdistricts is usually substantial, often exceeding the number in the nation's smaller districts in total. Some degree of fiscal control is often provided to the subdistricts and more often educational practices vary among subdistricts in a larger district. OCR should consider collecting subdistrict breakdowns for each large district and identifying each school by its subdistrict membership.

Checks on the Data

Because the data from OCR school and district surveys have profound implications both for the welfare of children and the legal and financial status of the schools, the panel recommends that a program of data validation be undertaken soon after questionnaire returns are obtained. This should include recounts of students enrolled in schools and school programs; a subset of elementary and secondary schools could be chosen within a sample of districts classified by demographic characteristics (e.g., size, racial composition, region). In each school and district revisited, respondents to the survey should be interviewed to compare the way in which questionnaire items were interpreted. The results of this investigation should be published with the summary and documentation of the data.

RESEARCH ON HISPANIC AND OTHER MINORITY GROUPS

The panel's analysis of OCR's 1978–1979 survey reveals that the pattern of disproportion for minority groups other than blacks varies considerably. In the case of Hispanic students, for example, there are numerous large EMR and SED (seriously emotionally disturbed) disproportions and many that are small or even reverse (i.e., few Hispanics in special programs). These trends appear to be a function of the availability of bilingual classes for children who have difficulty with English and of the racial or ethnic mix of the community. Further field-level research is needed to understand the processes of assessment and placement for Hispanic students. Trends among other non-English-speaking populations, including newly arrived Asian and other immigrants, also should be explored.

RESEARCH ON SMALL SCHOOL DISTRICTS

Small school districts tend not to be investigated in depth by federal agencies. However, the disproportion in EMR placement is particularly large among small districts in some parts of the country and may constitute a large-scale problem at the state or regional level. At the other extreme, many small districts in rural areas have small or nonexistent EMR or other special education programs. In general, special education practices among small school districts should be examined in detail to determine the extent and ways in which the educational needs of the students are being met.

RESEARCH ON SOUTHERN SCHOOL DISTRICTS

The panel's analysis of OCR survey data reveals that EMR disproportions for black students were high throughout most of the Southeast. Further investigation of this phenomenon is warranted, including an examination of state criteria for special education placement, the referral and assessment process, and the quality of educational programs being offered in both the regular and special education classrooms.

References

Alessi, G.
   1980 Behavioral observation for the school psychologist: responsive-discrepancy model. *School Psychology Review* 9:31–45.
Alessi, G., and Leys, W.
   1981 A Responsive-Discrepancy Consultation Model for Managing Referrals for School Psychological Services. Unpublished paper. Department of Psychology, Western Michigan University.
Algozzine, R., Whorton, J. E., and Reed, W. R.
   1979 Special class exit criteria: a modest beginning. *Journal of Special Education* 13:131–136.
Aloia, G. F., Beaver, R. J., and Pettus, W. F.
   1978 Increasing initial interactions among integrated EMR students and their nonretarded peers in a game-playing situation. *American Journal of Mental Deficiency* 82:573–579.
Alper, T. G.
   1978 IEP's: How Well Do They Work? Paper prepared under grant no. 77-37-B for the California State Department of Education.
Amira, S., Abramowitz, S. I., and Gomes-Schwartz, B.
   1977 Socially-charged pupil and psychologist effects on psychoeducational decisions. *Journal of Special Education* 11:433–440.
Anastasi, A.
   1976 *Psychological Testing.* 4th ed. New York: Macmillan.
Arter, J. A., and Jenkins, J. R.
   1979 Differential diagnosis—prescriptive teaching: a critical appraisal. *Review of Educational Research* 49:517–555.
Ashurst, D., and Meyers, C. E.
   1973 Social system and clinical models in school identification of the educable mentally retarded. Pp. 150–163 in R. K. Eyman, C. E. Meyers, and G. Tarjan, eds., *Sociobehavioral Studies in Mental Retardation*. Washington, D.C.: American Association on Mental Deficiency.

118

Association of State Directors of Special Education
  1980   *Summary of Research Findings in IEP's.* Washington, D.C.: Association of State Directors of Special Education.
Baker, E. H., and Tyne, T. F.
  1980   The use of observational procedures in school psychological services. *School Psychology Monograph* 4(1):25–44.
Ballard, M., Gottlieb, J., Corman, L., and Kaufman, M. J.
  1977   Improving the status of mainstreamed retarded children. *Journal of Educational Psychology* 69:607–611.
Bateman, B.
  1979   Teaching reading to learning disabled and other hard-to-teach children. Pp. 227–259 in L. Resnick and P. Weaver, eds., *Theory and Practice of Early Reading.* Vol. 1. Hillsdale, N.J.: Lawrence Erlbaum Associates.
Belmont, J., Butterfield, E. C., and Ferretti, R. P.
  In   To secure transfer of training, instruct self-management skills. In D. K. Detter-
  press   man and R. J. Sternberg, eds., *How and How Much Can Intelligence Be Increased?* Norwood, N.J.: Ablex.
Bennett, A.
  1932   *A Comparative Study of Subnormal Children in the Elementary Grades.* New York: Teachers College, Columbia University.
Benton, A. L.
  1974   Clinical neuropsychology of childhood: an overview. Pp. 47–52 in R. M. Reitan and L. A. Davison, eds., *Clinical Neuropsychology: Current Status and Applications.* New York: John Wiley & Sons, Inc.
Berk, R. A., Bridges, W. P., and Shih, A.
  1981   Does IQ really matter? A study on the use of IQ scores for the tracking of the mentally retarded. *American Sociological Review* 46:58–71.
Bersoff, D. N.
  1979   Regarding psychologists testily: regulation of psychological assessment in the public schools. *Maryland Law Review* 39(1):27–120.
  In   Larry P. and PASE: judicial report cards on the validity of individual intelligence
  press   tests. In T. Kratochwill, ed., *Advances in School Psychology.* Vol. II.
Birch, H., Richardson, S., Baird, D., Borobin, G., and Illsley, R.
  1970   *Mental Subnormality in the Community: A Clinical and Epidemiologic Study.* Baltimore, Md.: Williams and Wilkins.
Birman, B. F.
  1979   *Case Studies of Overlap Between Title I and P.L. 94–142 Services for Handicapped Students.* Research report EPRC 26 prepared for the U.S. Department of Health, Education, and Welfare. Menlo Park, Calif.: SRI International.
Bishop, Y. M. M., Fienberg, S. E., and Holland, P. W.
  1975   *Discrete Multivariate Analysis: Theory and Practice.* Cambridge, Mass.: MIT Press.
Blaschke, C. L.
  1979   *Case Study of the Impact of Implementation of P.L. 94–142.* Executive summary. Washington, D.C.: Education Turnkey Systems.
Blatt, B.
  1958   The physical, personality, and academic status of children who are mentally retarded attending special classes as compared with children who are mentally retarded attending regular classes. *American Journal of Mental Deficiency* 62:810–818.

Boll, T. J.
    1974   Behavioral correlates of cerebral damage in children aged 9 through 14. Pp. 91–120
           in R. M. Reitan and L. A. Davison, eds., *Clinical Neuropsychology: Current Status
           and Applications*. New York: John Wiley & Sons, Inc.
Bondy, A. S., and Erickson, M. T.
    1976   Comparison of modeling and reinforcement procedures in increasing question-
           asking of mentally retarded children. *Journal of Applied Behavior Analysis* 9:108.
Bradfield, R. H., Brown, J., Kaplan, P., Rickert, E., and Stannard, R.
    1973   The special child in the regular classroom. *Exceptional Children* 39:384–390.
Broman, S. H., Nichols, P. L., and Kennedy, W. A.
    1975   *Preschool IQ Prenatal and Early Developmental Correlates*. Hillsdale, N.J.: Law-
           rence Erlbaum Associates.
Brookover, W. B., and Lezotte, L. W.
    1979   *Changes in School Characteristics Coincident with Changes in Student Achieve-
           ment*. East Lansing: College of Urban Development, Michigan State University.
           ERIC Document Reproduction Service No. ED 181 005.
Brown v. *Board of Education*
    1954   347 U.S. 483.
Brown, A. L.
    1978   Knowing when, where, and how to remember: a problem of metacognition. Pp. 77–
           165 in R. Glaser, ed., *Advances in Instructional Psychology*. Vol. 1. Hillsdale,
           N.J.: Lawrence Erlbaum Associates.
Brown, A. L., and Barclay, C. R.
    1976   The effects of training specific mnemonics on the metamnemonic efficiency of
           retarded children. *Child Development* 47:70–80.
Budoff, M.
    1968   Learning potential as a supplementary assessment procedure. Pp. 293–343 in J.
           Hellmuth, ed., *Learning Disorders*. Vol. 3. Seattle, Wash.: Special Child Publica-
           tions.
Butterfield, E. C., Wambold, C., and Belmont, J. M.
    1973   On the theory and practice of improving short-term memory. *American Journal of
           Mental Deficiency* 77:654–639.
Calfee, R., and Brown, R.
    1979   Grouping students for instruction. Pp. 144–181 in D. L. Duke, ed., *Classroom
           Management*. The Seventy-Eighth Yearbook of the National Society for the Study
           of Education. Chicago, Ill.: University of Chicago Press.
Carnine, D., Zoref, L., and Cronin, D.
    1981   A Study of Implementation of Educational Change in an Urban Setting: Integrat-
           ing Teacher Effectiveness and Implementation Research. Unpublished paper. Col-
           lege of Education, University of Oregon.
Cassidy, V. M., and Stanton, J. E.
    1959   *An Investigation of Factors Involved in the Educational Placement of Mentally
           Retarded Children*. Columbus, Ohio: Ohio State University Press.
Chipman, S. F., Segal, J. W., and Glaser, R.
    In   *Thinking and Learning Skills: Current Research and Open Questions* (Vol. 2).
    press Hillsdale, N.J.: Lawrence Erlbaum Associates.
Christie, L. S., McKenzie, H. S., and Burdett, C. S.
    1972   The consulting teacher approach to special education: inservice training for regular
           classroom teachers. *Focus on Exceptional Children* 4:1–10.

Cole, L. J.
   1976   Adaptive Behavior of the Mentally Retarded Child in the Home and School En-
          vironment. Unpublished doctoral dissertation. School of Education, University of
          California, Berkeley.
Coleman, J. S., Campbell, E. Q., Hobson, C. J., McPortland, J., Mood, A. M., Weinfield,
F. D., and York, R. L.
   1966   *Equality of Educational Opportunity*. Washington, D.C.: Office of Education,
          U.S. Department of Health, Education, and Welfare.
Cooke, T. P., and Apolloni, T.
   1976   Developing positive social-emotional behaviors: a study of training and generaliza-
          tion effects. *Journal of Applied Behavior Analysis* 9:65–78.
Cooley, W. W., and Leinhardt, G.
   1980   The instructional dimensions study. *Educational Evaluation and Policy Analysis*
          2:7–25.
Corman, L., and Gottlieb, J.
   1978   Mainstreaming mentally retarded children: a review of research. Pp. 251–275 in
          N. R. Ellis, ed., *International Review of Research in Mental Retardation*. Vol. 9.
          New York: Academic Press.
Coulter, W. A., and Morrow, H. W.
   1978   *Adaptive Behavior: Concepts and Measurements*. New York: Grune & Stratton.
Cronbach, L. J., and Snow, R. E.
   1977   *Aptitudes and Instructional Methods: A Handbook for Research on Interactions*.
          New York: Irvington.
Cruickshank, W.
   1967   *The Brain-Injured Child in Home, School and Community*. Syracuse, N.Y.:
          Syracuse University Press.
Cruickshank, W., Bentzen, F. A., Ratzeberg, F. H., and Tannhauser, M. T.
   1961   *A Teaching Method for Brain-Injured and Hyperactive Children*. Syracuse, N.Y.:
          Syracuse University Press.
DeAvila, E. A., and Havassy, B.
   1974   *Intelligence of Mexican-American Children: A Field Study Comparing Neo Piage-
          tian and Traditional Capacity and Achievement Measures*. Austin, Tex.: Dissemi-
          nation Center for Bilingual Bicultural Education.
Diana v. *State Board of Education*
   1970   C. A. No. C-70-37 (N.D. Cal. 1970).
   1973   C. A. No. C-70-37 (N.D. Cal. 1973).
Doll, E. A.
   1941   The essentials of an inclusive concept of mental deficiency. *American Journal of
          Mental Deficiency*. 46:214–219.
Dunn, L. M.
   1968   Special education for the mildly retarded—is much of it justifiable? *Exceptional
          Children* 35:5–22.
   1973   *Exceptional Children in the Schools: Special Education in Transition*. New York:
          Holt, Rinehart & Winston, Inc.
Education Commission of the States
   1974   *National Assessment of Educational Progress. General Information Yearbook*.
          Report no. 03/04-GIY. Washington, D.C.: U.S. Government Printing Office.
Engle, R. W., and Nagle, R. J.
   1979   Strategy training and semantic encoding in mildly retarded children. *Intelligence*
          3:17–30.

Esposito, D.
  1973   Homogeneous and heterogeneous ability grouping: principal findings and implica-
         tions for evaluating and designing more effective educational environments. *Review
         of Educational Research* 43:163–179.
Farr, J. L., O'Leary, B. S., Pfeiffer, C. M., Goldstein, I. L., and Bartlett, C. J.
  1971   *Ethnic Group Membership as a Moderator in the Prediction of Job Performance:
         An Examination of Some Less Traditional Predictors.* AIR technical report no. 2.
         Washington, D.C.: American Institutes for Research.
Feuerstein, R., Rand, Y., and Hoffman, M. B.
  1979   *The Dynamic Assessment of Retarded Performers. The Learning Potential Assess-
         ment Device, Theory, Instruments, and Techniques.* Baltimore, Md.: University
         Park Press.
Feuerstein, R., Rand, Y., Hoffman, M. B., and Miller, R.
  1980   *Instrumental Enrichment.* Baltimore, Md.: University Park Press.
Fine, M.
  1967   Attitudes of regular and special class teachers toward the educable mentally re-
         tarded child. *Exceptional Children* 33:429–430.
Fisher, A. T.
  1977   Adaptive Behavior in Non-Biased Assessments. Revised version of paper presented
         at the meeting of the American Psychological Association. ERIC Document Repro-
         duction Service No. ED 150 514.
Fisher, C., Filby, N., Marliave, R., Cahen, L., Dishaw, M., Moore, J., and Berliner, D.
  1978   *Teaching Behaviors, Academic Learning Time, and Student Achievement. Final
         Report of Phase III-B, Beginning Teacher Evaluation Study.* Technical report U-1.
         San Francisco, Calif.: Far West Laboratory for Educational Research and Devel-
         opment.
Fox, W., Egner, A., Paolucci, P., Perelman, P., McKenzie, H. S., and Garvin, J.
  1973   An introduction to a regular classroom approach to special education. Pp. 22–47 in
         E. Deno, ed., *Instructional Alternatives for Exceptional Children.* Reston, Va.:
         The Council for Exceptional Children.
Goldman, R. D., and Hartig, L. K.
  1976   The WISC may not be a valid predictor of school performance for primary-grade
         minority children. *American Journal of Mental Deficiency* 80(6):583–587.
Goldschmid, M. L., and Bentler, P. M.
  1968   *Concept Assessment Kit: Conservation. Manual and Keys.* San Diego, Calif.:
         Educational and Industrial Testing Service.
Goldstein, H.
  1974   *The Social Learning Curriculum: Phases 1-10.* Columbus, Ohio: Merrill.
  1975   *The Social Learning Curriculum: Phases 11-16.* Columbus, Ohio: Merrill.
Goldstein, H., Moss, J. W., and Jordan, L.
  1965   *The Efficacy of Special Class Training on the Development of Mentally Retarded
         Children.* U.S. Office of Education, Cooperative Research Project report no. 619.
         University of Illinois, Urbana.
Goodman, J. F.
  1977   The diagnostic fallacy: a critique of Jane Mercer's concept of mental retardation.
         Journal of School Psychology 15:197–205.
Gresham, F. M.
  1981   Social skills training with handicapped children: a review. *Review of Educational
         Research* 51:139–176.

Grossman, H. J., ed.
  1977 *Manual on Terminology and Classification in Mental Retardation*. American Association on Mental Deficiency. Baltimore, Md.: Garamond/Pridemark.
Haring, N. G., and Krug, D. A.
  1975 Placement in regular programs: procedures and results. *Exceptional Children* 41:413-417.
Harris, C. W., Alkin, M. C., and Popham, W. J., eds.
  1974 *Problems in Criterion-Referenced Measurement*. Monograph no. 3. Los Angeles, Calif.: Center for Study of Evaluation, University of California, Los Angeles.
Hartman, W. T.
  1980 *Policy Effects of Special Education Funding Formulas*. Policy report no. 80-B1. Stanford, Calif.: Institute for Research on Educational Finance and Governance.
Hayden, A. H., and Haring, N. G.
  1977 The acceleration and maintenance of developmental gains in Down's syndrome school-age children. Pp. 129-141 in P. Mittler, ed., *Research to Practice in Mental Retardation*, Vol. I. Baltimore, Md.: University Park Press.
Hecaen, H., and Albert, L. M., eds.
  1978 *Human Neuropsychology*. New York: John Wiley & Sons, Inc.
Heintz, P.
  1974 Teacher expectancy for academic achievement. *Mental Retardation* 12:24-27.
Hewett, F. M., and Forness, S. R.
  1977 *Education of Exceptional Learners*. Boston: Allyn and Bacon.
Hobbs, N., ed.
  1975 *Issues in the Classification of Children*. 2 vols. San Francisco, Calif.: Jossey-Bass, Inc.
Hunt, J. McV.
  1961 *Intelligence and Experience*. New York: Ronald Press Co.
Jencks, C., Smith, M., Acland, H., Bane, M. J., Cohen, D., Gintis, H., Heyns, B., and Michelson, S.
  1972 *Inequality: A Reassessment of the Effect of Family and Schooling in America*. New York: Basic Books.
Jenkins, J. R., and Mayhall, W. F.
  1976 Development and evaluation of a resource teacher program. *Exceptional Children* 43:21-29.
Jensen, A. R.
  1969 How much can we boost IQ and scholastic achievement? *Harvard Educational Review* 39(1):1-123.
  1980 *Bias in Mental Testing*. New York: Free Press.
Jones, R. L.
  1979 Protection evaluation procedures: criteria and recommendations. Pp. 15-84 in *PEP: Developing Criteria for the Evaluation Procedures Provisions*. Philadelphia, Pa.: Research for Better Schools.
Jones, R. L., Gottlieb, J., Guskin, S., and Yoshida, R.
  1978 Evaluating mainstreaming programs: models, caveats, considerations, and guidelines. *Exceptional Children* 44:588-601.
Kaufman, M. E., and Alberto, P. A.
  1976 Research on efficacy of special education for the mentally retarded. Pp. 225-255 in N. R. Ellis, ed., *International Review of Research in Mental Retardation*. New York: Academic Press.

Kavale, K.
   1981   Functions of the Illinois Test of Psycholinguistic Abilities (ITPA): are they trainable? *Exceptional Children* 47:496–510.
Kirk, S. A.
   1958   *Early Education of the Mentally Retarded*. Urbana: University of Illinois Press.
Knight, M. F., Meyers, H. W., Paolucci-Whitcomb, P., Hasazi, S. E., and Nevin, A.
   1981   A Four-Year Evaluation of Consulting Teacher Service. Unpublished manuscript. College of Education, University of Vermont.
Kohlberg, L.
   1968   Early education: a cognitive-developmental view. *Child Development* 39:1013–1062.
Lambert, N. M.
   1978   The adaptive behavior scale—public school version: an overview. Pp. 157–183 in W. A. Coulter and H. W. Morrow, eds., *Adaptive Behavior: Concepts and Measurements*. New York: Grune & Stratton.
   1981   Psychological evidence in *Larry P.* v. *Wilson Riles*: an evaluation by a witness for the defense. *American Psychologist* 36:937–952.
Lambert, N. M., Windmiller, M., Cole, L. J., and Figueroa, R. A.
   1975   *AAMD Adaptive Behavior Scale Manual*. Rev. ed. Washington, D.C.: American Association on Mental Deficiency.
Lapouse, R., and Weitzner, M.
   1970   Epidemiology. Pp. 197–223 in J. Wortis, ed., *Mental Retardation—An Annual Review I*. New York: Grune & Stratton.
Larry P. v. *Riles*
   1972   343 F. Supp. 1306 (N. D. Cal. 1972) (order granting preliminary injunction).
   1974   502 F. 2d 963 (9th Cir. 1974) (per curiam) (affirming preliminary injunction).
   1979   495 F. Supp. 926 (N. D. Cal 1979) (decision on merits) *appeal docketed* No. 80.4027 (9th Cir., Jan. 17, 1980).
Lazarson, M.
   1975   Educational instructions and mental subnormality: notes on writing a history. Pp. 33–52 in M. J. Begab and S. A. Richardson, eds., *The Mentally Retarded and Society: A Social Science Perspective*. Baltimore, Md.: University Park Press.
Leinhardt, G., and Pallay, A.
   1981   Restrictive Educational Settings: Exile or Haven? Unpublished manuscript. University of Pittsburgh, Learning Research and Development Center.
Leinhardt, G., Bickel, W., and Pallay, A.
   In   Unlabeled but still entitled: toward more effective remediation. *Teachers College*
   press *Record*.
Lemkau, P., Tietze, C., and Cooper, M.
   1941   Mental hygiene problems in an urban district. *Mental Hygiene* 25:624–646.
   1942   Mental hygiene problems in an urban district. *Mental Hygiene* 26:100–119, 275–288.
Lerner, J. W.
   1976   *Children with Learning Disabilities*. Boston, Mass.: Houghton Mifflin.
Levine, M.
   1976   The academic achievement test: its historical context and social functions. *American Psychologist* 31:228–238.
Lezak, M. D.
   1976   *Neuropsychological Assessment*. Oxford University Press.

Loehlin, J. C., Lindzey, G., and Spuhler, J. N.
  1975   *Race Differences in Intelligence*. San Francisco, Calif.: W. H. Freeman.
MacMillan, D. L., and Borthwick, S.
  1980   The new educable mentally retarded population: can they be mainstreamed? *Mental Retardation* 18:155-158.
MacMillan, D. L., and Meyers, C. E.
  1979   Educational labeling of handicapped learners. Pp. 151-194 in D. C. Berliner, ed., *Review of Research in Education*. Washington, D.C.: American Education Research Association.
MacMillan, D. L., Jones, R. L., and Aloia, C. F.
  1974   The mentally retarded label: a theoretical analysis and review of research. *American Journal of Mental Deficiency* 79:241-261.
Martuza, V. R.
  1977   *Applying Norm-Referenced and Criterion-Referenced Measurement in Education*. Boston, Mass.: Allyn and Bacon.
Marver, J. D., and David, J. L.
  1978   *Three States' Experiences with IEP Requirements Similar to P.L. 94-142*. Menlo Park, Calif.: SRI International.
Matthews, C. G.
  1974   Applications of neuropsychological test methods in mentally retarded subjects. Pp. 267-287 in R. M. Reitan and L. A. Davison, eds., *Clinical Neuropsychology: Current Status and Applications*. New York: John Wiley & Sons, Inc.
Mattie T. v. Holliday
  1975   C. A. No. DC-75-31-S (N. D. Miss. 1975).
Matuszek, P., and Oakland, T.
  1979   Factors influencing teachers' and psychologists' recommendations regarding special class placement. *Journal of School Psychology* 17:116-125.
Medley, D. M., and Mitzel, H. E.
  1963   Measuring classroom behavior by systematic observation. Pp. 247-328 in N. L. Gage, ed., *Handbook of Research on Teaching*. Chicago, Ill.: Rand McNally.
Mercer, J. R.
  1973   *Labeling the Mentally Retarded: Clinical and Social System Perspectives on Mental Retardation*. Berkeley, Calif.: University of California Press.
  1979   *System of Multicultural Pluralistic Assessment Technical Manual*. New York: Psychological Corporation.
Mercer, J. R., and Lewis, J. F.
  1978   *System of Multicultural Pluralistic Assessment*. New York: Psychological Corporation.
Mercer, J. R., and Richardson, J. G.
  1975   "Mental retardation" as a social problem. Pp. 463-496 in N. Hobbs, ed., *Issues in the Classification of Children*. San Francisco, Calif.: Jossey-Bass, Inc.
Messé, L. A., Crano, W. D., Messé, S. R., and Rice, W.
  1979   Evaluation of the predictive validity of tests of mental ability for classroom performance in elementary grades. *Journal of Educational Psychology* 71:233-241.
Messick, S.
  1980   Test validity and the ethics of assessment. *American Psychologist* 35:1012-1027.
Meyen, E. L., and Hieronymous, A. N.
  1970   The age placement of academic skills in curriculum for the EMR. *Exceptional Children* 36:333-339.

Meyers, C. E., Nihira, K., and Zetlin, A.
    1979   The measurement of adaptive behavior. Pp. 431–481 in N. R. Ellis, ed., *Handbook of Mental Deficiency, Psychological Theory and Research.* Hillsdale, N.J.: Lawrence Erlbaum Associates.
Mills v. *Board of Education*
    1972   348 F. Supp. 866. (D.D.C. 1972).
Monteiro M.
    1981   Problems and Strategies in the Implementation of Direct Instruction in Public School Settings. Paper presented to the Association for Behavioral Analysis, Milwaukee, Wisc.
Mullen, F. A., and Itkin, W.
    1961   *Achievement and Adjustment of Educable Mentally Handicapped Children in Special Classes and in Regular Classes.* Chicago, Ill.: Chicago Board of Education.
Nihira, K., Foster, R., Shellhaas, M., and Leland, H.
    1969   *AAMD Adaptive Behavior Scale.* Washington, D.C.: American Association on Mental Deficiency. (Revised edition published in 1975.)
Oakland, T., ed.
    1977   *Psychological and Educational Assessment of Minority Children.* New York: Brunner-Mazel.
Parents in Action on Special Education (PASE) v. *Hannon*
    1980   No. 74-C-3586 (N. D. Ill. 1980).
Pennsylvania Association for Retarded Citizens v. *Pennsylvania*
    1971   334 F. Supp. 1257 (E. D. Pa. 1971).
    1972   *modified*, 343 F. Supp. 279 (E. D. Pa. 1972).
Petersen, C. R., and Hart, D. H.
    1978   Use of multiple discriminant function analysis in evaluation of a state-wide system for identification of educationally handicapped children. *Psychological Reports* 43:743–755.
Pickholtz, H. J.
    1977   The Effects of a Child's Racial-Ethnic Label and Achievement. Unpublished doctoral dissertation, Department of Education, Pennsylvania State University.
Pinard, A., and Laurendeau, M.
    1964   A scale of mental development based on the theory of Piaget. *Journal of Research Science in Teaching* 2:253–260.
Poland, S., Ysseldyke, J., Thurlow, M., and Mirkin, P.
    1979   *Current Assessment and Decision Making Practices in School Settings as Reported by Directors of Special Education.* Research report no. 14. Minneapolis, Minn.: Institute for Research on Learning Disabilities.
Reitan, R. M., and Davison, L. A., eds.
    1974   *Clinical Neuropsychology: Current Status and Applications.* New York: John Wiley & Sons, Inc.
Reschly, D. J.
    1978   WISC-R factor structures among Anglos, Blacks, Chicanos and native American Papagos. *Journal of Consulting and Clinical Psychology* 46:417–422.
    1979   Comparisons of Bias in Assessment with Conventional and Pluralistic Measures. Unpublished manuscript. Department of Psychology, Iowa State University.
Reschly, D. J., and Jipson, F.
    1976   Ethnicity, geographic locale, age, sex and urban-rural residence as variables in the prevalence of mild retardation. *American Journal of Mental Deficiency* 81:154–161.

Reschly, D. J., and Sabers, D. L.
    1979   Analysis of test bias in four groups with regression definition. *Journal of Educational Measurement* 16(1):1-9.
Reynolds, M. D., and Birch, J. W.
    1977   *Teaching Exceptional Children in All America's Schools: A First Course for Teachers and Principals*. Reston, Va.: The Council for Exceptional Children.
Rosenshine, B. V., and Berliner, D. C.
    1978   Academic engaged time. *British Journal of Teacher Education* 4:3-16.
Rutter, M., Tizard, J., and Whitmore, K.
    1970   *Education, Health and Behavior*. London: Longman.
Salvia, J., Clark, G., and Ysseldyke, J.
    1973   Teacher retention of stereotypes of exceptionality. *Exceptional Children* 39:651-652.
Sandoval, J.
    1979   The WISC-R and internal evidence of test bias and minority groups. *Journal of Counseling and Clinical Psychology* 47:919-927.
Sarason, S. B., and Doris, J.
    1979   *Educational Handicap, Public Policy, and Social History. A Broadened Perspective on Mental Retardation*. New York: Free Press.
Sattler, J. M.
    1974   *Assessment of Children's Intelligence*. Philadelphia Pa.: W. B. Saunders Company.
Schenk, S. J., and Levy, W. K.
    1979   *IEP's: The State of the Art—1978*. Hightstown, N.J.: Northeast Regional Resource Center. ERIC Document Reproduction Service No. ED 175-201.
Segal, J. W., Chipman, S. F., and Glaser, R.
    In   *Thinking and Learning Skills: Relating Instruction to Basic Research* (Vol. 1).
    press   Hillsdale, N.J.: Lawrence Erlbaum Associates.
Smith, E.
    1980   Test validation in the schools. *Texas Law Review* 58:1123-1159.
Smith, I. L.
    1980   Research in large-scale curriculum development for mildly retarded children. Pp. 148-175 in J. Gottlieb, ed., *Educating Mentally Retarded Persons in the Mainstream*. Baltimore, Md.: University Park Press.
Stallings, J. A.
    1977   *Learning to Look: A Handbook on Classroom Observation and Teaching Models*. Belmont, Calif.: Wadsworth Publishing Co.
Stearns, M. S., Greene, D., and David, J. L.
    1979   *Local Implementation of P.L. 94-142*. Menlo Park, Calif.: SRI International.
Stebbins, L. B., St. Pierre, R. G., Proper, E. C., Anderson, R. B., and Cerva, T. R.
    1977   *Education as Experimentation: A Planned Variation Model. An Evaluation of Follow Through*. Volume IV-A. Report no. 76-196A. Cambridge, Mass.: Abt Associates, Inc.
Stewart, M. D.
    1980   Melanin and Sensori-motor Development in the Afrikan Child: An Alternative View of the Developmental Style of the Afrikan Infant. Unpublished manuscript. Department of Psychology, George Peabody College of Vanderbilt University.
Strauss, A. A., and Lehtinen, L. E.
    1947   *Psychopathology and Education of the Brain-Injured Child*. New York: Grune & Stratton.

Tarjan, G., Wright, S., Eyman, R., and Keeran, C.
   1973   Natural history of mental retardation: some aspects of epidemiology. *American Journal of Mental Deficiency* 77:369–379.
Thouvenelle, S., and Hebbeler, K.
   1978   *Placement Procedures for Determining the Least Restrictive Environment Placement for Handicapped Children.* Silver Spring, Md.: Applied Management Sciences, Inc.
Thurlow, M. L., and Ysseldyke, J. E.
   1980   *Factors Influential on the Psychoeducational Decisions Reached by Teams of Educators.* Research report no. 25. Minneapolis, Minn.: Institute for Research on Learning Disabilities.
Tomlinson, J. R., Acker, N., Conter, A., and Lindborg, S.
   1977   Minority status and school psychological services. *Psychology in the Schools* 14:456–460.
Tuddenham, R. D.
   1970   A "Piagetian" test of cognitive development. Pp. 49–70 in W. B. Dockrell, ed., *On Intelligence.* London: Methuen.
Turnure, J., Buium, N., and Thurlow, M. L.
   1976   The effectiveness of interrogatives for promoting verbal elaboration productivity in young children. *Child Development* 47:851–855.
U.S. Department of Education
   1980   *Second Annual Report to Congress on the Implementation of Public Law 94-142: The Education for All Handicapped Children Act.* Office of Special Education. Washington, D.C.: U.S. Department of Education.
U.S. Department of Health, Education, and Welfare
   1978a *Fall 1976 Elementary and Secondary School Civil Rights Survey. Final File Documentation.* June. Office for Civil Rights. Washington, D.C.: U.S. Department of Health, Education, and Welfare.
   1978b *1978 Elementary and Secondary Civil Rights Survey. Sample Selection.* February. Office for Civil Rights. Washington, D.C.: U.S. Department of Health, Education, and Welfare.
   1979a *Progress Toward a Free Appropriate Public Education: A Report to Congress on the Implementation of P.L. 94-142: The Education for All Handicapped Children Act.* Office of Education. Washington, D.C.: U.S. Department of Health, Education, and Welfare.
   1979b *Progress Toward a Free Appropriate Public Education: Semi-Annual Update on the Implementation of P.L. 94-142—The Education for All Handicapped Children Act.* Bureau of Education for the Handicapped, U.S. Office of Education. 0-631-611/2923. Washington, D.C.: U.S. Government Printing Office.
   1979c Service Delivery Assessment: Education for the Handicapped. Unpublished report. Inspector General's Office, U.S. Department of Health, Education, and Welfare.
U.S. General Accounting Office
   1981   *Disparities Still Exist in Who Gets Special Education.* Report no. IPE-81-1. Washington, D.C.: U.S. General Accounting Office.
Uzgiris, I. C., and Hunt, J. McV.
   1975   *Assessment in Infancy: Ordinal Scales of Psychological Development.* Urbana, Ill.: University of Illinois Press.
Venezky, R. L., and Winfield, L. F.
   1979   *Schools That Succeed Beyond Expectations in Teaching Reading.* Final Report submitted to the National Institute of Education. University of Delaware.

Weber, G.
  1971 *Inner-City Children Can Be Taught to Read: Four Successful Schools.* Washington, D.C.: Council for Basic Education.
Werner, E. E.
  1972 Infants around the world: cross-cultural studies of psychomotor development from birth to two years. *Journal of Cross-Cultural Psychology* 3(2):111–134.
Wigdor, A. K., and Garner, W. R., eds.
  1982 *Ability Testing: Uses, Consequences, and Controversies.* Vols. 1 and 2. Report of the Committee on Ability Testing, Assembly of Behavioral and Social Sciences, National Research Council. Washington, D.C.: National Academy Press.
Williams, J. M.
  1972 Abuses and misuses in testing black children. *The Counseling Psychologist* 2:62–73.
Ysseldyke, J. E., Algozzine, R., Regan, R., and McGue, M.
  1979 *The Influence of Test Scores and Naturally-Occurring Pupil Characteristics on Psychoeducational Decision Making with Children.* Research report no. 17. Minneapolis, Minn.: Institute for Research on Learning Disabilities.

BACKGROUND
PAPERS

Biological and Social Factors Contributing to Mild Mental Retardation

JACK P. SHONKOFF

The concept of mental retardation has eluded clear definition for centuries. From the simplistic moralisms of preindustrial times to the complex "scientific" determinations of contemporary societies, the mentally retarded population has been to a great extent a cultural creation. As social and economic demands have changed, so have the names and the characteristics of the categories of intellectual deficit.

The debate over the relative etiological contributions of biological attributes in the individual, both inborn and acquired, and sociocultural factors in the environment has raged fiercely. It assumes particular significance in American society today with regard to the phenomenon of mild mental retardation. This paper provides an overview of recent research in areas directly relevant to these issues, formulates the current state of the art, and provides a framework for conceptualizing the available data in their imperfect form. In so doing, it attempts to specifically examine the contribution of biological and social factors to the disproportionate representation of minority students and males in education programs for the mildly mentally retarded.

HISTORICAL OVERVIEW

Shifting criteria for mental defectiveness have clearly mirrored changes in society. In early Western civilizations, handicapped children were fre-

I am grateful to Ian Canino, C. Keith Conners, Allen Crocker, Leon Eisenberg, Robert Haggerty, Jane Mercer, Julius Richmond, *and* Arnold Sameroff *for constructive reactions to an earlier draft of this paper.*

quently put to death, and those left to survive were often ostracized and cared for by the clergy (Menolascino, 1977). Before the development of the industrial revolution and universal public education, almost all of those now categorized as mildly retarded were undoubtedly indistinguishable from the general population. In medieval England, for example, a person merely had to be able "to count twenty pence, to tell one's age, and to name one's parents" in order to avoid designation as an idiot and thereby retain the right to the profits of his own property (Kirman and Bicknell, 1975:5).

In the aftermath of the political consciousness of individual rights stirred up by the American and French revolutions in the 18th century, attention began to be directed toward the human needs of the mentally handicapped. During much of the 19th century, medicine greatly influenced the societal response to the problem of mental deficiency. While detailed classifications of brain pathology were being compiled by such eminent neurologists as Jean Martin Charcot, the possibilities of education for the "feeble-minded" were being championed by such physicians as Edward Seguin (Blanton, 1975). In an era when universal public education was viewed in the United States as a solution to the growing social problems associated with the industrialization, urbanization, and ethnic diversity resulting from increased immigration from Europe, institutions for the feeble-minded were established in a spirit of educational optimism, not simply as custodial enterprises. As the belief in the reversibility of significant mental retardation weakened, however, the climate of hope and idealism diminished.

With the growth of the intelligence testing movement at the turn of the 20th century came fierce battles over the need to protect society from the threat of its defective members who could now be more readily identified. Inspired by the tenets of social Darwinism, some of the most influential American psychologists of the early 20th century, including such luminaries as Lewis Terman, Henry Goddard, and Robert Yerkes, joined well-organized efforts to advance the eugenic philosophy, popularized by Sir Francis Galton, by advocating compulsory sterilization and severe restrictions on immigration. Terman singled out the mildly mentally impaired as a serious threat to the health of the society. In the first edition of the manual for the Stanford-Binet scales, he wrote (Terman, 1916:6-7):

Intelligence tests will bring tens of thousands of these high grade defectives under the surveillance and protection of society. It is hardly necessary to emphasize that the high grade cases of the type now so frequently overlooked, are precisely the ones whose guardianship it is most important for the state to assume.

Mildly retarded people were feared for their assumed tendencies toward immorality, delinquency, criminality, and the propagation of "defective" children who would further dilute the competence and vitality of American society. The residential institutions that originated in a spirit of salvation evolved into bastions of isolation and educational vacuum.

In the years following World War II, encouraged by the work of such researchers as Heinz Werner and Alfred Strauss, interest in special education had a rebirth. In the decades that followed, with the increasing militancy of many parents of handicapped children, the dramatic focus in the 1960s on civil rights for victims of institutionalized discrimination, and the critical support given by President Kennedy to the needs of mentally retarded persons, a revolution began in the status of the developmentally disabled population in American society. The widely held belief in the benefits of segregated special education gave way to arguments for normalized "mainstreaming" in the public school system (Dunn, 1968), which culminated in the passage of the Education for All Handicapped Children Act of 1975 (P.L. 94-142).

Historically, the problem of the classification of children for educational purposes has been problematic. In England the passage of the Defective and Epileptic Children (Education) Act in 1899 authorized special classes for children who were deemed incapable of performing adequately in ordinary classes but who were not seriously enough impaired to be assigned to an institutional setting. The Education Act of 1921 specifically addressed the needs of the mildly retarded by creating a category of mental defect restricted to children ages 7–16 and based on educational but not social deficiencies (Blanton, 1975).

At the turn of the century, when the French minister of education commissioned Alfred Binet to develop a test to facilitate the early identification of children who could not meet the demands of regular schooling, the die was cast and the classification of school children was irrevocably altered. Although Binet himself believed in the value of compensatory instruction, his instrument has sometimes been used as a tool for limiting the educational options for intellectually impaired youngsters. The Binet-Simon scales were adapted for use in school systems throughout Europe and the United States. Data obtained in Belgium and Italy revealed significant differences in scores related to social class, and eminent cultural anthropologists argued that this "scientific" concept of measured intelligence was very much culturally determined (Blanton, 1975).

In the United States, revisions of the Binet scales were developed by Goddard, Kuhlman, and Terman, and the history of the use of these and other intelligence tests for the educational classification of children has been rich and controversial. At the heart of much ongoing debate has been the conflict between the "scientific," quantitative data obtained from standardized tests and the practical matter of educational classification and class placement, which is always affected by social values, attitudes, and beliefs. The changing nature of these values has been reflected in the changing definitions of mental retardation. In a presentation to the National Education Association in 1910, Goddard defined a "subnormal child [as] one who is unable to do school work at the usual rate, or any child who is behind his grade" (Goddard, 1910:242). He suggested the following classification (p. 242):

The temporarily subnormal ... whose backwardness is due to sickness, physical impairment, or unfavorable environment, [and the] permanently subnormal or "feeble-minded" which consists of three subgroups—"idiots" [who] are totally arrested before the age of three, [the "imbeciles" who] become permanently arrested between the ages of three and seven, [and the "morons" who] become arrested between the ages of seven through twelve.

Little attention was paid to individual differences in the mentally retarded population. Generally speaking, a simple quantitative concept of backwardness was accepted in educational circles, and similar curriculum materials were applied for a variety of children with diverse learning handicaps. It was not until Werner and Strauss (1939) began to talk about the importance of functional analyses of individual strengths and weaknesses rather than standardized test scores that the concept of mental retardation as a homogeneous condition was seriously challenged. Their popularization of the notions of endogenous (familial) and exogenous (secondary to prenatal, perinatal, or postnatal brain insult) mental retardation ushered in a new era of special education and laid the foundation for many of the modern concepts of specific learning disabilities.

In 1953 a committee of the World Health Organization defined mental deficiency as incomplete or insufficient general development of the mental capacities secondary to biological factors and defined mental retardation as the same condition secondary to social factors. The upper boundary of deficit was conventionally defined as two standard deviations below the mean on a standardized intelligence test.

In 1959 the American Association on Mental Deficiency (AAMD) proposed a system of classification that included a requirement for assessing adaptive behavior and created the category "borderline retardation" for those individuals with "subaverage intellectual functioning" as defined by a test score of between one and two standard deviations below the mean. Among the novel features of this model were its emphasis on current level of functioning and its focus on individuals whose deficits are manifested during the developmental period (Heber, 1959).

In 1973 the AAMD announced that "since 1959 numerous changes have taken place in the field and in the society which necessitate a new manual to reflect the knowledge and philosophy of the seventies" (Grossman, 1973:4–5). This new definition of mental retardation, which is still current, required "significantly subaverage general intellectual functioning," which was defined as two standard deviations below the mean, thereby eliminating the category of "borderline retardation." In their acknowledgment of "changing concepts regarding the social capability of persons with low intelligence" (p. 5), the AAMD arbitrarily transferred a segment of the mentally retarded population back into the "normal" fold with a simple stroke of the pen. As observed by MacMillan et al. (1980:112), "many of the children in a mildly retarded sample study conducted in 1965 would be 'nonretarded control' subjects today if they achieved an IQ of 75 to 85."

Diagnostic systems for retardation have changed in their conceptual as well as their quantitative dimensions. They have alternately stressed the functional interests of psychometricians and educators and the etiological curiosities of the medical profession. Perhaps the best analysis of the differential impact of diverse models of diagnosis is that of Mercer (1971). She defines the clinical perspective as one that considers retardation to be an intrinsic handicapping condition. The current AAMD definition reflects this perspective. It is a statistical and pathological model designed to serve the needs of the helping professions, e.g., medicine, psychology, and education. The clinical perspective implies that a person who fits the criteria is in fact mentally retarded, even if no one is aware of that fact and a definitive diagnosis has not been made. The social system perspective, by contrast, implies that the status is assigned to an individual within a specific social milieu. The implication of this sociological model is that a person is in fact mentally retarded only when he or she is designated as such by a social system and therefore is perceived that way by its other members. Generally speaking, the school has traditionally been the system that most frequently assigns the social status of mental retardation. It is therefore critical that we gain greater insight into the factors that contribute to those administrative decisions that can so dramatically affect children's lives. The need to recognize that we are dealing with values and not objective truths is an important beginning.

In summary, the concept of mental retardation is fluid and defies permanent definition. In its mild manifestations, it is less a vehicle for understanding those people whom it labels than a mirror of the society that determines its boundaries (Sarason and Doris, 1979). In this context of uncertainty this paper explores the data regarding the biological and social roots of mild retardation.

EPIDEMIOLOGY OF MILD MENTAL RETARDATION

In view of the continually changing definition of the mildly retarded population, it is not at all surprising to discover that this group is very difficult
to count. Indeed, the search for valid epidemiological data has been fraught
with frustration and inevitable limitations. Some of the confounding factors
are related to methodological difficulties, while others are inherent in the
chameleonlike nature of the condition itself.

Types of Data

Two types of data have been the focus of study: incidence and prevalence
rates. Incidence refers to the number of new cases of a condition that occur
in a given time interval. These kinds of data have been particularly problematic for the study of mental retardation because of the difficulty in determining the point at which the condition begins to exist. For children
whose diagnosis is specific and unequivocal (e.g., Down's syndrome), this
question has been relatively easy to answer. For the mildly retarded population, however, the point at which the diagnosis may appropriately be
made is often difficult to ascertain. The empirical observation that an individual may move in and out of the mildly retarded category further clouds
the usefulness of incidence data.

Prevalence refers to the number of individuals who have a given condition at a specific point in time. Although they are related to incidence data,
prevalence rates are affected by the duration of a condition and are therefore lowered by the removal of persons from the target population through
death, "cure," or diagnostic revision. This paper focuses primarily on
prevalence data, as these numbers are the most relevant for defining and
planning intervention services.

Limitations of the Data

The most fundamental dilemma is clearly related to the absence of a consistent definition of mild retardation. Whereas moderate and severe mental retardation have been relatively easy to identify, regardless of changing
nosologies, the boundary between "mildly defective" and "low normal" remains ambiguous and tentative. As discussed above, diagnostic criteria
have been altered as the values of the society have changed, and it is likely
that further modifications will be developed in the future. Moreover, the
present emphasis on concurrent adaptive behavior requires consideration
of abilities that have traditionally eluded reliable and valid quantification.

In the absence of a permanent, universally acceptable definition, it is not at all surprising that much of the available epidemiological data on all levels of mental retardation have been significantly influenced by the era during which they were collected, the target groups studied, and the disciplinary orientations of the investigators. Clinical and school populations, for example, are not at all comparable. On one hand, medically based studies are generally skewed by populations with a disproportionate number of "patients" with medically diagnosable conditions characterized by abnormal neurological signs and well-described clusters of findings (syndromes). Educationally based studies, on the other hand, understandably rely heavily on classifications related to school placement and pedagogical strategies. Thus, in some instances, a reported low prevalence of mental retardation may simply reflect limited resources for special education or a strong commitment to "mainstreaming" and individualized instruction; alternatively, a high prevalence rate may reflect artificially inflated figures designed to secure increased funding for service programs. MacMillan et al. (1980) examined the implications of these variations related to the sources of data for the planning and interpretation of relevant research. They differentiated between the mission of the school (which is to deliver education services) and the mandate of the psychological researcher (which is to build a model of retardation based on scientific rigor). The former is heavily influenced by variations in teacher behavior regarding referrals, differences in the way those referrals are screened, and the range of alternative placements and education options available within each school system. The latter should be characterized by strict adherence to objective and highly reproducible data. Consequently, meaningful comparisons among studies clearly require explicit information on the criteria for selection of each target group.

Sociological and anthropological investigations have employed yet another framework whereby retardation is defined in terms of a broad ecological analysis of social status within a specific cultural milieu. Robinson (1978) noted that the reported prevalence of mild mental retardation in the People's Republic of China is essentially zero; their technologically unsophisticated society places minimal value on individual achievement and maximal emphasis on social cohesion and mutual support. In Sweden, where industrial modernization and emphasis on achievement are more evident, the reported prevalence of mild retardation is also relatively low, in part because of social acceptance of educational mainstreaming of intellectually limited children (Grunewald, 1979). In both countries the prevalence of mental retardation at all levels is significantly lower than reported in most studies because they primarily consider the severely impaired. From the clinical perspective, the mildly retarded have been overlooked; from a sociological perspective, they do not exist as a discrete group.

In addition to the problems of disciplinary variation and changes over time in the definitions employed, methodological rigor within disciplines and contemporary studies has been wanting. The bulk of the epidemiological literature does not conform to the AAMD requirement that a diagnosis of mental retardation be based on well-standardized measurement of both adaptive and intellectual deficits. Smith and Polloway (1979), for example, found the inclusion of adaptive behavior measures in less than 10 percent of the recent research efforts that they reviewed. Cleland (1979) reported that many studies mismatched individuals' test scores with the appropriate level of retardation. In an analysis of 566 articles in the *American Journal of Mental Deficiency* and *Mental Retardation* from 1973 through 1979, Taylor (1980) found that only 28 percent included terminology consistent with the AAMD classifications, confirming Cleland's assertions by demonstrating that almost 20 percent of the studies he reviewed included subjects who had been inappropriately classified based on data presented in the article itself. Interpretation of such information clearly presents major problems.

The variety of data-collection methods employed has contributed additional confusion to the literature. Lemkau et al. (1942) studied the prevalence of mental disorders in Baltimore, Maryland, through an examination of the records of community and state agencies. Bremer (1951) surveyed the entire population (1,300 people) of a small Norwegian fishing village through interviews and personal observations. Wishik (1964) studied two Georgia counties through a combination of a communitywide campaign to solicit voluntary referrals and a canvass of 10 percent of the households in the area. Lapouse and Weitzner (1970) reviewed these and nine other epidemiological studies, whose case-finding mechanisms ranged from reviews of school and other agency records to sample surveys, interviews with key community informants, and individual testing by the investigators themselves. The prevalence rates for all levels of mental retardation generated by this wide variety of methods ranged from a low of 3.4/1,000 to a high of 77.0/1,000. When broken down by severity, the percentages of mild retardation within each group ranged from 63 to 92 percent, with a median of 80 percent. Clearly, the limitations of the available epidemiological data are formidable. With these caveats in mind, we now examine the numbers.

PREVALENCE OF MILD MENTAL RETARDATION

If intelligence were, in reality, normally distributed on a Gaussian curve, the prevalence of all degrees of mental retardation would be 2.28 percent. In fact, however, this is not the case. Several explanations have been offered to identify the reasons for the empirically observed variations from the statistically predicted rates.

Tarjan et al. (1973) have asserted that the true prevalence of mental retardation is closer to 1 percent. They explain the lower figure largely on the basis of the fact that not all people with IQ scores below two standard deviations from the mean have deficits in adaptive behavior (and therefore would not be appropriately classified as retarded). This position is supported by Mercer (1973), who found a prevalence estimate for IQ scores below 70 of 21.4/1,000 in Riverside, California, but a rate of mental retardation of 9.7/1,000 when an evaluation of adaptive behavior was added to the diagnostic criteria. Further arguments advanced by Tarjan et al. (1973) to support the lower prevalence figure include the assumption that severely retarded individuals have a shortened life span and the observation that "about two-thirds of the individuals diagnosed as [mildly] retarded lose this label during late adolescence or early adulthood" (p. 372).

Rutter et al. (1970) have added another consideration. They report an overall prevalence rate of 2.53 percent (based on IQ scores alone) among the 2,334 children ages 9–11 on the Isle of Wight and note that this confirmed a slightly higher prevalence than theoretically expected (2.28%) because of the increased number with severe mental retardation. Given the small absolute number of retarded children in their population (59), the authors did not subdivide their group by levels of severity.

The classic studies of Birch et al. (1970) in Aberdeen, Scotland, provide additional data, collected in a somewhat different fashion. Initial prevalence rates were obtained by ascertaining the number of children (ages 8–10) who were identified as subnormal by the local school authorities and placed in special programs based on evaluation of their social competence, school performance, medical status, and psychometric test scores. These children, whose diagnoses were confirmed after reexamination by the investigators, represented 1.26 percent of the population. Subsequent review of the scores of a psychometric test universally administered at school entry revealed an additional group of children who scored below the cutoff point at age 7 but who were not administratively designated as subnormal in the schools. This group represented 1.49 percent of the population of 8,274 children ages 8–10, giving a best estimate of overall prevalence of mental retardation of 2.75 percent. In the study, 50 percent of the children administratively diagnosed as subnormal had IQ scores of 60 or more, compared with 77 percent of the total group. The authors noted that their prevalence data for Aberdeen reflect the "demands of a modern industrial society with free, universal, and compulsory education and the psychometric screening of virtually all children at 7 years of age" (Birch et al., 1970:9).

In summary, valid prevalence rates for mild retardation are hard to come by. The overall prevalence of all levels of mental retardation is likely to be between 1 and 3 percent, with at least three quarters of that group probably falling within the range of mild impairment. Of all the methodological weaknesses throughout this literature, however, the major factor that sabotages efforts to get better numbers is the problem of definition. If it is true that mild retardation will always be a reflection of contemporary cultural values, and if it is true that the boundary between normality and subnormality is inevitably blurred, the hope for more precise prevalence data is fantasy.

VARIATIONS RELATED TO POPULATION SUBGROUPS

Despite the problems and disagreements described above, a number of strong relationships have consistently been reported regarding the relative prevalence rates of mild retardation among specific demographic subgroups.

SOCIOECONOMIC DIFFERENCES

In 1962, *The Report to the President* of the President's Panel on Mental Retardation noted (p. 9):

Epidemiological data from many reliable studies show a remarkably heavy correlation between the incidence of mental retardation, particularly in its milder manifestations, and the adverse social, economic and cultural status of families in these groups in our population. These are for the most part the low income groups—who often live in slums and are frequently minority groups—where the mother and the children receive inadequate medical care, where family breakdown is common, where individuals are without motivation and opportunity and without adequate education. In short, the conditions which spawn many other health and social problems are to a large extent the same ones which generate the problem of mental retardation.

The documentation of this phenomenon has been extensive and almost uniformly reproducible, although most reports have not included measures of adaptive behavior. In a 1937 study of educational backwardness in children in the regular public schools of London, Burt reported a frequency of greater than 20 percent in the poor districts as compared with 1 percent in the well-to-do areas (cited in Rutter et al., 1970). The New York State Department of Mental Hygiene (1955) in the early 1950s found a fourfold increase in the prevalence of mental retardation (loosely defined to include a variety of problems) from the highest to the lowest socioeconomic areas in Syracuse for children and youth under age 18. Stein and Susser (1969) collected data in the industrial city of Salford in northwest

England and found very few children with IQ scores between 50 and 79 in school districts with "high social standing," in contrast to large numbers in districts of "low social standing." The Isle of Wight investigations confirmed the reproducibility of these findings for small-town as well as inner-city populations (Rutter et al., 1970). In their elegant studies in Aberdeen, Birch et al. (1970) reported a prevalence of mild retardation approaching zero in the upper socioeconomic classes, with an increase in prevalence rates by a factor of two for each step down the class ladder, resulting in a summary conclusion that the prevalence of mild retardation (based on IQ greater than or equal to 60) was nine times higher in the lowest class than in the highest class. When within-class differences were examined, it was found that approximately 91 percent of the lower-class population of retarded children were mildly impaired (IQ greater than or equal to 50), while 89 percent of the retarded children in the highest class were moderately to severely subnormal (IQ less than 50). Detailed analysis of the data confirmed the fact that these marked discrepancies were accurate reflections of the prevalence rates based on the diagnostic criteria accepted for the study and were not an artifact related to class differences in administrative identification by the school system. Lapouse and Weitzner (1970) reviewed 12 epidemiological studies that further confirmed this inverse relationship between socioeconomic status and prevalence rates for mild retardation.

A recent analysis of data on more than 35,000 children from the Collaborative Perinatal Project of the National Institute of Neurological and Communicative Disorders and Stroke specifically looked at the relationship of race and socioeconomic status to the prevalence of mild retardation based on test scores of 50 to 69 on the (WISC-R at age 7). Rates for the white population were 3.34 percent for the lower socioeconomic group (bottom 25 percent), 1.31 percent for the middle group (middle 50 percent), and 0.30 percent for the upper group (top 25 percent), with an overall prevalence of mild retardation for the white children of 1.17 percent. Data for the black youngsters revealed a rate of 7.75 percent for the lower socioeconomic group, 3.59 percent for the middle group, and 1.19 percent for the upper group, with an overall rate of 4.83 percent (Broman, unpublished data, 1981).

Many investigators have tended to subsume the demographic characteristics of the lower socioeconomic classes under conceptualization designated as the culture of poverty, which implies a pervasive psychological sense of hopelessness and the inevitability of competitive disadvantage. Others have observed that such a view merely serves as an excuse for policy makers and educators to expect minimal benefits from intervention efforts (Ryan, 1971, cited in Eisenberg and Earls, 1975). Attempts to analyze variables within the lower socioeconomic groups have yielded inconsistent findings. In examining the relationship between mild retardation and class status, Birch et al. (1970) found an ever greater prevalence in the portion of the lowest socioeconomic classes living in large families in areas with particularly poor and overcrowded housing. Zajonc (1976) suggests that regional and ethnic differences in intellectual test performance are significantly related to family configuration, including factors such as the order and number of children and the time interval between their births. Firkowska et al. (1978) found that, although family size was an influential factor, parental education and occupation were the major variables affecting scores on the Ravens Progressive Matrices among 11-year-old children in Warsaw, Poland, where housing and community resources were of equal quality in the socially and economically heterogeneous neighborhoods that were created by the government following World War II.

RACIAL AND ETHNIC DIFFERENCES

Those studies that have systematically examined epidemiological data for racial differences in the reported prevalence of mental retardation have demonstrated consistent findings of disadvantage for minority groups. Four of the projects reviewed by Lapouse and Weitzner (1970) provide interesting insight into some fundamental issues. In a survey of the total population under age 18 in Onondaga County, in New York, in 1953 (342,000, 98 percent white), based on requested referrals from all possible community agencies, an overall mental retardation prevalence of 35.2/1,000 was found, based on an IQ cutoff score of 90. When analyzed for racial differences, the rate in the city of Syracuse for nonwhite children was 125/1,000 compared with 30.9/1,000 for white children. This fourfold discrepancy was reduced to a twofold difference (130.7/1,000 versus 63.9/1,000) when children from the same socioeconomic area in the city were compared. Rates for the remainder of the county were reported to be 88.9/1,000 for nonwhites and 30.0/1,000 for whites (New York State Department of Mental Hygiene, 1955). A major question obviously raised by this study relates to the validity of data obtained through soliciting records from community agencies whose individual identification and selection criteria are not clearly defined, especially with regard to race and ethnicity. Moreover, the establishment of an IQ score of 90 as the criterion for subnormality is highly problematic.

Studies by Lemkau et al. (1941, 1942) in the urban Eastern Health District in Baltimore, Maryland, provide fascinating data related to the interaction between race and age. Case finding was accomplished through record reviews of a wide range of community agencies, including schools, prisons, and courts for all age groups. Using an IQ score of 69 as the cut-off, a prevalence rate of 12.2/1,000 was calculated for the entire population of 54,600. Analysis of children ages 10–14 revealed prevalences of 98.2/1,000 for nonwhites and 26.1/1,000 for whites. Further examination of the data for people ages 20–60, however, revealed essentially no racial differences (7.2/1,000 for nonwhites versus 6.5/1,000 for whites) in IQ scores below 69. It appears that the racial differences as well as the overall changes in prevalence rates are related to issues that are peculiar to the school years.

Wishik (1964) reported an overall prevalence rate of 36.6/1,000 in a study population of 55,000 under age 21 in two counties in Georgia selected as being representative of the state regarding racial (27 percent black) and urban-rural characteristics. Individuals were located through a solicitation of referrals and a random household survey and were identified as retarded based on an IQ score less than 80 and the clinical judgment of pediatricians. Analysis of the target group revealed no significant racial differences in prevalence rates.

Reschly and Jipson (1976) administered individual IQ tests (WISC-R) to 950 of a stratified sample of 1,040 children in Pima County, Arizona. Scores revealed markedly increased prevalence rates of mild mental retardation for black, Mexican-American, and Papago Indian children compared to Anglo children when full-scale IQ scores were examined and a cutoff at 75 was used. When the cutoff score was reduced to 69 and the performance IQ was used as the criterion, however, the disproportionate classification was eliminated for the Mexican-Americans and greatly reduced for the black and Papago Indian children. Data from the Collaborative Perinatal Project of the National Institute of Neurological and Communicative Disorders and Stroke, based on IQ scores (WISC-R) between 50 and 69, revealed a prevalence rate for mild retardation of 4.83 percent among blacks and 1.17 percent among whites, with a persistence of at least a two-fold difference across all socioeconomic groups (Broman, unpublished data, 1981).

Perhaps the best-known and most influential work on ethnic disproportion in the classification of school children has been the studies conducted in Riverside, California. By critically examining the validity of standardized intelligence tests, Mercer (1973) demonstrated the overwhelming importance of culturally appropriate evaluations of adaptive behavior in order to justify a diagnosis of mental retardation. The addition of an assessment of adaptive behavior to the criterion of an IQ score less than 70 reduced the prevalence rate from 21.4/1,000 to 9.7/1,000. Of greater importance, however, was the observation that the decrease in diagnosed retardation was even more dramatic for black and Mexican-American children, with reductions of 44.9 to 4.1 and 149.0 to 60.0 per 1,000, respectively. The lack of change in the prevalence rate for Anglo children (4.4/1,000) clearly demonstrated the cultural discrimination of the IQ test and highlighted its contribution to the disproportionate classification of children from ethnic and racial minority groups. Controversies over racial and ethnic differences in IQ scores have been passionately raging since the introduction of intelligence testing in the early part of this century. These issues will not be addressed further in this paper.

Sex Differences

There can be little argument against the claim that much of the difference between the behavior of males and females in a given society is culturally determined. Nevertheless, biological differences between the sexes that are independent of social milieu have been well documented and must also be considered whenever specific characteristics are found to be distributed in a disproportionate manner. Two issues that bear some consideration in this regard are the greater susceptibility of males to a range of adverse conditions and their relatively slower rate of maturation for a variety of biological functions.

A substantial amount of data has accumulated demonstrating the greater biological vulnerability of males (Childs, 1965; Hutt, 1978; Winter, 1972). A review of mortality indices reveals a higher proportion of males reported in spontaneous abortions (Stevenson and McClarin, 1957) as well as in neonatal deaths (Naeye et al., 1971). In developing countries, male infants succumb to the intestinal complications of poor sanitation in greater numbers than females (Potts, 1970). Males are more susceptible to infectious diseases, including neonatal septicemia (Smith et al., 1956) and those that affect the central nervous system, such as meningitis and encephalitis (Carpenter and Petersdorf, 1962). The ratio of febrile seizures in boys compared with girls has been reported as 1.4:1.0 (Flor-Henry, 1974). Males have repeatedly been shown to have a much greater rate of involvement in accidents, especially after the first two years of life (Hutt, 1978; Winter, 1972).

The relatively slower rate of maturation of boys has also been well studied. Boys have lower growth velocity and later bone ossification and begin puberty on average about 2.5 years after girls (Nicolson and Hanley, 1953). Although some inconsistencies have been reported, a fair amount of data has been generated that indicates that girls mature cognitively and linguistically at a faster rate than boys in the early years (Waber, 1976). Hutt (1978) suggests that the relatively protracted period of development in boys may increase the length of any theoretically sensitive periods during which negative influences, such as malnutrition, could have an effect on brain development. Moreover, preliminary evidence suggesting more complete lateralization of language and spatial abilities in male brains might mean that the lesser degree of cerebral lateralization in female brains may reflect greater plasticity and therefore less susceptibility to the effects of unilateral insults (Lake and Bryden, 1976; Witelson, 1976).

Although it is generally said that mental retardation is more common in males than in females (Farber, 1968; Goodman et al., 1956; Kirk and Weiner, 1959), the literature on sex differences in prevalence rates is actually somewhat equivocal. Rutter et al. (1970) reports that although there is widespread agreement that severe mental retardation is somewhat more common in boys than girls, the sex distribution for mild retardation is fairly equal. They explain this discrepancy by distinguishing between mental retardation per se and educational backwardness. Data collected on the Isle of Wight, for example, revealed a prevalence rate for "intellectual retardation" of about 2.5 percent; a prevalence rate for specific reading retardation of about 4 percent; a prevalence rate for general "reading backwardness" of 6.5 percent; and, with some overlap among the groups, an overall prevalence rate for "severe intellectual or educational difficulties" of 8 percent. Although the male-female ratio for intellectual retardation was found to be essentially equal (0.9:1), the ratio for specific reading retardation was 3.3:1. It was suggested that the greater prevalence of school failure in boys is related to specific reading problems rather than global intellectual deficits.

Other investigators report different conclusions. Birch et al. (1970) found a slightly higher ratio of boys to girls who were rated abnormal (56 percent versus 44 percent), due largely to significant sex differences in those with IQ scores greater than 70, compared with little or no differences in the more severely impaired children. Lapouse and Weitzner (1970), in their review of 12 studies, reported a range of male-female ratios of mental retardation from a low of 1.1:1 to a high of 1.9:1, with only one exception reflecting a greater proportion of females. When levels of retardation were examined separately, however, the sex differences were inconsistent. In a study designed specifically to look at the prevalence of mild retardation based on IQ scores, Reschly and Jipson (1976) actually found a higher rate among females, although the differences were not statistically significant. Data from the Collaborative Perinatal Project corroborated that, for whites, girls have a higher rate of mild retardation (using scores of 50 to 69 on the WISC-R for children age 7) than boys (1.29 percent versus 1.03 percent) and, for blacks, boys have a higher rate than girls (4.99 percent versus 4.24 percent) (Broman, unpublished data, 1981).

Despite a substantial amount of evidence to suggest the greater biological vulnerability of males than females and in the face of well-documented greater numbers of boys than girls in special education placements, the epidemiological literature does not confirm a consistently higher prevalence of mild mental retardation in males.

GEOGRAPHIC DIFFERENCES

The differential impact of rural versus urban life on the prevalence of mental retardation has been difficult to ascertain. Some investigators have suggested that urban residence is correlated with higher levels of intelligence (Lehman, 1959; McNemar, 1942), while others have found no consistent differences (Jastak et al., 1963; Lapouse and Weitzner, 1970). Careful analysis of the confounding influences of socioeconomic and ethnic factors has not been done, and the data in this regard are therefore inconclusive.

AGE DIFFERENCES

One of the most consistent findings among epidemiological studies of mental retardation is the dramatic change in prevalence rates with age. Generally speaking, most retarded persons are mildly impaired, and the bulk of this group is not identified until the school years, with subsequent loss of official diagnostic classification in adult life (Farber, 1968; Goodman and Tizard, 1962). The 12 studies reviewed by Lapouse and Weitzner (1970) showed an increased prevalence in retardation (regardless of the definition used) between the first two 5-year periods (from birth to age 5 and ages 5–9), a larger increment during the next 5-year period (ages 10–14), a decrease in the prevalence rate by half during the next 5 years (ages 15–19), and a further decrease beyond age 20 to a prevalence rate that remains essentially stable throughout adult life. Gruenberg (1964) reported different prevalence rates in many countries (England, Formosa, Scandinavia, and the United States) but similarly shaped curves for age-specific rates—with a steady rise to peak levels during the school years and a steady decline thereafter. MacMillan et al. (1980) noted that the school has been the major identifier of mildly retarded people, those who are "not easily differentiated from non-retarded children in playground, marketplace, and employment situations that do not make school-like cognitive demands" (p. 109).

These trends in age-related rates, perhaps more than any other data, underline the role of the school in the pathogenesis of mild mental retardation. Although some might attribute the rising number during the school years to more effective diagnostic systems, the subsequent declining prevalence in late adolescence and adulthood provides a strong argument for the significance of extrinsic social factors in the assignment of this label. Further studies of the complex relationships among the demands of formal education and the requirements for competence in adult life are clearly needed to inform the development of policy guidelines in this critical area.

SUMMARY

In summary, the overall prevalence of mental retardation ranges between 1 and 3 percent, at least three quarters of whom are probably mildly retarded. Although precise data are most likely unachievable, there can be little question that ethnic minority groups and those in the lowest socioeconomic strata in society comprise a significantly disproportionate segment of those labeled as impaired. The data on sex distributions are more complex in that the numbers of boys assigned to categories of special educational need far outnumber those of girls, yet the epidemiological data on prevalence of mental retardation are less consistent and somewhat equivocal with regard to sex differences.

Perhaps the most striking finding in the epidemiological literature is the critical influence of age on diagnosis. In a variety of social contexts and regardless of the definition employed, the numbers of children identified as mentally retarded have been demonstrated to peak consistently in the elementary and junior high school years. This relationship between prevalence data and age confirms without question the fact that mild retardation is largely a creation of universal compulsory education.

Despite all the definitional confusion and methodological variation, the data show a consistent tension between the demands of the school and the performance of poor, nonwhite children, especially boys. The sociocultural explanations for this phenomenon are most compelling and unarguable, yet, as Birch and Gussow (1970) so eloquently warned (pp. 6–7):

There is some danger, however, that our initial focus on the social and cultural variables relevant to educational achievement may lead us to neglect certain bio-social factors which can directly or indirectly influence the developing child and alter his primary characteristics as a learner.... The fact is that the child who is both the subject and the object of all this concern, the individual who is interacting with these social, cultural and educational settings, is a biological organism.... As an organism the child is not only a mind and a personality capable of being unmotivated, unprepared, hostile, frustrated, understimulated, inattentive, distracted or bored; he is also a body which can be tired, hungry, sick, feverish, parasitized, brain-damaged or otherwise organically impaired.

The remainder of this paper examines the interplay between biological and social factors that may affect school achievement.

THE BIOSOCIAL ROOTS OF MILD RETARDATION

The question of etiology at all levels of mental retardation frequently goes unanswered. In a survey of 800 severely retarded, institutionalized persons, Berg (1963) was able to identify a definite cause or known syndrome in only one third of the cases. In a more recent study at the Fernald State School in Massachusetts, 34 percent of the 1,077 residents with IQ scores below 50 were designated as retarded for unknown reasons (Moser and Wolff, 1971). When one seeks to identify etiological mechanisms in the mildly retarded population, the task is even more formidable and unrevealing. In view of the fact that the frequency of abnormal neurological findings is negligible in most of the mildly impaired population (Rutter et al., 1970; Birch et al., 1970), there is often a tendency to minimize the importance of organic factors among the unknown (or at least unproven) causes of a child's diminished abilities.

Optimal competence and performance for any child, however, are dependent on the interplay between intrinsic biological integrity and an environment that facilitates the development of skills and positive self-esteem. The relationship between mild retardation and lower socioeconomic and ethnic minority status as well as the greater prevalence of school failure among boys have been extensively analyzed from educational, sociological, and political perspectives. Without minimizing the validity of cultural influences, however, it is important to keep in mind the very real discrepancies in the distribution of biological factors that predispose children to poor school performance. In very simple terms, brain function is a critical determinant of intelligence, and factors that may adversely affect brain function are found with greater frequency among males as well as in groups that are victims of institutionalized social disadvantage, such as members of ethnic minorities and the poor. Although the complexity of the data have so far precluded a clarification of the differential contributions of nature and nurture, we cannot justify a summary disregard for the causal role of organic vulnerabilities in mildly retarded school children.

PRECONCEPTION INFLUENCES

Before conception there are already two sets of variables that have potential effect on the developmental competence of the child who is ultimately born. The first involves the genetic contribution of each parent, and the second relates to those demographic factors that correlate with increased risks for the successful completion of gestation.

Genetic Factors

Genetic causes of mental retardation can be related to abnormalities of chromosomes, single genes, or multifactorial inheritance. Chromosomal disorders with associated mental retardation are generally characterized by moderate to severe intellectual deficits and/or atypical physical findings, including neurological abnormalities. Down's syndrome is the most common example. Others, such as Turner's and Kleinfelter's syndromes, may have associated mild retardation, but the majority of these children are of normal intelligence. The relatively low incidence of these conditions (1/10,000 female births and 1/1,000 male births, respectively), the low rate of intellectual impairment involved, and the absence of data to suggest disproportionate distribution among socioeconomic classes or ethnic minorities suggest that major chromosomal disorders do not contribute to the numbers of mildly retarded children in any appreciable way. Specific sex chromosome abnormalities have been associated with suggestions of developmental vulnerability, particularly for language but not with mental retardation (Leonard et al., 1974; Tennes et al., 1977). The recent discovery of the so-called fragile X chromosome in a number of institutionalized retarded males, whose causes of impairment were previously unknown, however, has opened up new areas of investigation that may shed light on the disproportionate number of males among the severely retarded (Gerald, 1980). The association of the fragile X chromosome with mild retardation in females has recently been noted, and further study is clearly needed (Turner et al., 1980).

Single-gene abnormalities may be inherited through autosomal dominant, autosomal recessive, X-linked dominant, or X-linked recessive mechanisms. Although many of these disorders (such as sickle-cell disease and cystic fibrosis) are not associated with intellectual deficits, a large number of inborn errors of metabolism (such as phenylketonuria) that are inherited as autosomal recessive disorders are accompanied by moderate to severe retardation. Some of these inborn errors have a high incidence in certain ethnic groups (e.g., Tay-Sachs disease among Ashkenazi Jews). No associations have been demonstrated, however, with social class or with those ethnic groups that have been disproportionately identified in the mildly retarded population. Again, the relatively low incidence of these metabolic disorders (e.g., 1/14,000 births for phenylketonuria) and their usual association with severe intellectual deficits often accompanied by progressive neurological deterioration eliminate their relevance for the mildly retarded population.

Multifactorial inheritance refers to the process whereby a disorder or condition is determined by the synergistic effects of one or more so-called minor genes and environmental factors. Often termed "polygenic," these mechanisms have been postulated by several investigators to explain the increased prevalence of mild retardation among ethnic minorities and lower socioeconomic groups as a result of genetic differences in intelligence. Such theorists have argued that poor people and blacks, for example, have lesser intellectual endowments, which they pass on to their children in a manner similar to other phenotypic characteristics, such as height or hair color. The polygenic inheritance mechanism is the core around which theories of racial intellectual inferiority have been built. The problem with its application to the study of intelligence is that the methods needed to analyze the relative contributions of biology and environment have not been adequately developed. There is little question that intellectual competence is significantly affected by both. How much of the variance is determined by each, however, varies with circumstances. That is to say, in a uniformly optimal environment, heritability accounts for a great deal of the variance; in a wide range of environmental situations, heritability will explain much less.

In summary, there is no evidence that discrete genetic disorders play any role in the incidence of mild mental retardation. The role of genetic factors in the increased frequency of developmental deficits in males appears to be restricted to more severe levels of retardation, but further work is needed to elucidate possible genetic contributions to the apparent developmental vulnerability of boys. Multifactorial inheritance, as it refers to the interaction between genetic predisposition and environmental contingencies, is more difficult to assess. As discussed in the remainder of this paper, many biological risk factors that are found disproportionately among ethnic minorities and boys have their onset in early life but are not genetic. Moreover, even if genetic differences did exist, their influence on outcome for the mildly retarded would be overshadowed by the effects of the suboptimal environments within which ethnic minorities and the poor reside.

Demographic Risk Factors

Pregnancies that involve factors that increase the likelihood of perinatal mortality, prematurity, low birth weight, or a wide variety of handicapping conditions, including mental retardation, are called "high risk." It has been estimated that such pregnancies account for more than half of all perinatal mortality and morbidity (Vaughan et al., 1979). Birch and Gussow (1970) report that "almost every complication of pregnancy, labor, delivery, and the perinatal period which is potentially damaging to children is excessively prevalent among economically depressed populations and particularly among those further handicapped by ethnic differences" (p. 46). Ramey and Finkelstein (1978) cataloged a variety of demographic variables found to be associated with "borderline mental retardation," including maternal IQ below 80, family disorganization, poverty, overcrowded housing conditions, parity greater than 5, race, maternal education less than 10 years, illegitimacy, and delayed prenatal care beyond the first trimester (Ramey et al., 1978). Despite the well-publicized value of prenatal care, approximately one quarter of all pregnant women in the United States receive none or only belated medical supervision (Select Panel for the Promotion of Child Health, 1981). They are more likely to be poor, black, adolescent, unmarried, and residing in rural areas. Low birth weight is reported to be three times as likely from such unmonitored pregnancies.

The issue of adolescent pregnancy provides a case study in demographic risk. Teenage pregnancies are more common among blacks than whites (Broman, 1980) and are more likely to result in the birth of a low birth weight infant, regardless of social class (American Academy of Pediatrics, 1979). Several investigators have suggested that the increased incidence of small neonates is related to the competition for nutrients between the fetus and the still-growing mother (Naeye, 1981). Nortman (1974) reported an increased prevalence of handicapped children born to adolescent mothers in Canada, while Baldwin (1976) found that 11 percent of children born to women less than age 16 had IQ scores of less than 70 at age 4, compared with 2.6 percent for the general population. Grant and Heald (1972) suggested that risk factors associated with ethnic and socioeconomic status may be the most influential determinants of poor outcome for a teenage pregnancy. This observation is supported by an analysis of data from the Collaborative Perinatal Project of the National Institute of Neurological and Communicative Disorders and Stroke, which found that differences in IQ scores at ages 4 and 7 were more highly correlated with ethnic and socioeconomic characteristics than with maternal age (Broman, 1980).

In reality, the relationships between discrete demographic variables that predict a high risk for unfavorable pregnancy outcomes and the incidence of specific consequences, such as mild mental retardation, are simply suggestive and always tenuous. In a sense a general discussion of demographic factors that increase the risk of mental retardation in a child from a group that is disproportionately represented within the mentally retarded population is an exercise in circular reasoning. A more careful analysis of the consequences of those specific biological factors that occur with greater frequency among such groups would be more fruitful. The process of development, however, defies the identification of simple, direct causal relationships. As stated by Birch and Gussow (1970:82): "When we deal with 'causes' singly, and as simply as the information permits, it is always within the understood context of a reality in which they are complex and interacting."

EARLY PRENATAL INFLUENCES

Until the past few decades, the human fetus was believed to be well protected within the mother's womb. Recent research, however, has provided more understanding of the variety of intrauterine factors that can have long-term adverse influences on the organism's ultimate developmental competence.

Intrauterine Infections

Acute intrauterine infection had long been viewed as a self-limited problem that resulted in either the death of the fetus or complete recovery through elimination of the invading organism by host defense mechanisms (Alford, 1977). The problem of low-grade, chronic, so-called latent infection, however, has become increasingly recognized as an important factor contributing to varying types of long-term sequelae, the dimensions of which are only beginning to be understood. Among the most important organisms in this group are cytomegalovirus (CMV), rubella, toxoplasmosis, and syphilis. They all have a chronic and/or recurrent nature in both mother and fetus and a capacity to adversely affect subsequent cognitive and perceptual development in children. Alford (1977) reported that the susceptibility to infection of women in the childbearing years, as determined by antibody prevalence, is approximately 10 percent for rubella, 15 percent for CMV, and 70 percent for toxoplasmosis. Major variables affecting susceptibility include age (younger mothers are more susceptible than older mothers) and socioeconomic status. For reasons that have been inadequately explained, in part because of insufficient data from developing countries, it has been stated that young women and poor women in industrial societies are the most likely to acquire chronic perinatal infections. The overall incidence of maternal infection during pregnancy has been reported as 14 percent, cytomegalovirus being the most common, representing about 13 percent of all infections (Alford, 1981). According to Alford (1977), between 1 and 7 percent of all infants born in the United States may be infected with one of these chronic organisms, and prevalence is even greater among adolescent women from lower socioeconomic classes. Since CMV is the most common of these infections, it would be instructive to examine its impact in detail.

The frequency of congenital cytomegalovirus infection ranges from 0.2 to 8.0 percent of all live births; the average in the United States is 1 percent. The highest rates are found in infants born to teenage mothers from lower socioeconomic groups (Hanshaw, 1981). Although approximately 4-5 percent of all women excrete CMV in their urine during pregnancy, most do not have infected infants (Hanshaw et al., 1973). This situation is complicated by the fact that the majority of women who have infections during their pregnancy are asymptomatic and are therefore unaware of the infection. Of the 33,000 infants born in the United States each year with CMV infection, it is estimated that less than 1,500 of them are symptomatic and therefore easily identifiable in the newborn period. Most of these obviously infected neonates have serious long-term sequelae, including a high rate of moderate to severe mental retardation.

Outcome for the asymptomatic newborn with so-called silent congenital CMV infection is less predictable than for newborns with symptoms but still somewhat worrisome. During the past decade, increasingly sensitive and specific laboratory techniques have facilitated the identification of greater numbers of infected neonates, thus providing an opportunity for prospective studies of both the symptomatic and asymptomatic groups. Results thus far have shown that, although the majority of those with silent infection appear to do well, as many as 10–20 percent develop intellectual or perceptual deficits as well as significant hearing impairment (Hanshaw et al., 1976; Kumar et al., 1973; Melish and Hanshaw, 1973; Reynolds et al., 1974). As noted by Pass et al. (1980), because of the relatively high frequency of asymptomatic congenital CMV (approximately 1 percent of live births), the occurrence of central nervous system damage in even 10 percent has significant public health implications.

Among those with silent CMV, the influence of socioeconomic status on developmental outcome appears to be important. Hanshaw et al. (1976) screened 8,644 newborns for the IgM antibody against CMV and found 53 children with positive titres. Although only 38 percent of the tested newborns were born to families in lower socioeconomic groups (Hollingshead groups 4 and 5), 68 percent of the CMV-positive group came from these families. In the study, 44 of the congenitally infected children had IQ tests administered between ages 3.5 and 7.0, and the results were compared with 44 matched and 44 random controls. Although the study sample was small and only 7 children had scores below 79 (all of whom were in the infected group), the difference in mean IQ between the CMV-positive and the matched control group was significant with a p value less than .025, after adjustment for social class. No significant IQ differences between the matched and random controls were found when social class differences were taken into account. Further analysis revealed significant differences in IQ scores between CMV-positive and control children from the lower socioeconomic families, with no significant IQ differences between those with and those without congenital infection in the middle-class groups. Predicted school failure, based on an IQ score of less than 90 in association with behavioral, neurological, and auditory evaluations, was not noted among any of the middle- or upper-class CMV-positive children. The lower-class CMV-positive children, on the other hand, had 2.7 times greater predicted school failure than the control children matched for social class. The significant risk for hearing impairment among the infected children (11 percent in this study) clearly contributes additional vulnerability.

In summary, the current state of knowledge regarding the influence of asymptomatic congenital cytomegalovirus infection on the prevalence of mild retardation among school children is highly suggestive but far from conclusive. Existing data certainly support the potential adverse effect of silent infection on higher cortical function. The greater prevalence of this condition among children of lower socioeconomic classes appears to be fairly well documented. Controlled studies have shown an effect of the virus on cognitive and perceptual skills independent of social class, yet evidence suggests that this may merely represent a subtle biological vulnerability that can be effectively neutralized by socioeconomic factors (not yet specifically analyzed) in the child-rearing environment. No sex differences have been reported regarding the long-term consequences of these infections. Although a great deal of work obviously remains to be done in this area, available data suggest that congenital infections such as cytomegalovirus may contribute to the disproportionate number of lower socioeconomic class children classified as mentally retarded.

Maternal Alcoholism

Substance abuse is a major public health problem with considerable attendant mortality and morbidity. The special implications of such sociomedical issues (excessive drinking, smoking, drug use, etc.) for the pregnant woman and her offspring have been the subject of increasing attention. Nevertheless, discrete teratogenic effects attributed to specific chemicals or drugs have been well documented in only a very small number of instances in comparison to the extensive array of substances that are ingested (both intentionally and inadvertently) by women during their pregnancies. The influences of alcohol on fetal and later childhood development are examined in this section to illustrate some of the problems associated with attempting to understand the relationships between such prenatal factors and the later consequence of mental retardation.

The association between maternal alcohol consumption during pregnancy and a constellation of adverse findings in the offspring has been a topic of significant interest and some degree of controversy since the concept of the fetal alcohol syndrome was introduced approximately 10 years ago. In its most complete form, this syndrome is characterized by (1) significant prenatal and postnatal growth deficiency; (2) a combination of characteristic phenotypic abnormalities, including atypical facial features, cardiac defects, and limb anomalies; and (3) central nervous system dysfunction with varying degrees of mental retardation (Clarren and Smith, 1978). A number of serious methodological deficiencies in the existing literature, however, compromise the reliability and validity of the available data.

Perhaps the most serious limitations of all studies in this area are related to the problem of the reliability of the amounts of alcohol women claimed they consumed during their pregnancies and the difficulty of establishing uniform criteria for defining such terms as "moderate" and "excessive" intake. Hanson et al. (1978), for example, studied infants born to mothers who reported either an average consumption of one ounce or more of absolute alcohol per day or "binges" during the pregnancy with ingestion of 5 or more drinks on a single occasion. Ouellette et al. (1977) calculated total monthly consumption of all alcoholic beverages, divided by 30 to get a daily volume, and defined heavy drinkers as those having more than 5 drinks on occasion with a consistent daily average of more than 45 milliliters of absolute alcohol. In fact, their group of heavy drinkers was found to consume an average of 174 milliliters of absolute alcohol per day. Streissguth et al. (1978) studied 20 individuals, ages 9 months through 21 years, born to chronically alcoholic mothers defined either by "self-report or by reports of social agencies, medical records, and/or family" (p. 364) and reported data that demonstrated a continuum of physical abnormalities and mental dysfunctions from severe to mild sequelae. Although careful analysis revealed a relationship between the degree of "dysmorphogenesis" and the extent of intellectual handicap, a considerable variability of IQ scores among children with similar phenotypic features was found. The hypothesis that the adverse affects of alcohol may in part be dose related is not an unreasonable one, but the methodological limitations of the current literature have precluded its evaluation. Moreover, the possible related influences of other ingested substances as well as poor nutrition have been extremely difficult to analyze.

As with all potentially teratogenic substances, the issue of host factors and variable susceptibility also must be addressed. The literature, at this stage of its development, is seriously deficient. Alcoholism is a common problem across a broad ethnic and socioeconomic spectrum. Possible differences in the vulnerability of pregnant women based on age, race, income, living conditions, general health, and nutritional status have not been adequately examined. Shaywitz et al. (1980) reported the results of a study of 15 children seen in a learning-disorders unit whose mothers had a history of "alcoholism" (undefined) during their pregnancy. All but one of the children were white and living in private suburban homes. They demonstrated a continuum of phenotypic features compatible with the diagnosis of fetal alcohol syndrome and were all experiencing persistent academic failure in school, yet their full-scale IQ scores ranged from 82 to 115, with a mean of 98. The authors concluded that the concept of the syndrome could be expanded to include more subtle manifestations of central nervous system dysfunction.

Common knowledge suggests that maternal alcohol ingestion can result in a variety of adverse consequences for the fetus, including varying degrees of mental retardation in later childhood. It is impossible, however, to determine from the available data the relevant variables that contribute to greater or lesser incidence of this syndrome or syndromes. The role of ethnic or socioeconomic factors has not been well studied, nor have patterns of sex difference been described. Moreover, children whose mothers have chronic drinking problems are obviously a highly vulnerable group from a child-rearing perspective. In view of the high prevalence of alcoholism, this may indeed represent a significant source of biological vulnerability in some groups within the population whose intellectual deficits are unexplained. At the present time, however, we have no basis for answering this question with much precision.

PERINATAL INFLUENCES

Perinatal risk factors for subsequent handicaps such as mental retardation have been the focus of extensive investigation, going back as far as Little's (1862) studies of the problem of brain damage related to asphyxia. In 1951, Lilienfeld and Parkhurst introduced the concept of a "continuum of reproductive wastage" to describe the range of possible outcomes, from death to cerebral palsy to varying levels of mental retardation, that were observed to follow difficulties encountered around the time of birth. Pasamanick and Knobloch (1961) suggested the alternative term "continuum of reproductive casualty" and expanded the spectrum of disorders to include a number of more subtle intellectual and functional deficits. Most recently, Sameroff and Chandler (1975) offered the phrase "continuum of caretaking casualty" to highlight the transaction between biological risk factors and environmental variables that eventually determine developmental outcome.

Regardless of the phrasing, the central issue relates to the degree to which the brain of a newborn is injured during labor, delivery, or the immediate neonatal period. Differential risks regarding the incidence of such cerebral insults and the degree to which some children are able to recover from a variety of untoward events raise important questions with regard to the prevalence of mild retardation. These issues are examined below within the context of both the general problem of low birth weight and the more specific problems related to discrete insults to the central nervous system.

Low birth weight in itself is important as a sign of increased risk for a broad array of pathological conditions that may result in a cerebral injury. Low birth weight as a result of prematurity, which is generally defined as a gestation of less than 37 weeks, is more likely to involve problems with hypoxia and/or ischemia affecting the cerebral circulation as a result of such disorders as respiratory distress syndrome, hypovolemic shock, and apnea with bradycardia. Additional threats to central nervous system integrity that occur with greater frequency among premature babies include hypoglycemia, jaundice, infection, postnatal malnutrition, and the increasingly recognized problem of intraventricular hemorrhage. When, however, the newborn's birth weight is significantly low for the expected range given his or her gestational age, the associated problems are different from many of those found in the premature infant. For a "small-for-gestational-age" infant, the issue is generally one of intrauterine growth retardation secondary to such factors as placental insufficiency, maternal malnutrition, intrauterine infection, or congenital abnormalities. Thus, low birth weight babies comprise a heterogeneous group with a variety of vulnerabilities.

The report of the Select Panel for the Promotion of Child Health (1981) states that "it is generally agreed that very low birth weight is among the most significant predictors of later neurological abnormalities and various cognitive and behavioral deficits" (p. 47). Many of the data regarding correlations between birth weight and developmental outcome, however, have been equivocal. Kiely and Paneth (1981) reviewed the methodological difficulties that have characterized these follow-up studies and found them to fall into two broad categories: limitations in study design and problems related to data analysis and reporting. The selection of single hospital samples, for example, has made generalization about the results extremely difficult. The absence of attention to socioeconomic status in the selection of control groups and in the analysis of data is another major shortcoming of many major follow-up studies. With regard to the issue of intelligence test results, studies vary in their reporting mechanisms—some neglect to specify the ages at testing or the instruments used, some indicate only mean IQ scores, and others report data on single cutoff points such as 90 or 70.

Problems of terminology also have plagued the literature. Caputo and Mandell (1970) noted that many studies used the terms "low birth weight," "immaturity," "prematurity," and "short gestation" interchangeably. In most of the early reports, birth weight of less than 2,500 grams (5.5 pounds) was generally employed as the sole criterion for determining prematurity; no distinctions were made for infants who were full-term but small for their gestational age. Data from those studies that failed to classify small infants are especially difficult to interpret.

An additional problem regarding longitudinal data of this type relates to the rapid rate of technological change in perinatal intensive care. That is to say, by the time school-age follow-up studies are completed, the care techniques for these small neonates have changed so dramatically that it is difficult to assess the validity of the findings for the new generation of tiny newborns.

Given these serious limitations in the literature, the difficulties we have in drawing definite conclusions from the existing data are not surprising. Many investigators have reported a high incidence of developmental morbidity in these groups. In a prospective study of 241 infants classified by birth weight, gestational age, and sex, Rubin et al. (1973) found that two thirds of low birth weight males and more than half of the total group of former small-for-gestational-age babies of both sexes had problems of sufficient magnitude to warrant a wide variety of special educational services (which were not well defined) in the elementary school grades. Analysis of all measures of mental development, language skills, school readiness, and academic achievement from preschool through age 7 revealed lower scores for low birth weight subjects as compared to a random control group. Ranges of scores, however, were not provided and analysis for socioeconomic differences was incomplete. Parkinson et al. (1981) studied 45 former full-term, small-for-gestational-age babies between ages 5 and 9 and 19 control children matched for age, sex, birth order, social class, and race. Based on teachers' assessments, the authors found that small-for-gestational-age children may have difficulties at school, the severity of which is related to sex (boys have more problems than girls), social class, and the stage of pregnancy at which slow head growth began. No formal test scores were obtained. Fitzhardinge and Steven (1972) conducted a prospective study of 96 full-term small-for-gestational-age infants and found virtually no major neurological defects (1 percent cerebral palsy, 6 percent seizures) but reported 25 percent diagnosed as having minimal cerebral dysfunction, and one third of the children with IQ scores greater than 100 failing consistently in school. Overall, 50 percent of the boys and 30 percent of the girls had poor school performance, although no analysis for ethnic or socioeconomic status was included. In a large study of prematures, Drillien (1964) found a direct relationship between birth weight and psychometric test scores at age 4, with the full-term control group having a mean IQ of 107 and those with birth weights below 3.5 pounds having a reported mean IQ of 80.

The literature on the follow-up of asphyxiated newborns also is equivocal. An extensive controlled study of several hundred hypoxic newborns followed to school age revealed poor performance on neonatal exams and persistent differences at age 4 on all tests of cognitive function but no significant IQ differences at 7 years (Corah et al., 1965). In a review of 20 studies related to perinatal asphyxia, Gottfried (1973) confirmed the impression that intellectual deficits were more prominent at younger preschool ages but noted that early hypoxia may increase the probability of occurrence of mental retardation in later childhood. Broman (1979) reported that the probability of retardation in asphyxiated groups was increased as much as twelvefold in infancy and sixfold at age 7 but demonstrated that the sequelae of retardation were, in fact, still relatively rare.

Sameroff and Chandler (1975) reviewed a considerable body of literature and concluded that socioeconomic and familial factors markedly overshadowed the effects of perinatal difficulties with respect to long-term developmental outcome. The painstaking longitudinal data collected on the children of Kauai over a 10-year period by Werner et al. (1968) provided one of the most dramatic documentations of the compensatory powers of well-organized families with adequate resources for nurturance. These findings were confirmed by analysis of data on the offspring of over 30,000 pregnancies followed through age 8 in the Collaborative Perinatal Project. According to Broman (1981), birth weight explained only 5–6 percent of the total variance in 8-month Bayley scores and less than 1 percent of the variance in Stanford-Binet IQ scores at age 4. Ethnic identification and maternal education were the best predictors, accounting for 16 percent and 6 percent, respectively, of the variance in IQ at age 4. These data suggest that low birth weight by itself is not a major risk factor for cognitive deficit. A related analysis revealed that 10 clinical signs of perinatal asphyxia explained less than 1 percent of the variance in IQ scores (WISC-R) at age 7 of both white and black children. A more extensive set of perinatal and demographic predictors, however, accounted for 25 percent of the variance in IQ scores among whites and 13 percent among blacks. The best predictor was a composite reflecting socioeconomic status, maternal educational level and performance IQ score, head circumference at birth, and, among whites, a clinical diagnosis of brain abnormality in the neonatal period (Broman, 1981).

In this context it is useful to examine the demographic distribution of low birth weight babies. During the 25 years from 1950 to 1976, the proportion of low birth weight newborns was consistently higher among non-

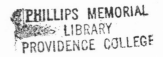

whites and the difference increased with time. At present, black babies have double the chance of weighing 2,500 grams or less at birth (Select Panel for the Promotion of Child Health, 1981). According to the National Center for Health Statistics (1980), the overall rate of low birth weight babies in 1976 was 6.1 percent for whites, 13.0 percent for blacks, and 6.9 percent for infants of other races. For babies who are small for their gestational age, the rates are 6.3 percent for blacks and 2.8 percent for whites.

It is clear from these data that low birth weight, with its associated increased risk of central nervous system insult, is considerably more prevalent among ethnic minority groups, particularly blacks. Moreover, the likelihood of a poor developmental outcome in a low birth weight or asphyxiated newborn is significantly increased for children in the lower socioeconomic classes. Further evidence suggests that although sex differences in IQ may not be significant, males may have a considerably higher incidence of subtle neurological and perceptual disabilities related to factors of perinatal stress that contribute to learning and behavioral profiles resulting in their disproportionate placement in special educational programs. Further study may provide more elucidation of these speculations.

POSTNATAL BIOSOCIAL INFLUENCES

Each child begins life with a set of biological strengths and weaknesses, among which is the relative integrity of the brain. Sociocultural and familial factors subsequently play a major role in shaping the ultimate development of potential abilities and skills. In the nature-nurture debate regarding the origins of mental retardation, however, not all sources of organic morbidity are immutably determined by the end of the neonatal period. On the contrary, a variety of biological influences can affect brain function throughout childhood and thereby contribute to the manifestations of mental retardation in its mild or severe forms. Some of the origins of brain insult are obvious—severe head trauma or an infectious process such as meningitis or encephalitis. Others are more controversial, especially in their mild to moderate forms. The issues of malnutrition and lead intoxication are reviewed below in some depth as representative of that type of biological influence whose dose-related effects are unclear and whose sociopolitical overtones are substantial.

Malnutrition

An extensive body of literature has documented an association between malnutrition in infancy and subsequent intellectual status, especially in developing countries (Cravioto et al., 1966; Hertzig et al., 1972; Stoch and

Smythe, 1963). In circumstances characterized by severe malnutrition during prenatal life and early childhood, the sequelae of mental retardation and behavioral disorders have generally been substantial and nonreversible. The effects of moderate or chronic low-grade malnutrition, however, are less well understood. Before considering the available data, we must review current knowledge on the relationship between nutrition and brain growth.

The results of extensive animal studies, and to a lesser extent human investigations, have supported the notion that there exists a critical period of "growth spurt" in the immature brain, during which it is most vulnerable with regard to inadequate nutrition. Studies in rats have clearly shown that comparatively mild nutritional restrictions during this sensitive period result in permanent changes in the adult brain associated with behavioral deficits that cannot be reversed by a better diet later. Significant undernutrition before or after the growth spurt period, however, produced no detectable effect that could not be "cured" by dietary rehabilitation (Dobbing and Sands, 1971). In humans the sensitive period of rapid brain growth appears to include two important phases: the first extends from mid-pregnancy until the end of the second year of life and is characterized by an early increase in neuronal and later in glial cell number; the second phase extends well into the third and fourth years and is characterized by rapid myelination in association with the continuous elaboration of increasingly complex dendritic branching and synaptic connections (Dobbing, 1974).

Thus, current evidence clearly suggests that the period of maximal vulnerability for brain growth in humans is much more postnatal than previously assumed. This by no means minimizes the critical impact of maternal and therefore fetal nutrition on prenatal brain growth, but it does support the notion that the consequences of intrauterine malnutrition may be reversible. Animal studies have demonstrated that growth retardation during only the first part of the sensitive period may not be sufficient to produce permanent deficits (Winick et al., 1968). If the same applies to humans, then adverse sequelae would be substantial only if malnutrition extended from mid-pregnancy through at least the first two years of life or if it were particularly severe over a portion of that period. In any event, Winick (1969) noted that "although the exact timing has yet to be worked out, it would appear that after infancy the brain is much more resistant to the effects of malnutrition" (p. 677).

The available data on the sequelae of significant malnutrition show high rates of intellectual impairment. In a review of seven studies, Chase (1973) reported significant deficits in test performance by malnourished children ages 2–14 in all but one report. Other investigators have noted greater deficits in behavioral phenomena such as attentiveness, curiosity, activity, and social responsiveness, while some have suggested that malnourished children may be particularly susceptible to the stresses and deprivations so frequently found in an environment of poverty (Read, 1975). This latter speculation was reinforced by data collected by Richardson (1976) in Jamaica that showed the consequences of severe malnutrition in infancy for later intellectual functioning to be correlated with social background and subsequent physical growth, rather than with malnutrition itself.

Methodological problems in human studies of the effects of malnutrition on intellectual development have been monumental. The most obvious relates to the almost universal association of poor nutrition with poverty and its constellation of associated factors that have their own additional negative influence on intellectual development. Cravioto et al. (1966) stated that malnutrition is never remote from impoverishment, and even studies in developed countries have observed a high degree of deprivation (Chase and Martin, 1970). Birch et al. (1971) attempted to control these variables by comparing school-age children with histories of hospitalizations in infancy for kwashiorkor (severe malnutrition) to their siblings who had never experienced malnutrition requiring a hospital admission. Mean IQ (WISC) differences were found to be statistically significant, favoring the nonmalnourished sibling.

A few reports have been published of studies involving malnutrition without the complicating factor of socioeconomic deprivation. Lloyd-Still et al. (1974) studied 41 middle-class subjects, ages 2–21, who were substantially malnourished in infancy secondary to cystic fibrosis or congenital defects of the gastrointestinal tract. Significant differences in scores on the Merrill-Palmer scales were found up to age 5, but no differences were observed on the Wechsler scales administered to the older subjects. Klein et al. (1975) reported follow-up data on 50 children, ages 5–14, who had brief periods of starvation in early infancy secondary to pyloric stenosis. Comparison to siblings and matched controls revealed no significant differences in global measures of intelligence, but significantly lower scores for the index children were found on subtests related to short-term memory and attention. Further studies of malnourished but socially nondisadvantaged youngsters are clearly needed; nevertheless, the Food and Nutrition Board of the National Research Council (1973) stated that "in spite of many serious methodological shortcomings in the studies that have been made, the weight of evidence seems to indicate that early and severe malnutrition is an important factor in later intellectual development, above and beyond the effects of socio-familial influences."

The extent to which the kinds of nutritional deficiencies commonly found in the United States may be sufficient to affect intellectual development in children was considered by Livingston et al. (1975) in their review of data on pregnant women, infants, and children under age 4 from the Ten State Nutrition Survey (U.S. Department of Health, Education, and Welfare, 1972) and children ages 1–4 from the study of the nutritional status of preschool children in the United States during 1968–1970 (Owen et al., 1974). They found that nearly 60 percent of all pregnant women living below the poverty level were apparently consuming calories at a rate low enough to adversely affect fetal brain development. At two to three times the poverty level, the proportion of vulnerable women was still 44 percent. Moreover, 14 percent of the pregnant women living below the poverty level were in jeopardy for both calories and protein. Of children ages 1–4 living in poverty, 18 percent were in jeopardy for defective brain development according to the data of the Ten State Nutrition Survey, while the preschool nutrition survey reported a higher frequency of 24 percent at risk. The Select Panel for the Promotion of Child Health (1981) states that approximately one third of all black children in the United States are estimated to suffer some kind of nutritional defect compared with less than 15 percent of white children. No data for Hispanic or other ethnic minorities were reported. It was noted that poverty and race are associated with deficiencies in six of eight specific nutrients. Even if these data are all high estimates of the extent of the nutritional problems of poor and ethnic minority children in this country, the potential contribution of this factor to the prevalence of mild retardation could be substantial.

Despite some of the inconsistencies and methodological dilemmas noted above, the relationship between prenatal malnutrition and severe or prolonged early childhood malnutrition and the increased risk of subsequent intellectual impairment is well accepted. Its association with poverty will always be inevitable and never easily separable. As noted by Winick (1969), it "is a self perpetuating problem, a vicious cycle which begins in infancy, condemns a person to a lifetime of perhaps marginal function, making it that much more difficult for him to extricate himself from the existing conditions and to create for his family an environment which will protect his children from the same 'disease' " (p. 677).

Lead Intoxication

The increased prevalence of lead intoxication in childhood among ethnic minorities and the poor as well as its association with neurological damage are well known (Byers and Lord, 1943; Lin-Fu, 1972; Perlstein and Attala, 1966). In its most severe form it is characterized by an acute encephalopathic process, the long-term sequelae of which frequently include moderate to severe mental retardation.

Multiple sources of lead in the environment have been identified; the most prominent include paint chips, household dust and dirt, newsprint, and contaminated air near smelting plants or in congested urban areas with high concentrations of automobile traffic. The urban poor have been consistently identified as the group at highest risk for excessive lead exposure. Prevalence rates in low-income, inner-city areas range from 4 to 40 percent positive in community screening programs (Lin-Fu, 1972). Moreover, among comparable socioeconomic groups in the population, lead absorption has been reported to be greater for black than for white children (Lin-Fu, 1979).

Although there are no disagreements about the definition or nature of significant lead poisoning, there has been considerable debate about the effects of an increased body burden of lead at low levels. Over the past 15 years, the upper limit of safety for blood levels of lead has gradually been lowered from 60 micrograms per 100 milliliters to a current level of 30 micrograms per 100 milliliters. As more attention has been focused on these asymptomatic, subclinical cases of increased lead burden, a great deal of controversy has been generated regarding its consequences. Many studies have suggested that moderate levels of lead intoxication often lead to significant attentional difficulties, with associated specific learning problems and behavioral disorders (Needleman et al., 1979; Pueschel, 1974). The influences of dysfunctional behavioral sequelae on adaptive performance in the school setting require more careful examination.

Whether mental retardation is involved is a far more complex matter. While some investigators have reported an inverse relationship between blood lead determinations and intellectual development (Beattie et al., 1975; de la Burde and Choate, 1975), others have found no consistent relationship between a low level of lead and developmental status (Kotok, 1972). Two recently published studies addressed the multiple methodological problems characterizing the literature and have attempted to critically analyze the subtle consequences of a low-level, chronic burden of lead. Needleman et al. (1979) administered an extensive battery of neuropsychological measures to 58 children with high dentine lead levels and 100 with low levels. Although the mean full-scale IQ scores (WISC-R) for each group were normal (102.1 versus 106.6, respectively), the difference between the two groups was statistically significant ($p < .03$). No sex differences were noted. Ernhart et al. (1981) studied 30 children comprising a "moderate lead group" and 50 comprising a "low lead group" five years after their initial identification in a summer screening clinic. All of the children were of low socioeconomic status, and the group was approximately half boys and half girls. Preliminary analysis of the scores on several subtests of the McCarthy Scales of Children's Abilities revealed significant impairment of the high lead group. When parental IQ was included in the analysis, however, the variance in the children's IQ scores associated with lead substantially decreased. The authors concluded from this work that if there are in fact behavioral and intellectual sequelae of low levels of lead intoxication independent of parental and social influences on development, they must be minimal.

Conclusions regarding this topic are extremely tentative. The ability of lead to damage the brain is well established. The upper limit of safety and the effects of low blood levels on intellectual abilities are being explored. The rate of increased lead exposure is highest among ethnic minority groups and the urban poor. In their follow-up study of 67 children age 7 who had asymptomatic lead exposure between ages 1 and 3, de la Burde and Choate (1975) found that the mean full-scale IQ of the index children was lower than that obtained for a control group ($p < .01$), and the former included a larger number of children in the borderline and mildly retarded range. Similarly, 67 percent of the control children received "normal scores" on all parts of an extensive test battery, while only 43.3 percent of the lead-exposed group had no failures in the entire series ($p < .01$). Thus, although the answers are not yet in, one cannot completely disregard the potential contribution of low levels of lead to the preponderance of mild retardation among ethnic minorities and poor children.

Family Resources, Child-Rearing Practices, and Individual Learning Styles

Contemporary conceptualizations of the process of human development place great emphasis on the transaction between biological predispositions and environmental contingencies as mutual determinants of developmental outcome. In this context a consideration of the social characteristics of early childhood and their possible contribution to the increased prevalence of mild retardation among ethnic minority and poor children is most important.

The specific characteristics that emanate from a "disadvantaged" sociocultural milieu can take many forms. Characteristics of a child's home environment, for example, and their relationship to the facilitation of optimal development have been shown to correlate with performance on standardized tests in the preschool years (Bradley and Caldwell, 1976; Elardo et al., 1975). In this context a great deal of data have been generated on the nature of the mother-child relationship and its influence on developmental competence. Ramey et al. (1979) reported that within an apparently homogeneous social class group, 50–65 percent of the variance in Stanford-Binet scores at age 3 could be accounted for by differences in the mothers' attitudes, behavior, and at-home interactions with their children during the toddler years. The authors cautioned, however, that these were correlations and were not presumed to reflect direct causal relationships. White (1975) found that "high competence" children generally engaged in more frequent interaction with their mothers, spent more time in "highly intellectual" activities, were the recipients of more maternal "teaching" and conversation, and received more encouragement than a "low competence" comparison group. Wilton and Barbour (1978) reported similar differences in the amount of didactic teaching and the frequency of encouragement of children's activities found in a comparison of high-risk (children with siblings diagnosed as having "cultural-familial retardation") versus control lower socioeconomic class children. Zajonc and Markus (1975) analyzed the impact of family size and spacing between births as two of many factors that might influence the degree of intellectual stimulation provided within a family. They reported a large body of data demonstrating an inverse relationship between intellectual performance and the number of children in a family. More marked adverse effects were found for younger siblings with brief intervals between births. Although these findings were noted to be independent of social class variables, Zajonc (1976) cited 1960 population data reporting larger families with shorter spacing between births among black American families compared with white American families. A more recent analysis of the influence of family configuration on Scholastic Aptitude Test scores, however, suggests that the amount of variance attributable to these factors is negligible (Zajonc and Bargh, 1980). Rutter (1979), in a review of the heterogeneity of so-called maternal deprivation and its consequences for developmental outcome, summarized these concepts by noting that "insofar as deprivation is a causal factor . . . intellectual retardation is a function of a lack of adequate meaningful experiences" (p. 298). The fact that the overwhelming majority of children from ethnic minority and poor families are not intellectually impaired reflects the essential resilience of most children and, more importantly, underlines the fact that we do not have good evidence that dysfunctional family relationships are typical of these groups. It is important to recognize, however, that the stresses of poverty and racism exact a severe price from many families, and the consequences for the emerging competence of young children are often formidable.

The concept of motivation and its relationship to developing self-esteem is another factor whose salience requires thoughtful consideration. In impoverished homes, where the expectations for future success may be blunted, the motivation of a constitutionally competent child to comply with the demands of an achievement-oriented learning situation may be considerably diminished. Zigler and Trickett (1978), emphasizing the potential central importance of this issue, charge that a considerable body of empirical evidence suggests that IQ changes resulting from preschool intervention programs reflect motivational changes that affect children's test performances rather than actual differences in their cognitive functioning.

The influence of sex differences on child-rearing practices and differences in learning styles is extremely complex. In a study of mother-child interaction in lower socioeconomic class preschoolers, Wilton and Barbour (1978) note that many of the dysfunctional encounters found were more pronounced for mothers and their daughters than for mothers and their sons. Although they could not explain the differences on the basis of their data, these investigators suggest that these differences might be related to cultural sex stereotypes reflecting greater efforts to promote the intellectual development of boys than girls. An alternative explanation suggests that the behavior characteristics of high-risk boys typically demand more maternal response. Similarly, the greater prevalence of aggressive and potentially disruptive behaviors in boys compared with girls may be a major determinant of more frequent referral for special class placement. A comprehensive analysis of sex differences in constitutional behavioral styles, child-rearing strategies and expectations, and intrafamilial relationships is beyond the scope of this paper. Its contribution to the disproportionate prevalence of school failure among boys, however, may very well be crucial.

SUMMARY AND CONCLUSIONS

Although its genesis may dig deeply into biological as well as social roots, the phenomenon of mild mental retardation is primarily a cultural construct. Its very nature has changed dramatically over time, and its contemporary definitions are highly influenced by differences among societies. Within the United States in the past 100 years, arbitrary shifts in diagnostic criteria have moved children in and out of the mildly retarded population. Moreover, as society becomes increasingly complex in its technological demands, new classifications of "defectiveness" will undoubtedly arise.

The charge that mild mental retardation is a creation of our system of universal, compulsory education is strongly supported by the consistent age distribution found across virtually all epidemiological studies. It is rarely diagnosed in the preschool years, begins to increase in incidence in the early elementary grades, reaches a peak in the junior high school population, and then progressively declines in frequency to a relatively low level that persists throughout adult life. The explanation for this inverted U shaped pattern of prevalence can be attributed to the extensive subjection of school-age children to formal testing and the relative inflexibility of school systems regarding the range of abilities and performance that they will accept without assigning a stigmatizing label. Thus, most of the children who are classified as mildly retarded during their school careers subsequently lose their labels and "disappear" into the general population as independently functioning citizens. Although they may be distinguished by the relatively low level of intellectual demand placed on them by their work and their recreation, they clearly assume the status of "normal" adults. Their early classification of defectiveness reflects a designation that primarily serves the administrative needs of the education system whose achievement criteria are set by the values and needs of the society.

Despite the serious methodological problems inherent in epidemiological studies of mild retardation, the consistency of the disproportionate diagnosis of children from ethnic minorities and lower socioeconomic groups has been impressive. Because of their high degree of overlap, it has often been difficult to tease out the relative contributions of ethnicity and poverty. Whatever the numbers may be, it is clear that children from socially and politically disadvantaged families are more likely to be labeled as mildly retarded in the United States than are white, middle-class children.

The data on sex differences are less straightforward. Boys are significantly more likely than girls to be classified as experiencing school failure, but the bulk of the literature on the prevalence of mental retardation demonstrates only a slightly greater proportion of boys among the severely retarded population and virtually no significant sex differences among the mildly impaired. This suggests that differences in educational classification are related to issues that go beyond general intellectual abilities. The list of variables that might explain the observed predominance of boys in special education placements includes differences in the prevalence of specific learning disabilities, attentional deficits, dysfunctional learning styles, and a wide variety of disruptive behavioral disorders as well as cultural differences regarding demands and expectations placed on boys and girls. Despite the well-documented greater biological vulnerability of boys, sex differences in the frequency of mild mental retardation have not been consistently found.

Ethnic and socioeconomic differences in the prevalence of mild retardation clearly demand a critical analysis. The sociopolitical arguments on this issue are highly persuasive. The debates over the cultural biases of psychometric tests, for example, have been well publicized, and their role in discriminatory diagnostic practices has been repeatedly charged. Moreover, marked inequities obviously exist in the availability of resources to facilitate optimal intellectual development within those population groups that have been subjected over many generations to the consequences of institutionalized discrimination. For these and related reasons, equalization of the distribution of mild retardation within the entire population is largely a political task.

A word must be said, however, about the distinction between intellectual impairment and cognitive differences that contribute to competitive disadvantage within a specific sociocultural system. IQ tests, with all of their problems, have been shown to do reasonably well in their originally intended function of identifying children who have an increased probability of failing in school. Thus, although changes in the criteria for making a diagnosis of mild retardation will liberate many children from the stigma of such classification, their performance in a traditional school curriculum is still likely to correspond to their scores on a "standardized" psychometric test. For many children whose life experiences differ from a typical middle-class upbringing, however, discrepancies in test scores and school performance may very well reflect a different kind of cognitive ability that does not necessarily imply intelligence. The tyranny of the dominant culture and its power over the standards of educational success will probably continue to undervalue such differences.

There is, however, another aspect of this problem, which has its roots in the cultural sphere but extends far into the area of biology—the issue of central nervous system function and brain integrity. Poor and minority children are not the victims of social discrimination alone. A considerable body of data suggests that they also carry a disproportionate burden of biological vulnerability that is largely related to the increased health risks of poverty. Much of the discussion of biological disadvantage among ethnic minorities and lower socioeconomic groups has traditionally focused on the issue of genetic differences in intellectual endowment. Biological differences in individuals, however, are determined by a great deal more than inherited traits. The developing brain, regardless of its genetic potential, is subjected to a variety of potentially damaging influences throughout its prenatal, perinatal, and postnatal life, which can have adverse effects on its ultimate functioning. Intrauterine factors such as cytomegalovirus and alcohol, complications during the newborn period related to prematurity and/or low birth weight, and early childhood insults such as malnutrition and lead intoxication can all inflict damage on an immature brain resulting in significant impairment in later intellectual functioning. These threatening influences and many others exist with greater frequency among poor and minority populations. The unequal distribution of these risk factors is certainly influenced by social and economic forces, but their existence creates very real, intrinsic biological vulnerabilities in the children who are so afflicted.

The ultimate roles of biological and social factors in the etiology of mild retardation can best be understood in the context of a transactional model of development applied to a basically resilient human organism. The overwhelming majority of poor and minority children are not retarded. Most low birth weight babies do well developmentally. Of those children who were exposed to noxious agents during their prenatal or postnatal life, some will have impairment of their intelligence and others will appear to escape unharmed. Many of those whose brains have been injured will not demonstrate abnormalities on traditional neurological examinations. Ultimate developmental outcome for all children appears to be a function of a highly complex series of transactions among a great number of biological and environmental facilitators and constraints.

Intelligence is determined by multiple factors, and its impairment rarely has a simple etiology. Some children are extraordinarily resilient and may have well-developed intellectual abilities despite minimal environmental supports. Others are constitutionally limited and will have significant deficits in the face of optimally facilitating experiences. Each child's abilities are dependent on the interplay between his or her biological equipment and life circumstances. Few individuals are without vulnerabilities—most manage to adapt reasonably well. The distribution of vulnerabilities within the general population, however, is grossly unequal. Poor and minority children bear a proportionately greater burden of them in both a biological and a social sense.

In conclusion, it is clear that mild mental retardation is largely a cultural invention and not an objective biological property. It reflects a society's expectations regarding intellectual performance and is subject to modification as values change. Children whose rearing and environmental resources differ from those of the dominant cultural group are at greater risk for having profiles of abilities that may very well be dysfunctional for the demands of the public school system. One must not underestimate, however, the fact that these same "disadvantaged" groups are victimized by a greater frequency of harmful biological factors that can adversely affect brain development in early life and later lead to very real intellectual deficits. Poor and minority children have the highest probability of sustaining injuries through both nature and nurture. Attempts to assign quantitative weighting to the relative contributions of each are thwarted by the limitations of available data. The synergistic effects of cumulative vulnerabilities in both spheres undoubtedly contribute to the greater prevalence of mild retardation in these groups. Thus, the ultimate resolution of these inequities will have to go beyond the very important social battles over evaluation and classification procedures, extending into the realm of maternal and child health.

REFERENCES

Alford, C.
  1977 Prenatal infections and psychosocial development in children born into lower socio-economic settings. Pp. 251-259 in P. Mittler, ed., *Research to Practice in Mental Retardation*. Vol. III. Baltimore, Md.: University Park Press.
  1981 Perinatal infections today and tomorrow. Pp. 81-93 in N. Kretchmer and J. Brasel, eds., *Biomedical and Social Bases of Pediatrics*. New York: Masson Publishing Co.
American Academy of Pediatrics
  1979 Statement on teenage pregnancy. Committee on Adolescence. *Pediatrics* 63:795-797.
Baldwin, W.
  1976 Adolescent pregnancy and childbearing—growing concerns for Americans. *Population Bulletin* 31:1-34; revised reprint May 1977.
Beattie, A., Moore, M., Goldberg, A., Finlayson, M., Mackie, E., Graham, J., Main, J., McLaren, D., Murdoch, R., and Stewart, G.
  1975 Role of chronic low-level lead exposure in the etiology of mental retardation. *Lancet* 1:589-592.
Berg, J.
  1963 *Proceedings of the Second International Congress of Mental Retardation—Part I.* Basel, Switzerland: S. Karger AG.
Birch, H., and Gussow, J.
  1970 *Disadvantaged Children: Health, Nutrition and School Failure.* New York: Grune & Stratton.
Birch, H., Pineiro, C., Alcalde, E., Toca, T., and Cravioto, J.
  1971 Relation of kwashiorkor in early childhood and intelligence at school age. *Pediatric Research* 5:579-585.
Birch, H., Richardson, S., Baird, D., Borobin, G., and Illsley, R.
  1970 *Mental Subnormality in the Community: A Clinical and Epidemiologic Study.* Baltimore, Md.: Williams & Wilkins.
Blanton, R.
  1975 Historical perspectives on classification of mental retardation. Pp. 164-193 in N. Hobbes, ed., *Issues in the Classification of Children*. Vol. I. San Francisco, Calif.: Jossey-Bass., Inc., Publishers.
Bradley, R., and Caldwell, B.
  1976 Early home environment and changes in mental test performance in children from 6 to 36 months. *Developmental Psychology* 12:93-97.
Bremer, J.
  1951 A social psychiatric investigation of a small community in northern Norway. *Acta Psychiatrica Scandinavica, Supplement* 62.
Broman, S.
  1979 Perinatal anoxia and cognitive development in early childhood. Pp. 29-52 in T. Field, ed., *The High Risk Newborn*. Jamaica, N.Y.: Spectrum Publications.
  1980 Long-term development of children born to teenagers. Pp. 195-244 in K. Scott, R. Field, and E. Robertson, eds., *Teenage Parents and Their Offspring*. New York: Grune & Stratton.
  1981 Risk factors for deficits in early cognitive development. Pp. 131-137 in G. Berg and H. Maillie, eds., *Measurement of Risks*. New York: Plenum Press.

Byers, R., and Lord, E.
   1943   Late effects of lead poisoning on mental development. *American Journal of Diseases of Children* 66:471–494.
Caputo, D., and Mandell, W.
   1970   Consequences of low birth weight. *Developmental Psychology* 3:363–383.
Carpenter, R., and Petersdorf, R.
   1962   The clinical spectrum of bacterial meningitis. *American Journal of Medicine* 33: 262–275.
Chase, H.
   1973   The effects of intrauterine and post-natal undernutrition on normal brain development. *Annals of the New York Academy of Science* 205:231–244.
Chase, H., and Martin, H.
   1970   Undernutrition and child development. *New England Journal of Medicine* 282: 933–939.
Childs, B.
   1965   Genetic origin of some sex differences among human beings. *Pediatrics* 35: 798–812.
Clarren, S., and Smith, D.
   1978   The fetal alcohol syndrome. *New England Journal of Medicine* 298:1063–1067.
Cleland, C.
   1979   Mislabeling and replication: methodological caveats. *American Journal of Mental Deficiency* 83:648–649.
Corah, N., Anthony, E., Painter, P., Stern, J., and Thurston, D.
   1965   Effects of peri-natal anoxia after seven years. *Psychological Monographs* 79(3) (whole no. 596):1–34.
Cravioto, J., DeLicardie, E., and Birch, H.
   1966   Nutrition, growth and neurointegrative development: an experimental and ecologic study. *Pediatrics* 38(Suppl.):319–372.
de la Burde, B., and Choate, M.
   1975   Early asymptomatic lead exposure and development at school age. *Journal of Pediatrics* 87:631–642.
Dobbing, J.
   1974   The later growth of the brain and its vulnerability. *Pediatrics* 53:2–6.
Dobbing, J., and Sands, J.
   1971   Vulnerability of developing brain: IX. The effect of nutritional growth retardation on the timing of the brain growth-spurt. *Biologia Neonatorum* 19:363.
Drillien, C.
   1964   *The Growth and Development of the Prematurely Born Infant.* Baltimore, Md.: Williams & Wilkins.
Dunn, L. M.
   1968   Special education for the mildly retarded—is much of it justifiable? *Exceptional Children* 35:5–22.
Eisenberg, L., and Earls, F.
   1975   Poverty, social depreciation, and child development. Pp. 275–291 in D. Hamburg and H. Brodie, eds., *American Handbook of Psychiatry.* Vol. 6—New Psychiatric Frontiers. New York: Basic Books.
Elardo, R., Bradley, R., and Caldwell, B.
   1975   The relation of infants' home environments to mental test performance from six to thirty-six months. *Child Development* 46:71–76.

Ernhart, C., Landa, B., and Schell, N.
   1981   Subclinical levels of lead and developmental deficit—a multivariate follow-up reas-
          sessment. *Pediatrics* 67:911-919.
Farber, B.
   1968   *Mental Retardation: Its Social Context and Social Consequences.* Boston, Mass.:
          Houghton-Mifflin.
Firkowska, A., Ostrowska, N., Sokolowska, M., Stein, Z., Susser, M., and Wald, I.
   1978   Cognitive development and social policy: the contribution of parental occupation
          and education to mental performance in 11-year-olds in Warsaw. *Science* 202:
          1357-1362.
Fitzhardinge, P., and Steven, E.
   1972   The small-for-date infant. II. Neurological and intellectual sequelae. *Pediatrics*
          50:50-57.
Flor-Henry, P.
   1974   Psychosis, neurosis and epilepsy. *British Journal of Psychiatry* 124:144-150.
Gerald, P.
   1980   X-linked mental retardation and an x-chromosome marker. *New England Journal
          of Medicine* 303:696-697.
Goddard, H.
   1910   What can the public school do for subnormal children? *The Training School*
          7(5):242-248.
Goodman, M., and Tizard, J.
   1962   Prevalence of imbecility and idiocy among children. *British Medical Journal* 1:
          216-219.
Goodman, M., Gruenberg, E., Downing, J., and Rogot, E.
   1956   A prevalence study of mental retardation in a metropolitan area. *American Journal
          of Public Health* 46:702-707.
Gottfried, A.
   1973   Intellectual consequences of perinatal anoxia. *Psychological Bulletin* 80:231-242.
Grant, J., and Heald, F.
   1972   Complications of adolescent pregnancy. *Clinical Pediatrics* 11:567-570.
Grossman, H.
   1973   *Manual on Terminology and Classification in Mental Retardation, 1973 Revision.*
          Special Publication Series No. 2. Washington, D.C.: American Association on
          Mental Deficiency.
Gruenberg, E.
   1964   Epidemiology. Pp. 259-306 in H. Stevens and R. Heber, eds., *Mental Retarda-
          tion—A Review of Research.* Chicago, Ill.: University of Chicago Press.
Grunewald, K.
   1979   Mentally retarded children and young people in Sweden. Integration into society:
          the progress in the last decade. *Acta Paediatrica Scandinavica, Supplement*
          275:75-84.
Hanshaw, J.
   1981   Cytomegalovirus infections. *Pediatrics in Review* 2(8):245-251.
Hanshaw, J., Schultz, F., Melish, M., and Dudgeon, J.
   1973   Congenital cytomegalovirus infection. *Ciba Foundation Symposium* 10:23. Am-
          sterdam: Associated Scientific Publishers.
Hanshaw, J., Scheiner, A., Moxley, A., Gaev, L., Abel, V., and Scheiner, B.
   1976   School failure and deafness after "silent" congenital cytomegalovirus infection.
          New England Journal of Medicine 295:468-470.

Hanson, J., Streissguth, A., and Smith, D.
  1978 The effects of moderate alcohol consumption during pregnancy on fetal growth and morphogenesis. *Journal of Pediatrics* 92:457–460.
Heber, R.
  1959 A manual on terminology and classification in mental retardation. *American Journal of Mental Deficiency, Monograph Supplement* 64(2).
Hertzig, M., Birch, H., Richardson, S., and Tizard, J.
  1972 Intellectual levels of school children severely malnourished during the first two years of life. *Pediatrics* 49:814–824.
Hutt, C.
  1978 Biological bases of psychological sex differences. *American Journal of Diseases of Children* 132:170–177.
Jastak, J., MacPhee, H., and Whiteman, M.
  1963 *Mental Retardation: Its Nature and Incidence*. Newark, N.J.: University of Delaware Press.
Kiely, J., and Paneth, N.
  1981 Follow-up studies of low-birth weight infants: suggestions for design, analysis and reporting. *Developmental Medicine and Child Neurology* 23:96–100.
Kirk, S., and Weiner, B.
  1959 The Onondaga census—fact or artifact. *Exceptional Children* 25:226–231.
Kirman, B., and Bicknell, J.
  1975 *Mental Handicap*. Edinborough, Scotland: Churchill Livingstone.
Klein, P., Forbes, G., and Nader, P.
  1975 Effects of starvation in infancy (pyloric stenosis) on subsequent learning abilities. *Journal of Pediatrics* 87:8–15.
Kotok, D.
  1972 Development of children with elevated blood lead levels: a controlled study. *Journal of Pediatrics* 80:57–61.
Kumar, M., Nankervis, G., and Gold, E.
  1973 Inapparent congenital cytomegalovirus infection, a follow-up study. *New England Journal of Medicine* 288:1370–1372.
Lake, D., and Bryden, M.
  1976 Handedness and sex differences in hemispheric asymmetry. *Brain and Language* 3:266–282.
Lapouse, R., and Weitzner, M.
  1970 Epidemiology. Pp. 197–223 in J. Wortis, ed., *Mental Retardation—An Annual Review I*. New York: Grune & Stratton.
Lehman, I.
  1959 Rural-urban differences in intelligence. *Journal of Educational Research* 53:62–68.
Lemkau, P., Tietze, C., and Cooper, M.
  1941 Mental hygiene problems in an urban district. *Mental Hygiene* 25:624–646.
  1942 Mental hygiene problems in an urban district. *Mental Hygiene* 26:100–119, 275–288.
Leonard, M., Landy, G., Ruddle, F., and Lubs, H.
  1974 Early development of children with abnormalities of the sex chromosomes: a prospective study. *Pediatrics* 54:208–212.
Lilienfeld, A., and Parkhurst, E.
  1951 A study of the association of factors of pregnancy and parturition with the development of cerebral palsy: a preliminary report. *American Journal of Hygiene* 53: 262–282.

Lin-Fu, J.
   1972   Undue absorption of lead among children—a new look at an old problem. *New England Journal of Medicine* 286:702–710.
   1979   Lead exposure among children—a reassessment. *New England Journal of Medicine* 300:731–732.
Little, W.
   1862   On the influence of abnormal parturition, difficult labor, premature birth, and asphyxia neonatorum on the mental and physical condition of the child, especially in relation to deformities. *Transactions of the Obstetrical Society of London* 3:293–344.
Livingston, R., Calloway, D., MacGregor, J., Fisher, G., and Hastings, A.
   1975   U.S. poverty impact on brain development. Pp. 377–394 in M. Brazier, ed., *Growth and Development of the Brain*. New York: Raven Press.
Lloyd-Still, J., Hurwitz, I., Wolff, P., and Shwachman, H.
   1974   Intellectual development after severe malnutrition in infancy. *Pediatrics* 54:306–312.
MacMillan, D., Meyers, C., and Morrison, G.
   1980   System-identification of mildly mentally retarded children: implications for interpreting and conducting research. *American Journal of Mental Deficiency* 85:108–115.
McNemar, Q.
   1942   *The Revision of the Stanford-Binet Scale*. Boston, Mass.: Houghton-Mifflin.
Melish, M., and Hanshaw, J.
   1973   Congenital cytomegalovirus infection: developmental progress of infants detected by routine screening. *American Journal of Diseases of Children* 126:190.
Menolascino, F.
   1977   *Challenges in Mental Retardation: Progressive Ideology and Services*. New York: Human Sciences Press.
Mercer, J.
   1971   The meaning of mental retardation. Pp. 23–46 in R. Koch and J. Dobson, eds., *The Mentally Retarded Child and His Family: A Multidisciplinary Handbook*. New York: Brunner/Mazel.
   1973   *Labeling the Mentally Retarded: Clinical and Social System Perspectives on Mental Retardation*. Berkeley, Calif.: University of California Press.
Moser, H., and Wolff, P.
   1971   The nosology of mental retardation: including the report of a survey of 1378 mentally retarded individuals at the Walter E. Fernald State School. *Birth Defects: Original Article Series* 7(1):117–134.
Naeye, R.
   1981   Teenaged and pre-teenaged pregnancies: consequences of the fetal-maternal competition for nutrients. *Pediatrics* 67:146–150.
Naeye, R., Burt, L., Wright, D., Blanc, W., and Tatter, D.
   1971   Neonatal mortality, the male disadvantage. *Pediatrics* 48:902–906.
National Center for Health Statistics
   1980   *Factors Associated with Low Birth Weight: United States, 1976*. S. Taffel. Publication no. 80-1915. Vital and Health Statistics, Series 21, Number 37. Washington, D.C.: U.S. Department of Health and Human Services.
National Research Council
   1973   Position paper on *The Relationship of Nutrition to Brain Development and Behavior*. Food and Nutrition Board. National Academy of Sciences, Washington, D.C.

Needleman, H., Gunnoe, C., Leviton, A., Reed, R., Peresie, H., Maher, C., and Barrett, P.
   1979   Deficits in psychologic and classroom performance of children with elevated den-
          tine lead levels. *New England Journal of Medicine* 300:689–695.
New York State Department of Mental Hygiene
   1955   A special census of suspected referred mental retardation. Data for Onondaga
          County, New York, in *Technical Report of the Mental Health Research Unit*.
          Syracuse, N.Y.: Syracuse University Press.
Nicholson, A., and Hanley, C.
   1953   Indices of physiological maturity: derivation and interrelationships. *Child Develop-
          ment* 24:3–38.
Nortman, D.
   1974   Parental age as a factor in pregnancy outcome and child development. *Reports on
          Population and Family Planning* No. 16.
Ouellette, E., Rosett, H., Rosman, N., and Weiner, L.
   1977   Adverse effects on offspring of maternal alcohol abuse during pregnancy. *New
          England Journal of Medicine* 297:528–530.
Owen, G., Kram, K., Garry, P., Lowe, J., and Lubin, A.
   1974   A study of nutritional status of preschool children in the United States, 1968–1970.
          Pediatrics 53:597–646.
Parkinson, C., Wallis, S., and Harvey, D.
   1981   School achievement and behavior of children who were small-for-dates at birth.
          Developmental Medicine and Child Neurology 23:41–50.
Pasamanick, B., and Knobloch, H.
   1961   Epidemiologic studies on the complications of pregnancy and the birth process. Pp.
          74–94 in G. Caplan, ed., *Prevention of Mental Disorders in Children*. New York:
          Basic Books.
Pass, R., Stagno, S., Myers, G., and Alford, C.
   1980   Outcome of symptomatic congenital cytomegalovirus infection: results of long-term
          longitudinal follow-up. *Pediatrics* 66:758–762.
Perlstein, M., and Attala, R.
   1966   Neurologic sequelae of plumbism in children. *Clinical Pediatrics* 5:292–298.
Potts, D.
   1970   Which is the weaker sex? *Journal of Biosocial Science* 2(Suppl.):147–157.
President's Panel on Mental Retardation
   1962   *Report to the President: A Proposed Program for National Action to Combat Men-
          tal Retardation*. Washington, D.C.: U.S. Government Printing Office.
Pueschel, S.
   1974   Neurological and psychomotor functions in children with an increased lead burden.
          Environmental Health Perspectives (May):13–16.
Ramey, C., and Finkelstein, N.
   1978   Psychosocial Mental Retardation: A Biological and Social Coalescence. Paper pre-
          sented at the Conference on Prevention of Retarded Development in Psychosocially
          Disadvantaged Children, Madison, Wis.
Ramey, C., Farran, D., and Campbell, F.
   1979   Predicting I.Q. from mother-infant interactions. *Child Development* 50:804–814.
Ramey, C., Stedman, D., Borders-Patterson, A., and Mengel, W.
   1978   Predicting school failure from information available at birth. *American Journal of
          Mental Deficiency* 82:525–534.
Read, M.
   1975   Behavioral correlates of malnutrition. Pp. 335–353 in M. Brazier, ed., *Growth and
          Development of the Brain*. New York: Raven Press.

Reschly, D., and Jipson, F.
 1976 Ethnicity, geographic locale, age, sex and urban-rural residence as variables in the prevalence of mild retardation. *American Journal of Mental Deficiency* 81: 154–161.
Reynolds, D., Stagno, S., Stubbs, G., Dahle, A., Livingston, M., Saxon, S., and Alford, C.
 1974 Inapparent congenital cytomegalovirus infection with elevated cord IgM levels—causal relation with auditory and mental deficiency. *New England Journal of Medicine* 290:291–296.
Richardson, S.
 1976 The relation of severe malnutrition in infancy to the intelligence of school children with differing life histories. *Pediatric Research* 10:57–61.
Robinson, N.
 1978 Mild mental retardation: does it exist in the People's Republic of China? *Mental Retardation* 16:295–298.
Rubin, R., Rosenblatt, C., and Balow, B.
 1973 Psychological and educational sequelae of prematurity. *Pediatrics* 52:352–363.
Rutter, M.
 1979 Maternal deprivation, 1972–1978: new findings, new concepts, new approaches. *Child Development* 50:283–305.
Rutter, M., Tizard, J., and Whitmore, K.
 1970 *Education, Health and Behavior*. London: Longman.
Ryan, W.
 1971 *Blaming the Victim*. New York: Pantheon.
Sameroff, A., and Chandler, M.
 1975 Reproductive risk and the continuum of care-taking casualty. Pp. 187–244 in F. Horowitz, ed., *Review of Child Development Research, Vol. 4*. Chicago, Ill.: University of Chicago Press.
Sarason, S. B., and Doris, J.
 1979 *Educational Handicap, Public Policy, and Social History: A Broadened Perspective on Mental Retardation*. New York: Free Press.
Select Panel for the Promotion of Child Health
 1981 *Report to the United States Congress and the Secretary of Health and Human Services on Better Health for Our Children: A National Strategy*. Publication no. 79-55071. Washinton, D.C.: U.S. Department of Health and Human Services.
Shaywitz, S., Cohen, D., and Shaywitz, B.
 1980 Behavior and learning difficulties in children of normal intelligence born to alcoholic mothers. *Journal of Pediatrics* 96:978–982.
Smith, J., and Pollaway, E.
 1979 The dimension of adaptive behavior in mental retardation research: an analysis of recent practices. *American Journal of Mental Deficiency* 84:203–206.
Smith, R., Platou, E., and Good, R.
 1956 Septicemia of the newborn. *Pediatrics* 17:549–575.
Stein, Z., and Susser, M.
 1969 Mild mental subnormality: social and epidemiological studies. *Social Psychiatry Research Publication* 47:62.
Stevenson, A., and McClarin, R.
 1957 Determination of the sex of human abortions by nuclear sexing the cells of the chorionic villi. *Nature* 180:198–199.
Stoch, M., and Smythe, P.
 1963 Does undernutrition during infancy inhibit brain growth and subsequent intellectual development? *Archives of Disease in Childhood* 38:546.

Streissguth, A., Herman, C., and Smith, D.
    1978   Intelligence, behavior, and dysmorphogenesis in the fetal alcohol syndrome: a
            report on 20 patients. *Journal of Pediatrics* 92:363–367.
Tarjan, G., Wright, S., Eyman, R., and Keeran, C.
    1973   Natural history of mental retardation: some aspects of epidemiology. *American
            Journal of Mental Deficiency* 77:369–379.
Taylor, R.
    1980   Use of the AAMD classification system: a review of recent research. *American
            Journal of Mental Deficiency* 85:116–119.
Tennes, M., Puck, M. Orfanakis, D., and Robinson, A.
    1977   The early childhood development of 17 boys with sex chromosome anomalies: a
            prospective study. *Pediatrics* 59:574–583.
Terman, L.
    1916   *The Measurement of Intelligence*. Boston, Mass.: Houghton-Mifflin.
Turner, G., Brookwell, R., Daniel, A., Selikowitz, M., and Zilibowitz, M.
    1980   Heterozygous expression of x-linked mental retardation and x-chromosome marker
            Fra(x) (927). *New England Journal of Medicine* 303:662–664.
U.S. Department of Health, Education, and Welfare
    1972   *Ten State Nutrition Survey*. Publication no. 72-81334. Washington, D.C.: U.S.
            Department of Health, Education, and Welfare.
Vaughan, V., McKay, R., and Behrman, R., eds.
    1979   *Nelson's Textbook of Pediatrics*. Eleventh Edition. Philadelphia, Pa.: W. B.
            Saunders.
Waber, D.
    1976   Sex differences in cognition: a function of maturation rate? *Science* 192:572–574.
Werner, E., Bierman, J., French, F., Simonian, K., Connor, A., Smith, R., and Campbell, M.
    1968   Reproductive and environmental casualties: a report of the ten year follow-up of
            the children of Kauai Pregnancy Study. *Pediatrics* 42:112–127.
Werner, H., and Strauss, A.
    1939   Problems and methods of functional analysis in mentally deficient children. *Jour-
            nal of Abnormal and Social Psychology* 34:37–62.
White, B.
    1975   Critical influences in the origins of competence. *Merrill-Palmer Quarterly* 21:243–
            266.
Wilton, D., and Barbour, A.
    1978   Mother-child interaction in high-risk and contrast preschoolers of low socioeco-
            nomic status. *Child Development* 49:1136–1145.
Winick, M.
    1969   Malnutrition and brain development. *Journal of Pediatrics* 74:667–679.
Winick M., Fish, I., and Rosso, P.
    1968   Cellular recovery in rat tissues after a brief period of neonatal malnutrition. *Journal
            of Nutrition* 95:623–626.
Winter, S.
    1972   The male disadvantage in diseases acquired in childhood. *Developmental Medicine
            and Child Neurology* 14:517–519.
Wishik, S.
    1964   Georgia Study of Handicapped Children. Report on a Study of Prevalence,
            Disability Needs, Resources, and Contributory Factors. Publications for Program
            Administration and Community Organization. Georgia Department of Public
            Health, Atlanta.

Witelson, S.
1976 Sex and the single hemisphere: specialization of the right hemisphere for spatial processing. *Science* 193:425-427.
Zajonc, R. B.
1976 Family configuration and intelligence. *Science* 192:227-236.
Zajonc, R. B., and Bargh, J.
1980 Birth order, family size, and decline of SAT scores. *American Psychologist* 35:662-668.
Zajonc, R. B., and Markus, G. B.
1975 Birth order and intellectual development. *Psychological Review* 82:74-88.
Zigler, E., and Trickett, P.
1978 I.Q., social competence and evaluation of early childhood intervention programs. *American Psychologist* 33:789-798.

Classifying Mentally Retarded Students: A Review of Placement Practices in Special Education

WILLIAM E. BICKEL

INTRODUCTION

The purpose of this paper is to describe what is currently known about placement processes in special education since the enactment of the Education for All Handicapped Children Act of 1975 (P.L. 94-142). Particular emphasis is on the relationship of these processes to the disproportionate representation of minorities in programs for educable mentally retarded (EMR) students. The paper is divided into six major sections. The first section describes several models of placement that have been offered by education theorists and professionals. The second section gives an overview of empirical research with a discussion of referral and screening processes. Sections three, four, and five review empirical research in the areas of evaluation, individual education plans and least restrictive environments, and parental involvement and due process procedures. The concluding section summarizes major trends in the empirical research on placement and minority representation in special education.

The focus of the paper is broad, and several limitations are in order to make the task more manageable. First, testing issues related to minority

This paper has benefited from the comments of a number of my colleagues. I would particularly like to thank Jack Birch, William Cooley, Alonzo Crim, Gaea Leinhardt, Thomas Oakland, John Ogbu, Jane Mercer, Daniel Reschly, Lauren Resnick, David Sabatino, *and* Naomi Zigmond *for critiquing early drafts. I would also like to acknowledge the assistance of* Rachel Kohnke *in research activities for this paper.*

placement are not examined in detail. Similarly, litigation and financial policies related to placement are not directly addressed. These issues are the subjects of other background papers prepared for the panel (see Magnetti, 1980; the papers by Magnetti and Travers in this volume). The review of the literature stresses those studies that have examined placement processes since the passage of P.L. 94-142. Finally, the representation of minorities in EMR classes is the primary program area of concern, although issues related to learning disabilities (LD) and compensatory education programs are discussed where appropriate. Explicit attention is given to the empirical research on placement practices directly related to minority representation. In the following discussions, "placement process" refers to the referral, preplacement, evaluation, classification, and assignment of an individual student to an individualized special education program. This is understood to be distinct from the location, room, or facility in which a specially classified child receives instruction.

PLACEMENT MODELS

Numerous models of what an effective placement process should consist of have been offered by education theorists and professionals in the field of special education. Jones reviews current models and offers a synthesis that suggests that these models have six basic components in common (Jones, 1979:17):

First, a school-related problem is identified. The problem may be one of behavior, of achievement, of appropriateness of the administrative arrangement, or some combination of the above. Second, if formal observations and/or assessments are deemed necessary, permission to engage in such activities is sought from parents/parent surrogates. Third, formal observations and assessments by various specialists (e.g., school psychologists, school social workers, resource consultants, speech therapists, physicians, and others) are obtained. Fourth, a planning team is constituted to integrate information received about a child and to make recommendations for further case disposition. Fifth, an instructional plan may be formulated. Sixth, follow-up is required.

A model proposed by Reynolds and Birch (1977) comprises the four fundamental steps of screening, educational diagnosis, development of short- and long-term objectives, and program evaluation. Particular emphasis is on the second step, in which there are at least four separate components: (1) obtaining available information, (2) standardized formal assessment (norm-referenced tests), (3) criterion-referenced tests, and (4) observation.

Poland et al. (1979), in the context of learning-disabled placement, offer the following detailed 13-step model, based on a survey of special education directors:

1. Child found or referred
2. Review of referral
3. Appoint assessment team
4. Obtain parental permission
5. Assessment
6. Review of assessment results
7. Eligibility determination
8. Contact parent
9. Develop individual education plan (IEP)
10. Placement decision
11. Parental permission for placement
12. Develop strategies to implement the IEP
13. Implement program

All of these theoretical models have in common what Oakland calls a commitment to fusing "assessment (i.e., placement) activities ... fused with intervention activities, creating a system in which the diagnostic processes find meaning by becoming interrelated with viable intervention processes" (1977:iii). This theme of relating intervention to assessment is at the heart of the panel's recommendations on assessment.

The Poland model provides (through step 11) a framework for the analysis of model placement processes. A child enters the placement process either through referral by a teacher, parent, or administrator or through identification by some routine screening process, such as a review of test scores in a district (step 1). The referral is reviewed by an individual or group of persons who function as gatekeepers in the system (step 2). A decision can be made at this point as to the appropriateness of the referral. For example, a school principal may decide that the child's problem can be worked out within the existing classroom assignment.

If the initial decision maker decides that further action is justified, an assessment team (also known as the placement team or the planning team) is appointed (step 3). The team might consist of several of the child's teachers, a school administrator, staff psychologists, counselors, and others. Each member of the team brings specific expertise to the placement process and is individually responsible for collecting information on the child in the relevant domain(s). Prior to actually collecting information on the child the placement team informs the parent(s) of the activity and their rights in the process (step 4). Ideally the parents will not only be informed of the process but will also contribute to it.

Once parental permission is obtained the actual evaluation activities are undertaken (step 5). The data are collected and reviewed by the placement team (step 6); on the basis of the review, a child may be determined to be eligible for special education services (step 7). If the child is found to be eligible, the child's parents are notified (step 8). A group consisting of a parent, the child's teacher, and at least one member of the placement team meets to develop an IEP (step 9). The content of the IEP specifies what services the child requires (step 10), and the child is assigned to a program. The final step (step 11), for the purpose of this paper, is the securing of parental permission for the program of services assigned. (Steps 12 and 13 of the Poland model are not directly relevant to this paper, since they relate to post-placement implementation issues.)

As the review of the literature below makes clear, Poland's model in many ways reflects the placement requirements of P.L. 94-142. The problems involved in the federal regulations lie not in their distance from model or ideal practices but in the difficulties of implementing them in the complex and variable world of local and state education agencies.

EMPIRICAL RESEARCH ON PLACEMENT

The literature on special education placement primarily addresses the extent to which the P.L. 94-142 regulations are in place and, to a far lesser extent, the degree to which they are having the intended effects. Most of the studies reviewed focus on the placement process, broadly defined, without specifically addressing the minority representation issue per se. However, much of what is uncovered is relevant to the question of minority representation in the sense that the results of these studies provide an important contextual background. Studies specifically addressing minority representation are discussed in detail in a final subsection of each major section.

The review of placement research has been organized into four major categories:

1. Referral and screening
2. Evaluation
3. IEPs and least restrictive environments
4. Due process/parental involvement

It should be noted that this review is confined basically to work that has been done since the passage of P.L. 94-142 in 1975. The literature is developing rapidly, and much relevant research is currently under way. Such work in progress is described in terms of the research design and data-collection procedures, as available.

The scarcity in some topic areas of research directly related to EMR placement processes has necessitated that the studies reviewed draw on the larger placement context (e.g., learning disabilities). The findings of these studies are relevant in that many if not all of the same placement mechanisms apply in all programs. The program area of each study is made explicit.

Each section begins with a brief description of the appropriate regulations and a general description of the studies relevant to a specific issue, followed by a review of findings, both convergent and conflicting. Studies that specifically investigate issues related to minority representation are described in detail. Finally, it should be noted that the methodological strategies used in each study are not reviewed in depth, although the studies reviewed were selected on the basis of three criteria: (1) the relevance of the questions addressed, (2) the representativeness of the samples and data base, and (3) the appropriateness of the analysis and conclusions given the data reported.

SCREENING AND REFERRAL

Federal Mandate

Requirements for screening and referral are contained in two sections of P.L. 94-142 (Sec. 300.128, Sec. 300.220). State and local education agencies must ensure that all handicapped children are identified, located, and evaluated. Although specific activities are not prescribed, these agencies must detail in their annual program plans what has been done to locate children in need of service.

Increases in Enrollment

The number of students in special education programs has steadily increased despite a drop in total public school enrollment. The continued growth in the special education population is, in part, a result of federal pressure to institute aggressive screening and referral procedures and the growing availability of alternatives to program placement (especially LD programs) at the state and local levels. This pressure emanates from P.L. 94-142 and the Office of Special Education (OSE), formerly the Bureau of Education for the Handicapped. In their semiannual report to Congress (U.S. Department of Health, Education, and Welfare, 1979b:xiii, hereafter referred to as USHEW), OSE noted that "almost 75% of the nation's handicapped school-age children are receiving special education ... today compared to less than half as estimated by Congress at the time P.L. 94-142 was enacted." The report goes on to state that 84 percent of the polled states and territories have reported increases over the previous year. Several states (Georgia, Indiana, North Carolina, and Ohio) increased their special education population by more than 10,000 students in a single year. OSE reports that by 1979 approximately 3.71 million children were receiving special education services (USHEW, 1979b).

As examples of the kinds of activities that are stimulating the growth in special education, the 1979 OSE report cites the involvement of parent groups, the use of print and electronic media to advertise the availability of assistance, and the availability of toll-free telephone numbers in numerous states. In some instances, new activities are the result of specific litigation. For example, the Philadelphia school district was ordered to institute LD screening procedures for the entire student population because of allegedly inadequate prior service (*Frederick L.* v. *Thomas*, 1980). OSE estimated that of 160,000 students evaluated nationwide as a part of screening and referral activities, "80% were identified as potentially requiring special services" (p. 15).[1]

Who Does the Referring?

Referrals represent the second major source of students identified for possible placement in special education programs. While the overwhelming opinion is that the classroom teacher is the major source of referral, relatively little direct research on this source has been uncovered.

Six studies have looked at some aspect of the question of who does the referring (Birman, 1979; Blaschke, 1979; Nelson, 1980; USHEW, 1979c; Stearns et al., 1979; Stevens, 1980). A range of states and local areas are to be found in the samples of these studies. In general, the major data-collection strategies involved interviews with special education personnel and/or reviews of referral documentation instruments.

Several conclusions are reported in this research. First, the teacher is still the most important source of referrals (Birman, 1979; Blaschke, 1979; Stearns et al., 1979; USHEW, 1979c). For example, Blaschke (1979:9) concluded that most "new students entered special education through the in-school referral process." This generally consisted of the teacher's reporting to the principal that "he/she is having difficulty teaching the child and needs assistance" (p. C-1). A second conclusion to be drawn from these studies is that there is also a trend toward the diversification of the source of referrals; other school personnel, parents, and health personnel are playing larger roles (Blaschke, 1979; Nelson, 1980; Stevens, 1980).

[1] Estimates were based on an OSE survey of 654 LEAs representing 50 percent of the school enrollment in 16 states. These figures were extended as estimates for the nation.

What Influences Screening and Referral Rates and Content?

The question of what influences referrals is a difficult one, especially since most studies have relied on self-reported descriptions of the process by special education personnel rather than on direct observation by researchers. Several studies, relying on interviews, report findings in this area (Blaschke, 1979; Stearns et al., 1979; USHEW, 1979a, 1979c).

A most significant finding in these studies concerns the role of program availability in influencing referrals. In effect, the presence or absence of a service in a local education agency (LEA) strongly influences whether children are referred (Stearns et al., 1979; USHEW, 1979c). One study found that "school districts with more special education staff, facilities, and services identify more children needing help" (USHEW, 1979c:3). This study reports one case of a district that has only EMR classes. This district, thus far, has identified only children with EMR handicaps. Not a single additional handicap has been uncovered. The finding that child identification and resources are related is not in itself surprising. However, this trend, if widespread, indicates the difficulty of implementing the section of P.L. 94-142 that requires first the identification of educational needs and then the provision of treatment based on the needs identified. Such a process requires a district to create a program if it is needed rather than to find students who fit into existing programs.

A second finding reported is that backlogs in processing assessments can reduce referrals (Blaschke, 1979; Stearns et al., 1979). The regular classroom teacher becomes frustrated with a process that does not seem to deliver help to the children rapidly enough and tends to refer them less and less often.

Another influence on referrals is the criteria for eligibility in a particular state or LEA (Stearns et al., 1979; USHEW, 1979c). Federal regulations and education theorists assume that eligibility criteria are applied after a child is evaluated. However, Stearns et al. (1979) found that eligibility criteria can heavily influence the process at much earlier stages. An extreme case is a state that has such rigid eligibility criteria that even the referral forms for use by a teacher are based on specific programs. Thus, a teacher would not refer a student for assessment, but for EMR, ED (emotionally disturbed), or LD assessment. The importance of eligibility criteria and the variations in them found across states mean that "whether or not a child is identified as in need of special education [very often] depends on the state of residence" (Stearns et al., 1979:45).

At the other extreme, the Stearns et al. (1979) study found some states with such ambiguous criteria that a great deal of discretion in interpretation is permitted at the local level. This encourages a "considerable lack of uniformity in who gets identified both across LEAs and even across schools within LEAs" (p. 46). (The ambiguity in criteria was documented by Huberty et al., 1980.) Great personal discretion in the referral process was also found by USHEW (1979c). The picture of wide variation from state to state in referral processes coupled with the possibility of significant personal discretion in the system supports the conclusion noted earlier that a child's referral for assessment may be as much a function of where he or she lives and attends school as it is of his or her actual learning capabilities and performance. This pattern of variation is an interesting contrast to the expectations of 27 special education directors in 1979, who indicated that the location and identification of children as required by P.L. 94-142 presented little difficulty (USHEW, 1979b).

Outcomes of Identification

It is not within the scope of this report to describe in detail the essential demographics of the students who are referred (see Finn in this volume). However, in reviewing the research on referrals, several interesting findings have been reported as to who is likely *not* to be referred. Stearns et al. (1979) found that referrals were generally on the increase in about half the sites in their study. They found a trend away from EMR and toward LD placements. (Such trends are further documented in Bickel, 1981.) They also found that five categories of children were *not* likely to be identified or referred:

1. Children who were LD at the high school level.
2. Children with emotional problems, especially at the intermediate and secondary school levels.
3. Children who were quiet and well behaved.
4. Children who did not have parents who influence the staff to act on their behalf.
5. Children who fall between the eligibility criteria for LD and EMR programs.

Minority Representation and Screening and Referral

Since P.L. 94-142 was enacted, little research has been conducted on the relationship of referral and screening practices to minority representation in special education classes. The obvious question is: Are minority students referred at a higher rate, thus influencing the higher placement rate in EMR classes? A few studies have looked at this question through the review of actual referral data. Several others have used referral simulations to examine the issue. Because of the small number of studies and their importance to this paper, these studies are reviewed individually. Tomlinson et al.'s (1977) study of 355 students referred for psychological services in an urban school system investigated the relationships among referral rates and "minority status, sex, ... types of presenting problems and the nature of subsequent psychological services" (p. 456). The minority populations represented in the samples consisted of 127 black, 42 native American, and 5 Oriental students. Tomlinson et al. report the following (1978: 457–458):

1. The referral rate of minority students was 14% higher than their enrollment in school.
2. Minority students did not differ significantly from white students with respect to the type of problem (academic or behavior) for which they were referred—with 41 percent of the minority students referred for academic problems and 59 percent for behavior, and 39 percent and 61 percent, respectively, for these problems among white students.
3. Referral rates for males were higher (68 percent) than those for females (32 percent).
4. There were no significant differences between males and females as to the type of problem identified for referral.

An interesting related finding was that "the schools [in the sample] referring the lowest percentage of minority students had been integrated the longest" (p. 458). These researchers theorize that there exists the possibility "that teachers, in making referrals of minority students, may in part be acting on a bias that decreases as their experience with minority students increases" (p. 458). (It cannot be overemphasized that this is pure speculation, unsupported in the study or in the literature; the question has simply not been addressed.) These researchers concluded their study with a call for further research to "determine if referral behaviors of minority students are quantitatively or qualitatively different from those of majority students, and the extent to which SES status alone would account for differences obtained" (p. 458).

The issue of socioeconomic status and its relationship to referrals and placements, largely unexamined in the literature, merits additional attention if for no other reason than for the statistical correlations that have been obtained between socioeconomic status and achievement in school.

A study in Florida (Lanier and Wittmer, 1977) investigated the relationships among teacher referral rates and students' minority status, sex, and socioeconomic level. A sample of 359 elementary teachers from a single county school system was asked to review 16 hypothetical fourth-grade students. The profiles contained similar information on age, socioeconomic status, behavior, achievement, intelligence, and family size. Only race and sex were varied in the samples. These researchers reported that "black students, although with the very same mental capacity and achievement test scores were referred to EMR classes ... more frequently than were their white contemporaries (regardless of race of referring teacher)" (p. 169).

Craig et al. (1978) compared the characteristics of 7,000 children recommended for special education by using indicators derived from teacher and parent recommendations, medical examinations, school behaviors, test scores, and developmental histories. Variations were investigated for six types of handicaps: hearing, vision, mental retardation, emotional disturbance, orthopedic, and speech. Data from the National Center for Health Statistics were used. Several findings are most relevant: (1) There was little agreement among the various indicators used for recommending students for special services (i.e., teachers and parents were not identifying the same groups of students). (2) Despite the inconsistency among indicators, more students from lower socioeconomic groups tended to be identified for many of the handicapping conditions. (3) Teachers tended to recommend greater numbers of blacks for EMR and ED placements. Teachers also tended to recommend more males than females for these categories. In addition, disruptive school behavior seemed to play a role in teacher recommendations.

The influences of race and sex were also investigated in a study of Hispanic students in the Southwest (Zucker et al., 1979). In this study, 180 second- and third-grade teachers were asked to evaluate a student file and rate the appropriateness for placement in an EMR program. The information used was designed to "create equivocal data," i.e., "no hard evidence to provide justification for special class placement" was present (p. 3). The student was shown to be functioning one year below academic grade level. Only race and sex were varied. The researchers reported that "regardless of sex ... teachers scored special class placement more appropriate for Mexican-American children than they did for white children" (p. 4).

Contrasting findings were uncovered in a recent review of a large urban school district in the Northeast undertaken by the Region III Office of OCR (Naidoff and Gross, 1980). Data were collected on the referral rates of children for psychological assessments. During the 1978–1979 school year, 978 students were referred for psychological testing for learning or behavioral problems. Approximately 49 percent of these students were black. Since the district population was 48 percent black at the time, it was determined that black students were not being referred disproportionately. It should be noted, however, that in this same district the percentage of students placed in EMR programs was higher for black students than their percentage in the district.

Although the studies discussed in the previous sections on referral did not address minority representation issues explicitly, one finding that turns up in several of these studies may be germane. Stearns et al. (1979) and USHEW (1979c) found that the availability of programs and staff has a positive effect on referrals. The more staff and programs there are, the more referrals are made. This may be significant for the issue of minority representation in urban districts with large concentrations of black students. If urban districts have more services available and more staff concerned with placement (this, of course, would have to be shown), this availability coupled with the concentration of black students may act to inflate referral rates for these populations overall. This question warrants additional research.

This review of the literature does not provide an adequate answer to the original question of whether referral rates are higher for minorities. The bulk of the studies, using real or simulated data, do show a tendency toward higher rates of referral for minorities. However, contrasting evidence in a large urban district was also uncovered. This evidence plus the limited number of studies addressing the question lead to the conclusion that more research must be undertaken to establish a more thorough understanding of the relationship between minority referrals and EMR placement rates.

Conclusion

In terms of the larger body of research, two findings stand out most clearly: (1) the tendency for referrals to be influenced by program availability and (2) the ambiguity in some instances and rigidity in others of the criteria for various categories. The next section reviews the literature on what happens after referral.

EVALUATION

The research discussed in this section describes some of the basic assessment practices currently in use. As noted earlier, detailed analysis of test issues is not a focus of this paper. The discussion here is divided into three major subsections: (1) How are evaluations conducted? (2) What influences evaluation processes? (3) What is the quality of the decision made? In theory, referral and assessment activities cannot be easily separated from the writing of IEPs and the assignment of least restrictive environments. The discussion here of these issues in separate sections, used simply as an organizational strategy, does not imply discrete separation in these processes.

Federal Mandate

Federal law and regulations require that, once identified or referred, a student must be assessed to determine his or her special education needs. The law requires three major steps in the process:

1. Evaluation of the individual child.
2. Development of an IEP.
3. The assignment of a least restrictive environment in which to receive services.

Some specific evaluation regulations also require that a variety of procedures be used that are validated for the purpose, that a variety of data be developed by a multidisciplinary team, that any tests must be administered in the child's native language by someone trained in their use, and that the assessment must be socially and culturally nondiscriminatory (Sec. 300.532-4). Specific requirements for IEPs are that the document be a written record containing current levels of performance, annual and short-term goals, designation of the least restrictive environment, objective criteria and evaluation procedures, expected duration of services, and provisions for annual and three-year reviews (Sec. 300.342-6). The requirement for the least restrictive environment attempts to ensure that a "continuum of alternative placements" is provided to students (Sec. 300.551-3).

How Are Evaluations Conducted?

An initial question concerns the current status of implementing the federal requirements. A number of studies have attempted to describe one or more aspects of the evaluation process (Marver and David, 1978; National Association of State Directors of Special Education, 1980; Poland et al., 1979; Stearns et al., 1979, Thouvenelle and Hebbeler, 1978). With the exception of the Thouvenelle and Hebbeler study, this research is based primarily on interviews and/or surveys of participants in the processes of special education assessment.

The findings reported to date indicate several important trends. A number of studies lend evidence to the trend reported by OSE toward general compliance, at least in form, with federal regulations by LEAs (Mar-

ver and David, 1978; Poland et al., 1979; Stearns et al., 1979; Thouvenelle and Hebbeler, 1978).

Descriptions of the process vary across studies, but in general the process has shifted away from one of a single psychologist administering one
or more tests toward the creation of assessment teams reviewing multiple
data sources, as described at the beginning of this paper. These data are
reviewed by members of the team and discussed with parents.

Within the overall picture of compliance, several studies report findings
that are in opposition to some of the major tenets of the law. For example,
three studies (Marver and David, 1978; Poland et al., 1979; Thouvenelle
and Hebbeler, 1978) report that "preassessment" meetings were held by
school officials prior to assessment meetings involving the parents. The
purpose of these preassessment meetings seems generally to be to prepare
a district's position on an individual child. However, the effect may be to
present the parent with a decision determined before the assessment meetings envisioned under P.L. 94-142 take place.

Poland et al. (1979) report that, despite the trend toward compliance,
there still exists a heavy reliance on psychological assessment data as the
basis for a decision. Marver and David (1978) found that data files tend to
be poorly kept and that assessment is often made by personnel not trained
in the procedures. Another study (National Association of State Directors
of Special Education, 1980) indicates that placement team meetings tend
to be dominated by administrative personnel or psychologists. Finally,
Stearns et al. (1979) report that there is clearly a tension in LEAs between
the need to do thorough, individualized case studies and the requirement
of many states for speedy processing. Not only can backlogs affect the
referral rates, as reported earlier, but they can also reduce the quality of
the assessments as a system attempts to catch up on its case load.

What Influences Assessment Decisions?

Only a few studies have directly investigated factors that may influence
evaluation decisions (e.g., Thouvenelle and Hebbeler, 1978). Such studies
are expensive and time-consuming in that direct observation of placement
meetings are probably required to supplement interviews or survey data.
A number of studies have investigated this question through interviews
and simulations (Poland et al., 1979; Thurlow and Ysseldyke, 1980;
Ysseldyke et al., 1979a, 1979b).

Based on the observations of a number of meetings, Thouvenelle and
Hebbeler (1978) report that it is difficult to determine when and how the
placement decision is made. It is therefore equally difficult to determine

precisely what influences the decision. These researchers report that the decision seems to be made by one or two school representatives and that the parent is not directly involved. Information on a student's academic achievement and social and behavioral needs seems to be the most important data used in the process. Program characteristics and specific goals are in the next most frequently discussed category.

The importance of achievement as a primary data source influencing the decision was generally confirmed by Poland et al. (1979) and Ysseldyke et al. (1979a). In addition, Poland et al. (1979) found that teachers' reports of achievement are particularly important. This finding to a certain extent parallels that of Thurlow and Ysseldyke (1980), Yesseldyke et al. (1979a), and Ysseldyke et al. (1980a). These studies found in simulation investigations that a final decision was heavily weighted by the original referral data. Since many referrals are made by teachers, the referral data may subtly influence the placement of the child. The importance of the referral statement to the final decision also adds additional significance to the findings cited above, that, on one hand, the referral process involved a great deal of personal discretion and that, on the other hand, in states with rigid criteria, the initial referral is made with a final potential placement already in mind. The net effect of these relationships may be to put a student on a preconceived track toward a placement prior to the actual evaluation process.

Several of the simulation studies explicitly investigated the potential influence on evaluation of sex, socioeconomic status, and physical appearance (Thurlow and Ysseldyke, 1980; Ysseldyke et al., 1979). In addition, Poland et al. (1979) studied the effects of student's race on evaluation. In general, these studies do not report a strong effect for these characteristics. The influence of referral information is much stronger. Thurlow and Ysseldyke (1980) indicate that special education directors rate the influence of student characteristics less highly than assessment and observation in the evaluation process. It is important to note, however, that these studies were simulations, and in the Thurlow and Ysseldyke (1980) study the researchers are reporting on what special education directors perceive to be influencing their decisions. From the evidence presented in these studies, it would be extremely unwise to dismiss without additional investigation the possible effects of student characteristics.

To summarize, the literature reviewed on what influences the final evaluation decision contains several relatively consistent findings. Student achievement, particularly as evidenced by reports of teachers, is of primary importance. Achievement, when coupled with initial referral information, represents the single most important data influence on the final decision.

What Is the Quality of the Decision?

The question of the quality of the decisions made can be addressed in several ways. One measure of quality may be found in discrepant classification rates across racial, sexual, and economic groups. Studies examining this measure are reviewed below. Some researchers have examined the consistency of the educational characteristics of children in a special program as compared with those placed in another classification, those referred but not placed, and those in the general population (Birman, 1979; Craig et al., 1978; Gajar, 1977; Hallahan and Kauffman, 1977; Hansche et al., no date; Larson, 1978; McDermott, 1980; Meyers et al., 1978; Petersen and Hart, 1978; Thurlow and Ysseldyke, 1979; Ysseldyke et al., 1979a). It is important to note that these studies looked at placement decisions across a number of special education categories and, in one instance (Birman, 1979), Title I placements as well. Furthermore, these studies generally used *post hoc* statistical analyses of placement data comparing the mean characteristics of one group (e.g., EMR students) with those of another (e.g., LD or ED or both). With these methodological limitations in mind, several interesting trends in the data are discernible.

One major impression to be drawn from these studies is that placement decisions are remarkably inconsistent. This seems to be particularly true in LD placements (Larson, 1978; Thurlow and Ysseldyke, 1979; Ysseldyke et al., 1979a). The single most consistent indicator distinguishing various groups seems to be IQ (Gajar, 1977; Larson, 1978; Meyers et al., 1978; Petersen and Hart, 1978).

Birman (1979:80) sums up inconsistency of placements in the following statements:

The characteristics of special education studies varied by schools, by district, and by state. Variability and ambiguity in the criteria used to select students for both programs [special education and Title I] implied that students who are viewed as Title I students in one school or district are seen as belonging in special education programs in other schools or districts, or vice versa.

The role of IQ is summed up by Petersen and Hart (1978:754) as follows:

Those diagnostic categories which are described in the guidelines in terms of explicit IQ ranges were the most clearly identifiable statistically.... But in the application of such labels as "emotionally handicapped" and "learning disabled" in which diagnosis is generally viewed as representing a complex, inferential process, there was little consistency in evidence.

The importance of the IQ score in describing, *post hoc,* the populations in various classifications lends credence to those who suggest that this single score still plays an inordinate role in placement decisions. This may be true despite the requirements of P.L. 94-142 that a broad data base be used in evaluating students. Heavy reliance on IQ scores also represents a significant departure from the theoretical models described in this paper. The findings on the use of IQ in placement decisions, coupled with those concerning the importance of achievement to initial referral, suggest a process in which poor achievement "nominates" a student for assessment and the IQ "anoints" him or her in a particular classification.

Minority Representation and Evaluation

The major issue, and the focus of most of the research related to evaluation procedures and minority representation, concerns test bias and the possibility of developing technically sound and culturally fair test instruments. A technical review of testing issues is not within the scope of this paper.[2] However, some research has investigated the effects of race on placement decisions not directly related to testing issues and is reviewed here.

One thesis about the cause of the high percentages of minorities in EMR programs is based on the perception that placement relies heavily on IQ scores as the major factor in the final decision (Mercer, 1972). This tendency, coupled with the finding that minorities tend to score lower on IQ tests (Kaskowitz, 1977:Appendix B), may explain much of the disproportionate representation of minorities in EMR classes. Studies reviewed earlier have documented the continuing emphasis that is generally given by the placement team to test scores.

A recent survey (Huberty et al., 1980) of state definitions for EMR populations confirms that the IQ score is still a major criterion for placement. Table 1, a summary of the variations found among the responding states, shows that significant variations do occur among the reporting states. Variations in definition concern the basic elements of the definition as well as the presence and nature of cutoff scores on IQ tests. It is important to note the number of states (15) that do not list adaptive behavior as part of their definitions and the number of states (24) that, while specifying adaptive behavior in their definitions, do not identify the criteria used. In such states it can be presumed that IQ scores continue to play a predominant role in the classification of EMR children.

The relationship between an emphasis on IQ scores in EMR placement and disproportionate representation of minorities is explored at some

[2]For detailed reviews of testing issues, see Bersoff (1979), Hobbs (1975), Oakland (1977), and Travers (in this volume).

TABLE 1 Summary of States' Guidelines Concerning IQ and Adaptive Behavior in Mentally Retarded Students

State	Date of Guidelines	Type of Definition	Intelligence Criteria	Include Adaptive Behavior in Definition	Adaptive Behavior Criteria Indicated	Adaptive Behavior Measures Indicated	Incorrect Use of Ratio IQ Concept
Alabama	1973	Other	30-80 IQ	No	No	No	Yes
Alaska	1975	Other	Not specified	Yes	No	No	No
Arizona	1977	Other	Not specified	No	No	No	No
Arkansas	1977	Other	≤ −2.0 S.D.	Yes	No	Yes	Yes
Colorado	1976	Similar	≤ −1.75 S.D.	Yes	No	No	No
Connecticut	1976	Other	Not specified	No	No	No	No
Delaware	1974	Other	Not specified	No	No	No	No
District of Columbia	Not specified	AAMD and BEH	≤ −2.0 S.D.	Yes	No	No	No
Florida	1976	AAMD	≤ −2.0 S.D.	Yes	Yes	Yes	No
Georgia	1975	Similar	≤ −2.0 S.D.	Yes	No	No	Yes
Hawaii	1966	Other	Not specified	No	No	No	Yes
Idaho	1975	Similar	≤ 75 IQ	Yes	No	No	Yes
Illinois	1976	Other	Not specified	Yes	No	No	No
Indiana	1973	Other	≤ 75 IQ	No	No	No	Yes
Iowa	1974	Other	≤ −1.0 S.D.	Yes	No	No	No
Kansas	1976	Other	Not specified	Yes	No	No	No
Kentucky	1975	Other	Not specified	No	No	No	No
Maine	Draft	Other	Not specified	No	No	No	No
Michigan	1973	Other	Not specified	Yes	No	Yes	No
Missouri	1976	AAMD	≤ −2.0 S.D.	Yes	No	No	Yes
Montana	Not specified	Similar	≤ 75 IQ −1.6 S.D.	Yes	No	No	No

State	Year	Definition	IQ				
Nebraska	1975	Other	Not specified	Yes	No	No	No
Nevada	1976	Other	≤75 IQ	No	No	No	No
New Hampshire	1976	Other	Not specified	No	No	No	No
New Jersey	1976	Other	≤ −1.5 S.D.	Yes	No	No	No
New York	1975	Other	≤ −1.5 S.D.	No	No	No	No
North Dakota	1976	Other	≤75 IQ	No	No	No	No
Ohio	1973	Other	≤80 IQ	No	No	No	No
Oklahoma	1976	Other	≤75 IQ	No	No	No	No
Oregon	1976	AAMD	≤ −2.0 S.D.	Yes	Yes	No	No
Pennsylvania	1976	Similar	≤80 IQ	Yes	No	No	No
Rhode Island	1963	Other	Not specified	Yes	No	No	No
South Carolina	1972	Other	≤70 IQ	Yes	Yes	No	Yes
South Dakota	1974	Similar	Not specified	Yes	No	No	No
Tennessee	1976-1977	Other	Not specified	Yes	No	No	Yes
Utah	1975	AAMD	≤75 IQ	Yes	Yes	No	No
Virginia	1972	Other	≤ −2.0 S.D.	No	No	No	No
Washington	1976	Other	≤75 IQ	Yes	No	Yes	No
West Virginia	1974	AAMD	≤75 IQ	Yes	Yes	No	No
Wisconsin	Not specified	AAMD	≤ −2.0 S.D.	Yes	No	No	No
Wyoming	1975	AAMD	≤ −2.0 S.D.	Yes	No	No	No

Key to abbreviations:

AAMD—American Association of Mental Deficiency.

BEH—Bureau of Education for the Handicapped.

Other—definition other than AAMD and BEH.

S.D.—standard deviation(s).

Similar—similar to AAMD definition, with only minor variations.

SOURCE: Huberty et al. (1980:258-259). Copyright © 1980 by the Council for Exceptional Children. Reprinted by permission.

length in a study on validation of state counts of handicapped children (Kaskowitz, 1977). In a review of a number of studies, Kaskowitz reports that, theoretically, an emphasis on IQ scores alone would invariably yield a disproportionately higher number of minority children in the EMR population. The range reaches proportions of 10 to 1 when IQ is the sole criterion and a cutoff score of approximately 70 is used.[3] Kaskowitz also reports that, when IQ scores are adjusted for socioeconomic and racial differences, prevalance rates diminish dramatically.

Several studies have investigated the consequences of manipulating IQ cutoff scores as a way to minimize disproportionate representation of minorities. For example, a study in Arizona (Reschly and Jipson, 1976) investigated the impact of IQ cutoff scores of 69 or 75 on minority placement in a sample of 1,040 randomly selected children. The researchers report the following (p. 160):

> If the cutoff point is 69 and the guidelines from the *Diana* and *Guadalupe* decisions applied (i.e., use of nonverbal intellectual measures with Mexican-American children), then overrepresentation of Mexican-American children in the mildly retarded classification is virtually eliminated. Application of the above procedure greatly reduces the overrepresentation of Blacks and Papago Indians. However, the IQ cutoff score of 75 leads to disproportionate representation of all non-Anglo groups in the mild retardation classification.

P.L. 94-142 states that a simple reliance on IQ scores to determine placement is no longer permissible. The regulations require that a variety of assessment measures be used, including ones that assess adaptive behavior. A similar position emerges from the review of theoretical models in this paper. Several studies have examined the impact that the use of such additional measures might have on minority representation measures. One study (Fisher, 1977) used three different classification schemes to assess and classify a sample of 46 students. The sample included black (4), Hispanic (30), and Anglo (12) students from low and middle socioeconomic backgrounds. The first classification scheme simply used a full-scale IQ score two standard deviations below the mean. The second scheme used multiple test criteria including subtest scores on an IQ measure, achievement scores, and performance on a visual-motor test. The third approach was a pluralistic model that included the traditional psychometrics of the second model and added the ABIC (Mercer, 1979), a

---

[3]It is interesting to note that this same study (Kaskowitz, 1977:80) cites research by Craig et al. (1978) to the effect that "if classification were based on teacher opinion, the difference in rates would be diminished [by almost one half]...."

measure of adaptive behavior of children. The results of the study indicate (Fisher, 1977:5) that:

The full scale IQ approach led to classification as EMR of 34 (75%) of the total 46 students. The psychometric approach led to 28 (60%) EMR classifications and the pluralistic approach led to 12 (26%) EMR classifications. Hence, the pluralistic approach decreased the number of students classified as EMR two to three times as compared to the other two approaches.

The majority of the differences among the three classification schemes occurred as a result of differing classification of Mexican-American students. The small number of blacks in the study prevents interpretation of significance in the changes that occurred among these students. This study also investigated socioeconomic trends within the sample and found that the pluralistic model tended to classify as EMR far fewer low-income students than the other models.

Findings similar to those of Fisher are reported by Reschly (in press). This researcher examines the application of procedures developed by Mercer and Lewis (1978): the System of Multicultural Pluralistic Assessment (SOMPA). A feature in this system is the inclusion of measures of adaptive behavior. (ABIC, the test used in Fisher's study, is part of SOMPA.) Reschly reports that the use of SOMPA can indeed produce a "reduction in the number of students, especially minority, eligible or classified for special education . . ." (p. 12).[4]

An interesting opportunity to study the effects of a deemphasis on IQ scores for EMR placement is occurring in California as a result of Judge Peckham's decision (*Larry P.* v. *Riles*, 1979) to impose a ban on their use. A recent study (Stevens, 1980) investigates this question in Los Angeles. Since the original ban on IQ testing, the Los Angeles district has used an elaborate assessment model that includes achievement tests, estimates of adaptive behavior, language assessment, school and family histories, and psychological measures other than IQ scores. Stevens reports that "the school district continues to have black EMR enrollment above the percent of its total black enrollment. However, the actual numbers of black students and the percentages have declined from 1976 to 1979 by 976 students or 19.6 percent" (p. 5).

Apart from variations in the assessment criteria and instruments used, the question remains as to whether a student's race affects the classification process through other mechanisms, such as expectations concerning

---

[4]It should be noted that Reschly is not without reservations concerning SOMPA, and he suggests that a great deal of work must be done to further refine measures of adaptive behavior.

various ethnic groups on the part of those making the assessment. Presumably such expectations may influence the selection of instruments and/or the interpretation of results. One survey mentioned earlier (Poland et al., 1979) examined the influence of race on placement decisions and did not find this kind of relationship: Special education directors judged that the factors of race and sex were not influential in making a placement decision. However, the fact that the data are self-reports by people who are significantly involved reduces the likelihood that the findings represent actual practice.

Matuszek and Oakland (1979) investigated factors that influence teachers' and psychologists' recommendations regarding assignment to various special class settings. In this study, 53 psychologists and 76 teachers were asked to review 10 cases and make recommendations for enrollment in a program continuum, from regular class to full-time special class. The participants were *not* asked to assign a special label. Sex, age, time of year, physical abnormalities, referral source, and teacher characteristics were held constant in the cases. Ethnicity, socioeconomic status, language preference, and home-related anxiety were some of the variables in the cases. Matuszek and Oakland (1979) report that, in general, (p. 116):

Both groups consider IQ, test achievement, class achievement, and home-related anxiety important in making recommendations, with IQ and test achievement weighted more heavily by psychologists than by teachers. SES is important only to psychologists, while adaptive behavior and self-concept are important only to teachers. Recommendations by both groups were not influenced by children's ethnicity, language, home values, classroom manageability, and interpersonal relationships.

Additional findings of interest in this study include the fact that teachers did not appear to make different program or setting recommendations on the basis of a child's manageability in the classroom. The authors speculate that this may be because the teachers in the study were making recommendations for enrollment in someone else's class and would not be responsible themselves for working with the child on a daily basis. Another interesting finding was that teachers did use measures of adaptive behavior in their decisions and recommended fewer special services for children with average performance on these measures. Finally, teachers in the study recommended more special placements for children with language backgrounds other than English.

Another study (Amira et al., 1977), investigating the impact of students' race and socioeconomic status on psychologists' decisions, used a sample of 217 members of the School Psychology Division of the American Psychological Association. The cases used for review varied only in the race (black/white) and socioeconomic level (middle/lower income) of the student. The participants were asked to "rate the severity of several diagnostic conditions, and the desirability of several remedial programs, and their attitude toward the boy" (p. 435). Measures of the professional experience of the psychologists as well as their personal value structures were obtained. The finding that is most relevant for the purpose of this paper concerns a three-way interaction effect in which more traditional psychologists tended to regard lower-income black students as less mentally retarded and less suitable for placement in a custodial care situation. Caution is warranted in interpreting such an interaction, as it would necessarily require further inspection and verification.

Johnson (1977), investigating the decision-making behavior of school psychologists, examined their behavior on being presented with data that suggest multiple problems when the available classification system permits only singularly defined disorders (as is generally the case in most special education contexts). Johnson hypothesized that in such cases nonsalient characteristics (e.g., age, socioeconomic level, sex) would be used over salient characteristics (e.g., IQ for EMR, behavior problems for ED, and achievement discrepancy for LD) to resolve the ambiguity and to reach a classification decision. While race was not included in the research as a nonsalient characteristic, the use of socioeconomic level, which overlaps heavily with race, makes a review of this study of interest. A total of 373 school psychologists were asked to review hypothetical cases; some were textbook cases based on unambiguous information, and some were cases based on conflicting information in which multiple disorders were present. Johnson reports that "recommendations were always based solely on the salient features. Rather than using age, sex, and social class . . . the psychologists appeared to weigh the significance of the salient features against each other [in conflict situations] to arrive at their placement recommendations" (p. ix).

As noted earlier, race was not included in this study. The finding of this research concerning the lack of effect of socioeconomic level is particularly interesting. This study's finding seems to contradict other studies that found correlational patterns between socioeconomic level and placement in special classes. The apparent contradiction may not exist if one takes the position that the correlations between socioeconomic level and placement are in fact a reflection of the well-documented relationship between socioeconomic level and income and achievement (Wolf, 1977). Given the importance accorded to achievement tests in determining placements, it is not surprising that a relationship to socioeconomic level would also show up in final placements. The Johnson (1977) study, on the other hand, attempts to measure *direct* socioeconomic bias on the part of psychologists.

Johnson's conclusion suggests that such a direct bias was not active in his sample. More research on the relationships among race, socioeconomic level, and placement is clearly in order.

Turning to other questions related to evaluation processes and minority representation, two studies (Mishra, 1980; Swanson and Deblassie, 1979) investigated the effects of test administration on their outcomes when bilingual Mexican-American students were involved. The Swanson and Deblassie study examines the question of whether "the use of an interpreter and/or a regular examiner in administering the WISC would affect the results of a group of Mexican-American children" (p. 231). In this study, 90 children were divided into 3 groups of roughly comparable levels of mental maturity. One group was administered the test in English; the second, in English with interpretation; and the third in Spanish. The researchers report a single subtest-language interaction in which the "administration of the verbal phase of the WISC in English and the performance phase in Spanish appears to be most efficacious in terms of eliciting optimum performance of Mexican-American children" (p. 235). In all other cases the interactions did not seem to be significant.

Mishra (1980) investigated the effect of the ethnicity of the examiner on intelligence test performances of Anglo and Mexican-American children. Verbal subtests of the Wechsler Intelligence Scale for Children (WISC) and the Raven Progressive Matrices (four in all) were used. Half of each subtest was administered by a Mexican-American examiner, and English was used exclusively in the testing situation. Mishra reported that on one of the four subtests—the WISC vocabulary—Mexican-American children scored significantly higher when the test was administered by Mexican-American examiners. It would be unwise at this point to draw any conclusions based on this evidence. Further exploration of the relationship among test performances, the ethnicity of the examiner, and special education seems to be warranted.

Several features of the research on assessment practices are most striking. First, there clearly remains a tension between the requirement to do more thorough, multidimensional assessments and the need to process students efficiently given due process mandates and limited resources. Second, the research indicates the continuing importance of IQ tests in the placement process, despite the federal mandate to broaden assessment strategies. Third, in their examinations of the question of quality in placement decisions, most researchers used consistency among categories as a primary criterion. To this writer the efficacy of the placement—and efficacy is taken to mean the impact on student growth under a special education program, as compared with previous growth or growth that may be attributed to alternative programs not considered to be part of special education—must remain the more important criterion in an evaluation of quality in placement decisions. Fourth, the continued importance of IQ scores has serious implications for minority placement, given the often noted differences in minority and majority group IQ means. This issue, however, is not easily amenable to a simple solution. Any new system of assessment (e.g., one not using IQ scores) must meet the test of being at least as accurate as the one currently used.

A final point on assessment concerns an agenda for future research. Useful research would include investigations of the innovative practices in assessment that are currently being implemented in various jurisdictions across the country. Of particular interest is the tendency to implement treatment strategies prior to a formal assessment process as a way of eliminating the need for an eventual special education assessment and placement. Magnetti (1981) reports on procedures in Louisiana that call for observations of children once they are referred but prior to formal assessment for the purpose of identifying changes that might be tried in the regular classroom that would alleviate the need for special education. Similar procedures have been noted by Bickel (1981) and Wang (1981). These innovations reflect the assessment philosophy of the panel, and the results obtained from such work would be important to examine in this context.

IEPs AND LEAST RESTRICTIVE ENVIRONMENTS

The development of an IEP in the theoretical model of placement discussed earlier in this paper occurs after a child's assessment and determination of eligibility. In theory, once an IEP is developed, a placement decision is reached. As noted in previous sections, these stages are often collapsed into one or two meetings, and the review of assessment data, the determination of eligibility, the development of an IEP, and placement decisions all occur at one time. The requirement of P.L. 94-142 that an IEP be developed before a child is placed and that it must be continually updated has sparked a great deal of discussion among educators across the country. The IEP requirement has also stimulated a large amount of research focused primarily on the status of the implementation of these regulations and the reactions of educators to them.

This section is divided into four parts: a discussion of the federal requirements and a review of the literature on the status of the implementation of IEPs, problems in implementation, the typical content of an IEP, and the implementation of requirements of least restrictive environments through IEP documentation.

Federal Mandate

P.L. 94-142 specifies that an IEP must be completed for each child receiving special services and the content areas that must be included in an IEP. Each IEP must contain a statement of "the child's present levels of performance; . . . annual goals including short term instructional objectives; . . . specific special education and related services . . . [and] the extent to which the child will be able to participate in regular education programs; the projected dates for initiation of services and [their] . . . duration; and . . . objective criteria and evaluation procedures and schedules for determining . . . on an annual basis whether the short term . . . objectives are being achieved" (34 CFR 300.346).

Status of Implementation

Several studies have examined the status of the implementation of IEP regulations (Blaschke, 1979; USHEW, 1979b; Research Triangle Institutes, 1980). In general, these studies found IEP regulations at the state level to be in place and that most LEAs actually had IEPs for individual students. For example, OSE reports (USHEW, 1979b) that state policies "regarding IEPs were found to be consistent with federal regulations in all but one state" (p. 19). This report also stated that a review of IEPs in 281 programs across the nation found 269 with IEPs in place.

Problems in Implementation

While most states and districts seem to be moving toward implementation in form, numerous problems have surfaced as state and local jurisdictions have attempted to move toward compliance (Blaschke, 1979; Marver and David, 1978; National Association of State Directors of Special Education, 1980; USHEW, 1979c). A primary problem in implementation concerns the management of the logistics necessary for each case (i.e., time, scheduling, etc.). A second problem concerns anxiety among participants over the use that was to be made of IEPs in evaluating special education services. Teachers and administrators seemed to be particularly concerned that IEPs would be used for purposes of accountability (Marver and David, 1978; National Association of State Directors of Special Education, 1980).

Two studies found that the relationship of IEPs to their use in instruction was unclear (Blaschke, 1979; USHEW, 1979c). There seemed to be particular difficulty in this regard when a student crossed organizational boundaries within a district (e.g., from junior to senior high school).

Several studies have found that there is difficulty in implementing IEP regulations involving parent participation (Blaschke, 1979; Marver and David, 1978; USHEW, 1979c). Problems ranged from LEAs that developed IEPs before meeting with parents, to difficulty in getting parents to meetings, to IEPs written with so much education jargon that parental understanding was hindered. In several of the studies, problems in implementation seemed to be reduced as an LEA gained experience with the process.

Content of IEPs

A number of studies have examined samples of IEPs to determine their content (Alper, 1978; Blaschke, 1979; Marver and David, 1978; Reisman and Macy, 1978; Research Triangle Institute, 1980; Schenck and Levy, 1980; Stearns et al., 1979; Wall, 1978). In general, most of the IEPs reviewed contained most of the requirements of the regulations. Within this broad framework of compliance, however, are some areas in which IEPs consistently fall short of the P.L. 94-142 mandate. For example, Alper notes (1978:64–69) that the principal language of the student was not specified in 89 percent of the cases and that evaluation procedures and/or criteria were infrequently specified.

Several studies confirm this lack of specification in evaluation procedures and/or criteria (Alper, 1978; Marver and David, 1978; Research Triangle Institute, 1980; Schenck and Levy, 1980). There also seems to be a tendency to stress long-term goals in IEPs, leaving short-term goals ambiguous or to be specified by the special education teacher.

The fact that many IEPs lack evaluation procedures and criteria makes it particularly difficult to monitor student progress. While the final regulations specifically exempt special educators from accountability for the progress of an individual student, it is nevertheless important to understand where progress is being made in order to develop a better picture of the efficacy of special education programs generally.

Requirements for Least Restrictive Environments

A specific component of the IEP is the specification of the final placement of a child and the amount of regular instruction he or she will receive. P.L. 94-142 requires that a placement be in the least restrictive environment, i.e., an environment as close to the home school and the regular classroom as is feasible. One study that actually observed placement meetings (Thouvenelle and Hebbeler, 1978) did not find much discussion of least restrictive environments but noted a general trend in placement that gave most of the students (78 percent) some contact with regular classrooms.

Another study reports a close link among least restrictive environments, program availability, and the label assigned to a child (Stearns et al., 1979); that is, a given district might only have one type of classroom setting (e.g., self-contained EMR instruction). If a child receives the EMR label, he or she is inevitably placed in the classroom setting available in the district, in this case self-contained, irrespective of his or her ability to adapt to a similar program offered in a less restrictive setting. It is important to recall that the significance of both single program availability in a variety of settings and various programs available in the same setting has surfaced in terms of the referral and evaluation processes. This issue is a key point of tension between the law, which requires a continuum of programs, services, and settings needed for an individual child and what seems to be the reality that most districts simply cannot provide such a range.

Minority Representation and IEPs

The writing of an IEP does not directly affect the numbers of minority children that are classified as EMR. However, it is important to know whether, in the process of writing IEPs and assigning the least restrictive environment, minority students are given significantly different goals and types of assignments. No research was found that directly examined the question of whether the content of IEPs (especially short- and long-term goals) varies by race. However, there is some information on the effects of race on the types of setting in which children are placed.

Tomlinson et al. (1977) investigated the question of whether race affects assignments to special education settings. These researchers report that "minority students were recommended more frequently for resource help, while majority students were recommended more frequently for placement in self-contained classes" (p. 459). It should be noted that this trend is in the context of an overall greater tendency to recommend minority students for some special education placements.

Another study (Matuszek and Oakland, 1979) also addresses the issue of variation in type of placement. Psychologists participating in this study chose from a program continuum of options, from regular-class placement with no additional help to placement in a full-time special class or special school. These researchers report that "the data from this study clearly indicate that they [the psychologists] did not make different recommendations on the basis of race" (p. 121). It is interesting to note that

these researchers indicate that socioeconomic status was a factor in determining the nature of the placements. In this regard, they found that psychologists tended to recommend more services (and a more restricted environment) for higher-income students.

Two issues identified by the research on IEPs are of particular importance to the panel's work. These concern (1) the failure in one study to
find a relationship between IEP content and classroom instruction and (2)
the more general finding that evaluation criteria and/or procedures are
often missing from IEPs. In each case the panel's interest in establishing
the efficacy of special placements is hindered by the absence of key links
or data.

PARENTAL INVOLVEMENT AND DUE PROCESS

Reviews of the research on due process and parental involvement are combined in this section because of the overlap in the literature. Research on
due process in placement has examined almost exclusively the interaction
between parents and schools.[5] Although due process must presumably include the role of students vis-à-vis school personnel as well as that of parents, these aspects have yet to receive much attention. Research on parental involvement includes, of course, the examination of procedural due
process mechanisms; it also extends to a consideration of the quality of the
interaction between parents and school personnel as students are being
identified, assessed, and placed in special education programs.

Federal Mandate

Specific due process regulations in P.L. 94-142 call for the right of parents
to information, to prior approval of preplacement and initial placement
activities, and to appeal (34 CFR 300.502-510). Beyond these procedural rights, parental involvement in the placement process is further
specified in regulations concerning the writing of IEPs (34 CFR 300.345).
The clear effect of these regulations is to encourage parental participation
in placement activities and to place the burden for ensuring their involvement on the schools.

---

[5]There has, of course, been a great deal of litigation on due process in special education.
Specific reviews of court cases are not within the scope of this paper. For good reviews of due
process litigation, see Bersoff (1979), Kotin (1976), and National Association of State Directors of Special Education (1978).

Status of Implementation

A number of studies have reported on the status of the implementation of due process procedures (Blaschke, 1979; Stearns et al., 1979; Thouvenelle and Hebbeler, 1978; USHEW, 1979b). In general, these studies, in reviewing the annual program plans and the procedures in place in LEAs, find that the regulations (if not necessarily the practice) within most jurisdictions are in compliance with the P.L. 94-142 requirements. For example, the OSE, in its report to Congress (USHEW, 1979b) confirms this status of compliance, concluding that "since September, 1977, approximately 40 states have changed their laws and/or regulations to meet the due process . . . requirements of P.L. 94-142" (p. xv).

In terms of parental involvement in the placement process, Blaschke (1979) reports that most attention has been given to their involvement with IEPs. He reports that "most district activities to involve parents focus upon obtaining written permission (e.g., for testing . . . IEPs, and for placement) and informing parents (e.g., assessment results, rights to participate, results of IEP reviews)" (p. 20).

Several studies have examined the content of due process hearings as part of the research on implementation (Blaschke, 1979; National Association of State Directors of Special Education, 1978; Stearns et al., 1979). Although the numbers of hearings reviewed in these studies are relatively few, the findings in several cases are reasonably consistent. Disputes over private school placements (i.e., the parents who want them and want the public school district to pay for them) and the provision of related services are the two most frequent topics of the hearings. However, earlier work (e.g., Buss et al., 1976) that examined due process data in Pennsylvania after the decision in *Pennsylvania Association for Retarded Citizens* (1971) adds an additional category of dispute between school officials and parents: the classification of children. Parents most often disputed the assignment of a label (especially that of mentally retarded) by school officials, preferring their child to remain classified as normal.

Problems in Implementation

Difficulties in implementing due process protections can be divided into two parts: one relating to parental involvement in decision making about placements and one relating to the use of hearings to resolve disputes. Several studies find that, while more parental contact has occurred in placement processes as a result of P.L. 94-142, parents have relatively little real involvement in decisions (Blaschke, 1979; National Association of State

Directors of Special Education, 1978; Stearns et al., 1979; Thouvenelle and Hebbeler, 1978; USHEW, 1979c). For example, Thouvenelle and Hebbeler (1978) report that "while parents were asked to contribute information about the child, decisions about educational placement were made primarily by the school district staff, and then presented to parents for approval" (p. 7). Blaschke (1979) confirms this finding when he writes that increased contact between parents and school officials resulting from P.L. 94-142 has not meant "a dramatic increase in shared parent/staff decision-making . . ." (p. 20).

Several studies have reported findings on what influences parental involvement (Blaschke, 1979; National Association of State Directors of Special Education, 1978, 1980; Stearns et al., 1979; USHEW, 1979c). Clearly, traditions within a school or district have much to do with the extent of parental involvement. The social class of parents also seems to be important; increased involvement was found among middle-class, suburban, nonminority populations. Reasons cited for noninvolvement cover a wide spectrum: parental lack of knowledge, school personnel resistance, difficulty in scheduling, mistrust between parents and officials, trust of school officials by parents, and proximity to the school.

Several studies cite problems attendant to the due process hearings themselves that militate against implementation of federal regulations (Blaschke, 1979; National Association of State Directors of Special Education, 1978; Stearns et al., 1979). Two findings are most common. First, the due process procedures have tended to formalize the interactions between school officials and parents to the point, in some instances, where recordkeeping takes precedence over communication. Second, the costs, in terms of time and attorneys' fees to parents and districts, may have the effect of depressing the use of due process hearings in cases in which it is warranted. The trauma of a hearing can negatively affect one party's willingness to exercise due process rights again. These studies also reported that in some school districts creative alternatives have been developed that can mitigate disagreements without resort to formal hearings. For example, Stearns et al. (1979) note the importance of mediators, advocacy groups, and the like in assisting parents and school officials in ironing out problems before a formal hearing becomes necessary.

Overall, the research literature provides a mixed picture of parental involvement and due process. Clearly, there has been significant movement as a result of P.L. 94-142; procedural forms are in place, meetings are held, parents sign approval forms, etc. The literature also indicates that the actual reality of compliance in many instances falls short of the objectives of the legislation.

Minority Representation, Parental Involvement, and Due Process

Have minority parents become more involved in placement processes? Do the requirements of P.L. 94-142 work to diminish the number of minority children that are placed in EMR classes? Have parents used due process procedures? Little research has been conducted that can directly answer these questions. Three studies (Blaschke, 1979; National Association of State Directors of Special Education, 1980; Stearns et al., 1979) do provide some information on the participation of minority parents. These studies indicate that a lower degree of participation tends to occur in urban areas, especially among minority populations. However, these studies do not provide specific information on the question of whether due process procedures are affecting the rates of minority representation in special education programs or whether they would affect these rates if parents were fully involved.

Several studies have addressed the question of whether black parents and white parents are differentially treated during the evaluation process. For example, Tomlinson et al. (1977) indicate that psychologists assessing students "made contact with the parents of majority students significantly more often (58 percent) ... than with parents of minority students (41 percent) ..." (p. 457). This occurred despite the fact that contacts with teachers for majority and minority students by psychologists were about the same. These researchers also report that the range of options presented to minority parents by psychologists when they were contacted was significantly more restricted than that presented to majority parents. Recommendations to parents of minority students most commonly involved program placement, while recommendations to parents of majority students were more varied across a number of categories (e.g., behavior management, help at home, counseling, etc.).

Lanier and Wittmer (1977) report findings similar to those cited above for teachers. These researchers state that teachers involved in an EMR referral process "were more likely to request a parent-teacher conference with the parents of white students than with black students" (p. 168). The important point is that too little is known about minority parental involvement to draw any but the most tentative conclusions.

It is clear from research on parental involvement and due process that much remains to be accomplished in the implementation of the P.L. 94-142 regulations. Some of the changes must come at the local level, in terms of knowledge and attitudes of school personnel and parents. Possibly some changes may have to occur at the national level, where emphasis on procedural swiftness in processing students at times runs counter to mandates to involve parents meaningfully in the decisions made. It is also clear that the research undertaken thus far on due process hearings raises as many questions as it answers. More detailed investigations are required as to what policies are in place and how they are working.

SUMMARY

Research on placement practices since the passage of P.L. 94-142 has emphasized investigation of the status of the implementation of the law's regulations. Table 2 reviews some of the questions addressed by the major national studies of the implementation of P.L. 94-142 as well as their basic characteristics and the methodologies used. Table 3 summarizes the significant problems in implementation that have been uncovered by these studies. To a far lesser extent, the literature on placement has also addressed questions related to whether the law is having the intended effects and the impact the regulations are having on minority students.

P.L. 94-142 has clearly had a great impact on state and local placement policies and practices. Since 1977, when the completed regulations became official, states and school districts have changed their policies to reflect the basic tenets of the federal requirements. However, the research demonstrates that more must be done to accomplish full implementation, especially in light of the spirit and intent of the specific regulations. The description here of the research on placement processes highlights both the progress made and the need for continued improvement. It also points out that gaps in knowledge still exist, particularly with regard to the impact of the law on minority students. This section summarizes what is currently known about these processes.

SCREENING AND REFERRAL

A student enters the placement process in one of two ways. The child may be identified through a district or statewide screening process, which often entails the systematic review of student performance on some standardized measure (e.g., achievement or IQ tests). Or the student may be referred for evaluation by someone who knows him or her. The person typically making the referral is the classroom teacher, although P.L. 94-142 has effectively broadened the participatory base in special education placement processes.

A minority student's chances for referral seem to be considerably higher in most instances than those of a majority student. Based on a very limited number of studies, there does not seem to be much difference between minority and majority students in the problems for which they are referred. There is some suggestion in the literature that the experience of

TABLE 2 Sample Characteristics and Methodologies of the Major Implementation Studies

Study	Sample Size	Sampling Method	Methodology	Major Question
Thouvenelle and Hebbeler (1980)	5 SEAs 15 LEAs 96 cases 134 PT meetings	*SEA*: Sampled to ensure variability on geography, funding, percentage served, and organization of service delivery. *LEA*: Sampled to ensure variability on location and size. *Cases*: For variability of handicap, age, degree of handicap, and difficulty of placement decision.	*Ethnographic case study*; structured observations of PT meetings.	Do school districts use the least restrictive environment provisions of P.L. 94-142 in making placement decisions?
Stearns, Greene, and David (1979)	9 SEAs 22 LEAs	*SEA*: Sampled to ensure variability in match of state and federal guidelines, funding, and organization. *LEA*: Sampled to ensure variability on resources and other factors such as presence of residential facilities.	*Case study*: structured interviews, case-file review.	How is P.L. 94-142 being implemented?

Study	Sample	Sampling	Method	Research questions
National Association of State Directors of Special Education (1980)	230 PT meetings 1,478 persons	Connecticut study: Random sample of schools within one SEA.	Survey	What are the levels of participation with planning team meetings among involved personnel and parents?
	4 SEAs 31 LEAs 1,000 persons	Alabama, Wisconsin, New Jersey, and Washington studies: Systematic for geographic location.	Interviews	What is the relationship of federal IEP guidelines to state and local guidelines, and what are the parents' and teacher's roles in IEP implementation?
Marver and David (1978)	3 SEAs 15 LEAs 150 IEPs	Sampled to ensure variation on district size, wealth, and population density within states with IEP provisions before P.L. 94-142.	Interviews, content analyses, observations of PT meetings.	Can local districts implement IEPs?
Thurlow and Ysseldyke (1979)	39 child service demonstration centers 26 SEAs	All 55 centers polled; 39 responded and had appropriate functions.	Questionnaire	What are currently used assessment and decision-making practices in learning disabilities child service demonstration centers?
Blaschke (1979)	3 SEAs 9 LEAs 1,500 persons	*SEA*: Sampled to ensure variability of match of state and federal regulations. *LEA*: Systematic to represent each geographic location and to have comparable PPE.	*Case study*: interviews, observations of PT meetings, case file review.	What are current implementation activities and consequences?

TABLE 2 (*continued*)

Study	Sample Size	Sampling Method	Methodology	Major Question
USHEW (1979c)	6 SEAs 24 LEAs	Systematic to represent high and low special education enrollment.	Interviews	Why do the proportions of handicapped served by local districts vary widely, and what is the degree of successful implementation of P.L. 94-142 as indicated by perceptions of people in the field?
Weatherly (1980)	1 SEA 3 LEAs	Systematic for similarity on community wealth, urban location, and per-pupil expenditure.	Case study	How is special education reform law implemented at the local level?
USHEW (1979a)	26 SEAs	Unspecified	"Program Administrative Reviews" and results from selected studies.	(1) Are intended beneficiaries being served? (2) In what settings are they served? (3) What services are provided? (4) What are the consequences of implementation? (5) What administrative procedures are in place? (6) Is the intent of the act being met?
USHEW (1979b)				

Alper (1978)	1 SEA 13 LEAs 286 IEPs	Random selection of IEPs within districts, systematic selection of districts.	IEP content analysis, interviews.	What are the differences in comprehensiveness, clarity, specificity, implementability and pupil change among IEPs written by three types of school committees in California?
Research Triangle Institute (1980)	42 SEAs 208 LEAs 507 schools 2,657 IEPS	Random sample of IEPS.	Content analysis, teacher and principal questionnaire, survey.	What is the current status of IEP implementation nationwide?
Portny (1980)	1 SEA 1 LEA 57 cases	Random sample of cases from 11,000.	*Case study:* file review interviews with personnel.	What does the placement process look like, how effective is implementation, and what are the problems?

Key to abbreviations:
SEA—state education agency.
LEA—local education agency.
PT—placement team.
IEP—individual education plan.

TABLE 3 Problems in Implementation of P.L. 94-142 Found Across Several Studies

	Thouvenelle and Hebbeler, 1978	Stearns et al., 1979	NASDSE, 1980	Marver and David, 1978	Thurlow and Ysseldyke, 1980	Blaschke, 1974	USHEW, 1976c	USHEW, 1979a	USHEW, 1976b	Weatherly, 1979	Alper, 1978	Research Triangle Institute, 1980	Portny, 1980
A. Referral													
1. Lengthy backlogs		—		—		—		—	—	—			
2. Overreliance on teacher referral		—				—	—			—			
B. Evaluation and Placement													
1. Lack of real group decision-making process in placement team meetings	—	—	—	—						—			—
2. Replacement meetings held without parents	—	—	—	—						—			
3. Placement not based on wide range of options	—						—	—	—	—			

4. Lack of direct link between test results and placement decision

C. IEP

1. Lack of specific short-term goals

2. Not used by service givers

3. Lack of specific procedures for monitoring success of placement

4. Absent or incomplete three-year reevaluation results

D. Overall

1. Variability in SEA guidelines

Key:
+ = not a problem.
− = problem found.
The blank cells mean that the study did not address that issue.

teachers in teaching minority students may be positively related to lower referral rates: that is, the greater the experience, the lower the rate. On these questions, like most questions related to minority issues, there are large gaps in our knowledge about the impact of the law; thus, conclusions at this juncture are premature.

Referral rates do not seem to be greatly influenced by the presence of federal money per se. There is no evidence that students are placed simply to increase a school district's budget by the federal increment that supports special education. However, this may be because of the relatively modest levels of support for new programming that currently exist. The availability of state and local resources was found to be highly significant: Students are referred to and placed in programs that exist.

Rigid eligibility criteria for specific programs in some districts actually influence the referral process. That is, students are not referred for a general assessment of needs, but rather for an ED, LD, or EMR evaluation.

Procedural requirements for assessment (e.g., extensive reviews, due process, etc.) within a state (most often) and within a district also influence referral rates. For example, the emphasis on individualized assessment (in part as a result of the federal mandate for IEPs) has tended to slow the evaluation process, creating a backlog in the referral process that in turn can discourage referrals.

Parental pressure was found to be a significant factor in referral. In some districts a history of strong parental involvement tended to discourage referrals because teachers (and presumably others) were hesitant to face the hostility that such a referral might entail. It is also true, however, that active parental pressure has acted to bring students' needs to the attention of school officials.

It is clear that a great amount of personal discretion still exists in the referral process, and as a result there is a tendency to refer children who have more severe problems or who disrupt school routines.

EVALUATION

Once a child is identified or referred, some individual or group determines whether the case merits further assessment. As the system currently functions, gatekeepers at this point in the process often use largely undetermined criteria to decide if an assessment should be made. The gatekeeper may be the school principal, counselor, or some district officer.

A decision to assess usually brings the involvement of additional participants, often the school psychologist and the parents (at some point). Additional participants can include regular and special education teachers and administrative personnel. This group, or key individuals in it, determine the areas in which the child should be evaluated.

There is wide variation in the areas in which a child might be assessed. Important trends have been documented indicating that a broadening in the domains assessed is occurring as required by P.L. 94-142. However, data clearly indicate a heavy reliance on traditional asessment information, especially IQ and achievement tests, in the EMR evaluation process.

The continued reliance on IQ tests in EMR placement has a significant impact on minority placements. Minority students, in the aggregate, do not do as well as majority students on these measures, a fact that may explain in part the higher placement rates among minority populations. The rate of placement of minority students diminishes as the IQ cutoff score is lowered. The use of measures of adaptive behavior also was found to lower the rate of placement of minority students, provided such measures were not simply standardized tests of in-school adaptive behavior.

Once the data are collected, a decision is made as to eligibility. The decision process often occurs with the ostensible participation of the entire placement team. There are some indications, however, that participation is often a formality, in which a key individual (e.g., an administrator or a school psychologist) makes a recommendation to the group for fairly routine approval.

A variety of factors influence the determination of eligibility. The most important seems to be not individual educational needs, as the law requires, but rather the availability of programs. The data clearly indicate that a child is rarely determined eligible for services that are not currently in place. Initial referral information and achievement and IQ test scores were also found to be very influential in the eligibility decision. Demographic factors such as race, socioeconomic status, and sex were in themselves not found to be directly significant in the limited number of studies that examined these variables. For example, race alone did not seem to determine placement when other variables were held constant. However, the correlation among socioeconomic status, race, and test scores clearly establishes a general pattern of higher placement of minority students when these measures are relied on heavily.

It should be noted that some interesting, contrasting findings to the above pattern are reported in several studies of the placement behavior of psychologists. Some psychologists tended to place minority students at a lower rate (or in less restrictive environments) than their majority counterparts when majority students had similar test scores. Researchers speculate that this pattern may be the result of a growing sensitivity within the profession to minority issues, perhaps as a result of P.L. 94-142.

Personal discretion on the part of team members also was found to be influential in the placement decision, particularly in the selection of the areas in which a student is evaluated. The evidence is too thin, however, to draw conclusions about this issue.

Additional factors that influence the placement decision include the existence of program alternatives outside special education (e.g., Title I) and ambiguity in state and federal criteria for placement. Ambiguity in the guidelines was especially significant for LD placements.

The federal regulations and the theoretical models reviewed in this paper indicate that an assessment of needs should precede a determination of eligibility, followed by the design of a program to meet the needs (IEP), and then an assignment to a context in which to implement the services (least restrictive environment). This sequence is rarely found in practice. The practical limitations of resources, noted above, in addition to the demands on the time of school personnel usually mean that the process is compacted into one or two meetings. And a placement decision is seldom separate from the program realities (i.e., the existence of services and available space) of a given local education agency.

A number of studies investigated the quality of placement decisions and the outcomes of those decisions. Consistency in the ability of placement procedures to discriminate between various populations needing services and those not needing services was the basic criterion used. Research on EMR programs generally indicates consistency in these placements; however, it tended to be the result of a single measure, IQ scores. Research on ED and LD placements demonstrated little consistency in these placements. Ambiguous disability guidelines, inadequate testing technology, and inconsistently applied psychological theory created patterns of placement in which inconsistency was more the rule than the exception.

It is important to remember that consistency is not the only measure of the quality of placement decisions. Ultimately, the efficacy of the placement for the child is the criterion that must be used to determine quality. Research on efficacy is needed, especially as efficacy relates to minority students.

IEPs AND LEAST RESTRICTIVE ENVIRONMENTS

Research on IEPs and least restrictive environments has investigated issues concerning the status of the implementation of P.L. 94-142 regulations, how IEPs and least restrictive environments are determined, and their content. A general trend of compliance with the form of P.L. 94-142 regulations in these areas is documented in the research; most states now have policies in place that reflect federal requirements.

Research examining the writing of IEPs supports the view that factors external to the assessment of needs often guide the final content of the individual program of services. That is, service availability may be more significant than the particular need of a child. An IEP is often written by some or all of the same group that determines placement and sometimes even at the same time.

A point of contention in the process seems to center on the federal requirement that IEPs include specific evaluation strategies to assess whether the goals are met. There seems to be a serious concern among educators that such evaluations will be used for accountability purposes. As a result there is a genuine reluctance among practitioners to be specific in the statement of goals. Another major point of tension related to IEPs concerns the amount of time that is required on the part of teachers to write them.

The quality and content of IEPs range dramatically from district to district and from state to state. In general, long-range, open-ended goals take precedence over short-term, specific objectives. As noted above, this may be the result of fears on the part of teachers and school officials that the IEPs will be used for accountability purposes. The special education teacher plays a key role in the writing of an IEP, especially when short-term goals are included.

Little research has been done to determine whether the content of IEPs varies with the ethnicity or social class of a student. The importance of this question is related to the issue of whether special education placements for minority students are dead-end placements or whether these students receive important services in these classes. The few studies that have reported information on this issue suggest that content is not dependent on the race or the social class of the student.

Decisions on least restrictive environments are similar to those on IEPs. That is, the close link between the availability of a program and a classification influences the determination of the least restrictive environment. Most districts simply do not have the range of program alternatives that is implied in P.L. 94-142. Thus, an EMR placement in a given district may automatically imply a certain decision on the least restrictive environment regardless of the capabilities and needs of an individual child.

Research on variations in least restrictive environments, like that on IEPs, is limited. One study that investigates the issue finds no relationship between the type of environment chosen for placement and the race of a student (Matuszek and Oakland, 1979). Another study finds a tendency to place minority students in less restrictive environments than their white counterparts (Tomlinson et al., 1977). This may be a result of a trend in the referral process that refers fewer majority students; these students presumably have more obviously serious problems than the larger numbers of minority students referred.

Parental Involvement and Due Process

Research on parental involvement and due process proceedings documents that, while the law has had an important impact, there is room for considerable improvement. Parents are becoming more involved in placement processes. They are important sources of initial referrals, and they are often an important source of pressure on school districts to provide additional or better services. For the most part, parents attend IEP meetings and sign forms approving assessments, placements, and service delivery. However, the research also demonstrates that participation is often superficial and that consent is seldom informed. Interestingly enough, the responsibility for shortcomings in this area is rather equitably distributed among all concerned. Parents often are unknowledgeable, apathetic, or too trusting. School officials often see parental involvement as an unhelpful intrusion on the exercise of their professional expertise. Unrealistic regulations place extreme burdens on the time and energy of parents and school personnel in requiring attention to IEPs, more comprehensive assessment, and increased parental involvement—all with due speed.

The history of school-parent interactions and the social class of parents are significant influences on involvement. The type of district (i.e., suburban or urban) was also important; parental involvement occurred to a lesser extent in urban districts. Each of these factors contributes to the lack of parental involvement in placement decisions. What little research exists on the involvement of minority parents suggests that they are not fully participating beyond the formal requirements of the law. There is some suggestion (based on only two studies) that even when minority parents do become involved, they receive different treatment (e.g., are given fewer program options) than that typically given to majority parents.

Due process procedures providing recourse for the parents and school personnel when there are disagreements are generally in place. The most common foci of these proceedings since P.L. 94-142 have been on acquiring public school support for private placement and the provision of related services. Clearly, more research is required in this area.

Factors that hinder the use of due process hearings by parents include (1) the complexity of the law and parental lack of understanding and (2) the costs of participation in terms of time and attorneys' expenses. The parents involved in due process hearings tend to be white, nonurban, and middle class. Interesting by-products of due process hearings have been an increasing formality and tension in communications between school officials and parents, with greater emphasis placed on recordkeeping and written agreements.

CONCLUSION

The research on placement processes for special education indicates that most of the P.L. 94-142 requirements are in place, at least in form. Great amounts of time and energy are being expended by school personnel, children, and parents in the implementation of specific regulations. However, additional time, resources, and effort will be required to fully implement the intent of the P.L. 94-142 regulations in placement. In terms of the impact that the placement provisions of P.L. 94-142 are having on the disproportionate representation of minorities in special education programs, research undertaken to date does not adequately address this issue. What indications there are suggest that much remains to be done to ensure that placement occurs in an accurate, fair, and efficacious manner for these students. It is also clear that research concerned with minority experiences in special education must extend to issues related to efficacy. Regardless of the circumstances of placement, one question remains: Does placement in special programs lead to the effective treatment of a child's actual problems? It is on these grounds that special education programs must justify themselves to minority students and to all other students who are placed in them.

REFERENCES

Alper, T. G.
 1980 IEPs, How Well Do They Work? Paper prepared under grant no. 77-37-B for the California State Department of Education.
Amira, S., Abramowitz, S. I., and Gomes-Schwartz, B.
 1977 Socially-charged pupil and psychologist effects on psychoeducational decisions. *Journal of Special Education* 11:433–440.
Bersoff, D. N.
 1979 Regarding psychologists testily: regulation of psychological assessment in the public schools. *Maryland Law Review* 39(1):27–120.
Bickel, W. E.
 1981 Second Assessment for Minority Students in Special Education. Paper presented at the annual meeting of the American Educational Research Association, New York.
Birman, B. F.
 1979 *Case Studies of Overlap Between Title I and P.L. 94-142 Services for Handicapped Students.* Research report EPRC 26 prepared for the U.S. Department of Health, Education, and Welfare. Menlo Park, Calif.: SRI International.
Blaschke, C. L.
 1979 *Case Study of the Impact of Implementation of P.L. 94-142.* Executive Summary. Washington, D.C.: Education Turnkey Systems.

Buss, W. G., Kirp, D. L., and Kuriloff, P. J.
    1976   Exploring procedural modes of special classification. Pp. 386–431 in N. Hobbs,
           ed., *Issues in the Classification of Children.* Vol. II. San Francisco, Calif.: Jossey-
           Bass, Inc.
Craig, P. A., Kaskowitz, D. H., and Malgoire, M. A.
    1978   *Teacher Identification of Handicapped Pupils (Ages 6–11) Compared with Iden-
           tification Using Other Indicators, Volume II.* Menlo Park, Calif.: Educational
           Policy Research Center, Stanford Research Institute.
Fisher, A. T.
    1977   Four Approaches to Classification of Mentally Retarded. Paper presented at the
           meeting of the American Psychological Association, Toronto. ERIC Document
           Reproduction Service No. ED 172-495.
Frederick, L. v. Thomas
    1980   408 F. Supp. 832 (E.D. Pa., 1976); 419 F. Supp. 960 (E.D. Pa., 1976); *aff'd.* 557
           F.2d 373 (3rd Cir., 1977), 578 F.2d 513 (3rd Cir., 1978); Stipulation, E.D. Pa.,
           4/7/80.
Gajar, A. H.
    1977   Characteristics and classification of educable mentally retarded, learning disabled,
           and emotionally disturbed students. Doctoral dissertation, University of Virginia.
           Dissertation Abstracts International 38:4090A. University microfilm no. 77-28,
           644.
Hallahan, D. P., and Kauffman, J.
    1977   Labels, categories, and behaviors: ED, LD, and EMR reconsidered. *Journal of
           Special Education* 11:139–149.
Hansche, J. H., Gottfried, N. W., and Hansche, W. J.
    No   Special Education Classification: A Multivariate Analysis and Evaluation of Clini-
    date   cal Judgments. Unpublished paper, Department of Psychology, Tulane University.
Hobbs, N., ed.
    1975   *Issues in the Classification of Children.* 2 vols. San Francisco, Calif.: Jossey-Bass,
           Inc.
Huberty, T. J., Koller, J. R., and Tenbrink, T. D.
    1980   Adaptive behavior in the definition of mental retardation. *Exceptional Children*
           46:256–261.
Johnson, V. M.
    1977   Salient features and sorting factors in the diagnosis and classification of excep-
           tional children. Doctoral dissertation, Pennsylvania State University. *Dissertation
           Abstracts International* 37:4282-A. University microfilm no. 76-29, 649.
Jones, R. L.
    1979   Protection evaluation procedures: criteria and recommendations. Pp. 15–84 in
           *PEP: Developing Criteria for the Evaluation of Protection in Evaluation Proce-
           dures Provisions.* Philadelphia, Pa.: Research for Better Schools.
Kaskowitz, D. H.
    1977   Validation of State Counts of Handicapped Children. Vol. II. Menlo Park, Calif.:
           Stanford Research Institute.
Kotin, L.
    1976   *Due Process in Special Education: Legal Perspectives.* Cambridge, Mass.: Re-
           search Institute for Educational Problems.
Lanier, J., and Wittmer, J.
    1977   Teacher prejudice in referral of students to EMR programs. *The School Counselor*
           24:165–170.

Larry P. v. Riles
1979   495 F. Supp. 926 (N.D. Cal. 1979) (decision on merits) *appeal docketed* No. 80.4027 (9th Cir., Jan. 17, 1980).

Larson, S. L.
1978   The implementation of labeling and diagnostic placements of children within schools in two southeastern Nebraska communities. Doctoral dissertation, University of Nebraska. *Dissertation Abstracts International* 39:1442A–1441A. University microfilm no. 78-14700.

Magnetti, S. S.
1980   The Legal Context of Special Education Placement. Background paper prepared for the Panel on Selection and Placement of Students in Programs for the Mentally Retarded, Committee on Child Development Research and Public Policy, National Research Council, Washington, D.C.
1981   Assessment Practice in Louisiana. Memorandum prepared for the Panel on Selection and Placement of Students in Programs for the Mentally Retarded, Committee on Child Development Research and Public Policy, National Research Council, Washington, D.C.

Marver, J. D., and David, J. L.
1978   *Three States' Experiences with IEP Requirements Similar to P.L. 94-142.* Menlo Park, Calif.: SRI International, Educational Policy Research Center.

Matuszek, P., and Oakland, T.
1979   Factors influencing teachers' and psychologists' recommendations regarding special class placement. *Journal of School Psychology* 17:116–125.

McDermott, P. A.
1980   Congruence and typology of diagnoses in school psychology: an empirical study. *Psychology in the Schools* 17:12–24.

Mercer, J. R.
1972   I.Q.: the lethal label. *Psychology Today* 6:44; 97.
1979   *System of Multicultural Pluralistic Assessment Technical Manual.* New York: Psychological Corporation.

Mercer, J. R., and Lewis, J. F.
1978   *System of Multicultural Pluralistic Assessment.* New York: Psychological Corporation.

Meyers, C. E., MacMillan, D. L., and Yoshida, R. K.
1978   Validity of psychologists' identification of educable mentally retarded students in the perspective of the California decertification experience. *Journal of School Psychology* 16:4–15.

Mishra, S. P.
1980   The influence of examiner's ethnical attributes on intelligence test scores. *Psychology in the Schools* 17:117–122.

Naidoff, S. W., and Gross, J. A.
1980   Memorandum prepared for Office of the Regional Attorney, Philadelphia, Pa.

National Association of State Directors of Special Education
1978   *The Implementation of Due Process in Massachusetts.* Washington, D.C.: National Association of State Directors of Special Education.
1980   *Summary of Research Findings on IEP's.* Washington, D.C.: National Association of State Directors of Special Education.

Nelson, F. H.
1980   Fiscal Determinants of the Provision of Services to Handicapped Children. Paper

presented at the meeting of the American Educational Research Association, Boston, Mass.

Oakland, T., ed.
1977   *Psychological and Educational Assessment of Minority Children*. New York: Brunner/Mazel.

Pennsylvania Association for Retarded Citizens v. *Pennsylvania*
1971   344 F. Supp. 1257 (E.D. Pa., 1971).

Petersen, C. R., and Hart, D. H.
1978   Use of multiple discriminant function analysis in evaluation of a state-wide system for identification of educationally handicapped children. *Psychological Reports* 43:743–755.

Poland, S., Ysseldyke, J., Thurlow, M., and Mirkin, P.
1979   *Current Assessment and Decision Making Practices in School Settings as Reported by Directors of Special Education*. Research report no. 14. Minneapolis, Minn.: Institute for Research on Learning Disabilities.

Portny, S. E.
1980   *An External Evaluation of Continuum Education in the Montgomery County Public Schools*. Alexandria, Va.: Portny & Associates.

Reisman, K., and Macy, J.
1978   Context Evaluation of IEPs in an Urban School District. Paper presented at the meeting of the Rocky Mountain Educational Association, Albuquerque, N.Mex.

Reschly, D. J.
In   Assessing mild mental retardation: the influence of adaptive behavior, sociocul-
press   tural status and prospects for non-biased assessment. In C. R. Reynolds and T. B. Gutkin, eds., *A Handbook for School Psychology*. New York: John Wiley & Sons.

Reschly, D. J., and Jipson, F. J.
1976   Ethnicity, geographic locale, age, sex, and urban-rural residence as variables in the prevalence of mild retardation. *American Journal of Mental Deficiency* 81:154–161.

Research Triangle Institute
1980   *A National Survey of Individualized Education Programs (IEPs) for Handicapped Children*. Final report, Vol. I, Executive Summary. Research Triangle Park, N.C.: Research Triangle Institute, Center for Educational Research and Evaluation.

Reynolds, M. D., and Birch, J. W.
1977   *Teaching Exceptional Children in all America's Schools: A First Course for Teachers and Principals*. Reston, Va.: Council for Exceptional Children.

Schenck, S. J., and Levy, W. K.
1980   *IEPs: The State of the Art—1978*. Hightstown, N.J.: Northeast Regional Resource Center. ERIC Document Reproduction Service No. ED 175-201.

Stearns, M. S., Greene, D., and David, J. L.
1979   *Local Implementation of P. L. 94-142*. Menlo Park, Calif.: SRI International.

Stevens, F. I.
1980   The Impact of the Larry P. Case on Urban School Districts. Paper presented at the meeting of the National Council on Measurement in Education, Boston, Mass.

Swanson, E. N., and Deblassie, R. R.
1979   Interpreter and Spanish administration effects on the WISC performance of Mexican-American children. *Journal of School Psychology* 19:231–236.

Thouvenelle, S., and Hebbeler, K.
1978   *Placement Procedures for Determining the Least Restrictive Environment Placement for Handicapped Children*. Silver Spring, Md.: Applied Management Sciences, Inc.

Thurlow, M. L., and Ysseldyke, J. E.

1979 *Current Assessment and Decision-Making Practice in Model Programs for the Learning Disabled.* Research report no. 11. Minneapolis, Minn.: Institute for Research on Learning Disabilities, University of Minnesota.

1980 *Factors Influential on the Psychoeducational Decisions Reached by Teams of Educators.* Research report no. 25. Minneapolis, Minn.: Institute for Research on Learning Disabilities, University of Minnesota.

Tomlinson, J. R., Acker, N., Conter, A., and Lindborg, S.

1977 Minority status and school psychological services. *Psychology in the Schools* 14:456–460.

U.S. Department of Health, Education, and Welfare

1979a *Progress Toward a Free Appropriate Public Education: A Report to Congress on the Implementation of P.L. 94-142: The Education for All Handicapped Children Act.* Office of Education, U.S. Department of Health, Education, and Welfare.

1979b *Progress Toward a Free Appropriate Public Education: Semi-Annual Update on the Implementation of P.L. 94-142: The Education of All Handicapped Children Act.* Office of Education. Superintendant of Documents no. 0-631-611/2923. Washington, D.C.: U.S. Government Printing Office.

1979c Service Delivery Assessment: Education for the Handicapped. Unpublished report. Inspector General's Office, U.S. Department of Health, Education, and Welfare.

Wall, C.

1978 Pennsylvania's Preschool Pilot Individualized Educational Program. Paper presented at the meeting of the American Educational Research Association, Toronto.

Wang, M. C.

1981 *The Adaptive Mainstreaming Learning Environments Project: An Interim Report.* Pittsburgh, Pa.: Learning Research and Development Center, University of Pittsburgh.

Weatherly, R. A.

1979 *Reforming Special Education: Policy Implementation from State Level to Street Level.* Cambridge, Mass.: MIT Press.

Wolf, F.

1977 *The Relationship between Poverty and Achievement.* Washington, D.C.: National Institute of Education.

Ysseldyke, J. E., and Algozzine, R.

1980 *Diagnostic Classification Decisions as a Function of Referral Information.* Research report no. 19. Minneapolis, Minn.: Institute for Research on Learning Disabilities, University of Minnesota.

Ysseldyke, J. E., Algozzine, R., Regan, R., and McGue, M.

1979a *The Influence of Test Scores and Naturally-Occurring Pupil Characteristics on Psychoeducational Decision Making with Children.* Research report no. 17. Minneapolis, Minn.: Institute for Research on Learning Disabilities, University of Minnesota.

Ysseldyke, J. E., Algozzine, R., Shinn, M., and McGue, M.

1979b *Similarities and Differences between Underachievers and Students Labeled Learning Disabled: Identical Twins with Different Mothers.* Research report no. 13. Minneapolis, Minn.: Institute for Research on Learning Disabilities, University of Minnesota.

Zucker, S. H., Prieto, A. G., and Rutherford, R. B.

1979 Racial Determinants of Teacher's Perceptions of Placement of the Educable Mentally Retarded. Paper presented at the meeting of the Council for Exceptional Children, Dallas, Texas. ERIC Document Reproduction Service No. ED 191 015.

Testing in Educational Placement: Issues and Evidence

JEFFREY R. TRAVERS

To write about testing in relation to the issues facing the Panel on Selection and Placement of Children in Programs for the Mentally Retarded is somewhat like testifying as a ballistics expert at a shooting trial: The topic invites discussion in almost limitless technical detail, but the details are significant only insofar as they help illuminate whether someone has injured someone else and by what means. Therefore, this paper focuses less on psychometric issues than on their interplay with the legal, political, and moral issues raised by testing in the context of educational placement.

The paper, in providing background and support for portions of the panel's report, attempts to accomplish two distinct but related tasks. First, given the controversy that has surrounded testing in the academic and popular literature as well as in recent court cases, the panel felt a responsibility to survey the scientific evidence bearing on relevant aspects of the controversy. This paper provides such a survey, albeit one that is condensed and selective and that covers material already well known to professionals in testing and related fields. Second—and more importantly—the panel wanted to place the testing controversy in proper per-

I would like to thank the panel members and the outside reviewers who commented on drafts of this paper. Among the panel members, special thanks go to Donald Bersoff, Asa Hilliard, Jane Mercer, and Samuel Messick. Outside reviewers were Lee Cronbach, Robert Linn, Richard Snow, and Mark Yudoff. Their thoughtful comments helped me to strengthen my arguments and correct various errors. For errors that remain, as well as for judgments with which a few reviewers disagreed, I alone am responsible.

spective. Issues surrounding testing are part of the larger complex of issues raised by the stubborn and tragic fact that large numbers of children, particularly minority children, are not learning in regular classrooms. Consequently, as the paper examines various controversies and the associated scientific evidence, it also examines their wider implications for educational policy and practice.

Several limitations on the scope of the paper should be made clear at the outset. It is not a comprehensive discussion of issues related to ability testing. (For such a discussion, see the report of the Committee on Ability Testing of the National Research Council, Wigdor and Garner, eds., 1982; see also the special issue of *American Psychologist*, Glaser and Bond, eds., 1981.) This paper focuses specifically on the issues that have figured in the debate over placement in programs for educable mentally retarded (EMR) children. It does not deal with research on mental retardation per se, nor does it make judgments about the validity or utility of the EMR category. It asks instead how tests contribute to classification or misclassification, given current professional and legal definitions of EMR. Finally, this paper does not deal directly with the consequences of classification—the effects of labeling or the educational benefits and costs of placement in EMR classes—although one of its major themes is that the consequences, not just the accuracy, of classification must be taken into account in deciding whether any assessment procedure is appropriate.

This paper focuses primarily on the widely used, individually administered tests that yield IQ scores, notably the Stanford-Binet and the revised Wechsler Intelligence Scale for Children (WISC-R), although other tests are mentioned. Much of the discussion applies to ability tests generally. Special issues raised by group testing and by various quick and dirty substitutes for the major tests are not discussed. (The fact that the Stanford-Binet and WISC-R are widely used and that IQ scores are important determinants of EMR placement are documented in Chapter 2 of the panel's report and in the paper by Bickel in this volume.) Here, these facts are taken as points of departure and concentration is not on describing how tests are used in educational placement but on elucidating the controversy surrounding their use.

Readers familiar with professionally recommended practices for administering and interpreting tests of mental ability and with the range of such tests currently available may be disturbed by the emphasis throughout this paper on single IQ scores and the occasional use of such words as "IQ test." Leaders in the field of assessment have long recommended the use of multiple tests and careful consideration of performance profiles across subscales within tests, and they have inveighed against the practice of recording only single, summary IQ scores. Unfortunately, data (cited in

Chapter 2 and in the paper by Bickel in this volume) indicate that in many school systems the single IQ score is accorded overwhelming weight in placement decisions. Although the extent of this practice cannot be gauged, it is an important source of the controversy over testing in educational placement. It may also be a source of miscommunication between professionals in testing and related fields, who think in terms of the best practices and proper test use, and some critics of testing, who focus on possible or actual misuse and misinterpretation of tests.

This paper assumes that the reader has at least a rudimentary knowledge of how tests are constructed and interpreted as well as of basic statistical concepts and procedures. The presentation is largely qualitative, however, and some background material is included.

It is useful to begin this inquiry with rough caricatures of the positions taken by proponents and opponents of mental ability testing. Though such caricatures ignore many significant distinctions and nuances within the two camps, they lay out most of the major points of dispute and illustrate the interrelatedness of the various issues from both perspectives. Subsequent sections of the paper will necessarily discuss selected issues seriatim. However, if one thing is clear in all of the debate, with its complex arguments and high emotions, it is that the positions of participants rarely rest on one or a few isolated facts or arguments; data and logic instead lodge within a web of assumptions, beliefs, and values that must be understood if rational analysis is to proceed.

TESTING ON TRIAL: BRIEFS FOR THE DEFENSE AND FOR THE PROSECUTION

Proponents of the use of tests of general ability in educational placement hold that such tests measure global, enduring qualities of cognitive functioning—not necessarily "native intelligence" but some broad ability to learn, reason, and grasp abstract concepts. Proponents deny that tests are culturally biased; while they recognize that children from certain ethnic and socioeconomic groups on the average score lower than white, middle-class children, they attribute these group differences in test scores to genuine differences in cognitive functioning, caused by heredity, environment, or both. Finally, in justifying the social uses of tests in educational and occupational selection and placement, proponents argue that tests offer individual members of disadvantaged groups, such as minorities and the poor, their best chance of distinguishing themselves and achieving educational and economic success; alternatives to testing, such as qualitative assessments by teachers and supervisors, are, claim the proponents of testing, likely to be more discriminatory than tests.

Critics of standardized tests hold that the tests fail to measure intelligence, aptitude, or global cognitive skill and instead measure specific skills and knowledge acquired through particular experiences or instruction. Moreover, critics charge, experiences leading to the acquisition of these skills are more accessible to white, middle-class children than to children of other ethnic and socioeconomic groups. Some critics also argue that the test situation itself is unfamiliar and threatening to low-income and/or minority children, further depressing their scores. Thus, argue the critics, tests are inherently biased against low-income and/or minority children and systematically underestimate their intellectual ability relative to that of middle-class whites. Finally, critics attack the social uses and social effects of testing. Tests, they allege, perpetuate race and class prejudices because they are widely interpreted as demonstrating the inherent intellectual inferiority of minorities and low-income groups. Similarly, they perpetuate racial and class inequities in income, job status, and other forms of success and achievement, because they channel children from minority and/or low-income families into educational settings that provide little intellectual stimulation, little opportunity to acquire the skills most valued by the society, and little in the way of prestigious credentials and social contacts that can influence occupational and economic success quite apart from ability and effort. The extreme case in point, of course, is placement in classes for mentally retarded students, which, it is alleged, stigmatizes the child unfairly and virtually guarantees a dead-end education leading to a menial job at best.

Even this brief summary, which has barely skimmed the surface of the debate, makes it clear that many profound issues divide the proponents and opponents of testing. Any list of the primary open questions would include at least the following:

1. *What do standardized ability tests measure?* To what degree do they measure deep-seated mental abilities as opposed to skills and knowledge that can be readily acquired by almost any child in the right environment?

2. *Are tests culturally biased?* To what degree do test scores understate or fail to measure the abilities of minority and/or low-income children?

3. *What are the causes of observed group differences in test performance?* To what degree are the causes genetic? To what degree do such differences arise from group differences in quality of prenatal care, nutrition, and health care? To what degree do they arise from differences in early experience or in the home environment? To what degree do they arise from differences in out-of-home educational environments and opportunities from the preschool years on?

4. *What are the social consequences of testing?* To what degree do tests

provide opportunities for gifted individuals from disadvantaged backgrounds to identify themselves? To what degree do they perpetuate disadvantage and prejudice? In the context of educational placement, do they, on balance, help or hinder the meeting of children's needs? To what degree do they identify children who need special help? To what degree do they lead to inappropriate classification and unfair allocation of educational opportunity?

Answers to these questions vary with particular tests and particular policies regarding their use. The partial answers offered below relate primarily to the use of major "IQ tests" in EMR evaluations during recent years and may not generalize beyond that context. The first three issues are discussed in separate sections below. The fourth is central to the mission of the panel and crosscuts the others; it is discussed in each substantive section and in the conclusion of this paper.

The possible contribution of testing to the disproportionate representation of boys in EMR classes—another concern of the panel—is not discussed explicitly since the controversy over testing has focused on ethnicity rather than gender. Important issues concerning possible interactions of gender and ethnicity and the reportedly greater vulnerability of boys than girls to environmental variations are likewise beyond the scope of this paper.

WHAT DO "INTELLIGENCE" TESTS MEASURE?

To discuss what such tests as the WISC-R and Stanford-Binet measure, it is first necessary to clear away a popular misconception about what they are supposed to measure. In the view of most professionals in psychology, psychometrics, and related fields, such tests do not and are not intended to measure the global, fixed native capacity that seems to be implied by the term "intelligence." Indeed, for these professionals the equation of intelligence with native intellectual capacity is entirely misleading and has been the source of much confusion and unnecessary acrimony in debates about testing and its uses. (For an authoritative statement of this position, see Cleary et al., 1975).

The gap between this view and that of many educators, policy makers, members of the public, and some social scientists is illustrated by federal Judge Robert Peckham's landmark decision in the case of *Larry P.* v. *Riles* (1979). In a section entitled "The Impossibility of Measuring Intelligence," the judge writes (*Larry P.* v. *Riles*, 1979, Section IVA):

While many think of the IQ as an objective measure of innate, fixed intelligence, the testimony of the experts overwhelmingly demonstrated that this conception of

IQ is erroneous. Defendant's expert witnesses, even those closely affiliated with the companies that devise and distribute the standardized intelligence tests, agreed, with only one exception, that we cannot truly define, much less measure, intelligence. We can measure certain skills, but not native intelligence.

The judge implies that in the common view intelligence is, by definition, a quality both innate and unchanging; and he apparently holds this view himself. (Generations of psychologists, most of them now deceased, advanced the same definition.) However, the judge rejects what he considers to be the popular view that IQ is an accurate measure of native intelligence. He himself was convinced that IQ tests measure something that is not fixed or innate—"certain skills"—and he does not seem to equate these skills with intelligence.

Presumably, however, the "experts" who "devise and distribute" intelligence tests must believe that they measure something that can legitimately be called "intelligence," even if it is ill defined and not fixed or innate. The experts seem to hold the view of those contemporary psychologists who think of intelligence as a kind of global ability to absorb complex information or grasp and manipulate abstract concepts—an ability that is not fixed but that develops continuously through a process of reciprocal interaction with the physical and social world, including, but not limited to, the world of formal education. This very general view is shared by psychologists who differ on many specific theoretical points—Piagetian developmental psychologists, cognitive psychologists oriented toward computer simulation and information processing, even some learning theorists committed to animal behavior models. For all of these psychologists, it is reasonable to speak of an individual's intelligence at a given point in his or her development, but there is no presumption that individual differences in intelligence are fixed or wholly determined by the genes.

From this perspective the central question is whether IQ is a valid measure of "developed intelligence." Questions about how much genes contribute, how genes and environment interact, and how much IQ can be modified by planned social intervention through education are separate. A few of these questions are discussed in a subsequent section on the causes of variation in IQ; selected aspects of the validity question are discussed here.

Inspection of one of the major intelligence tests, such as the Stanford-Binet or the WISC-R, reveals that items vary widely in content and that many plainly require learning of a very specific sort. Examples include verbal analogies, numerical computations, and questions about practical tasks and social norms (How do you make water boil? What should you do if a smaller child tries to start a fight with you?). Vocabulary items provide some particularly striking examples: At its most advanced adult level, the

Stanford-Binet asks the meanings of such esoteric words as "parterre" and "sudorific." This manifest emphasis on acquired knowledge and diversity of item content naturally raises questions as to how such tests can be said to measure any general mental property (as opposed to specific skills and knowledge) as well as how tests can be said to measure "ability" in any broad sense that goes beyond the ability to answer the specific questions and solve the specific problems presented by the test itself.

The generality of mental test scores has been the subject of a long debate in psychometrics. Early leaders in the field, notably Spearman and Thurstone, took opposed positions. The debate came to focus on the statistical issue of shared variation: What fraction of the variance in individual performance is shared by all items? What fraction is shared within distinct clusters of items but not across clusters (thus pointing to differentiated abilities rather than a single "intelligence")? What fraction is unique to individual items (pointing to "abilities" specific to the items)? Statistical techniques of principal components and factor analysis were developed largely to address these questions.

There is no universal agreement on precise, quantitative answers to these questions. Different analytic techniques yield different estimates of the relative importance of the general factor versus differentiated clusters. There is agreement, however, that a significant fraction of the variation is shared across items. The diverse items on such tests as the WISC-R and Stanford-Binet appear to measure (in part) the same thing or a small number of things; they are not merely a heterogeneous ragbag of skills and bits of knowledge. Item responses correlate with one another, with subscale scores, and with total scores on the test. Items load on a single general factor and on a small number of orthogonal factor scales. For example, several analyses of WISC-R scores, based on large samples comprised of several ethnic groups, have revealed independent "verbal" and "perceptual" factors and, occasionally, a third factor variously labeled "distractibility," "attention," "memory," and "sequential" (Kaufman, 1975; Mercer, in press; Reschly and Reschly, 1979). In addition, most tests of general abilities, even when apparently dissimilar in content, correlate positively and often highly with each other.

Covariance of scores across items and across tests is an established empirical fact. To identify common variance with ability or abilities requires inference and interpretation. The inference rests on an assumption: A child who possesses general perceptual and analytic abilities will make good use of experience and will master a wide range of specific facts, concepts, and principles. Conversely, a child who performs well on a wide variety of items is likely to have well-developed information-processing abilities of a general sort. An alternative interpretation of test and item covariance is that both the tests and the individual items reflect exposure to the mainstream culture, especially to the language, symbols, information, strategies, and tasks that are important in schools. These two interpretations are not necessarily opposed, so long as it is recognized that perceptual and analytic abilities may be developed in part through experience and exposure to appropriate stimulation. (There may of course be other broad perceptual and analytic abilities that are neither captured by existing tests nor fostered by the mainstream culture.)

It is important to recognize that all test performance depends on both general abilities and specific knowledge, both of which are products of learning, at least in part. For example, a test of an advanced, academic subject matter, e.g., one that requires the respondent to solve differential equations, clearly requires specific preparation. Nevertheless, general mathematical ability is likely to play a large role in individual performance. The relative contributions of general ability and specific learning are not fixed characteristics of the test itself but depend as well on the tested population and the circumstances of testing. Pursuing the example just given, if students in a calculus class are all drawn from a narrow, high band of the spectrum of general mathematical ability but vary widely in their previous preparation for calculus, the latter variations will be a relatively important determinant of test performance. If students in the class vary widely in ability but have all been exposed to the same mathematics curriculum in the past, variations in ability will be a more important factor.

Most school psychologists and educators who use IQ tests avoid the interpretive issues discussed above and justify their use of tests on grounds of "predictive validity," a purely empirical phenomenon. Many studies have shown that IQ scores predict (correlate with) "criterion" measures of scholastic success, such as later school grades or scores on standardized tests of achievement in specific subject areas. For elementary school children, validity coefficients (correlations) of .7 or higher have often been obtained using achievement tests as criteria (see Crano et al., 1972). Correlations with grades are typically somewhat lower. Values around .5 have been reported (Messé et al., 1979). Occasionally, much lower correlations with grades have been reported; however, technical limitations may account in part for these findings.[1]

---

[1]Lower and less consistent correlations with grades are to be expected for many reasons. IQ tests are more similar in style and content to standardized achievement tests than to classroom tests and other performance measures used in grading. Grades are likely to be less reliable than standardized achievement tests, and unreliability attenuates correlations. Grades are likely to be influenced by factors other than achievement, such as deportment or per-

It is not necessary to dwell on the evidence for predictive validity, because some degree of the predictive power of tests is generally conceded. What is sharply debated, however, is the interpretation of validity correlations. They are obviously consistent with the hypothesis that IQ tests measure academic ability, which is later manifested in scholastic performance, and they have been interpreted in this way, implicitly or explicitly, by many of those who use tests in schools. They are also consistent with the hypothesis that IQ tests, teacher-made tests, and standardized achievement tests all sample the same domain of acquired skills.

This ambiguity of interpretation points to an important fact, noted by Messick (1980), among others, that the term "predictive validity" is a misnomer. Prediction is not a kind of validity; prediction does not in itself guarantee that a test measures what it is supposed to measure. (Parental income predicts a child's IQ and school success, but it is surely stretching the term "measure" to call parental income a measure of the child's intelligence.) What is needed is an explicit theory of intelligence that links this construct to its measures and to other constructs and their associated measures. To draw a physical analogy, there is an explicit theory that links temperature to pressure and volume and, thereby, to the height of a column of liquid in a sealed tube. Without such a theory it would be hard to understand why a thermometer measures the entity that causes water to boil or one's hand to hurt when placed on a hot stove. Belief in the validity of the measure gains strength with repeated confirmation of the theory. In psychometric parlance, this process is "construct validation," and, as Messick and others have argued, construct validity is the only kind there is. Prediction is just one of several kinds of evidence that can be used to support claims of construct validity. Unfortunately, where intelligence is concerned, there are multiple, competing theories, few of them very precise; hence, the evidence of prediction is subject to multiple interpretations.

In sum, there are two principal pieces of evidence for the validity of IQ tests as measures of "developed intelligence." One is the convergence of different items and different tests. The other is the association between IQ scores and measures of academic achievement. Both are subject to varying interpretations. The question of interest here is how the evidence bears on the use of tests in educational placement.

---

ceived effort. Overall grade point averages may include nonacademic subjects, for which little effect of intellectual ability might be expected. Students are likely to be grouped by ability, formally or informally, and graded in comparison to their classmates; such practices imply that the same grade means different things for students in different classes or for students graded by different teachers and also that the restricted range of variation in IQ within classes will reduce the correlation between IQ and grades.

Critics of testing have argued vehemently that tests are invalid as measures of a child's potential and are, therefore, unfair devices to use for placement. However, they have not spelled out why they would be fair if they did measure potential nor why they are unfair if they measure only acquired skills or developed abilities. Defenders of testing have not contested the point about measurement of potential but have justified the use of tests on grounds of predictive validity, apparently believing that the use of tests in educational placement is fair even if tests measure skills that are partially or primarily acquired. In my view, neither the critics nor the defenders (exemplified by the plaintiffs and defendants in *Larry P.* and in *Parents in Action on Special Education* v. *Hannon*) have focused their arguments appropriately. Prediction in itself is not sufficient justification for using tests in educational placement. Nor is the critical shortcoming of tests their failure to measure "potential" or "native intelligence." The key issue is whether tests offer guidance in choosing among educational alternatives.

One relevant, if obvious, limitation of prediction has been mentioned in court cases concerned with the use of tests in EMR placement (e.g., U.S. Department of Justice, 1980:A7–A8): Prediction is probabilistic. The fact that a given IQ on the average predicts a specific grade level does not guarantee that any particular child who achieves the given IQ will achieve the predicted grade level. Variation around the predicted level can be quite wide. When the validity coefficient is as high as .6, a child who scores below the 10th percentile (an IQ of roughly 80) would have a 46 percent chance of achieving a grade point average in the bottom fifth of the class, hence a 54 percent chance of doing better. The child would have a 17 percent chance of being in the top half of the class. When the validity coefficient is as low as .2, the child would have only a 28 percent probability of being in the bottom fifth—just 8 percent higher than pure chance. The child would have a 40 percent likelihood of being in the top half of the class (Schrader, 1965). Even if it is conceded that IQ tests are among the best predictors of school success that we have, the margin of error in an individual case is substantial. (In principle, prediction can be improved by the use of other valid indicators in conjunction with IQ scores. In practice, as indicated earlier, this improvement may or may not be achieved, depending on whether additional indicators are in fact collected and used.)

A second limitation—somewhat paradoxical, given the first—is that the predictive information available in the IQ overlaps with that available in the child's grade record or achievement test scores, when the latter are available. Past and current achievement predicts future achievement, typically better than IQ (Crano et al., 1972). Although, as illustrated in the previous paragraph, a substantial portion of the variation in achievement is independent of IQ and vice versa, prediction based on both IQ and achievement is only a little more accurate than prediction based on achievement alone. (The fact that IQ and achievement measures are not entirely redundant does have important implications, however. In current practice, children are usually referred for testing only after experiencing serious and prolonged difficulty in the classroom. When testing reveals that such children have low IQs, it merely confirms expectations. In some individual cases, however, testing can make a distinctive and positive contribution: When children who are performing poorly in class prove to have IQs in the normal range, the discrepancy points to undetected problems that should be diagnosed—sensory malfunctions, emotional difficulties, poor or inappropriate instruction, etc. Obviously, this is not to say that high scores are somehow more valid or meaningful than low scores or that predictive equations are different for high and low scores. The point, rather, is that the functional contribution of testing is likely to lie less in improving prediction than in stimulating diagnosis.)

A more fundamental limitation concerns the underlying logic of using prediction as a basis for educational placement at all. Even if it could be predicted with certainty that a child with a low IQ will get low grades in a regular class, this fact would not in itself dictate or justify removing the child from the class. Judge Peckham recognized this point when he drew a distinction between testing for educational placement and testing for job placement. Courts have held that employers have a legitimate stake in employee performance and thus are justified in selecting employees on the basis of a test that has demonstrated predictive power (Bersoff, 1979). But the stake of educators in the performance of children is not analogous. Children, not educators, are the beneficiaries of education, and the public schools have an obligation to teach every child as well as possible. The paramount question is not how to select children who will perform well in regular classes but how to select classes or programs that best meet the needs of children.

To justify separate placement on the basis of an IQ score it would be necessary to show that children with low IQs require and profit from a different curriculum or different type of instruction from that available in regular classes. (Alternatively, separate placement might be justified if it could be shown that children with low IQs are not harmed by it, while children in regular classes are harmed when children with low IQs share those regular classes.) Educational researchers call situations in which different educational approaches work best with children of different initial ability "aptitude-treatment interactions" (Cronbach and Snow, 1977). It has been urged that demonstration of aptitude-treatment interactions is the appropriate way to validate tests for use in educational placement, although there may be severe difficulties in conducting such demonstrations in special education.[2] The more general point stands, however: Separate placement demands justification on grounds of educational consequences, not merely predicted failure in regular classes.

Such justification goes far beyond the boundaries of technical test validity, as demonstrated by item convergence and prediction. As Messick (1980) pointed out, even ironclad evidence of technical validity is insufficient to justify a particular use of a test. One must always consider whether the construct measured by the test is relevant to the decision to be made, and one must always consider the consequences of the decision. The case of educational placement is a dramatic illustration of these precepts, as was noted by Reschly (1981), among others. It is likely that the framers of the implementing regulations for P.L. 94-142 (see Chapter 2) had this broad range of information in mind when they required that tests be "validated for their intended use," i.e., educational placement.

Later in this paper I argue that the above arguments would apply even if IQ scores supported strong inferences about learning potential. That is, even if children with low IQs were genetically limited in their capacity to learn, the decision to separate them from other children (or to assign them to any sort of special program) should be based on the educational consequences for these children and their classmates. First, however, I will consider another issue, central to both the *Larry P.* and *PASE* cases, the issue of racial and cultural bias in tests.

ARE TESTS BIASED?

Do tests misrepresent the skills or abilities of minority children and those from low-income families? Are tests merely the bearers of bad news about genuine differences in academic functioning, or are they the creators of false differences? To address these questions it is necessary to clarify certain points of definition that have caused confusion and miscommunication between specialists in psychological measurement, on one hand, and lawyers, judges, many social scientists, and the public on the other.

Documents such as Judge Peckham's decision in the *Larry P.* case or the *amicus curiae* brief filed by the U.S. Department of Justice in *PASE* v.

---

[2]To demonstrate an aptitude-treatment interaction it is necessary to use similar outcome measures for the various children and classes, or "treatments," being studied. If EMR children are exposed to curricula with goals that are radically different from those of the regular class—e.g., teaching self-help and vocational skills rather than academic skills—the use of common measures is pointless. The situation is further complicated if EMR children are in fact given individualized treatment, as required by current law.

Hannon (1980) suggest that the authors define bias quite differently from the measurement specialists. For many nonspecialists (accustomed, as noted earlier, to thinking that tests purport to measure innate ability), tests are biased if group differences in test scores can be attributed to average differences in environmental advantage enjoyed by children from different ethnic or socioeconomic groups. The issue for nonspecialists is not whether tests capture genuine differences in skill or developed ability between groups; it is whether these differences are caused by cultural factors. Thus the Justice Department attorneys (1980:17) in their post-trial memorandum supported the plaintiffs in *PASE*:

Plantiffs argue that racial and cultural bias, demonstrated most graphically by the differences in the test scores by race, reflect differences in cultural patterns and levels of exposure to the dominant school culture between blacks and whites.

Judge Peckham, in supporting his conclusion that tests are biased, cited testimony by witnesses for both plaintiffs and defendants to the effect that racial differences in IQ scores are culturally caused. For example, he wrote (*Larry P.* v. *Riles*, 1979, Section IVC):

... there was general agreement by all sides on the inevitability of cultural differences on IQ scores. Put succinctly by Professor Hilliard, black people have "a cultural heritage that represents an experience pool which is never used" or tested by standardized IQ tests.

To be sure, the cited documents contain additional discussion suggesting that the writers are aware of other aspects of bias more closely akin to the concerns of the specialist, which are discussed below. It is clear, however, that for these (arguably) representative nonspecialists, evidence for cultural causation of group differences in test scores is sufficient to establish bias in the tests themselves. In effect, "bias," "cultural causation," and "unfairness" are equivalent concepts for many nonspecialists. From this perspective it seems unfair to categorize children or allocate educational opportunities on the basis of performance differences that are culturally caused, and it seems proper to characterize the instruments that effectuate this unfair categorization as biased.

For the specialist, questions of bias, fairness, and cultural causation are separate. In psychometric theory, bias is purely a measurement issue: A test is biased if and only if quantitative indicators of validity—internal structure and relationships to other variables—differ for different cultural groups. A test is held to be unbiased if these quantitative properties are invariant across cultural groups, even if different groups have different performance profiles due to differential opportunity and experience. The following quote from Jensen (1980:375) illustrates the strong methodological flavor of the measurement specialist's definition of bias and its kinship to mathematical definitions of the term:

In mathematical statistics, "bias" refers to a *systematic* under or overestimation of a population parameter by a statistic based on samples drawn from the population. In psychometrics "bias" refers to systematic errors in the *predictive validity* or the *construct validity* of test scores of individuals that are associated with the individual's group membership.

This definition separates bias from fairness. It makes bias a purely technical issue. No matter how good a test is technically, there is room for disagreement concerning the decision rules to be applied when the test is used for selection, placement, or other purposes. Questions of fairness apply to these rules and to test use, not to tests themselves.[3] (There have been a number of attempts to formulate explicit, quantitative criteria of "fairness" in the use of tests that show different performance profiles across social groups; see Petersen and Novick, 1976.)

Given this technical definition of bias, it is not inconsistent to argue that the use of a particular test for a particular purpose may be unfair even if the test is, in the sense defined, unbiased. For example, it is consistent to argue that IQ tests are racially unbiased measures of academic ability but that ability is affected by cultural experience and that it is, therefore, unfair to use IQ tests to make decisions that require inferences about innate potential. Thus a measurement specialist might agree with some of Judge Peckham's conclusions while rejecting the judge's claim that tests per se are biased.

What evidence could be adduced to show that IQ tests are unbiased in the technical sense, i.e., that tests are equally valid for children from different ethnic groups or markedly different socioeconomic and/or educational backgrounds? The answer is that there is *no* direct way to demonstrate that a test is culturally unbiased. (Jensen, who has devoted a 740-page tome to showing that bias is not a significant factor in mental testing, concurs with this point.) However, it is possible to show that a test is biased, in any of a number of specific ways. Conversely, by systematically ruling out each of the known potential sources of bias, it is possible to reduce the plausibility of the hypothesis that a test is biased, though never to falsify the hypothesis in a strict sense.

Three potential sources of bias have received the lion's share of atten-

---

[3]The usage here is fairly common but not universal. I use the term "bias" to refer to all potential group differences in quantitative measures of validity and the term "fairness" to refer to issues of test use. Others, such as Cole (1981), use "bias" and "fairness" to refer to different types of potential quantitative discrepancy between groups.

tion in the psychometric literature to date: (1) differences in performance induced by culturally sensitive features of the test situation, such as the race or dialect of the tester; (2) conspicuous differences across cultural groups in the difficulty of particular items or in other internal features of the pattern of responses generated by test items, which would indicate that the items do not tap the same underlying construct for different groups; and (3) differences in the external or predictive validity of tests for different groups.

BIAS IN THE TEST SITUATION

Many aspects of the test situation, aside from a child's actual skill or ability, are known or hypothesized to influence test scores. Any of these factors could in theory operate differentially by race, thereby artificially depressing the scores of black children relative to those of white children. The most complete list appears to be that in Chapter 12 of Jensen's (1980) book on bias and includes the following: familiarity with the particular test or type of test (coaching and practice); the race and sex of the tester; the language style or dialect of the tester; the tester's expectations about the child's performance; distortions in scoring or time pressure or lack thereof; and attitudinal factors such as test anxiety, achievement motivation, and self-esteem. Jensen characterizes the findings on the contribution of these aspects of testing to the racial gap in test scores as "wholly negative"; I would characterize them as equivocal, indicating a small degree of bias at best. (Jensen agrees that there is evidence for a language bias in the testing of bilingual children, but he denies the existence of bias due to racial dialects or any other bias linked to race.)

Many of these situational factors have statistically significant overall effects on test scores but show no interactions with race. For example, coaching and practice together can boost an individual's IQ score by about nine points, if the individual is retested after a fairly short time interval on a test that is highly similar to the practice one. However, blacks and whites profit almost equally from coaching and practice. Blacks do not gain much more than whites, as one might expect assuming that blacks are initially less familiar with tests and test-taking strategies. (Actually, a close look at the data reported by Jensen suggests that in several studies blacks did gain a point or two more than whites on some tests, while in other studies or on other tests they gained less. It is unclear whether the different outcomes are random or reflect some underlying phenomenon worthy of investigation.) There is little in the reported data to suggest that familiarization with tests can eliminate more than a small fraction of the IQ difference between the races. Not all of the other situational factors have significant overall effects on test scores, and none are as large as the effects of coaching and practice. More importantly, in no case is there a large interaction between a situational factor and race.

How can these equivocal-to-negative findings be reconciled with reports of large IQ gains when minority children who scored low are retested by persons of the same ethnic group under nonthreatening conditions? Cases of this sort have frequently been cited in the courts. There are at least two possible answers, with very different implications, indicating a need for research to resolve the issue.

One answer is that the people who retest children and boost their IQ scores drastically are merely making the test easier, e.g., by translating items containing difficult words into items with the same content but with easier words, by giving hints, by putting the most favorable interpretation on ambiguous answers, etc. Such changes in procedure may or may not be desirable, but the question of interest here is whether this approach to testing boosts the scores of minority children selectively. It might be the case that white, middle-class children would benefit as much or more than minority children from equivalent changes in procedure. If they did, the changed procedures would have nothing to do with cultural or ethnic bias in tests. If minority children benefited more, the changed procedure would point to bias and indicate that something was wrong or missing in the studies cited by Jensen.

What might that something be? One answer, a second potential explanation of the discrepancy between the null findings reported by Jensen and the substantial increases in IQ that are often reported, lies in the training of testers and the conditions under which tests are administered. It seems likely that the testers employed in research projects are likely to be particularly well trained, conscientious in their adherence to prescribed procedures, and sensitized to issues of bias. It may well be the case that situational distortions are minimized when such testers operate under such conditions. In contrast, it seems likely that school psychologists often work under considerable administrative pressure and less than optimal testing conditions, and their evaluations are less open to scrutiny by other professionals. If so, testing errors in general and bias in particular seem more likely to occur under "field" conditions. Some of the large increases attributed to retesting may have been genuine corrections of testing errors that would not have occurred in research settings. Studies that systematically compare the effects of the test situation on minority and white children under research and field conditions are needed to choose between the two explanations.

Item Analysis: Ruby is a Red Herring

Curiously, many critics and some proponents of testing share an exaggerated faith in the analysis of individual test items as a method for assessing cultural bias. In fact, item analysis is useful in addressing only limited aspects—and, as it happens, relatively unimportant aspects—of test bias.

A common approach to item analysis, which might be called "editorial," is to analyze the face content of items on logical or semantic grounds or on the basis of apparent or presumed connections to particular subcultural milieux. Judge John F. Grady's decision in *PASE* v. *Hannon* (1980) provides a dramatic and socially significant illustration of this approach. Setting aside a variety of statistical and empirical arguments for and against the use of tests in placing black children in EMR classes, the judge chose instead to examine test items individually and to decide in each case whether the item appeared *a priori* to present special difficulties for black children—rather like Judges Woolsey and Bryan, who read *Ulysses* and *Lady Chatterly's Lover*, respectively, to decide whether they were pornographic. Thus Judge Grady rejected the test question "What is the color of a ruby?" on the grounds that "Ruby" is a common name in the black community; hence, the name of the gem might be mistaken for a proper name and the child might answer "black." However, his "item analysis" led the judge to accept all but a few items on the Stanford-Binet and WISC-R and to uphold the use of these tests in educational placement by the Chicago public schools. Others have drawn diametrically opposed conclusions from similar editorial item analyses (e.g., Hoffman, 1962).

One obvious flaw in this approach is that it places "bias" in the eye of the editor, and different editors disagree. More important is the fact that judgments about item content (even if there is agreement) are neither necessary nor sufficient to prove that particular items discriminate against black children, in the sense of lowering their test scores. An apparently innocent item can be disproportionately difficult for minority children compared with whites, while an item that is problematic on its face can be equally difficult for all ethnic groups.

The foregoing sentence implicitly establishes one standard by which professionals in test construction determine whether items are biased: They examine proportions of children from different ethnic groups who get each item correct; when an item deviates markedly from the overall profile for any group (an item × group interaction), that item is assumed to confer an unacceptable advantage or disadvantage for one group or the other and is deemed to be "biased" in this precise and limited sense. Related psychometric approaches to assessing item bias focus on item-scale correlations and the factor loadings of items. If correlations or loadings for particular items differ conspicuously for children from different ethnic groups, such items are suspect on the grounds that they do not appear to measure the same construct for the various groups. Item analyses performed on IQ tests have tended to show that most individual items show about the same gap in performance between whites and other ethnic groups. There are statistically significant item × group interactions, but they are trivially small relative to overall group differences (Mercer, in press; Sandoval, 1979). Factor structures show only minor differences for most major ethnic groups (Reschly and Reschly, 1979). If there is bias in IQ tests, it is pervasive and not primarily linked to a few offending items. But bias can indeed be pervasive. It is possible that all items on a test systematically understate the abilities of minority children. Item analyses of the kind described cannot rule out this possibility.

In short, criticisms of tests based on the content of individual items are misplaced, insofar as those criticisms are meant to imply that particular, "culturally loaded" items account for the differential test performance of children from different ethnic groups. On the other hand, defenses of tests based on item analyses fail to address the issue of pervasive or global test bias. An independent case can be made that "editorial" or content bias in test items should be eliminated in order to enhance the credibility and acceptability of tests among minority cultural groups,[4] but current evidence does not warrant optimism that editorial changes will reduce differential performance.

DIFFERENTIAL PREDICTIVE VALIDITY

The logic of predictive validation of tests was explicated and critically examined earlier. A straightforward extension of that logic makes differential predictive validity a measure of bias, in a precise but rather narrow sense: If a test is a valid measure of some trait or skill for some social groups but not others, and if an independent criterion measure of the same trait or skill exists, it follows that the test should predict the criterion for those groups for which it is valid and fail to predict the criterion for those groups for which it is invalid. For example, if IQ tests measure intellectual skills or abilities more accurately for white children than for black children, IQ should correlate more highly with measures of future school

---

[4]There exist flagrant examples of racially offensive content in widely used tests. For example, prior to a recent revision, one popular test of "receptive vocabulary" incorporated only two pictures of black people among numerous pictorial stimulus items—a pullman porter and a Sambo figure. A case can clearly be made against the use of such materials without regard to their effects on performance.

success for whites than for blacks. Thus an empirical demonstration of differential predictive accuracy would tend to confirm the hypothesis of cultural bias, although bias in the test itself is not the only possible explanation for differential prediction. (For example, differential prediction could arise if tests measured ability accurately for both blacks and whites but the school performance of blacks was adversely affected by teacher attitudes and behavior.)

This question of differential validity can be addressed most clearly within the framework of statistical methods used to assess predictive power. In statistical terms, the question "Does a given test have equal predictive validity for blacks and whites?" translates into the questions "Do regression lines (relating the test to the criterion) for the two groups coincide, i.e., have the same slope and the same intercept?" and "Are the standard errors of estimate similar for the two groups? The first question has to do with whether the test predicts the same level of success on the criterion variable (e.g., school grades) for blacks and whites who score the same on the test. The second question has to do with whether the margin of error in predicting individual performance on the criterion is equal for both groups or greater for one group than the other.

These issues have been explored fairly extensively in a series of studies on the differential predictive validity of various ability tests applicable to young adults, such as the Scholastic Aptitude Test, the Law School Admission Test, and numerous tests of job aptitude. The criterion variables in these studies were college grades, law school grades, supervisor ratings on the job, and other indices of job performance. This literature was reviewed in a paper by Robert Linn (1982), commissioned by the Committee on Ability Testing of the National Research Council. Linn concludes that these studies consistently show that test scores overpredict the future success of blacks relative to that of whites; that is, blacks do less well in school or on the job than whites with similar test scores. There is also a tendency for the regression line for blacks to slope less steeply than the line for whites, so that overprediction is greatest for blacks who achieve the highest test scores.

With respect to the margin of error in prediction, Linn concludes that the evidence is less consistent but tends to show that tests predict less accurately for blacks than for whites, by a small margin in most studies. For example, 34 reported estimates of the multiple correlation between college aptitude tests and freshman or first-semester college grade averages yield a median of .302 for blacks and .385 for whites. Differences in predictive accuracy are essentially nonexistent for the Law School Admission Test and for most job-related tests; however, one large Air Force study found that the median correlation (across 39 different job areas) between the

Armed Forces Qualification Test and grades in Air Force technical training was .33 for whites and only .18 for blacks.[5]

Data like those presented by Linn, suggesting overprediction of black
scholastic success and roughly comparable errors of estimate, were cited
in defense of IQ testing in *Larry P.* and *PASE*. However, an obvious question that arises, in light of the matters at issue in those cases and of the
mission of the panel, is whether the findings apply to children of elementary and secondary school age, particularly those from minority groups
who score low enough on the IQ scale to be candidates for placement in
EMR classes. Unfortunately, there are surprisingly few studies of the differential predictive validity of IQ tests for black and white children of
school age, and fewer still that present regression data necessary to examine issues of underprediction and overprediction. (Most present only
correlations.)

As indicated in the earlier section on predictive validity, correlations between IQ scores and scores on standardized achievement tests are generally quite high. Typically they are only slightly lower for minority children
than for whites (see Sattler, 1974, for some representative findings).

Correlations with grades are typically lower and are less consistent
across studies, in part for the technical reasons mentioned earlier. Correlations reported for black children range from a high of .6–.7 (Sattler,
1974) to a low of zero (Green and Farquhar, 1965, quoted in Jensen,
1980:474). Correlations reported for whites are generally as high or higher
than those for blacks, sometimes substantially higher in the studies that
find the lowest correlations for blacks (e.g., Goldman and Hartig, 1976;
Green and Farquhar, 1965; Mercer, 1979). Goldman and Hartig, for example, found a correlation of only .27 between WISC IQ and later grades
for a large sample of elementary school children in California. For sub-
samples of black and Mexican-American children, correlations are in the
range of .12–.18. Mercer (1979) reports correlations of .46 for Anglo
children and .20 for black and Mexican-American children in an overlapping sample drawn from the same California school district. Judge
Peckham gave considerable weight to the Mercer and Goldman and Hartig results, although the latter have been criticized on methodological

---

[5]It must be kept in mind that observed differences in so-called validity coefficients (test-
criterion correlations) are affected by statistical factors that have nothing to do with "validity" as the word is commonly understood. In particular, if the range of variation in the test
score or criterion is less for blacks than for whites, the correlations between the test scores
and the criterion are lowered. Validity coefficients are, therefore, not always comparable.
Close examination of some of the data presented here and elsewhere in the text indicates that
relatively low validity coefficients reported for minority children are in fact due in part to
restricted variance in the IQ, the criterion, or both.

grounds similar to those mentioned earlier (e.g., by Messé et al., 1979). Mercer herself points out that her differential correlations are due in part to restricted variance in both WISC scores and grades in the minority samples; however, she also points out that essentially the same results are obtained when a semantic differential rating of student competence by teachers (which does not suffer from range restriction) is used as the criterion variable.

I have encountered only three studies that present full regression information for school-age children from different ethnic groups (Farr et al., 1971, quoted in Jensen, 1980:475–476; Mercer, 1979; Reschly and Sabers, 1979). Farr et al. examined the predictive validity of the California Test of Mental Maturity for black and white secondary school students, using grades and various teacher ratings as criterion variables. Reschly and Sabers used the WISC-R as a predictor and achievement test scores as criteria; their sample was a group of children in grades 1–9 and included Anglos, blacks, Chicanos, and Native American Papagos. Mercer's analysis, based on data from Goldman and Hartig, used the WISC (not the WISC-R) as a predictor and used grades as criteria; the sample included Anglo, black, and Hispanic children.

The Farr et al. and Reschly and Sabers studies produced complex patterns of results, varying with the ages of the children involved. On balance they indicated only minor differences in prediction for Anglos, blacks, and, in the Reschly and Sabers study, Hispanics. When patterns differed, they often revealed overprediction for blacks and underprediction for Anglos.[6] The Mercer analysis was unique in finding worse overall prediction, worse prediction for blacks and Hispanics than for Anglos, and underprediction of grades for minority children with IQs below the mid-70s—the range likely to be found among children being evaluated for placement in EMR classes. Mercer's findings suggest that, if the same cutoff scores were used to place children in EMR classes, minority children in those classes would be more academically able than their white counterparts. However, the findings are subject to some of the same caveats mentioned above in connection with the validity coefficients reported by Mercer.

In sum, within the measurement specialist's precise but narrow empirical framework for assessing bias, there are only a few studies indicating a relatively modest amount of distortion in test scores of minority children,

---

[6]Gordon (1980) reports partial results of a regression study, in which he found overprediction for Mexican-American students. Messé et al. (1979) report an analysis of data from a large, all-white British sample that revealed overprediction of grades for children of low socioeconomic status.

within the range of scores and ages most relevant to the panel's work. There is at best scattered evidence for bias in aspects of the testing situation external to the test itself; however, this issue merits further study under field conditions. There is little evidence that bias lodges in particular test items, but this does not preclude the possibility of generalized bias across all items. In general there has not been consistent evidence for differential predictive validity of tests across ethnic groups, although such evidence has been found in several influential but controversial studies.

On balance it must be concluded that bias in the technical sense contributes little either to explaining group differences in IQ or to shaping placement policy. No study I have encountered suggests that the magnitude of any bias effect, or even several combined, comes close to explaining all of the differences in IQs between whites and minorities. It is unlikely that elimination of psychometric bias, in the absence of other changes in policy and practice, would have much effect on the IQ scores of minority children or the proportion assigned to EMR classes.

It is important to recognize the limited import of this conclusion. The conclusion relates only to technical bias and says nothing about fairness in test use or about ethnic or racial bias in the interpretation of test scores or bias in the educational system or in society at large. Psychometric investigations of bias do not address many of the larger concerns of educators, policy makers, and the public, most of whom use the term "bias" more broadly than the technical definition allows. For example, these investigations ignore the problem of bias in the criteria: If school grades and/or achievement test scores underestimate the academic attainment of minority students—as tests allegedly underestimate their abilities—it would be no justification of testing, from a moral or policy standpoint, to find that prediction was perfect. In addition, as we saw at the beginning of this section, many persons outside the field of psychological measurement define bias as any contribution of sociocultural factors that raise or lower the IQ scores of one group relative to another. There is simply no doubt that there is some cultural contribution, as even the firmest believers in genetic determination of IQ would admit. I take up the issue of the relative size of this contribution in the next section, but I also argue that the issue is less important for policy in the area of educational placement than it may seem.

WHAT CAUSES INDIVIDUAL AND GROUP VARIATIONS IN IQ?

No question in psychology has provoked more bitter debate than that surrounding the determinants of variation in IQ scores. In recent years the controversy has centered on the relative contributions of heredity and environment to the 15-point average difference usually found between the IQ scores of blacks and whites. I survey some of the main lines of evidence briefly and then consider the relevance of the entire debate for educational policy and practice.

The hereditarian viewpoint has had a sporadic history in psychology generally and in the field of IQ testing particularly. Alfred Binet, whose work in the Paris schools in the early 20th century initiated modern ability testing, vociferously denied that his test measured innate ability. However, many of the American and British psychologists who translated, modified, and used Binet's instrument took the contrary view. Some expressed their opinions in the public-policy arena and were associated with the eugenics and anti-immigration movements (Kamin, 1974). As we have seen, the assumption that "IQ tests" measure or are supposed to measure innate intelligence is still shared by many outside the measurement field, although most professionals in the field reject it.

Arthur Jensen's article in the *Harvard Educational Review* (1969) revived the hereditarian viewpoint within the field and provoked a debate that still continues. Jensen's paper attempted to show that IQ tests measure general intellectual ability, that this ability is of great social importance, and that educational intervention has relatively little effect on individual differences in IQ. Examining correlations among IQs of persons in various biological kinship relations, Jensen concluded that the data can be well explained by postulating that intelligence is a polygenic trait and that 80 percent of its phenotypic variation is due to underlying genotypic variation.

Others, using similar techniques of "heritability estimation" but with somewhat different models, assumptions, or data, have arrived at lower estimates, in the neighborhood of 0.5 (e.g., Jencks et al., 1972; Plomin and DeFries, 1980). One thorough and dispassionate review (Loehlin et al., 1975) reached a summary estimate only a little lower than Jensen's for the heritability of individual variations in IQ within European and Caucasian populations. The reviewers found that estimates of heritability within the black population were less consistent and often lower than estimates for whites, although they still pointed to a substantial genetic component. However, Loehlin et al. note that there is considerable room for disagreement about the technical details of heritability calculations; existing evidence is hence consistent with a very broad range of within-group heritability coefficients.

A number of factors create difficulties for the statistical techniques, borrowed from population genetics, that are used to estimate heritability. For example, one widely noted problem is the confounding of heredity and environment: Innately bright parents are likely to provide their children with a lot of intellectual stimulation; innately bright children are likely to elicit stimulation from others and to find or create it in their physical environments (Scarr, 1981). Similarly, patterns of biological relationship are likely to mirror patterns of environmental similarity. For example, cousins share fewer genes than siblings, but they are also likely to grow up in less similar environments. As Loehlin et al. (1975) point out, most techniques for estimating heritability confound the purely genetic contribution with the contribution of the gene-environment correlation.

To get a meaningful heritability estimate for a given trait in a given population, it is necessary to sample the relevant ranges of genotypes and environments and to specify correctly the statistical model that describes their separate and joint contribution to the phenotype. Some skeptics (e.g., Layzer, 1972) doubt that techniques of heritability estimation can be legitimately applied to IQ data, given the limitations of existing data, the imprecision of existing definitions and theories of intelligence, and our ignorance about possible environmental influences and gene-environment interactions.

Probably this rather arcane controversy over the proper use of statistics in estimating the heritability of traits would have aroused little public attention had Jensen not gone beyond his discussion of individual differences in IQ to speculate that *group* differences, specifically black-white differences, are also partly genetic in origin. Jensen wrote (1969:82):

So all we are left with are various lines of evidence, no one of which is definitive alone, but which, viewed all together, make it a not unreasonable hypothesis that genetic factors are strongly implicated in the average Negro-white intelligence difference. The preponderance of the evidence is, in my opinion, less consistent with a strictly environmental hypothesis than with a genetic hypothesis, which, of course, does not exclude the influence of environment or its interaction with genetic factors.

This conjecture was not based on direct examination of data on the causes of racial differences but rather was an extension of Jensen's main discussion, which, as already noted, dealt with individual differences within ethnic groups. Jensen's critics have stressed that average group differences in a particular trait can be due mostly or entirely to the environment even if the heritability of the trait within groups is very high.

In an attempt to address the issue of between-group variance as directly as possible, Loehlin et al. (1975) reviewed a number of studies relating IQ to various indices of racial mixture. Some of these studies examined correlations between IQ and race-linked characteristics such as skin color and blood-group distributions. Others examined IQ distributions associated with various patterns of interracial mating. One particularly interesting study traced the genealogies of black children with extremely high IQs (and found no evidence for increased European admixture, compared with the black population at large). While careful to point out that the results of these studies "are consistent with either moderate hereditarian or environmentalist interpretations," Loehlin et al. (1975:238) suggest that the findings are "more easily accommodated in an environmentalist framework." (In an appendix they estimate between-group heritability at .125, though the estimate is cautious and tentative.)

A similar conclusion can be reached regarding other studies, indicating that the size of the IQ gap between blacks and whites is inversely related to the degree of the black child's exposure to white, middle-class culture and schooling. These include classic studies of black families who migrated from the rural South to the urban North (Klineberg, 1935), studies of interracial adoptions (Scarr and Weinberg, 1976), and studies of the effects of sociocultural variations within the black community (Mercer, 1979).

The foregoing cursory glance at a large and complex literature will not satisfy either supporters or critics of the hereditarian position. It merely indicates some of the areas in which scientific controversy exists. The important points for purposes of this discussion are (1) that controversy does exist; science has not yet provided definitive answers to the nature-nurture question and perhaps never will and (2) that virtually everyone involved in the controversy agrees that both genetic and experiential factors influence IQ; what is at issue is the degree of influence and the mechanisms involved. The relevant question is whether there are policy decisions or practices having to do with educational placement or instruction that hinge on resolution of the issue.

Courts have held that the issue is indeed central. In *Larry P.*, for example, Judge Peckham argued that EMR classes are (according to definitions adopted by the California Department of Education)[7] intended for children who are congenitally unable to learn in regular classes; to be valid for purposes of placing children in such classes, the judge reasoned, tests

---

[7]California's EMR classes were intended for "pupils whose mental capabilities make it impossible for them to profit from the regular instructional programs" (*Larry P.* v. *Riles*, 1979, Sec. IIIC). EMR children were distinguished (in a 1963 law) from "culturally disadvantaged minors," who are "potentially capable of completing a regular educational program" but unable to do so because of "cultural, economic and like disadvantages." EMR children were also distinguished from "educationally handicapped" children, who "cannot benefit from the regular educational program" because of "marked learning or behavioral disorders or both" (*Larry P.* v. *Riles*, 1979, Sec. IIIB). Given the historical definitions of the latter two categories, Judge Peckham not unreasonably construed the EMR category as applying to children who are congenitally unable to learn.

must be capable of identifying congenital disability. (See *Larry P.*, Sections IIIC and VB(4), and the analysis of the decision by Smith, 1980).

The assumption that mental retardation is by definition innate is one that professionals concerned with the problem abandoned long ago. The American Association on Mental Deficiency, for example, cites "significantly subaverage general intellectual functioning" and "deficits in adaptive behavior" as the defining conditions (Grossman, 1977:5). It can, of course, be debated whether this is an appropriate definition or whether IQ is an appropriate measure of intellectual functioning. Nevertheless, given the definition, it is not necessary to show that the deficient intellectual functioning (arguably) signalled by a low IQ is inborn in order to say that a child is "mentally retarded" according to the stated functional criteria. The medical profession has been more explicit in defining mental retardation as a purely functional category that may have many different causes, experiential as well as organic. (For a lucid discussion of contemporary definitions see Goodman, 1977.) It appears that there is a wide gap between the assumptions and definitions embraced by leaders in the field and those embodied in administrative procedures of some school systems. The latter assumptions apparently guided the *Larry P.* decision.

Professionals have abandoned the organic definition of mental retardation in favor of the functional definition for both scientific and moral reasons that seem compelling. Organic causes can be identified in a small proportion of cases of mild mental retardation. However, there is no evidence that different educational procedures are needed, or work better, for organically disabled children, compared with other children with similar functional abilities but no (known) organic deficit (Goodman, 1977). There is no evidence that it is any easier to teach the latter group than the former or that their prognosis for future success is any worse. Good teaching can do a great deal to help even children with organic disabilities meet their potential; conversely, poor performance that is socially caused is just as hard to correct as poor performance that is organically caused—at least up to the limits of present scientific knowledge and instructional techniques.

Moreover, different views of the relative contributions of genetic and environmental factors in no way affect the responsibility of schools to provide the best instruction possible. There will always be differences in ability and achievement among students, and schools will always have to deal with these differences, regardless of their causes. To be sure, schools face difficult questions about how to allocate resources among students with different levels of developed academic ability. However, there is apparently no basis in current knowledge for believing that investment in the education of students of low ability with environmentally caused deficiencies will pay off (in future performance or social contribution) more than investment in the education of those with congenital disorders.

If it is indeed the case that treatment of educational disability is independent of the cause of the problem, it is hard to see why different beliefs about the relative contributions of genes and environment to IQ should have any educational import. Earlier we saw that a wide range of academic performance is consistent with any given IQ score. The job of the educator is to make sure that performance is as good as it can be. Though a teacher, administrator, or policy maker with hereditarian views might be pessimistic about the likelihood of large gains in underlying intellectual ability, this pessimism would be no justification for failing to impart as many skills and as much knowledge as possible. I am not denying that negative expectations can potentially do harm; they probably can, whether they are based on beliefs in genetic *or cultural* inferiority of minority groups. I am arguing that they should not be allowed to do harm—that such beliefs provide no legitimate basis for educational policies or practices that would in any way restrict children's progress. Decisions about curricula and teaching methods to be used with children at different levels of initial performance as well as decisions about whether to teach these children separately or together can and should be based on the demonstrated pedagogical effectiveness of the various approaches, not on preconceptions about the causes of initial differences in performance.

Finally, one's position on the nature-nurture question gives little or no guidance as to the degree of racial imbalance in special education placement that one should be willing to tolerate. As long as there are separate classes or programs for children who are significantly lacking in traditional academic skills, both environmentalists and hereditarians would expect minority children to be overrepresented in such classes, at least for the immediate future.

Critics of IQ testing and EMR classes (e.g., the plaintiffs in *Larry P.* and *PASE*) have argued that the nativist connotations of terms such as "intelligence" and "mental retardation" are deeply ingrained. Children are harmed because people misinterpret the meaning of IQ scores and EMR placements, stigmatizing children and denying them educational opportunities. None of the evidence reviewed in this section bears on the truth or falsity of such claims. The arguments in this section of the paper have not dealt with the actual political and educational consequences of hereditarian versus environmentalist views. The arguments have been intended to make one fundamental point: Given current knowledge, there is no logical or necessary connection between the heritability of IQ and educational practice.

CONCLUSIONS

Two kinds of conclusions have been sprinkled liberally throughout this paper and need not be repeated here: judgments about the weight of the scientific evidence on various empirical issues that have been raised and value-based arguments about the implications of these judgments for education policy. In this final section I will draw a few more general lessons and reflect on their implications for the work of the panel.

One general lesson is that there is less articulation between the concerns of the public and the concerns of specialists in psychological measurement than might be expected, given their common agreement on the importance of the issues. Specialists have succeeded in formulating and answering an array of specific questions regarding aspects of test validity, bias, and the like. Other questions, however, remain ill formulated or unanswered; many of the latter questions are important to the nonspecialist and figure in his or her legitimate definition of validity, bias, etc., even if they do not figure in specialists' definitions. By the same token, nonspecialists—including some who are highly knowledgeable about education policy and legal aspects of testing—have often failed to recognize scientifically important distinctions among possible interpretations of connotatively loaded terms, such as intelligence, validity, and bias.

A second lesson is that standardized ability tests, as currently conceived and constructed, will inevitably contribute to disproportionate placement of minority children in classes for mildly mentally retarded students (or classes by any other name that are designed to serve children whose prognosis for success in school is poor). The reasons for this bleak conclusion are deeply rooted in the natures of the tests, of the schools, and of society. As long as new tests are built on the same logic as old ones, namely the logic of inferring ability from achieved performance across a wide variety of specific "intellectual" tasks, they will continue to tell us what we already know—that children who grow up outside the mainstream are likely to have trouble in school. They will not help us resolve the ambiguities of potential and achievement, of nature and nurture, that plague the existing tests. There are some new, experimental approaches to testing based on Piagetian developmental theory, on direct observation of the child's learning in novel situations, and even on measures of neurological functioning, such as electroencephalograms. It is impossible to say at this juncture, however, how much hope we should pin on them. For the foreseeable future, decisions about public policy and educational practice will have to be based on tests as they are.

Fortunately, many such decisions can be made in the face of a great deal of ambiguity about the meaning of tests. This is the third and most important lesson to be drawn from this paper. Debates over validity, bias, and the causes of group differences have a hypnotic quality because of the connotations of the word "intelligence" and the specter of genetic predestination. But the debate distracts our attention from what should be our central concern, namely how to improve education, particularly for children who are not doing well in the school system as it currently exists.

It is striking that some scholars who disagree fundamentally about the nature of IQ tests, such as Jane Mercer and Arthur Jensen, are in agreement about many aspects of the proper use of tests in evaluating children for placement in classes for mentally retarded children. Both Mercer and Jensen agree that tests tell us something about a child's level of school functioning and that they deserve a place in an assessment battery. Both agree that full diagnostic assessment should take place only when children have had trouble in the classroom; tests and other assessment procedures should not be used as general screening devices. Both agree that IQ tests alone should not determine placement but should be used in tandem with information about other characteristics of the child, notably the child's capacity to function in nonschool environments and roles, and the presence of any neurological, sensory, or other physical problems. To be sure, Mercer and Jensen would disagree about using information on the child's sociocultural background to interpret or adjust IQ scores, but the areas of agreement are substantial. It seems that serious theoretical disagreements are consistent with surprisingly similar practical recommendations. If so, one can only wonder about the wisdom of dragging the theoretical disagreements into the courts.

One consequence of the current focus of debate is that judges have been forced to deliberate about scientific controversies that they are ill equipped to consider. It is not surprising that their conclusions are sometimes contradictory. But judges (and policy makers) are well equipped to consider other kinds of issues; given the ambiguous meanings of test scores, and given the consequences of placement, is it consistent with established legal standards of fairness to use tests as placement devices? Are some uses fair, while others are not? This way of framing questions puts them squarely in the court of values and legal definitions and precedents.

The consequences of placement will surely play a central role in any such deliberation. Regardless of the intrinsic merits of tests or alternative placement procedures, it is hard to justify the use of any device to sort children or prescribe educational programs, unless there are demonstrated educational benefits attached to the sorting or prescription. In *Larry P*, Judge Peckham concluded that EMR classes are "educationally dead-end, isolated and stigmatizing." Given the issues raised in the case, it was necessary for the judge to go on to examine discrimination in placement procedures; had his purpose been to decide whether schools and society were meeting their responsibilities, however, he need not have looked further. If "special" classes (particularly EMR classes) convey no special benefits and involve no remedial instruction, it is hard to justify placing any children in them, regardless of race. If minority children are overrepresented in such classes, they are being disproportionately harmed; the basis for placement doesn't much matter. If, on the other hand, special classes do convey demonstrable benefits, disproportionate placement does not represent disproportionate harm. The benefits of the classes must be weighed against their costs, e.g., the cost of separateness per se.

If we are going to fight about IQ tests (or EMR classes) we should be fighting about what they do or do not contribute to learning. Proponents should try to show that tests give information, not available through other practical means, that can be used to match instruction to children's performance. Opponents should be trying to show that there are better ways to channel children into the most effective instructional situations. If the panel can help refocus public debate in this manner, it will have done a great service.

REFERENCES

Bersoff, D. N.
  1979 Regarding psychologists testily: regulation of psychological assessment in the public schools. *Maryland Law Review* 39(1):27–120.
Cleary, T. A., Humphreys, L. G., Kendrick, S. A., and Wesman, A.
  1975 Educational uses of tests with disadvantaged students. *American Psychologist* 30:15–41.
Cole, N. S.
  1981 Bias in testing. *American Psychologist* 36:1067–1077.
Crano, W. D., Kenny, D. A., and Campbell, D. T.
  1972 Does intelligence cause achievement?: a cross-lagged panel analysis. *Journal of Educational Psychology* 63:258–275.
Cronbach, L. J., and Snow, R. E.
  1977 *Aptitudes and Instructional Methods: A Handbook for Research on Interactions.* New York: Irvington.
Farr, J. L., O'Leary, B. S., Pfeiffer, C. M., Goldstein, I. L., and Bartlett, C. J.
  1971 *Ethnic Group Membership as a Moderator in the Prediction of Job Performance: An Examination of Some Less Traditional Predictors.* AIR technical report no. 2. Washington, D.C.: American Institutes for Research.
Glaser, R., and Bond, L., guest eds.
  1981 Testing: concepts, policy, practice and research. *American Psychologist* (special issue).
Goldman, R. D., and Hartig, L. K.
  1976 The WISC may not be a valid predictor of school performance for primary-grade minority children. *American Journal of Mental Deficiency* 80(6):583–587.

Goodman, J. F.
  1977 The diagnostic fallacy: a critique of Jane Mercer's concept of mental retardation. *Journal of School Psychology* 15:197–205.
Gordon, R. A.
  1980 Examining labeling theory: the case of mental retardation. Pp. 111–174 in W. R. Gove, ed., *The Labeling of Deviance: Evaluating a Perspective.* Beverly Hills, Calif.: Sage Publications.
Green, R. L., and Farquhar, W. W.
  1965 Negro academic motivation and scholastic achievement. *Journal of Educational Psychology* 56:241–243.
Grossman, H. J., ed.
  1977 *Manual on Terminology and Classification in Mental Retardation.* American Association on Mental Deficiency. Baltimore, Md.: Garamond/Pridemark.
Hoffman, B.
  1962 *The Tyranny of Testing.* New York: Crowell-Collier.
Jencks, C., Smith, M., Acland, H., Bane, M. J., Cohen, D., Gintis, H., Heyns, B., and Michelson, S.
  1972 *Inequality: A Reassessment of the Effect of Family and Schooling in America.* New York: Basic Books.
Jensen, A. R.
  1969 How much can we boost IQ and scholastic achievement? *Harvard Educational Review* 39(1):1–123.
  1980 *Bias in Mental Testing.* New York: Free Press.
Kamin, L. J.
  1974 *The Science and Politics of IQ.* New York: John Wiley & Sons, Inc.
Kaufman, A.
  1975 Factor analysis of the WISC-R at 11 age levels between 6½ and 16½ years. *Journal of Consulting and Clinical Psychology* 43:135–147.
Klineberg, O.
  1935 *Negro Intelligence and Selective Migration.* New York: Columbia University Press.
Larry P. v. *Riles*
  1979 495 F. Supp. 926 (N. D. Cal, 1979) (decision on merits) *appeal docketed* No. 80.4027 (9th Cir., Jan. 17, 1980).
Layzer, D.
  1972 Science or superstition?: a physical scientist looks at the IQ controversy. *Cognition* 1:265–299.
Linn, R.
  1982 Ability testing: individual differences, prediction, and differential prediction. Pp. 335–388 in A. K. Wigdor and W. R. Garner, eds., *Ability Testing: Uses, Consequences, and Controversies, Vol. II.* Report of the Committee on Ability Testing, National Research Council. Washington, D.C.: National Academy Press.
Loehlin, J. C., Lindzey, G., and Spuhler, J. N.
  1975 *Race Differences in Intelligence.* San Francisco, Calif.: W. H. Freeman.
Mercer, J.
  1979 *System of Multicultural Pluralistic Assessment Technical Manual.* New York: Psychological Corporation.
  In   What is a racially and culturally nondiscriminatory test? In E. R. Reynolds and R.
  press T. Brown, eds., *Perspectives on Bias in Mental Testing.* New York: Plenum.
Messé, L. A., Crano, W. D., Messé, S. R., and Rice, W.
  1979 Evaluation of the predictive validity of tests of mental ability for classroom performance in elementary grades. *Journal of Educational Psychology* 71:233–241.

Messick, S.
   1980   Test validity and the ethics of assessment. *American Psychologist* 35:1012–1027.
Parents in Action on Special Education (PASE) v. *Hannon*
   1980   No. 74-C-3586 (N. D. Ill. 1980).
Petersen, N., and Novick, M.
   1976   An evaluation of some models for culture-fair selection. *Journal of Educational Measurement* 13:3–31.
Plomin, R., and DeFries, J. C.
   1980   Genetics and intelligence: recent data. *Intelligence* 4:15–24.
Reschly, D. J.
   1981   Psychological testing in educational classification and placement. *American Psychologist* 36:1094–1102.
Reschly, D. J., and Reschly, J. E.
   1979   Validity of WISC-R factor scores in predicting achievement and attention for four sociocultural groups. *Journal of School Psychology* 17:355–361.
Reschly, D. J., and Sabers, D. L.
   1979   Analysis of test bias in four groups with regression definition. *Journal of Educational Measurement* 16(1):1–9.
Sandoval, J.
   1979   The WISC-R and internal evidence of test bias with minority groups. *Journal of Consulting and Clinical Psychology* 47:919–927.
Sattler, J. M.
   1974   *Assessment of Children's Intelligence*. Philadelphia, Pa.: W. B. Saunders Company.
Scarr, S.
   1981   Testing *for* children: assessment and the many determinants of intellectual competence. *American Psychologist* 36:1159–1166.
Scarr, S., and Weinberg, R. A.
   1976   IQ test performance of black children adopted by white families. *American Psychologist* 31:726–739.
Schrader, W. B.
   1965   A taxonomy of expectancy tables. *Journal of Educational Measurement* 2:29–35.
Smith, E.
   1980   Test validation in the schools. *Texas Law Review* 58:1123–1159.
U.S. Department of Justice
   1980   Post-Trial Memorandum of the United States. *Amicus Curiae* brief filed in *PASE* v. *Hannon*.
Wigdor, S., and Garner, W. R., eds.
   1982   *Ability Testing: Uses, Consequences, and Controversies*. Vols. 1 and 2. Report of the Committee on Ability Testing, National Research Council, Washington, D.C.: National Academy Press.

Effects of Special Education Placement on Educable Mentally Retarded Children

KIRBY A. HELLER

Research on the effects of placement in special education programs for educable mentally retarded (EMR) children has proliferated since the passage of the Education for All Handicapped Children Act of 1975 (P.L. 94-142). In part this research represents a response to the mandate of P.L. 94-142—a need to determine whether special education services can be effectively delivered in a less restrictive setting than self-contained classrooms[1] for EMR children; whether regular classroom teachers can instruct children previously assigned to special education teachers; and whether children in the regular classroom are adversely affected when EMR students are placed in their classrooms. These questions, however, did not arise solely in response to current educational policy. They have been asked repeatedly since the introduction of special education programs into the public school system. Even Binet, whose test was used to identify children needing special instruction, warned "it will never be to one's credit to have attended a special school" (cited in Lazarson, 1975:50).

---

[1]Throughout this paper, I use the term "special education" to cover all services provided to children who have been identified and labeled in the schools. I use the terms "segregated special education," "self-contained classrooms," and "special classes" interchangeably to refer to one type of administrative arrangement within special education.

I would like to thank James Gallagher, Jay Gottlieb, Samuel Guskin, Reginald Jones, Gaea Leinhardt, Lauren Resnick, *and* Melvyn Semmel *for their thoughtful and helpful reviews of earlier drafts of this paper.*

The long-standing debate over the efficacy of special education classes reflects a tension between the perceived need for educating the EMR student in a small class with a specialized curriculum and special teacher and the concern over the effects of segregating EMR children from the mainstream in classes that include a disproportionate percentage of minority students. The justification for educating the EMR child in a special class lies in the assumed benefits derived from such a class. If placement in a special program has harmful effects or an absence of beneficial effects, then the harms associated with special placement—pejorative labeling and segregation—appear indefensible. If, however, beneficial effects follow from a special placement, such programs may be successfully defended on educational grounds. For these reasons, answers to the question of the efficacy of special programs are important not only to special educators who seek to deliver better services but also to those concerned with the civil rights of minority and mentally handicapped children.

The purpose of this paper is to review the research on the effects of programs for EMR students. This research has almost exclusively focused on the effects of setting—whether EMR children should be educated in a regular classroom or in a self-contained classroom. To a large extent it ignores the processes that occur in these settings: those that lead to effective learning and those that provide barriers to further development. I argue that the goal of research should be to identify those factors that contribute to effective learning, rather than to arbitrate a final decision on setting, which must be determined by moral and legal concerns as well as by scientific evidence.

I begin with a brief description of the early studies, known as efficacy studies, on the effects of setting. This research has been widely reviewed and criticized for its methodological shortcomings (see, e.g., Guskin and Spicker, 1968; Kirk, 1964; Semmel et al., 1979). Methodological problems are discussed here because they provide an important caveat to the interpretation of the efficacy studies and because they illustrate the difficulties inherent in evaluating effects attributable to the settings in which EMR children are placed. The remainder of this paper is devoted to a discussion of the later research on the effects of mainstreaming. Included are studies on academic achievement and social adjustment of EMR children, studies on the attitudes of other children toward their EMR peers, and studies on the attitudes of teachers toward mainstreaming and their expectations for EMR children.

The literature on the consequences of special education for EMR children is voluminous, and this paper by necessity cannot be an exhaustive review of all relevant research. My approach has been to focus on representative, frequently cited, and, whenever possible, methodologically sound research. Because of the complexities involved in investigating the effects of educational programs on children, it is possible to criticize the methodology of almost every study undertaken in this area; yet it would be unfair to say that we know nothing about the effects of alternative educational arrangements on children and simply conclude that more research is needed. To some extent, however, it is impossible to avoid the cliche of more needed research since many mainstreaming programs are new and evaluation efforts are just beginning. Rather than focus on the lack of knowledge, I have tried to emphasize the issues consistently addressed in the literature and the specific research questions that need to be studied for a better understanding of the effects of special education on EMR children.

EFFICACY STUDIES

The efficacy studies hypothesized that children in special classes would achieve at higher levels and be better adjusted than their counterparts in regular classes. In most of these early studies the special class thus represented the treatment or experimental group and the regular classroom was the control group.

The efficacy studies have been reviewed thoroughly (e.g., Cegelka and Tyler, 1970; Gardner, 1966; Guskin and Spicker, 1968; Hammons, 1972; Kaufman and Alberto, 1976; Kirk, 1964; MacMillan, 1971; MacMillan and Meyers, 1979; Meyers et al., 1980), and their results are often too briefly summarized: The academic achievement of children in special classes was found to be lower than the achievement of children remaining in regular classrooms, whereas social adjustment was often lower for children remaining in regular classrooms. The reviewers note, however, that this generalization is misleadingly simple, for the results of many studies, including one of the better known and frequently cited efforts of this period (Goldstein et al., 1965) do not adhere to this pattern. In addition, all discussion of the efficacy studies includes, by necessity, an important caution: The literature suffers from serious methodological problems.

Sampling

A major problem in the research is the choice of an appropriate comparison group against which to measure the achievement of EMR children in self-contained classrooms. A typical strategy has been to compare EMR children to students with similar IQs who were perhaps matched on other variables as well, such as social class, age, sex, and achievement test scores (e.g., Baldwin, 1958; Kern and Pfaeffle, 1963). Since random sampling was not employed, the equivalence of the two groups is in doubt. In fact, it is likely that in most cases the groups were not equivalent. Children who have been identified as needing special education services are apt to differ from those who have never been so identified. Children who have been removed from the regular classroom may exhibit behavior or adjustment problems to a greater extent than those who remained in the regular classroom. To avoid these obvious problems, other sampling techniques have been adopted: matching EMR children in special classes with children on waiting lists for placement in special classes (e.g., Mullen and Itkin, 1961) or matching EMR children in special classes with children who attended schools in districts that did not have special education programs (e.g., Cassidy and Stanton, 1959; Johnson, 1961). Although well planned, these studies did not solve the problems created by a failure to randomly assign children to treatments. One can assume that children who are placed in special education differ in fundamental ways from children who await placement. Similarly, districts that do not provide special education services are likely to differ from those that do on many characteristics other than the availability of special education programs, such as size of school, expenditures, and educational philosophy (Kaufman and Alberto, 1976). The research also suffers from problems associated with matching students on selected variables, particularly the inability to generalize from the atypical matched samples to the original unmatched samples.

Only one of the efficacy studies attempted to eliminate these problems by a random assignment of students to classrooms. Goldstein et al. (1965) tested all students entering the first grade in 20 school districts and randomly assigned all those with IQ scores below 85 to either self-contained classes with carefully designed curricula and specially trained teachers or to regular classes. The children were tested periodically during the following four years using a variety of achievement and social adjustment measures. At the end of the four years no differences were found between the two groups in IQ gains, although both groups showed significant IQ increases, primarily during the first year of school. Results from academic achievement tests were mixed, depending on the specific subject matter tested, the IQ of the children, and the actual tests used.

Sociometric measures indicated that neither group was rejected by its peers, but children in the regular classes were more likely than their special-class counterparts to interact with other neighborhood children. In a study of self-concept using the data from the Goldstein et al. project, Meyerowitz (1962) found that students in the special classes applied more self-derogatory statements to themselves than did EMR children in regular classrooms.

Despite the strength of the methodology, there is a serious weakness in the study. Children were placed in the self-contained or regular classroom on the basis of IQ alone. Although this is not a methodological problem in the study itself, it does reduce the external validity of the project. Students are not usually placed in special classes unless they have been referred by a teacher (or someone else) who notices that the child has a specific problem (see the paper by Bickel in this volume). Thus the sample of children in the special classes in the Goldstein et al. (1965) study may not be equivalent to samples of children typically found in self-contained classrooms. In fact, many of the children who were originally placed in special classrooms later had IQ scores above 85. The study reveals little about the effects of special education on children who are placed when they are older than six or effects on children who have been chosen for placement using selection criteria other than the relatively high IQ scores used in this study.

This and other studies emphasize the importance of random sampling and standardized measures of cognitive ability and achievement. Other types of research designs, which often include less quantifiable measures, are relatively neglected in the literature. This is not meant to imply that studies that include randomization are not desirable. The measures employed must match the questions asked, and not all questions require randomization. To gain a more differentiated view of the effects of special education, a wide variety of outcome measures should be used, including naturalistic observations, descriptions of services provided, and more qualitative judgments of the experiences of EMR children in special and mainstreamed classes.

INSTRUMENTATION

The validity of the four instruments most commonly used to measure achievement in the efficacy studies—the Stanford Achievement Test, the Wide Range Achievement Test, the California Achievement Test, and the Metropolitan Achievement Test—has been questioned for use in regular classes (Kaufman and Alberto, 1976). In special classes, with modified curricula and students with IQs not represented in validation samples, the validity of these instruments is even more doubtful. Instrumentation problems are even more serious in the measurement of social behaviors. Many researchers attempt to measure ill-defined constructs with instruments of unknown reliability and validity.

The instrumentation problem involves more than the use of invalid measures. It is difficult to determine which measures are appropriate when two different types of programs with nonoverlapping goals are being compared. For example, it may be more appropriate to judge the effectiveness of special classrooms on the basis of outcomes other than academic achievement, since instruction is often geared toward acquiring social and vocational skills. The differences typically found between EMR children in special and regular classrooms could simply reflect the lack of emphasis on academic subjects in special classes.

IDENTIFICATION OF TREATMENTS AND POPULATIONS

The sampling and instrumentation issues discussed above are examples of specific problems that limit the inferences that can be drawn from the efficacy studies. There are, in addition, two other, more fundamental and pervasive problems that undermine efforts to synthesize results from the efficacy research. First, studies on the effectiveness of special education fail to delineate the treatment or curriculum that is being evaluated. One cannot assume that children educated in special classes share anything besides a common administrative arrangement. Differences found among classes include class size, curricula, the materials used, the professional backgrounds of the teachers, the attitudes of the teachers, and the educational needs of the students within the classroom. To understand the effects of special classes, the actual classroom operation, the nature of teacher-student interactions, the sequencing of ideas and materials, and the consequences of treatment rather than the administrative arrangement must be identified (Gallagher, 1967; Jones et al., 1978).

A similar problem is that the studies fail to describe the children being evaluated. Children labeled EMR do not belong to one clearly identifiable group. Rather, their membership is determined by the state in which they live as well as by idiosyncratic factors associated with individual school districts. For example, states employ different criteria in the definition of mental retardation, so that a child may be eligible for EMR programs in Illinois (with no specified IQ cutoff score) but ineligible in neighboring Indiana (with an IQ cutoff score of 75) Similarly, in 1959 the American Association on Mental Deficiency (AAMD) revised its system of classification of mentally retarded children by including in the definition of mild mental retardation deficits in adaptive behavior as well as subaverage intellectual functioning (test scores between one and two standard deviations below the mean). Thus, studies done prior to this revision included samples that may have been significantly different from those that were used after the new classification system was adopted.[2]

---

[2]The AAMD again revised its classification system in 1973, eliminating the category of "borderline retardation," thereby reducing further the generalizability of studies from decade to decade.

Children with varying learning characteristics and educational needs are likely to be found in EMR classes. These may include bilingual children who need help with English, children from impoverished environments who may be lacking experience or materials that aid in school adjustment, children with motivational problems, and children with emotional problems that depress test scores (MacMillan, 1971). For these reasons, studies that focus on the effects of special and regular classes without specifying the population under study and the actual classroom operations may fail to identify significant findings and relationships.

RESEARCH IN THE POST-EFFICACY STUDY ERA: THE EFFECTS OF MAINSTREAMING

The increased role of the judiciary in special education, the growing disenchantment with segregated special classes among influential educators (Dunn, 1968; Johnson, 1962), and the attendant restructuring of the laws governing the education of handicapped children led to a renewed interest in research on the effects of special education in the 1970s. The research addressed questions similar to those of the earlier efficacy literature, but the hypotheses of the later studies reflected a different bias. Children in mainstreamed classes were now considered the experimental group and children in special classes the control. This shift was partially the result of provisions of P.L. 94-142, which require the placement of children in the least restrictive environment.

Because of persistent attacks on the earlier studies, researchers investigating the effects of mainstreaming attempted to randomly assign subjects to groups (this, of course, is not always possible nor desirable, as argued previously), to more adequately describe classroom curricula and functioning, and to utilize more sophisticated measures. To this end two methodologies have been employed: (1) large-scale planned or natural experiments, which resemble the actual conditions found in classrooms and (2) smaller-scale controlled studies, which maximize control but are limited in their applicability to real classroom conditions. The synthesis of both leads to a more complete understanding of the potential and real effects of educating EMR children in regular classrooms.

DEFINITIONS OF MAINSTREAMING

The terms "mainstreaming" or "mainstreamed classroom" have been used simply to assert that some degree of integration of handicapped and nonhandicapped students occurs in the same classroom. This unqualified usage of the concept of mainstreaming reveals little about the educational environment experienced by a handicapped child. Variations include the number of hours of integration in the regular classroom, the academic and nonacademic subjects taught in integrated settings, the types of transitional programs that are provided, the supports given to handicapped children in the regular classroom, and the teaching strategies used to accommodate handicapped children. Meyers et al. (1980) list four forms of regular-class placement for special learners, each of which is considered an example of mainstreaming:

1. The special student is in the regular class for one half of the time and is aided in a resource room or taught by a tutor for the other half.

2. The special student is in the regular class for most of the time and gets periodic help when it is needed.

3. The special student is in the regular class and gets no direct special help, but the teacher is assisted by a consultant.

4. The special student is in the regular class and gets no extra assistance.

Kaufman et al. (1975:40–41) formulated a definition of mainstreaming that has been widely adopted as a model by many special education researchers (e.g., Jones and Wilderson, 1976; MacMillan and Semmel, 1977):

Mainstreaming refers to the temporal, instructional and social integration of eligible exceptional children with normal peers, based on an ongoing individually determined educational planning and programming process and requires clarification of responsibility among regular and special education administrative, instructional, and supportive personnel.

To satisfy the criteria set forth in this definition, a handicapped child must receive more than a desk and chair in the regular classroom. The additional requirements—a sharing of responsibility among educators and instructional and social integration—are precisely the factors most difficult to implement. As a result, it is unlikely that mainstreaming, as it is currently practiced, meets the standards set forth in Kaufman et al.'s definition or that evaluations of current practices are evaluations of mainstreaming in its intended form.

Guerin and Szatlocky (1974) conducted one of the few studies that compared various models of mainstreaming programs. They identified four models of integration that were used in eight school districts in California. These models included (1) primary assignment to a special class with partial integration into regular classrooms; (2) placement in combination classes in which the EMR children were in regular but small-sized classes all day, with access to aides and supplementary materials; (3) assignment to regular classrooms in a centralized school that maintained a resource center for the regular as well as the handicapped school population (the EMR children were helped by a special education teacher who assisted the other teachers in the resource center); and (4) attendance at local schools with help from a special teacher for an hour or two a day. Guerin and Szatlocky found that the type of integration affected students' behavior in the classroom as well as the attitudes and plans of the staff. The results from this study are described in greater detail in subsequent sections.

Research on the extent of mainstreaming indicates that the percentage of time a child is instructed in the regular classroom is not necessarily based on specific information about that child. For example, Semmel et al. (1979) noted that in a large-scale study in Texas (Project PRIME), administrative considerations probably determined the child's placement and that correlations between learners' characteristics and hours of integration were quite low. Determination of the least restrictive environment frequently is inextricably tied to the child's label—e.g., if a child is labeled EMR, his or her placement is in a self-contained classroom (Stearns et al., 1979). (These findings are part of a larger pattern, discussed in the paper by Bickel in this volume, in which service availability affects types of referrals, labeling practices, and final placements.)

ACADEMIC ACHIEVEMENT OF EMR CHILDREN

This research was recently reviewed by Semmel et al. (1979) and Corman and Gottlieb (1978). The conclusions of these reviewers are strikingly similar to those reached by reviewers of the efficacy literature. Corman and Gottlieb note (p. 257):

Studies on achievement of EMR pupils in a variety of school settings reveal inconsistent results. As a whole, these studies suggest that particular instructional techniques may be of greater relevance to improved achievement than the fact that these techniques are used in one of many possible integrated settings. Unfortunately, the designs of most achievement studies have failed to isolate particular treatment methods so that it is impossible to determine which treatment components were responsible for improvement.

Exceptions to this generalization—i.e., studies that do describe the educational program—generally follow behavior modification principles. For example, Bradfield et al. (1973) studied the progress of three EMR and three educationally handicapped children placed in regular third-grade classrooms. The trained teachers took a learning center approach, emphasizing individualized instruction and behavior modification techniques. At the end of the first year, the achievement scores of the handicapped children in the regular classrooms were similar to those of children who remained in the special classrooms, but the achievement scores of the nonhandicapped children in the mainstreamed classrooms were below those of other children in regular classes. During the second year of the program, the consultants were replaced and the program was altered. The curriculum relied less on traditional textbooks, and the staff developed their own materials. The emphasis was on precision charts that indicated each child's progress and on tangible reinforcements, such as food. All work was done on an individualized basis, and cross-age tutoring was employed. After the second year, the EMR children in the fourth-grade integrated classrooms gained more than their special-class peers in reading and arithmetic. There were no differences between third-grade EMR children in the model and control programs. Fourth-grade nonhandicapped students in the model program had higher achievement scores than other nonhandicapped students in regular classes. No other differences were found between these two groups, indicating that their performance did not deteriorate when EMR children were their classmates.

Haring and Krug (1975) did not initially investigate mainstreamed classes but did study the effects of curricula based on behavior modification techniques. In this study, 48 children who had been diagnosed as mentally retarded were randomly assigned to either experimental or control classrooms. The two experimental classrooms included precision charts showing daily achievements, a highly structured reading program, and a token reinforcement system in which students could earn rewards for good behavior. Teachers specified the programs in the two control classrooms. The experimental group gained significantly more in reading and arithmetic than the control group. Following the termination of the project, 13 of the 24 children in the experimental group returned to the regular classroom. None of the children in the control classrooms was transferred.

The one-year follow-up study is more relevant to a discussion of mainstreaming. Teacher ratings of the 13 EMR students who were reintegrated into the regular programs were compared with those for nonhandicapped children in the regular classrooms. The teachers indicated that on some specific items (e.g., the student follows directions, the student has basic skills) the experimental EMR students were superior to regular-class students. None of the former special-class students was perceived to need special-class help, and 76 percent of them did not require any extra assistance. The authors concluded that children who received adequate preparation in special classes can function effectively in regular classes.

As noted previously, characteristics of children labeled EMR may be more diverse than the single label implies. It is possible, and in fact likely, that some children labeled EMR may profit from instruction in the regular classroom, while others may advance under the conditions offered in special classes. A study described earlier (Goldstein et al., 1965) found that children with borderline IQs (in this case, 80–85) in regular classrooms had slightly although not significantly higher reading, arithmetic, and basic social information achievement test scores than did the equivalent IQ group in the special classes. The opposite pattern was found for children with IQ scores lower than 80. Children in this IQ range in the special classes had higher achievement test scores than did the children in the regular classes.

Budoff and Gottlieb (1976) studied the interaction between educational placement and "learning potential"—the ability to use prior training to solve new tasks. EMR children were divided into two groups: those that had high learning potential and those that exhibited low learning potential. Half the children in each group were randomly assigned to segregated classrooms or integrated programs supplemented by remedial learning centers. Achievement test scores as well as data from other measures were collected during the spring prior to placement, two months after the beginning of the school year, and at the end of the school year. Results indicated that the students with high learning potential had higher arithmetic and reading test scores than did the children with low learning potential at all three times of measurement. No differences were found between children in the two placement groups on achievement test scores.

The studies described above, with the exception of the older Goldstein et al. study, were experimental in design, using small samples and few classrooms. A different strategy, possible because of large-scale changes in special education following the implementation of P.L. 94-142 and revised state regulations, would be to monitor the effects of districts' efforts to educate EMR children in less restrictive environments.

One example is the Texas PRIME project (Kaufman et al., in press), which was based on a naturally occurring change in special education in Texas. Districts were required to choose either self-contained classrooms for EMR students or adopt mainstreaming plans. Anglo, Chicano, and black children in grades 3, 4, and 5 in special and regular classes were studied. Considerable data were collected concerning the types of programs into which children were placed, the percentage of class time that was integrated, the amount of one-to-one instruction, and the types of instruction provided. Although the final report has not yet been published, drafts indicate that the scores of the mainstreamed EMR students were roughly equivalent to those of the nonmainstreamed EMR students on various standardized achievement tests. The scores of both groups of EMR students were below those of the regular students.

A second study, capitalizing on changes in the special education system in California, followed students who, after reassessment, were returned to regular classrooms (Meyers et al., 1975). Students who were decertified under new state guidelines were compared with EMR children who were not decertified and a matched group of regular students. The regular students were chosen from the classrooms of the decertified students and were in the lower half of the class in achievement. Although the EMR students and the decertified students had similar IQ and achievement test scores at the time of the original placement in special classes, at the time of decertification the EMR students had lower IQs (and therefore were not returned to the regular classroom). On mathematics and reading achievement tests, the regular students had the highest scores, the EMR students had the lowest, and the decertified students fell between the two. There tended to be greater differences between the decertified and the EMR students than between the regular and the decertified students. Teacher grades were similar for the decertified and the regular students. Both decertified and regular students were several years below grade level.

The results from the studies reviewed can be interpreted according to one's expectations about mainstreaming. If one expects mainstreaming to be the panacea for all of special education's ills, clearly the results are disappointing. The two large-scale studies discussed here indicate that the EMR children may be progressing in the regular classroom but are still behind their peers, who themselves are not achieving at grade level. In fact, the most consistent finding from the studies reviewed is the rather poor prognosis for EMR children, whether in a special or a regular class. In their review of the literature, Semmel et al. (1979) note that mean reading scores of EMR pupils never reached a grade level beyond 4.0. A mainstreamed setting may be at least as effective as a segregated setting, but under either condition the reading skills of the children are deficient.

The studies reviewed also highlight the need to determine individuals' strengths and weaknesses rather than rely on a global label. Why, for example, did some students in the California decertification study (Meyers et al., 1975), who were originally quite similar on test scores to the EMR population, progress so that they were able to return to the regular classroom? The authors hypothesize that the decertified students might have had an enriched or stimulating home environment, yet this does not explain the initial low IQ of the decertified children. It also is possible that the decertified students improved because of their prior educational experiences in the special class. Identification of the factors that led to the improvement of the decertified students is critical.

Social Adjustment

Research on the social adjustment of EMR children who are mainstreamed into regular classrooms has focused on two general areas: the self-concept of the mainstreamed students and their attitudes toward learning and school. The commonly held belief, based on the early efficacy studies, is that attitudes about self and school suffer when EMR children remain in the regular classroom because of their obvious inferiority to their non-EMR peers. As noted previously, these studies are methodologically weak and the finding is an oversimplification at best.

In an attempt to specify one aspect of self-concept that should be affected by classroom placement, Schurr et al. (1972) measured the self-concept of ability in children four times during their first year of special education. The Michigan State University Self-Concept of Academic Ability Scale, used extensively in research by Brookover and his colleagues (Brookover and Erickson, 1975), indicates perception of one's ability to achieve on a task compared with others engaged in the same task. This measure has been found to be correlated with academic achievement, even when social class, intelligence, past achievement, and the expectations of others were controlled. However, the measure had not been used previously with EMR children.

Across the four times of measurement there was an increase in scores. In the second year of the study, seven children were reassigned to the regular class. The self-concept of ability of these children decreased, while that of those remaining in the special class continued to increase. This study highlights the importance of the children's comparison (or reference) group.

Strang et al. (1978) directly assessed the effect of the reference group on self-concept. Elementary school children who had been randomly chosen to participate in a partially integrated program were compared with children remaining in special classes by using the Piers-Harris self-concept scale. Self-concept was measured prior to mainstreaming, one month after mainstreaming and at the end of the school year. The children in the integrated classes had higher adjusted self-concept scores than the children who remained in the special classes. The authors hypothesized that the augmentation of self-concept could be due to one of two factors. The children in integrated programs may have been using multiple reference groups to evaluate their performance. Alternatively, the children in the mainstreamed classes may have interpreted their change in placement as an indication of success, which affected their self-concept.

To further understand the importance of reference groups, a second study was conducted. Children who were partially integrated into regular classes were randomly assigned to experimental or control groups. Both groups completed the Piers-Harris scale before mainstreaming and six weeks after mainstreaming. To increase the salience of the regular-class placement the experimental group was told to compare their performance with their non-EMR classmates. Consistent with hypotheses, the scores of the experimental group decreased and the scores of the control group increased (replicating the results of the first study). This study has interesting implications for mainstreaming. Programs that are based on partial integration, in which the EMR child interacts with EMR as well as non-EMR peers, allow the child to choose among multiple reference groups and select similar others (i.e., EMR children) as a comparison group, while disregarding dissimilar others (i.e., non-EMR children). In contrast, the entirely mainstreamed child may have a single reference group, one that is superior in many realms of behavior.

Two studies reviewed in the section on academic achievement also contain information about self-concept and attitudes toward school. Budoff and Gottlieb (1976) investigated the effects of class placement and learning potential on academic self-concept, attitudes toward school, and locus of control. After one year the children in integrated classrooms were more internally motivated and felt more positive about themselves and toward school than did the EMR children in self-contained classrooms. There was also an interaction between learning potential and placement. Children high in learning potential in integrated classrooms were more positive about school and themselves than children high in learning potential in segregated classrooms; children low in learning potential in segregated classrooms felt more positive about school and themselves than did children low in learning potential in integrated classrooms. Thus, the effects of placement are mediated by certain student characteristics.

Adjustment also was investigated in the California decertification study (Yoshida et al., 1976) and in Project PRIME (Kaufman et al., in press). The Project PRIME data indicate that EMR children in both settings as well as the non-EMR children had roughly equivalent academic self-concepts, feelings of isolation, and attitudes toward school.

The California decertification study obtained information from student files on attendance and on whether the student had dropped out of or had graduated from school. They found that more decertified students than EMR students graduated from school in two of the eight districts studied. Adjustment, as defined by remaining or dropping out of school, was similar for the two groups in the other six districts.

The results from these studies are clearly contradictory. Some show positive effects on social adjustment due to mainstreaming, some show negative effects, and some show no effects at all. Even the Budoff and

Gottlieb (1976) study, perhaps the most comprehensive and methodologically sound of all those reviewed, contains a critical shortcoming: While the students who were integrated into regular classrooms were placed in different classrooms with many teachers, the special-class children were all placed in one class with one teacher. The results could, therefore, be due to the behavior of the specific teacher rather than to the effects of placement in a self-contained classroom.

Under any conditions the measurement of self-concept is difficult and elusive. It is not surprising that results from studies using different measures and special populations do not converge. In addition, it is perhaps naive to expect that current educational placement, to the exclusion of a child's history of success and failure, will singularly modify self-concept or other deep-rooted attitudes toward learning. Perhaps the only conclusion that can be reached at present is that mainstreaming does not necessarily lead to a lowered self-concept and that other school and home factors probably have more powerful effects on a child's adjustment than does the influence of classroom setting alone.

SPECIAL EDUCATION PLACEMENT AND THE MINORITY CHILD

As mentioned previously, controversy over special education placement stems in part from concern about the overrepresentation of minorities in EMR programs. Studies of this problem typically have focused on the issues of assessment and placement (see Jones, 1976; see also the papers by Bickel and Travers in this volume) rather than the effects of special education programs for different subgroups of students. For example, the research reviewed in the previous sections often did not include descriptions of the racial composition of the samples; when this information was given, race was not used as an independent variable in analyzing the data.

If a greater percentage of minority children than white children are inappropriately placed in EMR programs, one might hypothesize that mainstreaming and the provision of less intensive remedial help may be more likely to benefit (or less likely to harm) minority students than white students. Data on this issue are not available. A related question for which data are available concerns the degree of integration (e.g., the number of hours or percentage of time in which a student is mainstreamed) for minority versus white children. In an analysis of Project PRIME data, Gottlieb et al. (1976) found that Chicano children were more likely than Anglos to receive reading, arithmetic, and nonacademic instruction in the regular classroom. These findings may reflect the fact that Anglo children had more severe disabilities and therefore were viewed as inappropriate candidates for mainstreaming; alternatively, greater political pressure may have resulted in the mainstreaming of the Chicano children.

Along with monitoring of the extent of mainstreaming and the impact of mainstreaming on disproportion in EMR programs, research is needed to document the effects of alternative educational placements on the academic performance and social adjustment of minority children. Although one goal of current mainstreaming efforts may be to decrease the disproportion of minorities in EMR programs, careful study is needed before one can conclude that any resultant reduction of disproportion necessarily implies that minority children are receiving a more appropriate education.

EFFECTS OF MAINSTREAMING ON NON-EMR CHILDREN

Effects on Academic Achievement

There has been almost no research on the effects of mainstreaming on non-EMR children's academic achievement, despite the fears of many critics that placing EMR children in regular classrooms will adversely affect the other children's learning. For example, opponents of mainstreaming believe that teachers will have to spend a disproportionate amount of time with the slower learners, neglecting the average and above-average students. Neither the Project PRIME data nor related research on the frequencies of interactions that teachers initiate with children of low versus high ability within a classroom, however, supports this hypothesis. While extreme variation exists among teachers, children of high ability are generally not ignored because of teachers' attentiveness to the slower learning students (Brophy and Good, 1974; Wang, in press).

Only one study reviewed investigated the achievement of non-EMR children in a mainstreamed setting (Bradfield et al., 1973); the results were summarized in a previous section. After the first year of an experimental program, the non-EMR children in the model program were adversely affected compared with a control group not involved in any special program. These negative effects could have been due to the presence of EMR children in the classroom or some aspect of the experimental program that may not have been appropriate for average and above-average students. After the second year, however, the achievement of the children in the model program was equal to or better than that of children in the control groups.

No conclusions about this important phenomenon can be based on the results of one sketchily described study. It does emphasize the need to investigate further this variable as well as the mediators of positive or negative effects of mainstreaming (e.g., changes in teachers' behaviors, changes in regular students' behaviors as a result of mainstreaming).

Effects of Labels

This research is only marginally relevant to an understanding of children's attitudes toward their EMR peers. Most of the studies use stories, audiotapes, or videotapes to portray labeled or unlabeled hypothetical children, rather than ask the children to rate people they actually know. Thus, the research indicates how children in regular classrooms might react to the integration of handicapped and labeled children into their classrooms rather than describing how they actually feel or behave.

The effects of labeling on children's attitudes and perceptions stem from a vast literature based in sociological, psychological, and educational theory. A review of this research is beyond the scope of this paper, but an excellent synthesis and critique can be found in an article by MacMillan et al. (1974).[3]

One issue that is relevant to an understanding of the effects of mainstreaming involves differentiating the effects of the behavior that led to the issuance of the label from the effects of the label itself (e.g., Budoff and Siperstein, 1978; Gottlieb, 1974, 1975a; Strichart and Gottlieb, 1975). Two conflicting hypotheses are plausible. First, the label may serve a protective function, resulting in more tolerant behavior by the non-EMR child to the potentially negative or unusual behavior of an EMR-labeled peer. Similarly, standards may be more lenient when judging an EMR child. Or in contrast, the label may exacerbate a child's reaction to the behavior of an EMR classmate. Inappropriate behaviors may be perceived more negatively, and positive behaviors may be misinterpreted.

The results of the research are affected by a number of factors: the behavior displayed by the actor and its congruence with the label, the sex and social class of the respondents, and the dependent measures used. In a typical study, children see a videotape or hear an audiotape of an actor performing a task either competently or incompetently. They are told that

---

[3]In this article the authors conclude that currently available data do not support the assertion that the mentally retarded label by itself has detrimental or long-lasting effects. In research, as in reality, labeling is confounded with different classroom experiences and interactions with significant others. For example, do children labeled mentally retarded have lower self-esteem? This is impossible to determine since those who are labeled are also in special classes and are treated differently by parents, peers, and teachers. Labeling initiates a chain of events that has a cumulative effect; therefore, it is impossible to isolate the consequences of the label itself.

the actor is either mentally retarded or are given little or no information about the actor and are asked to rate the actor by a series of adjectives or to indicate how much they want to be friends with the actor. Gottlieb (1974) found that labels did not affect the ratings of children from either an affluent suburb or a low-income urban neighborhood. The children in the middle-class sample had more positive attitudes toward competent than incompetent spellers regardless of the label. However, when subjects in the urban sample saw a videotape of a black rather than a white actor, neither levels of competence nor labeling affected their attitudes. A replication of this study using slightly different dependent measures (as well as different age groups and audiotapes rather than videotapes) revealed that subjects were equally positive toward labeled and unlabeled competent spellers but that boys were more negative toward incompetent, unlabeled spellers than were girls (Budoff and Siperstein, 1978).

When aggression rather than competence in spelling was the target behavior, an EMR child was rated less positively than an unlabeled child, and an actor behaving in a socially appropriate manner was rated more favorably than an actor behaving aggressively (Gottlieb, 1975a).

Freeman and Algozzine (1980) hypothesized that labeling effects could be diminished if positive behaviors were made salient. Fourth-grade children from middle to low socioeconomic status groups observed a videotape of a boy engaging in a variety of academic tasks as well as in free play. They were told he was either mentally retarded, learning disabled, or emotionally disturbed or that he was not given a label. After seeing a portion of the tape the children completed questionnaires revealing their perceptions of the actor. The investigators either described positive attributes of the actor or presented nonevaluative information. After viewing the latter part of the videotape, in which the actor behaved more negatively, the children completed a second series of ratings.

Labels had no effects on ratings. Children who were not told about the positive attributes assigned lower ratings to the boy on the videotape than those who had heard the positive description. Children who knew of the actor's positive attributes did not alter their ratings after viewing the end of the videotape, despite the actor's seemingly negative behaviors. The authors suggested that assigning positive attributes to an actor can offset the effects of negative behavior if the information provided is credible. Labels can lose their effects in the context of salient and believable behaviors.

A study by Foley (1979) illustrates the influence of teachers' reactions on students' attitudes. Fourth-grade children in a rural town saw a videotape of either a positive or negative reaction from a teacher to the academic and social behaviors of a child labeled mentally retarded, learning disabled, or average. Children were more accepting of actors who elicited positive rather than negative reactions from the teacher. Surprisingly, the acceptance scores were highest for actors labeled mentally retarded.

In summary, with the exception of one study (Gottlieb, 1975a) the results consistently indicated that children do not respond negatively to a peer labeled mentally retarded and that the actor's behavior is a more influential determinant of children's ratings. Generalizations to actual classroom situations must be made cautiously, however. First, characteristics of the population and of the behaviors exhibited influence the effects of labels. In addition, the paradigm used is rather contrived since the experimenter overtly assigns a label to the target child. Subjects in the studies may feel compelled to apply (which in these cases may mean to ignore) this information by behaving tolerantly or in a socially appropriate and desirable manner in front of an adult experimenter. The results from the study by Foley (1979) are otherwise difficult to interpret. Is it possible that these children truly preferred mentally retarded children in their reading groups, in their classrooms, and as partners? Children's behaviors in the classroom toward EMR peers may be less affected by the desire to behave in a socially desirable way, unless the teacher is watching. The salience of the label in the classroom probably is continually shifting, depending on the behaviors exhibited. Thus, the findings from the research reviewed above need to be validated in the classroom.

Social Acceptance of EMR Children by Their Non-EMR Peers

Numerous studies have established that mentally retarded children are less socially accepted than are nonretarded children by their nonretarded peers (Baldwin, 1958; Gottlieb, 1978; Hartup, 1970; Johnson, 1950). This consistent finding is a special case of the positive correlation that is found between IQ and social status, as measured by sociometric instruments (Dentler and Mackler, 1962; Hartup, 1970). What is less clear is the precise relationship between mental retardation and social status. Some reports suggest that the mentally retarded child is simply isolated from nonretarded peers (Lapp, 1957; Sheare, 1974); others suggest that the mentally retarded child is actually rejected (Gottlieb, 1978; Johnson, 1950) or barely tolerated (Morrison, 1981). Because the measures used differ in the various studies, the results cannot be easily synthesized. For example, some investigators used nomination measures (e.g., "Who is your best friend?" "With whom would you like to be grouped in a sports activity?"), while others used semantic differentials or rating scales (e.g., "How much do you like to play with _____?").

What factors account for the generally low sociometric position held by

EMR children? One possible cause of their low social status is that children in regular classes lack knowledge of and familiarity with mentally retarded children. A hypothesis frequently offered is that children who have had interactions with mentally retarded children have more positive attitudes toward them (e.g., Christoplos and Renz, 1969; Goodman et al., 1972). Obviously, the nature of the interactions should influence the effects of contact. If mainstreamed EMR children are disruptive or act bizarrely in the regular classroom, contact should lead to negative attitudes toward EMR children. Alternatively, the better-behaved EMR children may be those who are chosen for reintegration, and their behavior may be more conforming than those children remaining in the special classes (Gottlieb, 1975b).

The research thus far on this issue reveals that integrated EMR children are not more accepted than EMR children remaining in special classes (Goodman et al., 1972; Gottlieb and Davis, 1973; Morrison, 1981; Rucker et al., 1969; Strauch, 1970), although there are some exceptions to this pattern (Leinhardt and Leinhardt, in press; Sheare, 1974).[4]

Gottlieb et al. (1978) studied the effects of perceived misbehavior by and academic ability of EMR children in integrated classrooms on their non-EMR peers' (and teachers') ratings of social acceptance and rejection. Teachers and students completed questionnaires in which they nominated the children who were most disruptive (e.g., "Who does the teacher have to scold all the time?") and those who were low in achievement (e.g., "Who never knows the answers in class?"), and scores were derived for each EMR student from these ratings. Each EMR student also received a score of social acceptance and rejection as rated by his or her classmates. The measure used was a sociometric scale called "How I Feel Toward Others." Subjects colored in either a smiling face, a straightmouthed face, a frowning face, or a question mark (to signify unfamiliarity) to indicate their feelings toward each of their classmates. Ratings of cognitive ability by teachers and peers related to social acceptance scores, while ratings of misbehavior by teachers and peers related to social rejection scores.[5]

---

[4]In a reanalysis of Project PRIME data on social acceptance, Leinhardt and Leinhardt (in press) found that mainstreaming did have a positive effect on the attractiveness of the mainstreamed EMR child. They emphasize the importance of using a multivariate approach to the study of social acceptance and caution that univariate analyses may lead to erroneous conclusions.

[5]These results were not replicated by MacMillan and Morrison (1980). However, their study was conducted with EMR children in special classes. The authors discuss the importance of considering the characteristics of the setting and rater when interpreting results.

This study suggests that EMR children's misbehavior in the classroom may cause their lower social status and that brighter EMR children may be more accepted by their peers. Only a few studies have tested this hypothesis by including naturalistic observations of children's behaviors in mainstreamed classrooms. Two studies by Gottlieb and his colleagues investigated the effects of classroom placement and IQ on classroom behavior (Gampel et al., 1974; Gottlieb et al., 1975). In one study, EMR children were randomly assigned to self-contained or integrated classrooms, and these two groups were compared to children with low IQ scores who had never been identified for placement in a special class as well as to children with average IQs (Gampel et al., 1974). They found that the EMR children in the self-contained classrooms more frequently displayed hostile and aggressive behaviors than did the other three groups, which did not differ. In a similar study, Gottlieb et al. (1975) compared students who were randomly assigned to integrated or self-contained programs. Both groups were infrequently hostile, but the integrated EMR children engaged in prosocial behavior more frequently.

Observations in classrooms participating in the Project PRIME study yielded similar results. All groups of learners—mainstreamed EMR children, nonmainstreamed EMR children, and non-EMR children—displayed similar levels of cooperative and friendly behaviors and antisocial actions.

Guerin and Szatlocky (1974) conducted classroom observations in schools with different mainstreaming models, using Spaulding's Coping Analysis Schedule for Educational Settings (see Simon and Boyer, 1967). They observed each child for only about five minutes, and their data therefore can be considered only suggestive. They found very few behavioral differences between EMR children and other children. Students in programs that were integrated for most of the day were more self-directed than those in programs with limited integration.

Although these results are based on only a few small-scale studies, they indicate that mainstreamed EMR children do not misbehave in the classroom and that there are very few behavioral differences between EMR and other children. Differences in behavior may be more subtle or occur infrequently and remain undetected by the observational systems that were used.

Efforts have been made to alter the social skills and status of mentally retarded children. This research, recently reviewed by Gresham (1981), is primarily derived from social learning theory and uses such techniques as token reinforcement programs, differential reinforcement of behaviors other than the target response (presumably a negative behavior), removing the child from a reinforcing situation, modeling, coaching, and self-control training. The social skills of handicapped children improve under each of these approaches, although little is known about the maintenance and generalization of effects following termination of the intervention.

Four studies have specifically attempted to increase social acceptance by manipulating events in the EMR child's social environment (Aloia et al., 1978; Ballard et al., 1977; Chennault, 1967; Rucker and Vincenzo, 1970). For example, when group activities were organized and low-status EMR children were assigned to groups that included higher-status EMR peers, the sociometric scores of the low-status children improved more than those of the EMR children who did not participate in the group activity (Chennault, 1967). However, when Rucker and Vincenzo (1970) tried to replicate the Chennault findings with low-status EMR children and high-status non-EMR children, they found that the gains in social status were not sustained for more than one month.

Ballard et al. (1977) studied the effects of EMR children's participation in a group activity on acceptance (using a forced-choice sociometric instrument) of the EMR children by their non-EMR peers. Groups of four to six children planned and executed a cooperative multimedia project. Each group included one mainstreamed EMR child, and the acceptance of this child improved after participation in the group, even among classmates who were not originally members of the group.

Finally, after providing non-EMR children with information concerning the competencies of an EMR child in a game-playing situation, Aloia et al. (1978) found that the EMR children were more accepted by their peers.

Taken together, the studies reviewed do not indicate that mainstreaming alone has a positive effect on the acceptance of EMR children in the regular classroom. The picture is not entirely gloomy, however. First, a distinction can be made between methods that assess friendship and those that assess general acceptance. In an analysis of various sociometric measures, Asher and Taylor (in press) noted that handicapped children often are not chosen on measures that tap "best friendship" but that general acceptance rating scales reveal less negative pictures of the handicapped child's sociometric position. For example, the Project PRIME data revealed that nearly all of the mainstreamed EMR children were accepted by at least three of their non-EMR peers. In addition, there is considerable overlap in sociometric scores between EMR and non-EMR children (Gottlieb, 1981; Iano et al., 1974). It is important for research to focus on the types and quality of friendships and social networks that mentally retarded children may have rather than to simply rely on their sociometric position in class. A more differentiated view of the relationship between behavior and social acceptance is also needed. For example, a non-EMR child may not want an EMR peer as a spelling partner or as the baseball captain but may choose to sit with the same child on the bus. Children may not hold uniformly accepting or rejecting attitudes across all situations, since differing contexts may elicit differentiated behaviors from EMR children. Finally, sociometric status can be altered by certain group activities and by training social skills. Thus placement in a mainstreamed setting does not necessarily doom an EMR child to permanent social rejection.

EFFECTS OF MAINSTREAMING ON TEACHERS

As for most educational innovations, it is the teachers who are ultimately responsible for the success or failure of proposed changes in programming. Despite expressed concern about the ability and willingness of regular classroom teachers to adapt and cope with handicapped children in their classrooms, little research has been directed toward understanding the effects of mainstreaming on teachers.

The existing literature can be divided into two categories: survey studies on teachers' attitudes toward mainstreaming and the effects of labeling on teachers' expectations for EMR children. The first category clearly is relevant to the concerns of this paper. However, this research does not provide an in-depth investigation of teachers' feelings and behaviors as they are affected by mainstreaming. The usefulness of research in the second category is based on an important but debatable assumption; namely, that teachers' expectations ultimately influence the behaviors of children. In fact, one of the major criticisms directed at special education, emphasized by Dunn (1968), is that special classes are dead-end placements precisely because of the low expectations that teachers hold for EMR children.

Effects of Teachers' Expectations

The effects of teachers' expectations on children's achievement are less clear-cut than Dunn's (1968) original description. Rosenthal and Jacobson's (1968) book *Pygmalion in the Classroom* sparked considerable interest in research on teachers' expectations, demonstrating that children who were expected by teachers to show intellectual gains did, in fact, show them. Much criticism has followed publication of this study (Elashoff and Snow, 1971; Thorndike, 1968), and the results have been difficult to replicate. To briefly summarize the great deal of research that has been done in this area, it is fair to say that teachers' expectations are related to teachers' behaviors toward their students as well as to students' behaviors (e.g., Brophy and Good, 1974; Cooper, 1979; Rothbart et al., 1971; Rubovits and Maehr, 1971). Whether teachers' expectations directly cause achievement gains or losses is less clear. Teachers' expectations in the classroom may reflect actual differences in achievement as well as cause them, and the direction of causality is difficult to ascertain. Studies that measure naturally occurring expectations in the classroom cannot tease out the causal agent in the relationship between expectations and achievement. Studies in which expectations are artificially created before any interactions occur in the classroom have not shown consistent effects on students' achievement.

What are the effects of labeling children as mentally retarded on teachers' perceptions of or expectations for their students? Salvia et al. (1973) showed videotapes of children performing various tasks to students in regular and special education programs. The children were labeled mentally retarded, gifted, or normal. Subjects also rated a hypothetical child who was supposed to be a typical mentally retarded, normal, or gifted child. Responses to the stereotype were most affected by labeling. The students responded least favorably to their stereotypes of a mentally retarded child. In contrast, the label mentally retarded had few effects on the ratings of the children portrayed in the videotape. In a similar study, Yoshida and Meyers (1975) found no effects for labels. Subjects changed their expectations when the performance of the child on the videotape improved, indicating that reliance on the label was reduced when other cues (i.e., actual behavior) were present.

Several researchers have investigated teachers' attributions of hypothetical academic performance by children labeled EMR. Severance and Gasstrom (1977) found that subjects rated ability and task difficulty as more important causes of failure for mentally retarded children than for normal children, while effort was perceived as a more important cause of success for the mentally retarded children. They also believed that normal children were more likely to succeed in the future than were mentally retarded children and that past success was more influential in predicting future success for normal children. Similarly, Palmer (1979) found that when teachers were told that EMR, educationally handicapped (EH), or normal children were performing below grade level, the teachers perceived that lack of ability was more influential in determining performance for EMR children than for EH or normal children. Information about labels, however, was not applied when subjects were told that children were performing at grade level. Palmer also asked the teachers to recommend remedial programs and placements for the hypothetical children. Teachers initially prescribed more remedial programs and settings for the EMR and EH children than for the normal children, but as they continued to receive consistent feedback about the child's performance (the child performed either at grade level or below grade level at three points in time), instructional recommendations converged for the three groups of children. Thus, subjects differentially interpreted and applied information about children's initial performance for normal versus handicapped students, but the labels lost significance when information about current performance was consistently given to the teachers.

Using a different approach to the study of teachers' expectations, Meyen and Hieronymous (1970) asked special education teachers and curriculum specialists to determine the appropriate time in the child's schooling at which various skills should be introduced into the curriculum. Subjects indicated that most of the academic skills should be introduced into the EMR curriculum when children were approximately 11 through 14 years old. A sample of 1,405 students between the ages of 9 and 18 was also tested on the various items, and most of the EMR children achieved these skills between the ages of 12 and 15. In contrast, the same skills were acquired by non-EMR children by age 8. Thus, a seven-year lag often separated the achievement of EMR and non-EMR children. The authors speculated that the poor performance of the EMR children was only partially due to their slower intellectual development; it also reflected low expectations by teachers for their EMR students' attainment of the skills, which resulted in a relatively late introduction of the skills into the curriculum. Similar low expectations by special education teachers for reading achievement in EMR students have been demonstrated (Heintz, 1974).

Mainstreamed children participating in Project PRIME sensed their teacher's low expectations (Velman, 1973, cited in Brophy and Good, 1974). EMR students thought that teachers made fewer cognitive demands and expected less of them than their nonhandicapped classmates.

This body of research does not directly assess the effects of labels on teachers' behaviors in their classrooms and their attitudes toward EMR students.[6] It suggests, however, that teachers' expectations can affect their perceptions of children as well as the instructional strategies they use. The relationship between labels and teachers' attitudes and behaviors is not a simple or straightforward one. A label elicits many attitudes and feelings. In the research cited, the term mentally retarded connoted low ability rather than other transient factors as a cause of failure and led to initial low expectations for performance. Yet these expectations and attributions are not irreversible. Teachers change their expectations when

---

[6]Only one study was found in which observations of teachers' behaviors toward EMR and non-EMR children were conducted (Raber and Weisz, 1981). The EMR children received more negative feedback than non-EMR students; in addition, the patterns of feedback received by EMR children were those that often lead to learned helplessness in children. While the differences in teachers' behavior may have been due to differences between the groups, the authors selected the samples in ways that would minimize such differences.

behavior changes, and the label loses its salience when conflicting behavior is exhibited.

Teachers' Attitudes Toward Mainstreaming

Findings from studies that assess teachers' attitudes toward mainstreaming are inconsistent. Regular classroom teachers participating in the California decertification study (Meyers et al., 1975) experienced no particular problems with the decertified mainstreamed students in their classes, and only 29 percent mentioned that the decertified students needed additional assistance (e.g., different materials, assistance from aides). Only a few thought that the decertified students were disruptive. Their views of the accompanying transitional programs that were supposed to aid the decertified students were less positive. Less than half the teachers thought the transitional programs were helpful, and more than one third reported that no special help was given. Only 85 of the 262 regular-class teachers found the transitional programs useful.

Results from Project PRIME were similar. Teachers of mainstreamed classes had generally favorable attitudes toward mainstreaming and thought the appropriate placement for most EMR children was a regular classroom with added instruction in a resource room. Although a majority of the teachers received some form of supportive services (in-service training, consultation, education plans, special materials), they felt in general that these services were only somewhat effective.

The importance of supportive services was highlighted in a study of 941 regular-class teachers in New England (Larrivee and Cook, 1979). Teachers' attitudes generally were positive, and the availability of extra resources and administrative support had a significant impact on their attitudes toward mainstreaming. Guerin and Szatlocky (1974) also found that the teachers of mainstreamed classes had positive attitudes toward the integration of EMR students into the regular classroom. Only 19 percent of the teachers had negative views. Teachers in the same schools had similar attitudes, especially the regular-class teacher and the special-class teachers with whom he or she worked. For example, if the teacher in a resource room was opposed to mainstreaming, the regular-class teacher working with this individual also was likely to be opposed to mainstreaming. The authors also noted that the type of program adopted was based on the attitudes of the staff rather than on the behavior or abilities of the children. Thus, children attending totally integrated programs were not necessarily more advanced than children who attended resource rooms and were only partially integrated into regular classrooms.

In contrast, Shotel et al. (1972) studied the attitudes of regular-class teachers before and after a resource room model was introduced into their schools. Their attitudes were compared with those of teachers in schools that maintained self-contained classrooms. Before the resource-room program began, teachers in those schools had attended orientation meetings about the goals and philosophies of the program. The teachers in the schools that were mainstreamed initially had less negative attitudes toward mainstreaming (63 percent disapproved of placing handicapped children in regular classrooms with resource-room help) than did teachers in schools with self-contained classrooms (93 percent disapproved of mainstreaming). At the end of the year the attitudes of the teachers in the schools that were mainstreamed became even more negative (87 percent did not favor mainstreaming). Integration of students into the regular class thus had adverse effects on teachers' attitudes.

Gickling and Theobold (1975) questioned regular- and special-class teachers in Tennessee about their attitudes toward mainstreaming. In this study, 85 percent of the regular-class teachers and 82 percent of the special-class teachers recommended the use of resource rooms for EMR students. However, 46 percent of the regular-class teachers and 42 percent of the special-class teachers also recommended the use of self-contained classrooms for EMR children. Thus, some teachers seemed to favor both options, perhaps indicating that mainstreaming is appropriate for some students, while self-contained classrooms are better for others.

The research reviewed above just begins to tap the effects of mainstreaming on teachers. Many questions remain unexplored. What are the major problems that teachers experience? Which children are best suited for mainstreaming? What types of children have problems in regular classrooms? What kinds of special assistance would be helpful to teachers? Before the consequences of mainstreaming on children can be assessed, the effects on teachers, who mediate program success or failure, must be understood.

Factors Affecting the Implementation of Mainstreaming

The regular classroom is probably not the appropriate placement for all EMR children. How does one differentiate between those children who will adapt well to mainstreaming and those who will not? There has been surprisingly little research addressing this question. Budoff and Gottlieb (1976) provided some relevant evidence when they investigated the interaction of classroom placement (integrated versus self-contained classrooms) and levels of learning potential. On most achievement and motivational variables, children high in learning potential scored higher than children low in learning potential. As noted previously, children with high learning potential in integrated classrooms had more positive attitudes about school and themselves and were more reflective than the equivalent group of children in self-contained classrooms. Children with low learning potential in integrated classrooms, however, had less positive attitudes about school and themselves than did the children with low learning potential in self-contained classrooms. Thus, EMR children who have the ability to use past experiences to solve new tasks may be better suited to a regular class than children low in this ability.

The authors of the California decertification study (Meyers et al., 1975) attempted to identify variables that could predict which children would eventually be decertified. They found no differences (between children who retained the EMR label and those who were later decertified) at initial time of placement into EMR classes on IQ scores; grades in reading, mathematics, and citizenship in the regular classrooms before EMR placement; or in comments made by teachers or psychologists concerning adjustment problems. Their results indicate that for reasons not yet identified, the educational prognosis of some children improves, while the performance of others with similar characteristics at the time of original placement is less likely to warrant a change in status. Thus, continual re-evaluations and an openness to the possibility of changing children's placements are necessary.

Changes in the composition of EMR populations may also affect the likelihood of mainstreaming for those children who now receive the EMR label. The last few years have witnessed a significant decline in the number of children labeled EMR. In addition, fear of litigation may be reshaping the EMR population in several states (e.g., California), so that children labeled EMR may be more disabled than children with this label in other, less litigious states (MacMillan and Borthwick, 1980; MacMillan and Semmel, 1977).

Characteristics other than those pertaining to the child may also facilitate or hinder effective mainstreaming. These include the attitudes and practices of teachers (reviewed above), attitudes of administrators (Guerin and Szatlockly, 1974; Larrivee and Cook, 1979), and organizational structure of the school (e.g., flexible age groupings, open classrooms, team teaching; Budoff, 1972). For example, the Project PRIME data (cited in Semmel et al., 1979) revealed that classroom environment influences the social adaptation of EMR children. Regular classrooms that were characterized as more harmonious and cohesive were more likely to elicit positive social adaptation by EMR children than were classrooms in which there were higher levels of disruptiveness and dislike among the non-EMR children.

Jones et al. (1978) described three conditions that must be met for effective instructional integration to occur:

1. The educational needs of the EMR children must be compatible with the instruction given to non-EMR students.

2. Teachers must modify their instructional practices to accommodate the special needs of the EMR students. Large-group instruction is inappropriate in most cases.

3. There must be cooperation between regular teachers and personnel providing supportive services.

Simply returning the child to the regular classroom without the aid of transitional programs or other supportive services is unlikely to result in effective mainstreaming. In almost all cases, these children had been in the regular classroom and had failed. Unless some intervening experience has remedied the child's previous problems, the conditions that contributed to the labeling of the child as EMR probably will have a similarly detrimental effect on the child's future educational attainments.

CONCLUSION

The major theme emphasized throughout this paper is that evaluations of mainstreaming must expand beyond an investigation of setting. The child must be studied in context. Without a knowledge of the teaching processes employed in the classroom, teacher-student interactions, the teacher's organization of his or her time, patterns of feedback, curricula used, etc., the attributes of the mainstreamed or special classroom that contribute to program success and failure cannot be determined. Furthermore, the cumulative effects of various instructional options should be studied. A child's academic performance and self-concept, for example, are not merely the result of current school practices but of long-standing influences both inside and outside the school. This perspective calls for longitudinal research, tracing the EMR-labeled child through elementary and secondary school as well as the child's life adjustment after his or her schooling is completed.

Studies of setting alone allow few conclusions. In general, the evidence falls into one of three categories: (1) the data are contradictory, neither supporting nor refuting the efficacy of mainstreaming; (2) the data indicate that mainstreamed settings are more effective, or at least less harmful, than segregated classrooms; or (3) the data reveal the opposite pattern—segregated settings are more effective or less harmful than mainstreamed settings.

The first category, characterized by the research on self-concept, is the most troublesome. Can one make a policy recommendation concerning educational placement when the data are so contradictory? Balla and Zigler (1978:156) favor one interpretation:

While there does not seem to be a convincing rationale to reconcile these discrepant findings, it appears that there is insufficient empirical evidence in the self-concept area to support the predominant thrust in social policy in the area of the mentally retarded—that retarded persons be mainstreamed in regular classes to the greatest extent possible.

In cases that are truly ambiguous, I would favor an alternative interpretation. Unless there is evidence that the benefits derived from special classes outweigh the potential stigma and civil rights' infringements of segregation, the child should not be removed from the regular classroom. Thus, I would place the burden of proof on those who want to educate the child in a separate setting.

Most of the research falls within the second category—indicating that mainstreamed settings are more effective (or at least less harmful) than segregated classrooms. The parenthetical phrase is important, for it indicates that at best children in mainstreamed settings are performing equally to or slightly better than their special education peers. Mainstreaming does not miraculously cure an EMR child. It is more likely to facilitate the occurrence of certain positive events (e.g., higher expectations held by teachers) or shield the child from other negative factors associated with special class placement (e.g., stigma). The academic achievement of children in mainstreamed versus self-contained classrooms exemplifies the research in this category. As suggested in previous sections, mainstreamed children may score higher on standardized achievement tests because the curricula used in regular classrooms are more likely to emphasize academic subjects than are programs in special classes.

Research on the sociometric position of children in integrated classrooms lies within the third category of evidence—indicating that segregated settings lead to more positive, or less negative, effects than do mainstreamed settings. Children in mainstreamed classrooms may be less tolerated or more actively rejected than children in self-contained classrooms because regular classroom children spend considerably more time with the EMR children in their own classrooms than those in separate classes. It is perhaps easier to express tolerance for peers with whom one seldom interacts or encounters. Studies on classroom behavior, however, suggest that integrated EMR children do not act in ways that would necessarily lead to poor acceptance by their regular-class peers. More research is needed on the types of behaviors exhibited by EMR and non-EMR children that may contribute to the generally low sociometric position of EMR children in mainstreamed classrooms.

The interpretation of ambiguous and weak results as support for mainstreaming (or, more accurately, evidence against the value of self-contained classrooms) is consistent with the thrust of P.L. 94-142 toward education in the least restrictive environment. Yet neither the law nor the position advocated above implies that children should be "dumped" into the regular classroom and forever ignored. Clearly, these children need alternative services, for they were first identified on the basis of their inability to function adequately in the regular classroom. This view suggests that special services should be offered to the child, and the goals of these services should be to maintain the child in the regular classroom and to minimize the amount of time the child is separated from peers.

Education in a mainstreamed setting need not preclude provision of special services. A number of programs, some of which are still in the experimental stages, provide encouraging examples of special education services delivered within a mainstreamed program. These include the Consulting Teacher Approach to Special Education used in many districts in Vermont (Christie et al., 1972; Fox et al., 1973; Knight et al., 1981), the Instrumental Enrichment Program (Feuerstein et al., 1980), and the Adaptive Learning Environments Model (Wang, 1980, in press). Resource rooms in which a child receives more intensive instruction in a small group from a special education teacher may also provide the traditional benefits associated with special education programs while minimizing the associated harms (see Leinhardt and Pallay, 1981, for a review of this literature).

The segregative impact of various settings becomes increasingly troublesome as the effectiveness of programs becomes increasingly less evident. The segregation of children in self-contained classrooms is problematic because the costs are clear and the benefits are less than obvious. If specified instructional techniques led to successful outcomes, the importance of setting would become less significant. Its role, under these conditions, would be to facilitate effective practices rather than determine them, and its importance in research could diminish. The evaluation of programs could appropriately focus not merely on the setting in which these programs are implemented but also on the success of the programs in achieving specified goals.

REFERENCES

Aloia, G. F., Beaver, R. J., and Pettus, W. F.
  1978 Increasing initial interactions among integrated EMR students and their

nonretarded peers in a game-playing situation. *American Journal of Mental Deficiency* 82:573–579.

Asher, S. R., and Taylor, A. R.
In   The social outcomes of mainstreaming: sociometric assessment and beyond. *Express ceptional Education Quarterly.*

Baldwin, W. K.
1958   The educable mentally retarded child in the regular grades. *Exceptional Children* 25:106–108.

Balla, D., and Zigler, E.
1979   Personality development in retarded persons. Pp. 143–168 in N. R. Ellis, ed., *Handbook of Mental Deficiency, Psychological Theory and Research.* 2nd edition. Hillsdale, N.J.: Lawrence Erlbaum.

Ballard, M., Gottlieb, J., Corman, L., and Kaufman, M. J.
1977   Improving the status of mainstreamed retarded children. *Journal of Educational Psychology* 69:607–611.

Bradfield, H. R., Brown, J., Kaplan, P., Rickert, E., and Stannard, R.
1973   The special child in the regular classroom. *Exceptional Children* 39:384–390.

Brookover, W. B., and Erickson, E. L.
1975   *Sociology of Education.* Homewood, Ill.: Dorsey Press.

Brophy, J. E., and Good, T. L.
1974   *Teacher-Student Relationships Causes and Consequences.* New York: Holt, Rinehart & Winston.

Budoff, M.
1972   Providing special education without special classes. *Journal of School Psychology* 10:199–205.

Budoff, M., and Gottlieb, J.
1976   Special class students mainstreamed: a study of an aptitude (learning potential) × treatment interaction. *American Journal of Mental Deficiency* 81:1–11.

Budoff, M., and Siperstein, G. N.
1978   Low-income children's attitudes toward mentally retarded children: effects of labeling and academic behavior. *American Journal of Mental Deficiency* 82:474–479.

Cassidy, V. M., and Stanton, J. E.
1959   *An Investigation of Factors Involved in the Educational Placement of Mentally Retarded Children.* Columbus: Ohio State University Press.

Cegelka, W. J., and Tyler, J. L.
1970   The efficacy of special class placement for the mentally retarded in proper perspective. *Training School Bulletin* 67:33–65.

Chennault, M.
1967   Improving the social acceptance of unpopular educable mentally retarded pupils in special classes. *American Journal of Mental Deficiency* 72:455–458.

Christie, L. S., McKenzie, H. S., and Burdett, C. S.
1972   The consulting teacher approach to special education. Inservice training for regular classroom teachers. *Focus on Exceptional Children* 4:1–10.

Christoplos, G., and Renz, P. A.
1969   Critical examination of special education programs. *Journal of Special Education* 3:371–379.

Cooper, H. M.
1979   Pygmalion grows up: a model for teacher expectation communication and performance influence. *Review of Educational Research* 49:389–410.

Corman, L., and Gottlieb, J.
  1978 Mainstreaming mentally retarded children: a review of research. Pp. 251–275 in N.
         R. Ellis, ed., *International Review of Research in Mental Retardation*. Vol. 9. New
         York: Academic Press.
Dentler, R. A., and Mackler, B.
  1962 Ability and sociometric studies among normal and retarded children: a review of
         the literature. *Psychological Bulletin* 59:273–283.
Dunn, L. M.
  1968 Special education for the mildly retarded—is much of it justifiable? *Exceptional
         Children* 35:5–22.
Elashoff, J., and Snow, R. E.
  1971 *Pygmalion Reconsidered: A Case Study in Statistical Inference: Reconsideration of
         the Rosenthal-Jacobson Data on Teachers Expectancy*. Belmont, Calif.: Wads-
         worth Publishing Co.
Feuerstein, R., Rand, Y., Hoffman, M. B., and Miller, R.
  1980 *Instrumental Enrichment*. Baltimore, Md.: University Park Press.
Foley, J. M.
  1979 Effect of labeling and teacher behaviors on children's attitudes. *American Journal
         of Mental Deficiency* 83:380–384.
Fox, W., Egner, A., Paolucci, P., Perelman, P., McKenzie, H. S., and Garvin, J.
  1973 An introduction to a regular classroom approach for special education. Pp. 22–47
         in E. Deno, ed., *Instructional Alternatives for Exceptional Children*. Reston, Va.:
         The Council for Exceptional Children.
Freeman, S., and Algozzine, B.
  1980 Social acceptability as a function of labels and assigned attributes. *American Jour-
         nal of Mental Deficiency* 84:589–595.
Gallagher, J. J.
  1967 New directions in special education. *Exceptional Children* 33:441–447.
Gampel, D. H., Gottlieb, J., and Harrison, R. H.
  1974 Comparison of classroom behavior of special-class EMR, integrated EMR, low IQ,
         and nonretarded children. *American Journal of Mental Deficiency* 79:16–21.
Gardner, W. I.
  1966 Social and emotional adjustment of mildly retarded children and adolescents:
         critical review. *Exceptional Children* 33:97–105.
Gickling, E. R., and Theobold, J. J.
  1975 Mainstreaming: affect or effect. *Journal of Special Education* 9:317–328.
Goldstein, H., Moss, J. W., and Jordan, L.
  1965 *The Efficacy of Special Class Training on the Development of Mentally Retarded
         Children*. U.S. Office of Education, Cooperative Research Project report no. 619.
         University of Illinois, Urbana.
Goodman, H., Gottlieb, J., and Harrison, R. H.
  1972 Social acceptance of EMRs integrated into a nongraded elementary school.
         American Journal of Mental Deficiency 76:412–417.
Gottlieb, J.
  1974 Attitudes toward retarded children: effects of labeling and academic performance.
         American Journal of Mental Deficiency 79:268–273.
  1975a Attitudes toward retarded children: effects of labeling and behavioral ag-
         gressiveness. *Journal of Educational Psychology* 67:581–585.
  1975b Public, peer, and professional attitudes toward mentally retarded persons. Pp.

   99-125 in M. Begab and S. Richardson, eds., *The Mentally Retarded and Society: A Social Science Perspective*. Baltimore, Md.: University Park Press.

1978   Observing social adaptation in schools. Pp. 285-309 in G. P. Sackett, ed., *Observing Behavior, Vol. 1: Theory and Applications in Mental Retardation*. Baltimore, Md.: University Park Press.

1981   Mainstreaming: fulfilling the promise? *American Journal of Mental Deficiency* 86:115-126.

Gottlieb, J., and Davis, J. E.

1973   Social acceptance of EMR children during overt behavioral interactions. *American Journal of Mental Deficiency* 78:141-143.

Gottlieb, J., Gampel, D. H., and Budoff, M.

1975   Classroom behavior of retarded children before and after integration into regular classes. *Journal of Special Education* 9:307-315.

Gottlieb, J., Semmel, M. I., and Veldman, D. J.

1978   Correlates of social status among mainstreamed mentally retarded children. *Journal of Educational Psychology* 70:396-405.

Gottlieb, J., Agard, J., Kaufman, M. J., and Semmel, M. I.

1976   Retarded children mainstreamed: practices as they affect minority group children. Pp. 195-214 in R. L. Jones, ed., *Mainstreaming and the Minority Child*. Reston, Va.: The Council for Exceptional Children.

Gresham, F. M.

1981   Social skills training with handicapped children: a review. *Review of Educational Research* 51:139-176.

Guerin, G. R., and Szatlocky, K.

1974   Integration programs for the mentally retarded. *Exceptional Children* 41:173-197.

Guskin, S. L., and Spicker, H. H.

1968   Educational research in mental retardation. Pp. 217-278 in N. R. Ellis, ed., *International Review of Research in Mental Retardation*. Vol. 3. New York: Academic Press.

Hammons, G.

1972   Educating the mildly retarded: a review. *Exceptional Children* 38:565-570.

Haring, N. G., and Krug, D. A.

1975   Placement in regular programs: procedures and results. *Exceptional Children* 41:413-417.

Hartup, W. W.

1970   Peer interaction and social organization. Pp. 361-456 in P. H. Mussen, ed., *Carmichael's Manual of Child Psychology*, 2nd ed. Vol. 2. New York: John Wiley & Sons, Inc.

Heintz, P.

1974   Teacher expectancy for academic achievement. *Mental Retardation* 12:24-27.

Iano, R. P., Ayers, D., Heller, H. B., McGettigan, J. F., and Walker, U.

1974   Sociometric studies of retarded children in an integrative program. *Exceptional Children* 40:267-271.

Johnson, G. O.

1950   A study of the social position of mentally handicapped children in the regular grades. *American Journal of Mental Deficiency* 55:60-89.

1961   *A Comparative Study of the Personal and Social Adjustment of Mentally Handicapped Children Placed in Special Classes with Mentally Handicapped Children who Remain in Regular Classes*. Syracuse, N.Y.: Syracuse University.

1962   Special education for the mentally retarded—a paradox. *Exceptional Children* 29:62–69.

Jones, R, L., ed.
1976   *Mainstreaming and the Minority Child*. Reston, Va.: The Council for Exceptional Children.

Jones, R. L., and Wilderson, F. B.
1976   Mainstreaming and the minority child: an overview of issues and a perspective. Pp. 1–13 in R. Jones, ed., *Mainstreaming and the Minority Child*. Reston, Va.: The Council for Exceptional Children.

Jones, R. L., Gottlieb, J., Guskin, S., and Yoshida, R.
1978   Evaluating mainstreaming programs: models, caveats, considerations, and guidelines. *Exceptional Children* 44:588–601.

Kaufman, M. E., and Alberto, P. A.
1976   Research on efficacy of special education for the mentally retarded. Pp. 225–255 in N. R. Ellis, ed., *International Review of Research in Mental Retardation*. New York: Academic Press.

Kaufman, M. J., Agard, J. A., and Semmel, M. I.
In   *Mainstreaming: Learners and Their Environment*. Baltimore, Md.: University press Park Press.

Kaufman, M. J., Gottlieb, J., Agard, J. A., and Kukic, M. B.
1975   Mainstreaming: toward an explication of the construct. *Focus on Exceptional Children* 7(3).

Kern, W. H., and Pfaeffle, H. A.
1963   A comparison of social adjustment of mentally retarded children in various educational settings. *American Journal of Mental Deficiency* 67:407–413.

Kirk, S. A.
1964   Research in education. Pp. 57–99 in H. A. Stevens and R. Heber, eds., *Mental Retardation: A Review of Research*. Chicago, Ill.: University of Chicago Press.

Knight, M. F., Meyers, H. W., Paolucci-Whitcomb, P., Hasazi, S. E., and Nevin A.
1981   A Four-Year Evaluation of Cousulting Teacher Service. Unpublished manuscript. College of Education and Social Services, University of Vermont, Burlington.

Lapp, E. R.
1957   A study of the social adjustment of slow-learning children who were assigned part-time to regular classes. *American Journal of Mental Deficiency* 62:254–262.

Larrivee, B., and Cook, L.
1979   Mainstreaming: a study of the variables affecting teacher attitude. *Journal of Special Education* 13:315–324.

Lazarson, M.
1975   Educational institutions and mental subnormality: notes on writing a history. Pp. 33–52 in M. J. Begab and S. A. Richardson, eds., *The Mentally Retarded and Society: A Social Science Perspective*. Baltimore, Md.: University Park Press.

Leinhardt, G., and Leinhardt, S.
In   The evaluation of social outcomes in education. In E. Yaar and S. Spiro, eds., *Pro-press ceedings of the Pinchas Sapir Conference on Development. Social Policy Evaluation: Health, Education, and Welfare*. New York: Academic Press.

Leinhardt, G., and Pallay, A.
1981   Restrictive Educational Settings: Exile or Haven? Unpublished manuscript. Learning Research and Development Center, University of Pittsburgh.

MacMillan, D. L.
   1971   Special education for the mentally retarded: servant or savant? *Focus on Exceptional Children* 2:1–11.
MacMillan, D. L., and Borthwick, S.
   1980   The new educable mentally retarded population: can they be mainstreamed? *Mental Retardation* 18:155–158.
MacMillan, D. L., and Meyers, C. E.
   1979   Educational labeling of handicapped learners. Pp. 151–194 in D. C. Berliner, ed., *Review of Research in Education*. American Educational Research Association.
MacMillan, D. L., and Morrison, G. M.
   1980   Correlates of social status among mildly handicapped learners in self-contained special classes. *Journal of Educational Psychology* 72:437–444.
MacMillan, D. L., and Semmel, M. I.
   1977   Evaluation of mainstreaming programs. *Focus on Exceptional Children* 9:1–14.
MacMillan, D. L., Jones, R. L., and Aloia, G. F.
   1974   The mentally retarded label: a theoretical analysis and review of research. *American Journal of Mental Deficiency* 79:241–261.
Meyen, E. L., and Hieronymous, A. N.
   1970   The age placement of academic skills in curriculum for the EMR. *Exceptional Children* 36:333–339.
Meyerowitz, J. H.
   1962   Self derogations in young retardates and special class placement. *Child Development* 33:443–451.
Meyers, C. E., MacMillan, D. L., and Yoshida, R. K.
   1975   Correlates of Success in Transition of MR to Regular Class. Final Report. Grant no. OEG-0-73-5263. Prepared for the U.S. Department of Health, Education, and Welfare.
   1980   Regular class education of EMR students. From efficacy to mainstreaming. Pp. 176–206 in J. Gottlieb, ed., *Educating Mentally Retarded Persons in the Mainstream*. Baltimore, Md.: University Park Press.
Morrison, G. M.
   1981   Sociometric measurement: methodological consideration of its use with mildly handicapped and nonhandicapped children. *Journal of Educational Psychology* 73:193–201.
Mullen, F. A., and Itkin, W.
   1961   *Achievement and Adjustment of Educable Mentally Handicapped Children in Special Classes and in Regular Classes*. Chicago, Ill.: Chicago Board of Education.
Palmer, D. J.
   1979   Regular-classroom teacher's attributions and instructional prescriptions for handicapped and nonhandicapped pupils. *Journal of Special Education* 13:325–337.
Raber, S. M., and Weisz, J. R.
   1981   Teacher feedback to mentally retarded and nonretarded children. *American Journal of Mental Deficiency* 86:148–156.
Rosenthal, R., and Jacobson, L.
   1968   *Pygmalion in the Classroom*. New York: Holt, Rinehart & Winston.
Rothbart, M., Dalfen, S., and Barrett, R.
   1971   Effects of teacher's expectancy on student-teacher interaction. *Journal of Educational Psychology* 62:49–54.

Rubovits, P., and Maehr, M.
   1971   Pygmalion analyzed: toward an explanation of the Rosenthal-Jacobson findings. *Journal of Personality and Social Psychology* 19:197-203.
Rucker, C. N., and Vincenzo, F. M.
   1970   Maintaining social acceptance gains made by mentally retarded children. *Exceptional Children* 36:679-680.
Rucker, C. N., Howe, C. E., and Snider, B.
   1969   The participation of retarded children in junior high academic and nonacademic regular classes. *Exceptional Children* 35:617-623.
Salvia, J., Clark, G., and Ysseldyke, J.
   1973   Teacher retention of stereotypes of exceptionality. *Exceptional Children* 39:651-652.
Schurr, K. T., Towne, R. C., and Joiner, L. M.
   1972   Trends in self-concept of ability over two years of special class placement. *Journal of Special Education* 6:161-166.
Semmel, M. I., Gottlieb, J., and Robinson, N. M.
   1979   Mainstreaming: perspectives on educating handicapped children in the public schools. Pp. 223-279 in D. C. Berliner, ed., *Review of Research in Education*. Vol. 7. Washington, D.C.: American Educational Research Association.
Severance, L. J., and Gasstrom, L. L.
   1977   Effects of the label "mentally retarded" on causal explanations for success and failure outcomes. *American Journal of Mental Deficiency* 81:547-555.
Sheare, J. B.
   1974   Social acceptance of EMR adolescents in integrated programs. *American Journal of Mental Deficiency* 78:678-682.
Shotel, J. R., Iano, R. D., and McGettigan, J. F.
   1972   Teacher attitudes associated with the integration of handicapped children. *Exceptional Children* 38:677-683.
Simon, A., and Boyer, E. G., eds.
   1967   *Mirrors for Behavior*. Vol. 5. Philadelphia, Pa.: Research for Better Schools.
Stearns, M. S., Greene, D., and David, J. L.
   1979   *Local Implementation of P.L. 94-142*. Menlo Park, Calif.: SRI International.
Strang, L., Smith, M. D., and Rogers, C. M.
   1978   Social comparison, multiple reference groups, and the self-concepts of academically handicapped children before and after mainstreaming. *Journal of Educational Psychology* 70:487-497.
Strauch, J. D.
   1970   Social contact as a variable in the expressed attitudes of normal adolescents toward EMR pupils. *Exceptional Children* 36:485-494.
Strichart, S. S., and Gottlieb, J.
   1975   Imitation of retarded children by their nonretarded peers. *American Journal of Mental Deficiency* 79:506-512.
Thorndike, R. I.
   1968   Review of *Pygmalion in the Classroom* by R. Rosenthal and L. Jacobson. *American Educational Research Journal* 5:708-711.
Wang, M. C.
   1980   Mainstreaming Exceptional Children: Some Instructional Design and Implementation Considerations. Learning Research and Development Center, University of Pittsburgh.

In   Development and consequences of students' sense of personal control. In J. Levine
press   and M. C. Wang, eds., *Teacher and Student Perceptions: Implications for Learn-ing*. Hillsdale, N.J.: Lawrence Erlbaum.

Yoshida, R., and Meyers, C.
1975   Effects of labeling as EMR on teachers' expectancies for change in a student's per-formance. *Journal of Educational Psychology* 67:521–527.

Yoshida, R., MacMillan, D. L., and Meyers, C. E.
1976   The decertification of minority group EMR students in California: student achieve-ment and adjustment. Pp. 215–233 in R. L. Jones, ed., *Mainstreaming and the Minority Child*. Reston, Va.: The Council for Exceptional Children.

Some Potential Incentives of Special Education Funding Practices

SUZANNE S. MAGNETTI

Although various studies have indicated that special education services are cost-effective for society in terms of the increased lifetime earnings of the students in such programs (Conley, 1973; Schweinhart and Weikart, 1980; Weber et al., 1978), special education is a costly enterprise for local school jurisdictions in the short term. Because of the inability or unwillingness of local jurisdictions to assume the costs of these programs, states (and later the federal government) began to provide financial aid for those services to encourage the efforts of local jurisdictions to educate handicapped children. State and federal financial aid for special education constitutes a substantial portion of local budgets for special education.

The manner in which states and the federal government transfer funds to localities for special education services and the conditions placed on those funds may influence the types and amounts of services offered. At a very basic level, the amount of money a school district has available to spend on special education programs affects the quality and coverage of each district's special education program. From a more removed perspective, the multiple tiers of governmental funding (federal, state, and local) and related funding policies for special education programs may create fiscal incentives and disincentives that vary across jurisdictional lines.

I would like to thank Donald N. Bersoff, Alonzo Crim, Jerry Gross, William T. Hartman, Richard A. Rossmiller, *and* Frederick J. Weintraub *for their helpful comments on earlier drafts of this paper.*

These incentives and disincentives may affect the rate at which children are placed in special education clases. For example, where the fiscal implications of counting more children as handicapped are favorable to a school district or school, proportionally larger numbers of children might be classified as handicapped.

The panel was concerned with the phenomenon of minority students in the special education population, particularly in classes for educable mentally retarded (EMR) children, in proportions that far exceed their proportional enrollments in the public education systems. A number of factors have been pointed to as contributing in some way to this phenomenon, among them the methods used to fund special education programs. The purpose of this paper is to examine the fiscal incentives and disincentives that may result from state and federal funding methods and, when possible, to relate these to the patterns of minority enrollments in special programs for EMR children.

Fiscal incentives and constraints may arise from state and federal funding formulas and policies, state and local perceptions of funding and regulations, the interaction of federal policies with state and local programs and priorities, and the combined use of special education programs for the handicapped and other special-needs programs. In addition, the particular conditions that face a given school district—e.g., the relative geographic isolation or population density of the area, the wealth of the tax base of the area, the number of children served, and the availability of resources for handicapped children outside the school system—enhance or diminish the district's reaction to a source of funding. The combination of these interactions and conditions in the state or school district dictates what the particular fiscal incentive of an offer of funds to that jurisdictional unit will be.

An exploration of all these interactions was not possible within the context of the panel's work, but this paper identifies some of the forces contributing to fiscal incentives. Certain aspects of special education funding that appear to have had an effect in jurisdictions across the country are examined, e.g., the federal special-needs programs may create incentives to include or exclude children from special education classes. However, this focus on the federal programs is not exclusive; state funding plays a major role in the financing of special education programs. In past research, state schemes for funding special education have been grouped into a few rough categories. The possible effects of each of these categories on the provision of special education services are examined here. In addition, certain potential implications of these funding schemes that may affect the number of children identified and the placement of children with special needs are discussed.

THE FEDERAL SPECIAL-NEEDS PROGRAMS

Three federal funding programs are most frequently mentioned in discussions of the fiscal incentives involved in federal policies to place children in classes for the handicapped: (1) the Education for All Handicapped Children Act (20 U.S.C. 1401-1461, known as P.L. 94-142), which creates requirements and provides federal funds for special education programs for handicapped children; (2) Title I of the Elementary and Secondary Education Act of 1965 as revised by the Education Amendments of 1978 (P.L. 95-561) and by the Education Consolidation and Improvement Act of 1981, which funds compensatory education for the educationally deprived; and (3) the Bilingual Education Act of 1978, which funds bilingual education programs. Taken together, these three statutes comprise a substantial portion of the federal involvement in special-needs programming. Individually and as a group they provide funds and policies that can create inducements to expand or reduce the number of children receiving special education and that can affect the structure and quality of special education programs.

The Education for All Handicapped Children Act

The Education for All Handicapped Children Act (P.L. 94-142) is designed to provide a free, appropriate, public education to all handicapped children in this country. It is a grant-giving statute, allocating funds to states if they agree to meet detailed requirements for identifying, evaluating, and placing handicapped children. P.L. 94-142 potentially affects all handicapped children in this country, but the statute limits the number of children for which it will provide funds to 12 percent of all school-age children in the United States (20 U.S.C. 1411(a)(15)(A)(i)).[1]

For fiscal 1980 the federal allocation for P.L. 94-142 was $804 million (U.S. Department of Health, Education, and Welfare, 1979b), or about $217 per child served. For that same period the states spent an estimated $3.4 billion for special education programs (Odden and McGuire, 1980), a national average of $900-$1,000 per child, although wide variations existed across the states. And, as local governments also contribute to the costs of special education, the federal contribution mandated under P.L. 94-142 appears to be about 15 percent of the total cost of special education programs.

---

[1]Congress imposed a 12 percent ceiling on the number of children that could be served by P.L. 94-142 based on estimates developed near the time of enactment of the prevalence rates of handicaps in the United States.

Funds appropriated under P.L. 94-142 are allocated to the states on the basis of the number of children served. The P.L. 94-142 grant to each state increases by an incrementally greater amount for each child counted as served by the state's special education program. The dollar amount of the federal grant to each state is arrived at by multiplying the number of children served in special education programs in the state by the national average per-pupil expenditure for students in kindergarten through the twelfth grade. The states are reimbursed a set percentage of this amount (20 U.S.C. 1411(a)(1)).[2] For fiscal 1980 the federal contribution to special education was allocated among the states based on a count of 3,709,639 handicapped children served by special education programs.

The federal program establishes some limitations on how this money may be spent. State education agencies may retain up to 25 percent of the P.L. 94-142 grant. One fifth of that amount may be used by the state to cover the administrative costs of carrying out the provisions of P.L. 94-142, and the remainder of the state grant may be used to provide support services or direct services to children who are identified as handicapped but who are not receiving any special education services or are served inappropriately. Federal funds used by a state to provide support or direct services must be matched on a program basis by state funds for the same purpose (20 U.S.C. 1411(c)).

The remainder of the federal grant is distributed to the local-education agencies (LEA) or intermediate units. Each LEA is entitled to an amount that bears the same ratio to the total amount, minus the state's share, as the number of handicapped children served in that LEA bears to the total number of handicapped children served in the state (20 U.S.C. 1411(d)). This formula does not consider the variations in expenditures necessary to serve particular children. LEAs are not automatically eligible for P.L. 94-142 funds; in the same way that states must make application to the federal programs, LEAs must apply for funds and make satisfactory assurances that programs using that money satisfy the substantive requirements of P.L. 94-142 (20 U.S.C. 1414(a)).

No funds may be distributed to an LEA that is not entitled to at least $7,500 (20 U.S.C. 1411(4)(A)), but small districts may consolidate their applications and offer a joint program. Funds provided under P.L. 94-142 can be used only to cover the excess costs of special education and may not be used to reduce previous levels of state or local expenditures for special education (20 U.S.C. 1414).

---

[2] For fiscal 1980 the authorized reimbursable percentage was 30 percent, but only two thirds of that amount was appropriated by Congress.

TITLE I OF THE ELEMENTARY AND SECONDARY EDUCATION ACT OF 1965

Title I of the Elementary and Secondary Education Act of 1965, now administered by the U.S. Department of Education, provides for the largest federal program of assistance to elementary and secondary education. For fiscal 1980 (school year 1979–1980) the total Title I allocation was more than $3 billion (U.S. Department of Health, Education, and Welfare, 1979a). It is designed to meet the special education needs of school-age children by funding special programs of compensatory education for selected groups of educationally deprived children. Educationally deprived children are defined by regulation as ". . . (1) children who have need for special educational assistance in order that their level of educational attainment may be raised to that appropriate to their age, and (2) children who are handicapped" (45 C.F.R. 116a.2).

Title I comprises several smaller programs, each having a different target group (i.e., migrants, children in institutions for delinquents, children in institutions for handicapped children, children of low-income families), different grant requirements, and different procedures for counting children. The largest Title I program is directed to children of low-income families. Grants under this program are based on a count of the number of pupils from low-income families, the number of children living in institutions for neglected and delinquent children, and the number of children supported by public funds in foster care. The level of funding per state for this program is computed by multiplying the child count by 40 percent of the average per-pupil expenditure in that state within a range 20 percent above or below the average per-pupil expenditure in the United States (20 U.S.C. 2711). Like that of P.L. 94-142, Title I funding is based on a count of children. Under Title I, however, the criteria used to determine which children should be counted in arriving at the size of the grant (e.g., whether they are children of low-income families) are distinct from the reason for which individual children are selected to participate in the program, i.e., to provide compensatory education services to children who are educationally deprived. The other Title I programs have similar funding formulas, although the criteria used for counting children and the ways in which they are counted vary slightly.

One section of Title I (referred to as the P.L. 89-313 program) provides funds for the education of children in state-run or state-supported institutions for handicapped children (and, under certain conditions, to children who have been in such institutions and have subsequently returned to their local schools). The current method of allocating funds under this program is such that states and localities receive substantially more on a per-child-served basis under P.L. 89-313 than under P.L. 94-142. Children who receive services under P.L. 89-313 may not also receive services under P.L. 94-142, although other children counted under Title I can also be served with funds provided by P.L. 94-142.

The federal program also sets certain limits on how Title I money may be used. States electing to participate in Title I programs must file an application with the Department of Education. Participating states must agree to abide by Title I's no-supplant provision; Title I funds are intended to provide a supplement to regular education, not to supplant funds already available for the education of these children, and states must demonstrate that no state or local money was replaced with the federal funds. States must also demonstrate that comparable state and local funds are expended in Title I schools and other schools (20 U.S.C. 2736). State education agencies administer the Title I program within the state and report to the department.

Local education agencies that apply are awarded Title I funds in proportion to the number of eligible children in their districts. The LEAs must use those funds in areas with high concentrations of children from low-income families (20 U.S.C. 2732). Within those "target schools," Title I services should be made available to those children with the "greatest need for special assistance" whether or not they were originally counted as low-income children (20 U.S.C. 2733).

Title I also provides some stimulus for states to develop their own compensatory education programs. In addition to the basic Title I grant, the Education Amendments of 1978 created an incentive program that provides a special grant to each participating LEA in a state that offers its own compensatory education program (20 U.S.C. 2721). These incentive grants offer up to an additional 50 percent of the amount of state funds for compensatory education expended in a district. To be eligible for these matching funds, state compensatory education programs must offer categorical funds for the education of educationally disadvantaged children, the funds must be supplemental to other state education funds, and there must be program accountability based on performance objectives related to educational achievement (20 U.S.C. 2721).

THE BILINGUAL EDUCATION ACT

Through the Bilingual Education Act the federal government provides funds to local school districts and state departments of education for the operation of bilingual programs to assist children of limited proficiency in speaking and writing English (20 U.S.C. 3223). In fiscal 1979, federally funded programs served about 3.6 million students, and federal funds for bilingual education amounted to more than $158 million (about $44 per child served).

Grants are funded under the act on the basis of applications from school districts and state education agencies. There is no formula funding (20 U.S.C. 3231). These grants are available to establish, operate, and improve bilingual education programs; to provide supplemental community education activities; to train bilingual education personnel; and to provide technical assistance for the development of bilingual education programs. Grant applications compete for funds on the basis of several broad criteria: the geographic distribution of children of limited English-speaking proficiency, the relative needs of persons in different geographic areas, the relative ability of state or local agencies to provide these services, and the relative number of persons from low-income families who would benefit from these services (20 U.S.C. 3231).

OTHER PROGRAMS

Other federal education programs may also have some effect on special-needs populations. For example, school districts eligible for assistance under the Emergency School Aid Act are also entitled to a proportional amount of a second category of aid under the Bilingual Education Act. These grants are made to fund projects designed to meet the "special educational needs of minority group children who are from environments in which the dominant language is other than English" to develop language and cultural skills (20 U.S.C. 3261).

THE STATE ROLE IN FINANCING SPECIAL EDUCATION

Historically, public elementary and secondary education has been funded by a variety of federal, state, and local funds, the bulk of these funds coming from local sources. The trends of the late 1960s and 1970s, however, showed a gradual reduction in the percentage of education funding picked up by local governments and an increase in the size of the state role; the federal contribution has remained relatively stable at about 8 percent of the total funds expended for elementary and secondary education. By school year 1978–1979, local revenues accounted for less than 50 percent of the cost of elementary and secondary education. The state role in financing education now approaches 50 percent of the cost of education (Odden and McGuire, 1980).

State support for special education also appears to be increasing rapidly. In part, this increase is a response to the federal requirements for special education programs in P.L. 94-142, but substantial expansion of special education programs was already under way before the enactment of this legislation. Between 1975 and 1980 the national total of state budgets for special education grew by more than 66 percent (Odden and McGuire, 1980). For fiscal 1978 and fiscal 1979, state funds for special education increased by a national average of 16.1 percent (Hodge, 1979), although, of course, state funding varied considerably across the states. It is estimated that for 1980 the states spent more than $3.4 billion for the education of handicapped children.

The states have moved to address the needs of other special groups. Following the lead of the federal government in compensatory education (Title I), as of school year 1979–1980, 16 states funded state-run compensatory education programs. In addition, 6 other states provided supplemental support for compensatory education programs as a factor in their general aid formula (Education Commission of the States, 1979b, 1980). In school year 1978-1979, states spent approximately $700 million for their state compensatory education programs. Most of these programs were directed at children who were eligible for the federal Title I program but who were not served by it because of insufficient federal funding.

States are also addressing the need for additional bilingual education services; 22 states now offer bilingual-bicultural education programs. In school year 1979–1980, states spent approximately $98.4 million on these programs (Education Commission of the States, 1979a).

The state role in funding and operating special-needs programs is large and is increasing. While these issues are beyond the scope of this paper, the expanding role of the states in special education financing puts additional emphasis on the question of taxpayer equity, i.e., the extent to which these services should be paid for with revenue raised at the local level (property taxes) or at the state and federal levels (income, excise, and sales taxes). States have a substantial influence on the number of children reached by special education programs and the content of that education. In particular, the role of a state in financing special education programs for handicapped children affects the number and type of services available to such children. Complex layers of fiscal incentives and disincentives may affect state and federal policy objectives. Among the most important forces influencing these incentives and disincentives are the mechanisms states use to transfer state funds to LEAs for special education.

States employ several different types of financing formulas to transfer funds from state coffers to local education agencies. If a state has set aside or budgeted a certain amount of money to be distributed to its LEAs for a particular special education program, the type of financing formula used will not affect the total amount transferred (Bernstein et al., 1976). The formula used provides the method for dividing the state appropriation but will not increase or decrease it. The state funding formula is most important, therefore, not for the total amount of money transferred through its application, since that total may well be fixed by other forces, but for the messages it conveys to local jurisdictions on the relative value of various types of programs and services. The emphasis created by the funding formula may influence decisions of the LEA about the nature and quality of individual programs.

Besides the funding formula, other constraints imposed by the state to reinforce the program structure, to prevent waste, and to regulate the flow of funds also affect the transfer of funds to local jurisdictions. Thus, for example, states may define handicaps loosely or distinctly, may place ceilings on the number of children to be served, and may mandate services and programs. Other constraints imposed on the use of state money may be limits on the number of children to be served by each teacher or on the categories of services or personnel eligible for funding. Cost and program accountability requirements may also be used to regulate funding (Kakalik, 1979). Because actual or perceived fiscal incentives are dependent on the environment in which special education programs operate, it is not possible to determine absolutely what effect a given funding formula has by itself. However, within the separate contexts of the legal, political, social, and educational factors that affect a state's special education program, the funding formula influences the use of these funds and may also affect future programming. While the incentives and disincentives of various funding mechanisms are best explored within that environment, the basic form and implications of the various funding formulas provide the tools for a more particular investigation.

Types of Funding Formulas

Analysts have identified six types of funding formulas for special education (Bernstein et al., 1976; Hartman, 1980; Thomas, 1973). In practice, these formulas may be used as they are portrayed here or may be combined to serve the practical purposes of the state. The manner in which a particular state's formula varies from these basic types may be noteworthy and may be a result of particular conditions (e.g., population sparsity) or specific policy decisions. For example, a state is making a definite policy statement about its interest in supplying a basic education to all children with the use of a weighted formula that assigns a greater value to elementary education than to secondary education, even though secondary education costs more. The six types of funding formulas are described below:

1. *Unit*. Under a unit financing formula a fixed amount of money is provided by the state for every qualified unit of instructional, administrative, and/or other services. For example, a district may be reimbursed a set amount for each special education class. This type of funding formula is designed to cover some or all of the expenditures necessary to the operation of that particular unit, based on an averaged, actual, standard, minimum, or prorated expenditure per unit across the state.

2. *Personnel*. Under a personnel formula the state provides funds to LEAs to cover some or all of the costs of hiring special education staff. The amount reimbursed by the state may be determined by the duties of that staff. For example, under this formula an LEA could receive more for a teacher than for a program aide.

3. *Weight*. Under a weighted system the LEA is reimbursed an amount equal to the regular per-pupil reimbursement multiplied by a factor or weight that represents the increased cost of the special program. Generally, the weight varies by the type or severity of the handicap, so that, for example, a district might receive twice the base rate per child for multiply handicapped children and 1.5 times the base rate for hearing-impaired children.

4. *Straight Sum*. With a straight-sum formula the state reimburses LEAs a fixed amount of money for each handicapped child served. This amount usually varies by type of handicap. For example, the state may reimburse the district $1,000 for each EMR child served and $1,500 for each trainable mentally retarded child served.

5. *Percentage*. Under this type of formula a percentage of the local expenditures for educating a handicapped child are assumed by the state. For example, the state may reimburse a school district 30 percent of the district's excess cost of providing a program for seriously learning-disabled children, of the expenditures incurred for a set unit, or of the cost of necessary special personnel.

6. *Excess costs*. Under this formula the state assumes full or partial responsibility for the expenditures incurred in educating a handicapped child, above the average costs of a regular education.

For the purposes of this analysis, these six types of funding formulas can be further grouped by the characteristic factor on which payment is based. The unit and personnel formulas are resource-based formulas: Payment to local jurisdictions is based on the resources used, and the amount of money paid by the state is regulated at the state level by limits on allowable costs and on the number of children served per unit of payment. The weighted and straight-sum formulas are child-based formulas: Payment is based on the number of children served and is regulated by the costs of special education incurred and the amount of resources used. The percentage and excess-cost formulas are cost-based formulas: Payment is based on actual local expenditures, with state limits on the number of children served and the amount of resources used.

Each of these funding formulas, in conjunction with fiscal and program constraints and regulations, can affect policies and decisions at the level at which children are directly served and can provide feedback to those same constraints and regulations. The potential incentives and disincentives that these formulas provide in the making of special education policy and local programming decisions are diverse. For the purposes of this study, among the most noteworthy of these incentives and disincentives are those affecting labeling and classification of children, selection of the most appropriate program, class size, and support for placing children in the least restrictive environment.

IMPLICATIONS OF FUNDING ARRANGEMENTS

As noted above, the actual effects of a particular funding formula must be considered with reference to other factors that contribute to the operation of a given special education program. These factors vary considerably among the states and, in combination with each state's funding mechanism, create a spectrum of potential incentives and disincentives. An examination of these incentives and disincentives is beyond the scope of this paper; however, the potential effects of the state funding formulas grouped by the characteristic factor on which payment is based have been identified elsewhere (Kakalik, 1979; Hartman, 1980). These potential effects should be considered in conjunction with the incentives and constraints of the federal programs and the implications arising from the overlapping coverages of federal, state, and local programs.

Resource-Based Formulas

Under a resource-based formula (those based on units of service or staff costs) the incentive to overclassify students as handicapped is relatively low: Depending on the state-defined size of a unit, the number of additional students needed to fund an additional unit of services or justify an additional staff member is often relatively large. No funds accrue to the local jurisdiction for the classification of any one child. Nor do these formulas require the labeling of children; funding is based on the number of units of service or personnel needed and not the particular labels given to the children. These formulas provide at best rather weak support for systemic resistance to changes in student placements because relatively large numbers of students must move in or out of a program to change the number of resource units reimbursed by the state.

Among the problems involved with resource-based formulas is that they may encourage maximization of class size as a means of reducing per-pupil costs. This problem can be alleviated by manipulating other factors. For example, if the state sets levels of class or unit size relatively low, and if they are to a large degree funded with state or federal money, resource-based formulas can actually act as inducements to reduce class size so as to provide better services to handicapped children at little cost to the local jurisdiction. If resource-based formulas are based on the unit or teacher of a special class, placement in less restrictive environments is generally discouraged, but if resource reimbursements are defined to include alternative placement units and support personnel, then consideration of a variety of placements is reinforced.

Resource-based formulas may have other consequences as well. Small jurisdictions may not have the minimum numbers of students served to qualify for resource reimbursement. Jurisdictions with too few special education students to receive reimbursement for a given unit or personnel member may have to form cooperative arrangements with neighboring jurisdictions. A state may establish relatively high or low minimum and maximum class sizes and caseloads, but its ability to do so may be limited by the number of resource units it can afford to finance.

Child-Based Formulas

Child-based formulas (weighted and straight sum) appear to offer the greatest incentive among the types of funding formulas to overclassify children. Under these formulas the reimbursement for expenditures a jurisdiction receives from the state depends directly on the number of children identified as handicapped. When, for example, a jurisdiction's allocation from the state is decreasing, it may feel the need to classify more children as handicapped in order to get the same amount from the state as in previous years. However, local districts will also be increasing their costs by increasing the number of children served.

With a weighted formula that gives different weights to different handicaps, there is an incentive to classify more children in those categories that have a greater reimbursement rate. With a straight-sum formula, in which each child, regardless of handicap, generates the same amount of money, the incentive is greater to classify more children in the mildly handicapped categories and to reduce the number of seriously handicapped children served who require more, and more costly, services. For these same reasons the child-based formulas encourage labeling. Furthermore, even under the weighted formula that awards different handicaps varying amounts of money, no allowance is made for the fact that the extent of a child's handicap and educational needs can range widely in any given category; the incentive is to provide children with the lowest-cost programming alternative. Of course, many of these problems are not inherent in the formulas themselves and can be adjusted for by regulating the proportion of students in the fiscally preferred categories. These formulas do provide a strong incentive to identify previously unserved children, at least in some categories. Child-based formulas also provide an apparent incentive to increase class sizes and caseloads as a means of maximizing reimbursement while minimizing costs to the local jurisdiction.

The weighted formulas can provide a financial incentive to remove children from low-reimbursement categories and place them in high-reimbursement categories. This process would be cost-effective to a local jurisdiction only if net costs in the higher categories are lower than those in the lower categories. The weighted formulas can be used to encourage placements in less restrictive environments, however, by means of larger reimbursements, relative to the lower costs, for children in less restrictive settings. On one hand, child-based formulas provide a considerable inducement to avoid removing a child entirely from special education programs because that action would result in the loss of a reimbursable entity without reducing by very much the fixed costs of the program. On the other hand, child-based formulas are also cited as providing an incentive to serve children only briefly in the course of a year, or otherwise limiting the services provided to them, to get full reimbursment at a very limited cost. If an enrollment or a one-time count qualifies a child for a full reimbursement there may be a strong inducement to move that child quickly through a limited program. This problem can be solved by adjusting the formula reimbursement rate to recognize the duration of services for any child.

Small districts may have trouble collecting enough state money to support their special education program because reimbursement under these formulas is based on a count of eligible children and not on the costs of the complete program. With a weighted or straight-sum formula, reimbursement per child is usually based on the costs of an average class size, and a small district may have too few students to fill an average class. This may encourage some overclassification and mislabeling in small districts. However, states may adjust their reimbursement formula to solve this problem. For example, in some states that use a weighted formula, an additional weight or factor is added to the weight for children from small districts to ease the cost burden to these districts. Other states may choose to use the funding mechanism to encourage cooperative arrangements among neighboring small districts.

Cost-Based Formulas

The cost-based formulas—percentage and excess costs—reimburse jurisdictions on the basis of expenditures and not on the basis of the resources used or the number of students served. The percentage-based formula may encourage placement in the least expensive program available since local jurisdictions must assume some percentage of the costs of those placements and services. The excess-cost formulas would not appear to create any type of incentive when the state absorbs all costs associated with the special placement. On one hand, however, with the high levels of reimbursement often made with these formulas, there may be some incentive to mislabel. On the other hand, a fully funded excess-cost formula would allow jurisdictions to make the best appropriate placement for a child with no thought to cost. From the point of view of state planners, excess-cost formulas without some kind of cost constraints on local jurisdictions are a nightmare.

The percentage formulas do provide an incentive for jurisdictions to maximize class size to reduce the percentage that they themselves must pay. A jurisdiction that pays a significant percentage of the costs of a special education program may have additional incentives to reduce expenditures by placing students in the low-cost programs and may have disincentives to move children to higher-cost programs. The excess-cost formulas should not create any incentives that relate to class size, program content, or placement decisions, since all the expenditures associated with the special education program are reimbursed by the state. Placements outside of special education classes would not be discouraged by either the percentage or excess-cost formulas because the most restrictive placement would not cost the local jurisdiction any more.

Small districts should not be harmed by the excess-cost formulas if the state assumes all the extra costs of providing special education. However, if the state pays only a portion of the excess costs or if reimbursements are limited by minimum class size regulations and constraints on the categories of approvable costs, the ability of small districts to pay for special education may indeed be curtailed. The ability of small districts to afford a full special education program under a percentage formula depends on whether the reimbursable percentage is high or low.

A Comparison of Formulas

Forty-five states use a formula for funding special education programs clearly like one of the three discussed above (Education Commission of the States, 1980). To compare the three formulas and their relationship to disproportionate placements by race and sex, states were classified by the formula used and by geographic region. The means for geographic regions and funding formulas were compared statistically on the percentage of students enrolled in EMR programs, an index of racial disproportion in EMR classes, and an index of sex disproportion in EMR classes. The results are summarized in Table 1.[3]

There is a statistically significant difference among formulas, both in the average size of the EMR program and the average disproportion by race or ethnicity; there is no significant difference in disproportion by sex. Specifically, states employing resource-based formulas have on the average the largest EMR programs and also the largest minority-white difference in the percentage of students classified as EMR. States using cost-based formulas have the smallest average EMR programs and also the smallest racial differences.

There is also, however, a tendency for states in different geographic regions to employ different formulas. For example, more than half the states using resource-based formulas are located in the South or in states bordering the South. These states also have the highest average placement

TABLE 1   Relationship of Funding Formula to EMR Placement Rates and Disproportions by Race and Sex

Funding Formula	Number of States	Mean Percentage of Students in EMR Classes	Mean Disproportion by Race or Ethnicity	Mean Disproportion by Sex
Resource-based	13	1.95	0.87	0.44
Child-based	12	1.46	0.40	0.40
Cost-based	20	1.23	0.27	0.39

[3]The index of disproportion is the log-odds index described in the paper by Finn in this volume. The values in Table 1 are all positive, indicating that on the average a greater percentage of minority students is enrolled in EMR classes than white students, as is a greater percentage of males than females. Statistical comparisons were made by fitting a two-way fixed-effects analysis-of-variance model to the data, using an exact least-squares approach for unequal cell frequencies. All tests were made with $\alpha = .05$.

rates and the highest minority-white disproportions. Cost-based formulas are in more common use in the Northeast, Midwest, and West, where EMR programs and disproportions are generally lower. When the effects of different regions using different formulas are controlled statistically, no significant differences remain among the three formulas. Thus, it cannot be concluded that any particular funding formula produces certain levels of enrollment or disproportion. The funding approach for special education services is one of many factors—including geographic region, minority population density, and the relative size of the special education program—that varies systematically with the extent of racial disproportion.

INCENTIVES IN THE FEDERAL APPROACH TO FUNDING SPECIAL SERVICES[4]

P.L. 94-142, which is the principal means of channeling federal funds to special education, can be thought of as a civil rights requirement or entitlement law for handicapped children that also provides some share of the costs of the required programs. The major portion of funding for special education, however, comes from state and local governments. Few estimate that the federal government picks up more than 15 percent of those costs (Hartman, 1980). Current appropriations for P.L. 94-142 are less than half their authorized level, and future authorizations have been sharply reduced. Yet, on the whole, states, which are loath to lose federal support, accept the federal requirements. The funding provisions of P.L. 94-142 appear to provide some incentive for compliance with the substantive and procedural requirements of federal law, although some aspects of the funding provisions may negate the policy aims and priorities expressed elsewhere in the statute. It may be useful to examine the funding structure and the potential fiscal incentives created by the law before attempting to describe the effect of its fiscal provisions on the achievement of its policy goals.

P.L. 94-142 employs a straight-sum funding formula—a child-based formula—to transfer federal funds to local jurisdictions and states. Each state receives a fixed amount for each handicapped child receiving special education. The state is permitted to retain a relatively small, fixed percentage of this money and transfers the remainder to local jurisdictions in proportion to the number of children they serve. The federal formula does not make distinctions in the amount of funds generated on the bases of type or severity of handicap or the cost of the necessary program.

---

[4]The following discussion of the incentives created by the federal legislation was drawn largely from Hartman (1980:23-31).

One of the primary purposes of P.L. 94-142 was to expand special education services to an allegedly large but unknown population of handicapped children who were thought to be unserved. Studies conducted for the Bureau of Education for the Handicapped when enactment of P.L. 94-142 was under consideration suggested that about 12 percent of all school-age children were in need of special education services and that states were providing services to only a small proportion of this potential total.[5] The straight-sum funding formula complements this purpose and encourages states to identify and serve additional students. This type of formula can also be viewed as supplying a rather strong incentive to overlabel and misclassify students. The incentive is direct: For each additional child served the state will receive an additional fixed amount of money. This incentive applies until 12 percent of the school-aged population of a state is served—the goal embodied in the statute. In other words, the federal government will reimburse a state a fixed amount per child only up to that 12 percent limit. On one hand, this limit may be considered to be the goal of full implementation of the act; on the other hand, it also acts to curb the potential incentive of the funding formula to overclassify children.

The straight-sum formula may provide a strong incentive to states and local jurisdictions to identify and serve children in the mildly handicapped categories and to reduce the number or percentage of children served in the most costly programs. For many children who are classified in the mildly handicapped categories and who receive or need only limited services, the federal reimbursement could cover a sizable part of the costs of the additional services. The level of federal funding may create its own incentives with respect to the number of children served and the extent of services provided. If the level of federal funding is relatively low, resulting in a small per-pupil reimbursement, local jurisdictions probably would not increase the number of children served and would minimize the costs of educating those children identified as needing services, by maximizing class sizes and limiting the extent of the services provided.

The straight-sum funding formula itself creates an incentive to local jurisdictions to provide special education programs at least cost as a means of limiting their expenditures. However, other provisions of the act (e.g., the requirement of individual education plans for each child) should operate to prevent abusive placements in low-cost programs. Placing children in less restrictive educational settings is actively encouraged by

[5]This figure was based on estimates of the nationwide incidence of various handicapping conditions; there is little hard evidence of what these incidence rates actually are and little agreement on how many handicaps are defined.

this type of funding; since less restrictive programs are of relatively lower cost, there are positive incentives to local jurisdictions to place children in these programs. This is true only up to a point: Unless a state has reached the 12 percent limit in the number of children it can count as handicapped, there would be a distinct disincentive to return children to the regular education system.

The federal regulations also require that each child served be labeled and counted by category of handicapping condition. These requirements strengthen the practice of labeling and may result in the mislabeling or miscategorization of children.

As a general rule, the federal funds can be used only to supplement existing state and local supports for special education services (20 U.S.C. 1413(a)(9)). The emphasis of the federal law is to encourage the delivery of services to all needy children. States that can prove that all children in need of services are served, however, can apply for a waiver of the no-supplant rule. (One way to do so would be to identify as handicapped and serve 12 percent of their school-aged population). If such a waiver is granted, P.L. 94-142 funds can be used by the state essentially as general aid money (Barro, 1978).

The federal program may limit the ability of some small school districts to offer special education programs with its requirement that no funds be distributed to districts that are not eligible for at least $7,500 (20 U.S.C. 1411(c)(4)(A)). The purpose of this provision is to prevent the fragmentation of services. Small districts are permitted to file joint applications for the funding of special education programs.

Other requirements of P.L. 94-142 may create additional financial incentives that are not directly tied to its funding provisions. For example, the use of administrative hearing procedures established under the act adds to the costs of placing a handicapped child in special education. School districts may weigh the costs of a placement requested by a child's parents against the costs of fighting that request through an administrative hearing process. In fact, the opportunity of parents to impose these costs on a school district may be their greatest leverage against the school district. Some states may limit the extent of this leverage and thereby reduce the incentive of school districts to comply with such parental requests by reimbursing school districts for all or part of the costs of using the administrative hearing process.

Although these implications can be drawn from the funding mechanism and some of the regulations and statutory provisions of P.L. 94-142, federal law does not exist in a vacuum, and the implications for service delivery that appear to exist in P.L. 94-142 must be considered in light of the policies and regulations of individual state laws. The federal statute provides a direction or emphasis for state programs to follow, but much of the substance of special education programs comes from states or even local jurisdictions. Many of the implications created by the federal funding arrangement may be blunted or altered by conflicting incentives created at the state level. For example, if a state reimburses a local jurisdiction for only a small percentage of the costs of its program, the incentives created by the federal funding arrangements will probably have a considerable impact on its decisions about costs and, consequently, service delivery. If, on the other hand, a state reimburses all the excess costs of a local jurisdiction's program, federal funding arrangements will have little influence. In fact, if state funding is relatively high, local jurisdictions should be much more responsive to the incentives produced by the state requirements than they will be to the federal ones (Barro, 1978).

The effect of the federal incentives is also influenced by the interactions of special education programs with other special-needs programs. Several of these programs—most notably the federal compensatory education and bilingual education programs—are frequently cited as factors that can conflict with or confuse the policies expressed in P.L. 94-142. In part, these interactions are a result of the overlap in the populations served and the services provided between these programs and special education programs. These interactions also are, in part, the result of fiscal incentives that occur in the combined action of these programs.

Overlap in program participants exists because each of these programs is designed to serve a discrete group of children, and in reality the target groups are not discrete. For example, a child with a perceptible physical handicap may also need bilingual education services. The target groups as defined by each program are frequently vague and indefinite. This overlap may be important for several reasons. First, some children could be served under two or even more of these programs. Second, since each of these programs is often operated as a "pull-out" program (children served are taken out of the regular class for a portion of the day), children participating in two or three programs may lose class time in moving from program to program and may receive most of their education outside the regular school environment. As a result, fewer children may receive less core education in the regular class (Kimbrough and Hill, 1981). One large study undertaken to consider the problems of overlaps in special-needs services and populations found that, although schools frequently attempted to prevent duplication of services within the programs, some children did receive services from several programs (Birman, 1979). Multiple enrollment resulted in some disruption of students' base programs. Multiple enrollments were found most frequently where special-needs programs were nearly fully funded by state and federal funds. In jurisdictions where no state or federal funds were available to provide special-needs services, multiple enrollments of any one student were infrequent.

NEW DEVELOPMENTS AND CONSIDERATIONS FOR THE FUTURE

Recent economic and political developments indicate that, at least for the immediate future, federal and state governments will have or will make available fewer resources for special education programs. Local school districts must contend with declining enrollments, reduced revenues, and demands for a greater variety of services (Kirst and Garms, 1980). Given these diminished resources, the ability of schools to meet the needs of a diverse population may be considerably strained.

In addition, recent developments, at least at the federal level, suggest that not only will the funds going to special education programs be reduced but also that the method through which those funds reach states and local jurisdictions may be altered. In 1981 the Reagan administration announced that it would attempt to consolidate the federal categorical education programs into two block grants. Although the administration-backed Elementary and Secondary Education Consolidation Act of 1981 failed to be passed by Congress, Congress did pass a modified block-grant proposal—the Education Consolidation and Improvement Act of 1981, which modifies Title I of the Elementary and Secondary Education Act and consolidates most of its other titles (with the exception of the Bilingual Education Act and the Women's Educational Equity Program) into a block grant to the states effective in fiscal 1983. While P.L. 94-142 remained a categorical program, authorization levels for fiscal 1983 and fiscal 1984 were reduced, perhaps presaging an even more limited federal role in the future. The Reagan administration remains committed to shifting responsibility and control for education programs back to state and local authorities. It argues that block grants are a means of reducing the administrative costs associated with running the large numbers of federal categorical education programs and of increasing the flexibility of state and local governments to meet the education demands of their populations.

Opponents of block-grant funds argue that such grants would destroy the intent of the categorical programs by eliminating the commitment of funds to the particular populations in need. Most of those populations are minorities and lack the political power necessary to garner funds to meet their particular needs. Coupled with a general decline in federal funds, the consolidation of federal programs into block grants could have a deleterious impact on the disadvantaged, the handicapped, and other minorities.

CONCULSION

Fiscal incentives that may affect the behavior of a school district are functions of the environment of legal, social, political, financial, and educational considerations within which a school district must operate. The extent to which a given activity is more or less costly may influence the choices that school districts make about the number of children classified as handicapped, the types of handicaps identified, the placement of children in regular classes or in special environments, the length of time a child may spend in a special education program, the quality and type of programs and services provided, and the size of classes and support personnel's case loads. Although a description of the funding formula used to transfer special education funds to a local jurisdiction is useful for understanding the financial considerations that may be directing its actions, the funding formula cannot be viewed alone. A variety of factors are at work to create the incentives and disincentives that can affect the nature and quality of special education. For example, regulations and guidelines that define handicaps, describe programs and services, and limit class sizes act as constraints on the funding formula. Other factors—such as the level of funding, the history of special education in the jurisdiction, the relationship of education agencies to other government agencies, the interaction of special education programs and such activities as mental health programs and child welfare services, and the activities of special interests—also contribute to the fiscal incentives under which school districts operate. Since funding is provided through several federal and state programs, potential fiscal incentives should be considered in light of these various sources of funding.

REFERENCES

Barro, S. M.
  1978 Federal education goals and policy instruments: an assessment of the "strings" attached to categorical grants in education. Pp. 229-285 in M. Timpane, ed., *The Federal Interest in Financing Schooling*. Cambridge, Mass.: Ballinger.
Bernstein, C. D., Kirst, M. W., Hartman, W. T., and Marshall, R. S.
  1976 *Financing Education Services for the Handicapped: An Analysis of Current Research and Practices*. Reston, Va.: The Council for Exceptional Children.
Birman, B. F.
  1979 *Case Studies of Overlap Between Title I and P.L. 94-142 Services for Handicapped Students*. Research report EPRC 26 prepared for the U.S. Department of Health, Education, and Welfare. Menlo Park, Calif.: SRI International.
Conley, R. W.
  1973 *The Economics of Mental Retardation*. Baltimore, Md.: Johns Hopkins University Press.

Education Commission of the States
  1979a *1978-79 Bilingual Education Survey.* Education Finance Center. Denver, Colo.:
        Education Commission of the States.
  1979b *1978/79 State Compensatory Education Program Characteristics and Current
        Funding Levels for Sixteen States.* Education Finance Center. Denver, Colo.:
        Education Commission of the States.
  1980 *School Finance at a Fifth Glance.* Wall chart. Education Finance Center. Denver,
        Colo.: Education Commission of the States.
Hartman, W. T.
  1980 *Policy Effects of Special Education Funding Formulas.* Policy report no. 80-B1.
        Stanford, Calif.: Institute for Research on Educational Finance and Governance.
Hodge, M.
  1979 State Financing of Special Education. Unpublished paper prepared for the U.S.
        Department of Health, Education, and Welfare.
Kakalik, J.
  1979 Issues in the cost and finance of special education. Pp. 195–222 in *Review of Re-
        search in Education.* Vol. 7. Washington, D.C.: American Educational Research
        Association.
Kimbrough, J., and Hill, P. T.
  1981 *The Aggregate Effects of Federal Education Programs.* Report no. R-2638-ED.
        Santa Monica, Calif.: Rand Corporation.
Kirst, M. W., and Garms, W. I.
  1980 *The Demographic, Fiscal, and Political Environment of Public School Finance in
        the 1980's.* Policy Paper No. 80-61. Stanford, Calif.: Institute for Research on
        Educational Finance and Governance.
Odden, A., and McGuire, C. K.
  1980 *Financing Educational Services for Special Populations: The State and Federal
        Roles.* Working paper no. 28. Education Finance Center. Denver, Colo.: Educa-
        tion Commission of the States.
Schweinhart, L. J., and Weikart, D. P.
  1980 *Young Children Grow Up: The Effects of the Perry Preschool Program on Youths
        Through Age 15.* Monographs of the High/Scope Educational Research Founda-
        tion, No. 7. Ypsilanti, Mich.: High/Scope Press.
Thomas, M. A.
  1973 Finance: without which there is no special education. *Exceptional Children*
        39:475–480.
U.S. Department of Health, Education, and Welfare
  1979a Elementary and Secondary Education Act of 1965, P.L. 89-10 as Amended, Title I,
        Assistance for Educationally Deprived Children, Allotments for Fiscal Year 1980.
        Table dated March 30, 1979. Office of Education. Washington, D.C.: U.S.
        Department of Health, Education, and Welfare.
  1979b *Progress Toward a Free Appropriate Public Education: Semi-Annual Update on
        the Implementation of P.L. 94-142: The Education for All Handicapped Children
        Act.* Office of Education. Superintendent of Documents no. 0-631-611/2923.
        Washington, D.C.: U.S. Government Printing Office.
Weber, C. F., Foster, P. W., and Weikart, D. P.
  1978 *An Economic Analysis of the Ypsilanti Perry Preschool Project.* Monographs of the
        High/Scope Educational Research Foundation, No. 4. Ypsilanti, Mich.: High/
        Scope Press.

Patterns in Special Education Placement as Revealed by the OCR Surveys

JEREMY D. FINN

Since 1968 the Office for Civil Rights (OCR) has surveyed schools and school districts regarding student enrollment and placements. This paper describes the results of an analysis of the OCR survey data pertaining to the 1978-1979 school year. The original data consist of simple counts of students obtained from school and district offices at one point in time: October 1978. The data do not describe the processes whereby one student (or a group of students) is placed in special programs in any particular setting and, therefore, cannot explain how differences in placement rates are created. The data do, however, document the extent of disproportion in special programs by race/ethnicity and gender as well as the demographic conditions under which smaller or larger disproportions are found.

It is clear that the placement rates in special education programs are very different both for minority and white students and for males and females. Table 1 gives nationwide percentages of students in each of five special programs. Minorities are classified as educably mentally retarded (EMR) at a rate that is substantially higher than that for white students both in absolute and relative terms. By comparison, the male-female ratio in EMR programs is smaller, but 3 times as many males as females are classified as emotionally disturbed, and almost 2.5 times as many males as females have specific learning disabilities.

I am grateful to Robert Serfling, Amado Padilla, Reginald Jones, Richard Eyman, Lyle Jones, Ingram Olkin, *and* Miron Straf *for their reactions and suggestions for improvements to an earlier draft of this paper.*

The purpose of this analysis is to illuminate the differences in placement rates and, to the extent possible from the survey data, to describe the context in which they arise. This paper summarizes the results of the data analysis in a progression from general to more specific findings. Differences between minority and nonminority students in EMR placements are described, and the examination is specified by separate racial or ethnic classifications and by special education programs other than EMR programs.

THE 1978 OCR SURVEY

In its 1978 Elementary and Secondary School Civil Rights Survey, OCR sampled approximately 6,000 school districts, or about one third of the districts in the United States. Questionnaires were sent to all district offices and to every school in the 6,000 districts, requiring counts of the number of students enrolled, the number enrolled in special education programs, and additional global characteristics of the student population. All student counts were classified by racial or ethnic identity, and some were also classified by gender.[1] Both racial/ethnic and gender classifications were required for students in five special programs, which are, according to the general instructions (Form OS/CR 102), as follows:

1. Educable mentally retarded (or handicapped)—a condition of mental retardation which includes pupils who are educable in the academic, social, and occupational areas even though moderate supervision may be necessary.
2. Trainable mentally retarded (or handicapped)—a condition of mental retardation which includes pupils who are capable of only very limited meaningful achievement in the traditional basic academic skills but who are capable of profiting from programs of training in self-care and simple job or vocational skills.

---

[1] According to the "general instructions to the fall 1978 school survey" (Form OS/CR 102), the following racial or ethnic categories are recognized:

American Indian or Alaskan Native: A person having origins in any of the original peoples of North America and who maintains cultural identification through tribal affiliation or community recognition.

Asian or Pacific Islander: A person having origins in any of the original peoples of the Far East, Southeast Asia, the Pacific Islands, or the Indian subcontinent. This area includes, for example, China, India, Japan, Korea, the Philippine Islands, and Samoa.

Hispanic: A person of Mexican, Puerto Rican, Cuban, Central or South American, or other Spanish culture or origin—regardless of race.

Black, not of Hispanic origin: A person having origins in any of the black racial groups of Africa.

White, not of Hispanic origin: A person having origins in any of the original peoples of Europe, North Africa, or the Middle East.

TABLE 1 Nationwide Special Education Placements, by Sex and by Race or Ethnicity

Classification	Race or Ethnicity				Sex			
	Percentage		Log-Odds (Male-Female)	Q	Percentage		Log-Odds (Male-Female)	Q
	Minority	White			Male	Female		
Educable mentally retarded (EMR)	2.54	1.06	0.89	.42	1.65	1.19	0.37	.18
Trainable mentally retarded (TMR)	0.33	0.19	0.55	.27	0.25	0.20	0.26	.13
Seriously emotionally disturbed (SED)	0.42	0.29	0.37	.18	0.48	0.16	1.14	.52
Specific learning disabilities (SLD)	2.29	2.30	0.01	.01	3.22	1.33	0.92	.43
Speech impaired (SI)	1.82	2.02	−0.09	−.04	2.40	1.53	0.48	.24
None of the above	92.60	94.12			92.00	95.59		

SOURCE: Weighted projections to national totals, from *State, Regional, and National Summaries of Data from the 1978 Civil Rights Survey of Elementary and Secondary Schools*, prepared for OCR by Killalea Associates, Inc., April 1980.

3. Seriously emotionally disturbed—a condition exhibiting one or more of the following characteristics over a long period of time and to a marked degree, which adversely affects educational performance: an inability to learn which cannot be explained by intellectual, sensory, or health factors; an inability to build or maintain satisfactory interpersonal relationships with peers and teachers; inappropriate types of behavior or feelings under normal circumstances; a general pervasive mood of unhappiness or depression; or a tendency to develop physical symptoms or fears associated with personal or school problems. The term includes children who are schizophrenic or autistic. The term does not include children who are socially maladjusted, unless it is determined that they are seriously emotionally disturbed.

4. Specific learning disability—a disorder in one or more of the basic psychological processes involved in understanding or in using language, spoken or written, which may manifest itself in an imperfect ability to listen, think, speak, read, write, spell, or to do mathematical calculations. The term includes such conditions as perceptual handicaps, brain injury, minimal brain dysfunction, dyslexia, and developmental aphasia. The term does not include children who have learning problems which are primarily the result of visual, hearing, or motor handicaps, of mental retardation, or of environmental, cultural, or economic disadvantage.

5. Speech-impaired—a communication disorder, such as stuttering, impaired articulation, a language impairment, or a voice impairment, which adversely affects a child's educational performance.

The sample consists of both "forced" districts, which OCR required to be included because of their compliance status or because they had applied for funds under the Emergency School Aid Act, and "drawn" districts, chosen at random from within a sampling frame organized by 13 demographic characteristics to ensure that all characteristics of importance to OCR were represented.[2] Of the total 6,079 districts sampled, 6,040 provided responses; of these, 2,146 districts were "forced." The total number of schools represented in the sample is 54,082. Because the data are not a simple random sample of the districts of a state or region, sampling weights are provided to allow estimates of state totals or averages. Checks on the accuracy of these projections were made from the 1976 school survey (U.S. Department of Health, Education, and Welfare, 1978a), which followed a similar sampling plan and yielded very reasonable results.

The number of districts actually responding to the survey is given for each state in Table 2.[3] The District of Columbia and Hawaii each have a

---

[2]Details of the sampling design for 1978 are given in U.S. Department of Health, Education, and Welfare (1978b).

[3]The sampling plan caused the District of Columbia and eight states to be surveyed exhaustively (Alabama, Florida, Georgia, Hawaii, Louisiana, Mississippi, North Carolina, and South Carolina).

TABLE 2   Districts Sampled and Responding to Question on
EMR Programs

State	Approximate Number of Districts in State*	Number Sampled	Percentage with EMR Programs
Alabama	125	125	100.0
Alaska	50	22	100.0
Arizona	223	81	96.3
Arkansas	348	237	94.9
California	1,022	326	66.6
Colorado	117	58	91.4
Connecticut	162	74	90.5
Delaware	24	12	100.0
District of Columbia	1	1	100.0
Florida	67	67	100.0
Georgia	183	187	99.5
Hawaii	1	1	100.0
Idaho	111	42	95.2
Illinois	958	320	68.8
Indiana	280	123	91.9
Iowa	389	138	60.9
Kansas	301	105	79.0
Kentucky	159	108	95.4
Louisiana	66	66	100.0
Maine	172	72	93.1
Maryland	25	21	100.0
Massachusetts	336	126	47.6
Michigan	565	202	88.1
Minnesota	405	142	81.0
Mississippi	150	150	98.7
Missouri	419	197	95.4
Montana	521	62	82.3
Nebraska	996	66	92.4
Nevada	17	9	100.0
New Hampshire	142	43	93.0
New Jersey	556	197	75.1
New Mexico	88	51	94.1
New York	716	263	62.0
North Carolina	144	145	100.0
North Dakota	287	53	62.3
Ohio	566	245	92.2
Oklahoma	596	193	92.7
Oregon	327	64	87.5
Pennsylvania	479	317	83.3
Rhode Island	39	27	88.9
South Carolina	92	92	100.0
South Dakota	174	58	63.8

TABLE 2   (*continued*)

State	Approximate Number of Districts in State*	Number Sampled	Percentage with EMR Programs
Tennessee	140	110	99.1
Texas	1,077	573	90.8
Utah	39	19	100.0
Vermont	232	58	56.9
Virginia	132	101	99.0
Washington	301	91	87.9
West Virginia	49	28	100.0
Wisconsin	406	143	85.3
Wyoming	48	29	89.7

*From 1976 OCR survey, which surveyed districts exhaustively.

single administrative school district. Elsewhere the number of districts in a state varies immensely, as do the ways in which districts are defined. A number of states that are predominantly rural have many small districts—e.g., Nebraska, which has a large number of one-school districts—a situation that creates unique problems both for the organization of special education programs and for studying enrollment patterns. These districts, which often have small proportions of minorities, cannot be readily compared with those with much larger enrollments.

To date, OCR has not conducted any checks on the accuracy of the school or district reports. The 1976 survey requested data from all school districts in the country, and the response rate was at least 95 percent in every state. School districts are obligated under Title VI of the Civil Rights Act of 1964 to respond to the survey in a timely and accurate fashion and are reminded of this in the survey instruments. Thus, while the data have not been and should be verified, the conditions under which they are obtained suggest that respondents would take reasonable care with their reports.

TECHNICAL ISSUES

MEASURING GROUP DIFFERENCES IN PLACEMENTS

The results by sex in Table 1 show that disproportions may appear larger or smaller depending on whether they are based on the differences of percentages or on ratios. Because the percentage scale is bounded by zero at one end and 100 at the other, absolute differences between values close to either end are generally limited to being relatively small. In other words, a program for the seriously emotionally disturbed (SED), which has a small proportion of pupils enrolled in total, does not have a large absolute disproportion by gender, even though the process of classifying students as emotionally disturbed results in a male-female ratio of about 3:1. At the same time, there is a greater percentage of females who are not in special education. In comparison to the nonclassified group, the 3:1 disproportion is still more extreme.

In the analysis presented in this paper, these problems were addressed by using an index of disproportion derived from recent statistical developments termed log-linear analysis (Bishop et al., 1975). The basic element in the index is the "odds" of being assigned to a particular special education category. For example, a measurement of the odds of a minority student's being assigned to an EMR class is the percentage of minority students who are classified as EMR divided by the percentage of minorities who are not in special programs. From Table 1, this is $2.54/92.60 = 0.027$. The odds of a white student's being designated EMR is $1.06/94.12 = 0.011$. The disproportion index is the ratio of these two odds, scaled by being transformed to a natural logarithm;[4] that is, $\log_e(0.027/0.011) = 0.89$.

The log-odds index is positive because the EMR odds for minorities is larger than those for whites; it would be zero if the odds for minorities and whites were equal and negative if the odds for minorities were lower than those for whites. The index is not simple to interpret since the measure is unbounded, i.e., it can vary from $-\infty$ to $+\infty$ depending on the magnitude of the disproportion. As a rough interpretive device, however, the log-odds index can be transformed to a measure of association, Yule's Q-statistic, which, like a correlation, is limited to values between -1 and $+1$.[5] Thus the association of race or ethnicity (minority versus nonminority) with placement (EMR versus none) is $+.42$.

To see the degree of change in either the log-odds index or Q with a change in disproportion, suppose that the minority-white EMR ratio was 5:1 instead of the actual ratio of approximately 2.5:1.0. That is, suppose that 5.30 percent of racial/ethnic minorities were enrolled in EMR programs—

[4]This is also equivalent to the difference of the logarithms of the two odds, i.e., $\ln(0.027) - \ln(0.011) = 0.89$.

[5]The relationship is given by $Q = (a - 1)/(a + 1)$, where $a = e^x$ and x is the log-odds index. This transformation is the inverse of Fisher's z for correlations and maps x onto the zero-one interval. Q is normally distributed in large samples and attains a value of unity whenever either odds is zero.

about double the Table 1 value—and that 89.84 percent of minorities were not enrolled in any special program—instead of the actual value of 92.6 percent. These hypothetical values would increase the log-odds index to 1.66 and the measure of association to $Q = .68$.

DISAGGREGATION OF DATA

A second technical issue is the extent to which data on disproportion should be disaggregated. For example, Table 3 presents the percentage of students in each special program for specific racial/ethnic populations. It is clear that the relatively large minority-white differences in EMR placements are even more extreme for black students alone (3.46 percent of black students are classified EMR), who also comprise the largest minority population in this country. The disproportions in programs for the trainable mentally retarded and for emotionally disturbed children are also due in large part to the disproportionate representation of blacks in these classifications. At the same time, for Hispanic students—the second largest minority group—placement rates in EMR, TMR, and SED programs are very close to those for non-Hispanic whites on a nationwide basis. Asian and Pacific Island students have the lowest placement rates of all groups in the same three programs.

Table 3 also provides information on the apparent lack of difference between minority and white placements in specific learning disabilities programs. A slightly larger percentage of whites is classified as having specific learning disabilities than blacks, unlike the difference in other special programs, while a still larger percentage of Hispanic students is classified as having specific learning disabilities.

Disaggregation by race or ethnicity provides information that is not apparent in Table 1.[6] To simplify the data presentation, this paper first presents results for all minorities combined; the results are then subdivided for separate racial/ethnic groups. It is an important characteristic of the log-odds index of disproportion that it can be validly computed for each minority group separately, by replacing the odds of placement for all minorities with the odds for a particular subpopulation (e.g., blacks or Hispanics). Other approaches—e.g., the comparison of the proportion of

---

[6]Some further disaggregation by grade is possible with the OCR data, by locating schools within each district that serve only grades kindergarten-6, 7-8, and 9-12, respectively. About three fourths of the schools in the sample can be classified in this manner. While some age-related analysis is possible, the various levels are not comparable because of different dropout rates; dropout information was not gathered in the OCR's 1978 survey.

TABLE 3 Nationwide Special Education Placements for Specific Racial and Ethnic Groups

	American Indian/ Alaskan Native	Asian/ Pacific Island	Hispanic	Black	White	Percentage of All Students
Percentage of Student Population[a]						
Total	0.79	1.42	6.75	15.72	75.32	100.00
Percentage in special education programs[b]						
Educable mentally retarded (EMR)	1.73	0.37	0.98	3.46	1.07	1.43
Trainable mentally retarded (TMR)	0.23	0.15	0.24	0.39	0.19	0.23
Seriously emotionally disturbed (SED)	0.33	0.10	0.29	0.50	0.29	0.32
Specific learning disabilities (SLD)	3.49	1.27	2.58	2.23	2.32	2.31
Speech impaired (SI)	1.87	1.85	1.78	1.87	2.04	1.99

[a]From *State, Regional, and National Summaries of Data from the 1978 Civil Rights Survey of Elementary and Secondary Schools*, prepared for OCR by Killalea Associates, Inc., April 1980. Based on estimated total school enrollment of 41,836,257 students.
[b]Percentages are based on weighted projections to national totals from 1978 OCR survey data.

EMR students who are black with the proportion of the total school population that is black—do not give an accurate portrayal of disproportion in settings with multiple minority groups. This is because the denominators of the EMR proportion and of the total proportion are inflated differentially by the number of minority students included who are not black.

Further disaggregation by geographic or administrative unit can reveal trends that would not be apparent if the number of children enrolled in each school or district was disregarded. For example, consider a hypothetical geographic unit (a state or nation) that has only two school districts. District 1 has a total enrollment of 3,000 students, consisting of 1,000 white and 2,000 minority students. Of these, 20 white (2 percent) and 20 minority students (1 percent) are classified as EMR. While the rate for minorities in District 1 is slightly lower than that for whites, the situation is the opposite in District 2. The total enrollment is 600, consisting of 400 white and 200 minority students. Four of the white students (1 percent) and 18 minority students (9 percent) are enrolled in EMR classes, reflecting a relatively large disproportion.

If the geographic unit's total alone is examined, there are 1,400 white students of whom 24 are assigned to EMR classes, yielding a 1.7 percent placement. There are 2,000 minority students, of whom 38 (also 1.7 percent) are in EMR classes. While the two percentages are the same at the state level, they disguise several more detailed outcomes—the large disproportion in the small district and the variability between district practices. This stems from the tendency of large districts to obscure data for small districts in aggregations.

Districts that have no students classified in a special program inflate the state's total enrollment proportionate to the percentage of minority students in the district, distorting aggregate measures of disproportion further. For example, according to the 1978 OCR survey, in only 12 states did all districts report having EMR students. In 19 of the remaining states, more than 10 percent of the school districts reported having no EMR students at all, and in 8 states more than 25 percent of the districts reported having no EMR students. The average enrollment of 887 districts having no EMR students was 1,336, well below the average of 5,911 students in districts having EMR programs. While many smaller (often rural) districts maintain other special programs, including those for trainable mentally retarded, emotionally disturbed, or specific learning-disabled students, about one third of the districts having no EMR programs do not operate any of these other programs. Thus, there are essentially two populations of school districts represented in the survey data—those with and those without EMR programs. Statistical information regarding racial or sex differences in EMR placement rates can be obtained only from the former set.[7]

Placement in special education programs is a district-by-district process, and a wide range of placement rates and racial disproportions may be found among districts operating under the same state guidelines. It is essential that an analysis of special education trends reflects this variability.

Scoring Disproportion for Districts and States

The 1978 OCR survey provides data from which placement rates and the disproportion index may be calculated for each school district. Of the 5,153 districts in the 1978 sample that have students enrolled in EMR programs, 236 districts do not have both whites and minorities in their student populations. The distribution of the log-odds index for EMR placements in the remaining 4,917 districts is given in Table 4 for all minorities combined. A log-odds index of 1.6 ($Q = .66$) separates 20 percent of the districts with the highest degree of disproportion from those with less disproportion; an index value of 2.1 ($Q = .78$) separates 10 percent of the districts with the most extreme disproportions from the rest. The index values in every column of Table 4 have a nearly normal distribution and may be used in normal-theory statistical analysis (e.g., t-tests or F-tests).

Small districts present a special problem to the investigation of special education placements, which is reflected in any measure of proportionality. A typical rural district or one in a small New England community, for example, may have 500 students of whom all but 20 are white. One student of the 20 classified as EMR results in a EMR rate of 5 percent for minorities. If two are classified as EMR, the minority rate is 10 percent, which is unusually high, and so on. In other words, in districts with a very low number of minorities enrolled (or with a very low number of whites), small differences in the number of placements create large disproportions that may not reflect a serious problem of overrepresentation or underrepresentation. Furthermore, if none of the minority students (or none of the whites) is in an EMR class, the odds for that group are zero, and the logarithm is not defined.

Recent advances in the analysis of contingency tables provide methods for "smoothing" proportions so that they allow finer differences than the 5-10-15 percent values of the example above. The method of "iterative

---

[7]The proportion of the nation's school districts having no EMR programs may be larger than the OCR's 1978 survey indicates. In 1976, OCR surveyed all districts in the country, and approximately 45 percent reported no EMR enrollment. The 1978 sampling plan may have tended to overrepresent those districts having EMR classes.

TABLE 4   Relative Frequency Distribution of Log-Odds Measure for All Minorities in EMR

Interval	All	District Enrollment (in thousands)				
		Less Than 1	1 to 3	3 to 10	10 to 30	More Than 30
−5.0 and below	0.3	0.5	0.2	0.1	—	—
−4.9 to −4.5	0.1	0.2	0.1	0.2	—	—
−4.4 to −4.0	0.4	0.4	0.6	0.1	—	—
−3.9 to −3.5	0.6	1.2	0.5	0.2	0.2	—
−3.4 to −3.0	0.6	0.5	1.1	0.3	—	—
−2.9 to −2.5	1.2	2.0	1.1	1.0	0.4	—
−2.4 to −2.0	3.2	3.9	3.8	2.3	—	—
−1.9 to −1.5	4.6	5.6	5.3	3.7	0.7	0.7
−1.4 to −1.0	6.7	6.0	9.4	5.3	0.8	—
−0.9 to −0.5	8.2	9.8	10.4	4.4	3.9	—
−0.4 to 0	10.9	15.0	10.9	7.7	10.4	3.7
0.1 to 0.5	13.4	13.1	11.6	13.9	23.1	18.4
0.6 to 1.0	15.6	10.2	13.0	22.0	23.8	30.1
1.1 to 1.5	13.5	7.2	13.5	18.0	19.2	25.8
1.6 to 2.0	10.6	7.8	9.7	13.7·	12.7	14.7
2.1 to 2.5	5.1	6.7	4.2	4.9	4.4	5.1
2.6 to 3.0	2.2	3.8	2.2	1.5	0.2	0.5
3.1 to 3.5	1.0	1.7	1.0	0.4	0.2	—
3.6 to 4.0	0.5	1.3	0.3	0.1	—	—
4.1 to 4.5	0.3	0.7	0.3	0.1	—	—
4.6 to 5.0	0.2	0.4	0.0	—	—	—
5.1 to 5.5	0.2	0.8	0.1	—	—	—
5.6 to 6.0	0.1	0.3	0.2	—	—	—
6.1 to 6.5	0.2	0.4	0.2	—	—	—
6.6 to 7.0	0.2	0.2	0.2	0.1	—	—
7.1 and above	0.1	0.3	0.1	—	—	—
Number of districts in sample	4,917	1,074	1,785	1,507	418	133
Mean	0.42	0.37	0.25	0.59	0.77	1.02
Standard deviation	1.55	1.88	1.57	1.25	0.83	0.67

NOTE: Projections are weighted to nationwide percentages; weights are the inverse of sampling probabilities.

proportional fitting" (Bishop et al., 1975) is most commonly used when there are many cells in a complex contingency table with few observations (or zeros) but may also be used for smaller tables. In this application it is assumed that any district with few whites or few minority students does not permit accurate estimation of the odds for that group, because of the scale restriction described.[8] If all such districts within the state are summed, however, sufficient whites and minorities will be included to obtain fairly accurate estimates of EMR proportions. The state table becomes a "target," and the coarse figures for each small district in the state are adjusted slightly toward those target values. The adjustments are small in all cases but are relatively greater in the smallest districts, where the initial scale intervals may be very large. The adjusted proportions are used in the log-odds measure in place of the unadjusted rates. Experience with this procedure has shown that the difference in odds for minorities and whites is changed very little through smoothing, while the estimates of proportions obtained from small samples are refined, and district indexes may be calculated when one entry is zero. (Several examples of the procedure are given in the appendix to this paper.)

Summary statistics for a state are obtained by averaging the log-odds measure across all districts or subsets of districts (e.g., all districts of similar size). Dispersion measures (e.g., the range or standard deviation) provide an indicator of variability within the state. In every case the descriptive statistics presented in this paper are weighted by the inverse of the sampling probabilities provided from the survey, so that the mean or standard deviation for the entire state is more accurately approximated. Degrees of freedom for tests of significance, however, are based on the actual number of districts in the sample or subsample.

GEOGRAPHIC VARIATION IN DISPROPORTION

Table 5 presents a summary of disproportion in EMR classes by state and region, as calculated from the 1978 OCR survey. The percentages of minority and white students and males and females who are classified as EMR are calculated for each district having EMR programs, as is the log-odds scoring of the difference. The weighted average and the standard deviation are calculated to estimate the summary statistics for all districts having EMR programs in the state.

The average percentage of minority students in EMR classes exceeds

---

[8]The criterion used to identify small districts for this analysis was any district having fewer than 100 minority students enrolled or fewer than 100 whites enrolled.

TABLE 5 Summary of EMR Assignments by State

State	Race or Ethnicity						Sex				
	Percentage of Minority Enrollment	Average EMR Percentage		Log-Odds Index		Q	Average EMR Percentage		Log-Odds Index		Q
		Minority	White	Average	Standard Deviation		Male	Female	Average	Standard Deviation	
Northeast											
Connecticut	16.37	2.01	0.71	0.75	1.01	.36	0.94	0.67	0.28	0.57	.14
Maine	0.95	2.31	1.52	-0.41	1.53	-.20	1.78	1.27	0.41	0.81	.20
Massachusetts	9.53	1.44	1.04	0.06	1.38	.03	1.32	0.81	0.30	0.71	.15
New Hampshire	1.09	0.83	0.90	-0.93	1.27	-.43	1.01	0.78	0.16	0.81	.08
New Jersey	26.15	1.83	0.76	0.78	1.41	.37	1.08	0.94	0.20	0.70	.10
New York	31.06	3.35	1.17	0.09	1.77	.04	1.35	0.97	0.29	0.63	.14
Pennsylvania	14.01	2.05	1.60	-0.12	1.28	-.06	2.01	1.30	0.44	0.40	.21
Rhode Island	7.11	3.91	0.66	1.26	1.33	-.56	0.77	0.58	0.50	0.62	.25
Vermont	0.80	0.46	2.31	-1.35	1.34	-.59	2.61	1.99	0.30	0.68	.15
Border											
Delaware	25.73	5.20	1.23	1.51	0.47	.64	2.42	1.93	0.26	0.17	.13
District of Columbia	95.99	0.36	0.23	0.41	—	.20	0.50	0.21	0.90	—	.42
Kentucky	8.76	6.74	2.55	0.57	1.42	.28	3.43	2.19	0.54	0.47	.26
Maryland	31.71	2.54	0.70	1.44	0.57	.62	1.51	0.85	0.58	0.32	.28
Missouri	15.48	5.12	2.41	0.75	1.00	.36	3.16	2.10	0.46	0.49	.23
Oklahoma	22.81	3.31	2.15	0.19	1.28	.09	2.77	1.83	0.38	0.63	.19
West Virginia	5.03	1.47	2.11	-1.64	2.44	-.67	2.65	1.61	0.59	0.29	.28

TABLE 5 (continued)

State	Percentage of Minority Enrollment	Race or Ethnicity					Sex				
		Average EMR Percentage		Log-Odds Index			Average EMR Percentage		Log-Odds Index		
		Minority	White	Average	Standard Deviation	Q	Male	Female	Average	Standard Deviation	Q
South											
Alabama	34.21	9.09	2.07	1.55	1.31	.65	4.81	2.97	0.52	0.28	.25
Arkansas	23.56	6.28	2.23	0.93	1.45	.43	4.23	2.69	0.48	0.62	.24
Florida	30.46	5.33	0.93	1.86	0.41	.73	2.25	1.56	0.39	0.29	.19
Georgia	35.39	6.20	1.44	1.66	1.02	.68	3.46	2.27	0.48	0.31	.24
Louisiana	42.17	4.01	0.93	1.50	0.39	.63	2.66	1.66	0.51	0.24	.25
Mississippi	48.51	5.59	1.87	1.34	1.24	.59	3.99	2.31	0.58	0.40	.28
North Carolina	31.41	7.30	1.72	1.54	0.56	.65	4.17	2.65	0.51	0.25	.25
South Carolina	41.86	7.11	1.72	1.57	0.54	.65	4.96	3.17	0.51	0.26	.25
Tennessee	21.52	6.16	1.99	1.07	1.07	.49	3.29	1.98	0.57	0.43	.28
Texas	41.16	3.60	0.84	1.35	1.77	.59	1.71	1.28	0.33	0.68	.16
Virginia	27.07	4.06	1.14	1.34	0.84	.59	2.42	1.55	0.46	0.33	.23
Midwest											
Illinois	26.58	3.07	1.47	0.12	1.48	.06	1.80	1.33	0.38	0.64	.19
Indiana	11.06	2.83	1.50	-0.36	1.62	-.18	1.86	1.21	0.46	0.51	.23
Iowa	3.69	1.40	1.95	-1.25	1.45	-.55	2.28	1.60	0.36	0.72	.18

Kansas	11.33	4.52	1.60	0.09	1.48	.05	1.91	1.39	0.28	0.74	.14
Michigan	17.53	1.57	1.07	-0.09	1.42	-.04	1.30	0.93	0.31	0.64	.16
Minnesota	4.66	2.39	1.29	-0.03	1.11	-.02	1.54	1.08	0.39	0.70	.19
Nebraska	8.81	4.45	1.91	0.61	1.01	.29	2.47	1.65	0.37	0.63	.19
North Dakota	6.81	3.23	1.66	-0.11	1.86	-.06	2.12	1.52	0.26	0.57	.13
Ohio	14.26	5.42	2.46	0.05	1.37	.03	3.00	2.05	0.40	0.40	.20
South Dakota	7.83	1.93	0.80	0.29	1.35	.14	1.23	0.66	0.58	0.64	.28
Wisconsin	7.65	1.91	1.40	0.02	1.18	.01	1.70	1.15	0.38	0.62	.19
West											
Alaska	28.86	2.47	0.59	2.28	2.24	.81	2.01	1.49	0.45	0.76	.22
Arizona	33.28	1.35	0.71	0.36	2.21	.18	1.16	0.93	0.20	0.59	.10
California	36.03	0.85	0.61	0.33	0.96	.16	0.71	0.54	0.28	0.66	.14
Colorado	20.35	1.48	0.80	0.18	1.67	.09	1.09	0.79	0.39	0.70	.19
Hawaii	77.84	0.96	0.49	0.67	—	.32	0.97	0.74	0.31	—	.15
Idaho	6.16	1.31	1.24	-0.31	1.46	-.15	1.49	1.07	0.30	0.69	.15
Montana	9.59	1.43	0.89	0.23	2.20	.12	1.25	1.01	0.13	0.80	.07
Nevada	17.10	1.36	0.77	0.46	1.03	.23	1.25	0.53	0.77	0.62	.37
New Mexico	53.25	2.51	0.83	1.30	0.78	.57	1.93	1.26	0.59	0.73	.29
Oregon	7.72	0.97	0.71	-0.14	1.31	-.07	0.89	0.56	0.49	0.78	.24
Utah	6.96	2.00	0.82	0.93	0.50	.43	1.04	0.78	0.35	0.49	.17
Washington	10.72	2.62	1.17	-0.23	1.61	-.11	1.37	1.05	0.28	0.53	.14
Wyoming	8.61	1.16	0.45	0.84	2.08	.40	0.63	0.45	0.35	0.76	.18

NOTE: All figures except percentage of minority enrollment and Q are obtained by calculating the respective value for each district in the sample. The values for the districts in each state are weighted by the inverse of the sampling probabilities. The weighted averages and standard deviations are presented in the table as statewide estimates. Q is calculated directly from the estimated statewide average log-odds index.

the average percentage for whites in every state except New Hampshire, Vermont, West Virginia, and Iowa—states with a very small number of minority students. Of those states with more than 10 percent minority enrollments, the average EMR rates for minorities range from 0.85 percent to 9.09 percent with a median of 3.35 percent; for whites the average EMR rates range from 0.59 percent to 2.46 percent with a median of 1.17 percent. While the magnitude of the difference varies from state to state, as does the degree of consistency among districts within states, EMR disproportion by race or ethnicity is a nationwide phenomenon.

There is also systematic regional variation in the extent to which EMR placements for minorities and whites differ. The median state log-odds index for nine northeastern states is 0.06 ($Q = .03$), while state averages range from −1.35 in Vermont to 1.26 in Rhode Island. None of the northeastern states has an average log-odds index over 1.6, indicating no serious disproportion on a state level. The Midwest is even more homogeneous, with all average disproportion indexes near zero. In the West, 11 of 13 states have low or nonexistent disproportions by race, while New Mexico's average log-odds index is 1.30 ($Q = .57$) and that for Alaska is 2.28 ($Q = .81$). Each of these states has more than one large minority group.

The border states are a more diverse group, with average log-odds indexes ranging from −1.64 in West Virginia, where the percentage of whites in EMR classes is almost 1.5 times that of minorities, to 1.51 in Delaware ($Q = .64$). The average disproportion for Maryland is almost as high as that of Delaware.

The average disproportion in the southern states is consistently high, ranging from a log-odds index of 0.93 in Arkansas ($Q = .43$) to 1.86 in Florida ($Q = .73$), with a median state value of 1.50 ($Q = .63$). Except for Alaska, only southern states have average disproportion indexes that approach or exceed the 1.6 value that separates the 20 percent most extreme individual districts in the country.

The extent to which the same racial difference occurs throughout a state is revealed partially by the standard deviation of the log-odds index. In particular, seven states have relatively small standard deviations (less than .60), indicating relatively homogeneous racial differences throughout: Delaware, Florida, Louisiana, Maryland, North Carolina, South Carolina, and Utah. With the exception of Utah, all of these states have more than 25 percent minority enrollment and are located in or near the South. While the high minority enrollment implies that relatively large numbers of minority students attend school in most parts of a state, it does not imply that the EMR disproportion is necessarily as high everywhere. For example, Alabama, Mississippi, and Texas also have at least 25 percent minority enrollments and are more heterogeneous in placements from one district to another.

The average percentage of males in EMR classes is higher than that of females in every state, although the difference on a nationwide basis (Table 1) is not as large as the minority-white disproportion. The state averages for sex disproportion range from 0.13 ($Q = .07$) in Montana to 0.77 ($Q = .37$) in Nevada. The standard deviation of the sex difference within each state is relatively small; thus, the extent to which males outnumber females in EMR classes is more consistent across districts throughout the nation than differences by racial or ethnic identity.

Within this limited range, there are still some regional trends. The log-odds or association (Q) values are relatively homogeneous in the South and are among the largest average values found anywhere in the nation. The border states of Kentucky, Maryland, and West Virginia also have larger disproportions by sex. To some extent this pattern is similar to that for disproportion by race/ethnicity. It is possible that in these states large percentages of minority males in particular are assigned to EMR programs, creating a sex and a race disproportion simultaneously. Unfortunately, the data do not include sex-by-race tabulations, so this possibility cannot be explored.

The simultaneous occurrence of disproportion by race or ethnicity and by gender can be explored across states and districts, however. At the state level, the log-odds index for race was ranked for the 31 states having more than 10 percent minority enrollment. The rank-order correlation between these and the rankings by sex disproportion is $+.42$;[9] there is a moderate trend for states that have the largest disproportionate assignment of minorities to EMR classes also to have the largest relative proportion of males in them. At the district level the disproportion index for race was correlated with the index for sex separately within each of the five geographic regions, for each of three district size categories (fewer than 1,000 students; 1,000–9,999 students; and 10,000 or more students). The 15 correlations range from $-.20$ to $+.19$, with a median value of $-.01$; none exceeds the .01 value for a two-sided test of significance. When geographic regions are combined, the correlation for districts with fewer than 1,000 students is .03; for districts with 1,000–9,999 students it is .01; for larger districts it is .13.

There is no evidence of a relationship between disproportionate placement in EMR classes by sex and disproportion by race/ethnicity on a district-

[9]Statistically significant at $p < .05$, using a two-sided test.

by-district basis. There is an association at the state level, however. To the extent that males and minorities are represented in EMR classes in greater proportions than females and whites, respectively, the phenomenon reflects practices that vary from one state or region to another more than from one district to another.

THE AVAILABILITY PHENOMENON

States and regions vary in the proportion of minority and white students actually assigned to EMR classes. The percentages from Table 5 are summarized by regions in Table 6 for 31 states with more than 10 percent minority enrollment.[10] The five geographic regions are relatively homogeneous in the minimum and maximum average placement rates for whites, although the low EMR rate for whites in the West does stand out from the other regions. By comparison, there are dramatic differences in both minimum and maximum values for minorities. The South, with the most consistent disproportions in EMR placement, has the highest minimum and maximum average placement rates of any of the geographic regions, up to an average of 9.09 percent of minorities in EMR classes in Alabama. The Northeast and the Midwest, with generally small disproportions, have smaller average placements in EMR classes for minorities. At the low extreme, the minimum and maximum average placements for minorities in the West are similar to those for whites in other parts of the country.

TABLE 6   Minimum and Maximum Average EMR Percentages by Region

Region	Number of States	Minority		White	
		Minimum	Maximum	Minimum	Maximum
Northeast	4	1.83	3.35	0.71	1.60
Border	4	2.54	5.20	0.70	2.41
South	11	3.60	9.09	0.84	2.23
Midwest	5	1.57	5.42	1.07	2.46
West	7	0.85	2.51	0.59	1.17

NOTE: For 31 states with more than 10 percent minority enrollment. Minima and maxima were obtained from weighted projections to statewide average values; weights are the inverse of the sampling probabilities.

[10]Hawaii and the District of Columbia, each representing only one administrative school district, were not included.

TABLE 7   Correlations of Disproportion in EMR Placements
With Overall Placement Rates

District Size	N	Correlations With Proportion of All EMR Students	Correlations With Proportion of All Students in Special Education
Fewer than 1,000 students	1,074	0.07	0.07
1,000 to 2,999 students	1,785	0.12*	0.12*
3,000 to 9,999 students	1,507	0.17*	0.17*
10,000 to 29,999 students	418	0.30*	0.22*
30,000 or more students	133	0.06	0.34*
All districts	4,917	0.09*	0.09*

NOTE: Correlations are the weighted projections to nationwide values; weights are the inverse of sampling probabilities.
*Significant at $p < .01$ (two-sided test).

On a regional basis the evidence suggests that larger differences between minority and white EMR placements occur in areas where the percentage of children—both minority and white—who are placed in EMR classes is high. To explore this relationship further the same 31 states were ranked on EMR placement rates for all students in a state, and each state was classified as being above or below the median. States were also classified as having an average log-odds index for minorities compared with whites above or below the median value for all 4,917 districts (approximately 0.5). Of the 16 states with "low" EMR rates, 11 have "low" disproportion values, while 5 states with "low" rates have higher disproportions by race. Among states with "high" placement rates, 13 of the 15 states have disproportions above the median. The regional trend is thus supported at the state level as well.

Disproportion is also associated with the overall percentage of students in EMR programs and, for all special education programs, at the district level. The correlations of placement rates with racial disproportion are given in Table 7 for districts in each size category. All correlations are positive, and most are statistically significant when $p < .01$.[11] The relationship is strongest among districts with 10,000–29,999 students and is positive but nonsignificant among very small districts. Many of the latter

[11] The correlations of the size of the EMR program with disproportion by sex (M − F) are positive, ranging from .04 for the smallest districts to .36 for districts with 10,000–29,999 pupils. The correlations of the size of the entire special education program with sex disproportion are all small and nonsignificant.

enroll only white or only black students, so that disproportion is largely a function of the size of one student group or the other; these tend to cancel each other across many districts.

The positive relationship between the size of EMR programs and the disproportionate placement of minorities in those programs occurs at district, state, and regional levels. The association may be interpreted in one of several ways. First, it is possible that the high proportion of minorities is creating an overall EMR program that is large. This may be an artifact since a relatively large number of EMR students of any group will tend to inflate the overall size of the program. Second, the size of the program may encourage greater disproportion in placements. That is, a large EMR program may open the door to mechanisms that allow minorities to be placed in these classes in relatively larger proportions. Third, both the size of the program and the disproportion may be simultaneous results of other exogenous factors, e.g., relatively large groups of educationally handicapped children, state or district guidelines for the classification of EMR students, and inferior instruction for minority (and white) students. It is clear that when the size of an EMR program is curtailed—i.e., its availability reduced—fewer students are involved, whether or not the relative degree of disproportion is changed. The data do indicate that, in general, smaller degrees of disproportion occur in relatively smaller EMR programs.

DEMOGRAPHIC CHARACTERISTICS AND DISPROPORTION

ENROLLMENT

The correlation between racial disproportion and total district enrollment is .05 for all districts. (Table 4 provides more detail.) Except for the smallest districts the average disproportion increases with district size. The standard deviation decreases as district size becomes larger, reflecting the absence of extreme disproportions in either direction. The mean disproportion among districts with 30,000 or more students is the highest, not because of many high disproportions but because very few districts have small or negative minority-white differences. On one hand, the size of larger districts in general appears to play a limiting role in the magnitude of racial disproportion in EMR classes. Districts with very small enrollments, on the other hand, sometimes have extreme disproportions in both directions. While few students are affected within any one district, the disproportions may involve a sizable number of students when totaled to the state or regional level.

PERCENTAGE OF MINORITY ENROLLMENT

To examine the relationship of racial composition to EMR disproportion, districts were classified as having 0-10, 10-30, 30-50, 50-70, 70-90, or 90-100 percent minority enrollment. A two-way fixed-effects analysis-of-variance model was fit to the average log-odds index with percentage of minority enrollment and geographic region as factors of classification. Orthogonal polynomial contrasts for unequal intervals were tested for the minority enrollment factor to determine the degree of complexity of the relationship of racial composition to disproportion. Individual districts in a particular size interval were considered as replicated observations; five separate analyses were conducted, one for each size interval. The mean disproportion index for each size of district and each minority enrollment division is given in Table 8 and Figure 1.

Tests of significance indicate a distinct relationship of minority enrollment to EMR disproportion for each district size category. Specifically, a cubic trend is significant at the .01 level for both the smallest districts (fewer than 1,000 pupils) and for districts with 1,000-2,999 students. This appears in Figure 1 as an increase in disproportion from close to zero, when minority enrollment is 10 percent or less, to values between 1.1 and 1.5 that remain relatively constant for districts with up to 70 percent minority enrollment. Additional minority enrollment causes the curves to turn upward again and peak with very high disproportion as the minority enrollment approaches 90-100 percent.

The interaction of region and percent minority is also statistically

TABLE 8   Mean Log-Odds Index for Districts by Percentage of Minority Enrollment

District Size	Percentage of Minority Enrollment					
	0 to 10	10 to 30	30 to 50	50 to 70	70 to 90	90 to 100
Fewer than 1,000 students	−0.07	1.21	1.48	1.12	1.52	4.17
1,000 to 2,999 students	−0.09	1.24	1.37	1.35	0.98	2.03
3,000 to 9,999 students	0.32	1.15	1.41	1.29	0.82	0.01
10,000 to 29,999 students	0.58	1.15	1.11	0.99	0.59	0.06
30,000 or more students	1.13	1.34	1.00	0.97	0.66	−0.02

NOTE: Percentages are the weighted projections to nationwide values; weights are the inverse of sampling probabilities.

344

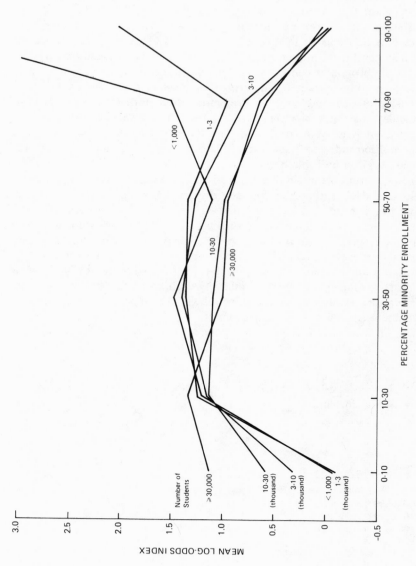

FIGURE 1 Mean log-odds index by district size.

significant for small districts. Border states with few minorities (0–10 percent) have minority-white differences that are larger than the slightly negative values given in Table 8, while northeastern states tend to have still more negative differences (i.e., greater proportions of whites in EMR classes than minorities). Also, small districts in the southern states with 90 percent or more minority do not attain the extremely large racial differences exemplified by the average values. A substantial portion of the nation's small all-minority school districts are in the South (15 of 41 in the sample). While EMR disproportion is relatively large, it is not as extreme as, for example, small all-minority districts in the West. Placement practices in small school districts in particular are worthy of further investigation.

The analyses for districts with 3,000–9,999 students and 10,000–29,999 students each produced a significant quadratic pattern of disproportion. This is apparent in Figure 1 as the parabolic curves for the two sets of districts. Each has a low, positive disproportion when the percentage of minority enrollment is small. The mean disproportion increases and peaks for districts with 10–70 percent minority enrollment, much like the smaller districts. The average disproportion becomes lower again, however, when the minority enrollment is 70–90 percent and approaches zero for districts that are essentially all minority.

For both medium-sized intervals, the interaction of region with percentage of minority enrollment is also significant, indicating that not all regions follow the pattern exemplified by the average curve. The most noteworthy exception occurs for districts with 10,000–29,999 students. As with the smaller districts, northeastern states with less than 10 percent minority enrollment are substantially below the nationwide average of 0.58; the Northeast mean disproportion is 0.33. Neither value is large, however.

The disproportion curve for the largest districts yields a significant linear effect, indicating that it is statistically indistinguishable from a monotonically decreasing pattern of means. The average disproportion for large districts is more than 1.1 when the proportion of minority students is 10 percent or less, increases slightly for districts with 10–30 percent minority enrollment, and decreases and approaches zero as the minority enrollment increases to 90–100 percent. The interaction of this trend with region is nonsignificant, so that the same pattern is characteristic of all five geographic areas.[12]

---

[12]It should be noted that not all regions have very large districts with the entire range of minority proportions. The Northeast, in particular, contributes only eight districts to this analysis, none of which has less than 30 percent minority enrollment. Since the northeastern average disproportion is generally low, this may partially account for the higher disproportions among large districts with small minority enrollments (see Table 8).

In general, the size of larger districts may impose constraints on programs for mentally retarded students that both limit the degree of disproportion and mediate the effects of greater minority enrollments. Among medium-sized and large districts, increased minority enrollments are not associated with increased racial disproportion in EMR classes. In fact, the opposite is true. Detailed analysis (not shown) indicates that as the percentage of minority enrollment increases, the minority EMR placement rate diminishes to close to that for whites, and the difference between white and minority rates approaches zero. Whether this is due to different assessment and placement procedures in districts with large numbers of minorities, different definitions of retardation, or different dropout rates[13] or whether it is a function of the availability of other facilities and resources (e.g., Title I programs) is not addressed by the survey data. At the same time, small districts with more than 50 percent minority enrollment exhibit increasing disproportions that are worthy of further study.

SOCIOECONOMIC STANDING

The 1978 OCR survey provides limited data on the socioeconomic standings of families whose children attend school in a given district. The school questionnaire requires a count of the number of students who pay full price for a daily lunch, the number of lunches that are served free under government subsidy, and the number of reduced-price lunches. It is not clear that all parents whose children qualify for reduced-price or free meals were informed of the program and made formal application or that the application reached the appropriate school officials. Further, the income cutoffs by which eligibility is determined depend on the number of children in a family, so that eligibility does not directly imply a given income level. Also, schools in middle- or high-income areas having entirely full-price lunch programs cannot be differentiated by socioeconomic status (SES) from the survey data. Under these conditions, only a gross index of SES is possible. The measure used was simply the proportion of lunches served in the district for which full price was paid.

The correlations of SES with EMR disproportions by race/ethnicity are given in Table 9. The association is significantly negative for all districts combined ($r = -.20$) and similar for districts with up to 9,999 students. However, correlations for separate geographic regions (not shown) indicate exceptions in the northeastern and border states, where the correla-

---

[13]According to the OCR's 1978 survey, the proportion of students suspended is inversely related to minority enrollment, so suspensions are probably not a contributing factor.

TABLE 9 Correlations of Socioeconomic Status With Disproportions in EMR Placement

District Size[a]	N[b]	Correlation With Disproportion (Minority-White)[c]
Fewer than 1,000 students	1,037	−0.22[d]
1,000 to 2,999 students	1,754	−0.23[d]
3,000 to 9,999 students	1,493	−0.15[d]
10,000 to 29,999 students	412	−0.07
30,000 or more students	131	+0.35[d]
All districts	4,827	−0.20[d]

[a]The correlation of district size with socioeconomic status for the entire sample is −.08.

[b]Ninety districts were eliminated that did not provide lunch program information.

[c]Correlations are the weighted projections to nationwide values; weights are the inverse of sampling probabilities.

[d]Significant at $p < .01$ (two-sided test).

tions are low positive. For medium-sized districts (up to 29,999 students) the correlation is negative but nonsignificant. This is supported by very small positive and negative values for separate geographic regions.

For districts with 30,000 or more students the correlation is significant and positive. Among the largest districts, relatively more minority students are enrolled in EMR classes when the population served has higher income levels. These figures may disguise a plethora of more complex factors, however.[14] For example, the correlation of district size with SES is itself negative, so that the positive .35 value is specific to a set of districts with relatively low income levels. The lower SES districts within this group are the same districts that have 60 percent or more minority enrollment as well as EMR rates for minorities that are close to those for whites. The higher SES districts in this group tend to have more part-time EMR placements (see the section below on time spent in EMR classes).

There is a general tendency for greater EMR disproportions to occur in lower SES districts. This is attributable in part to the percentage of students in EMR programs in a district. The relative size of EMR pro-

[14]The correlation may also be biased by regional differences. The largest districts are primarily "forced" into the sample, such that 79 of 131 districts were in the border or southern states. These regions have much higher disproportion levels and somewhat higher mean SES levels.

grams has a strong and consistent association with SES ($r = -.31$ for all districts in the sample). EMR classes may be small or nonexistent in upper-class communities and are accompanied by little racial disproportion. In lower SES communities, both the program size and racial difference are larger.

The association of SES with EMR disproportion, however, is mediated by a number of additional factors and even contradicted in some subsets of school districts.[15] Minority enrollment—a significant concomitant of SES—has a strong but complex relationship to disproportion as well. Unfortunately, the OCR survey does not provide cross-tabulations of race by participation in the subsidized lunch program, so the two characteristics cannot be disentangled.

DESEGREGATION AND RACIAL BALANCE

It has been hypothesized that court-ordered desegregation can become an antecedent of high EMR disproportions if classes for mentally retarded students are perceived as an alternate route toward class or school "resegregation." The OCR questionnaire data cannot reveal whether this is the case since the survey provides no time frame to interpret the question. A positive response to the OCR survey may indicate a program implemented in the recent past, in the more distant past, or perhaps still in preparation. Nevertheless, it is possible to compare the districts under court order with others in the same state that are not. Also, the racial balance among schools in each district may be examined, apart from the official desegregation status.

In general, districts subject to desegregation orders are larger than those that are not (average enrollment of 14,722, compared with 3,707) and have higher percentages of minorities enrolled (average percentage of 39.9, compared with 13.7). These differences may reflect the tendency of courts or federal agencies to focus their attention on large cities where minority populations are extensive. Table 10 provides several ways of examining the differences between the two groups of districts on a state-by-state basis.

The average log-odds index of disproportion was calculated separately for districts under court order to desegregate and those not under court order. They reveal few if any differences. The means for 38 states were

---

[15]The correlation of SES with disproportion by sex (M − F) is consistently negative and significant for all but the smallest districts. That is, in general, more males are assigned to EMR programs in lower SES districts.

TABLE 10 Districts Under Court Order to Desegregate

State	Number of Districts		Average Disproportion		Exceed State Average		Exceed Average +1 Standard Deviation	
	Court Order	Not	Court Order	Not	Court Order	Not	Court Order	Not
Northeast								
Connecticut	9	125	0.65	0.75	45.7	53.6	0.0	9.9
Maine	0	102						
Massachusetts	2	134	0.53	0.05	100.0	48.4	0.0	14.8
New Hampshire	0	63						
New Jersey	9	336	1.84	0.75	100.0	51.8	33.3	12.5
New York	9	395	0.45	0.08	66.7	54.2	11.1	13.4
Pennsylvania	10	406	-0.09	-0.12	70.1	48.5	0.0	16.9
Rhode Island	2	29	0.50	1.32	0.0	42.6	0.0	15.3
Vermont	4	44	-2.11	-1.27	0.0	51.3	0.0	13.0
Border								
Delaware	1	15	1.10	1.54	0.0	61.3	0.0	0.0
District of Columbia	0	1						
Kentucky	9	179	1.16	0.54	100.0	52.3	0.0	12.8
Maryland	2	22	1.25	1.46	57.9	53.5	0.0	16.9
Missouri	7	327	1.33	0.74	85.7	47.7	14.3	13.1
Oklahoma	5	300	0.61	0.18	56.9	53.9	0.0	11.4
West Virginia	2	31	0.85	-1.79	100.0	52.2	50.0	7.5

TABLE 10 (continued)

State	Number of Districts		Average Disproportion		Exceed State Average		Exceed Average +1 Standard Deviation	
	Court Order	Not	Court Order	Not	Court Order	Not	Court Order	Not
South								
Alabama	68	55	1.72	1.35	54.4	50.9	7.3	3.6
Arkansas	20	224	1.10	0.92	66.1	52.6	0.0	11.3
Florida	0	67						
Georgia	55	126	1.76	1.62	43.6	52.4	7.3	8.7
Louisiana	45	21	1.50	1.50	46.7	42.9	15.6	19.1
Mississippi	79	67	1.29	1.41	48.1	65.7	8.9	1.5
North Carolina	17	130	1.64	1.53	52.9	55.4	11.8	11.5
South Carolina	21	70	1.60	1.55	66.7	52.9	0.0	8.6
Tennessee	18	122	1.44	1.02	77.8	51.6	22.2	9.0
Texas	51	685	1.23	1.36	41.2	56.3	0.0	9.1
Virginia	22	109	1.60	1.28	54.3	47.3	18.1	11.5
Midwest								
Illinois	9	456	0.85	0.11	66.7	46.3	11.1	14.1
Indiana	17	252	0.02	−0.38	40.6	51.9	21.5	10.1
Iowa	0	141						

Kansas	4	189	0.95	0.08	100.0	47.6	0.0	11.1
Michigan	4	463	0.44	-0.09	100.0	52.8	0.0	14.3
Minnesota	4	287	0.59	-0.04	100.0	48.8	0.0	13.3
Nebraska	1	110	1.42	0.60	100.0	44.7	0.0	20.9
North Dakota	0	58						
Ohio	6	556	0.38	0.05	100.0	50.2	0.0	14.0
South Dakota	0	65						
Wisconsin	7	298	1.29	-0.01	100.0	49.0	42.7	14.9
West								
Alaska	0	35						
Arizona	1	129	0.92	0.35	100.0	58.9	0.0	5.4
California	17	446	-0.01	0.34	29.4	52.7	0.0	10.3
Colorado	5	100	-0.18	0.20	40.0	59.2	0.0	10.0
Hawaii	0	1						
Idaho	0	79						
Montana	1	89	1.01	0.23	100.0	50.9	0.0	11.2
Nevada	0	19						
New Mexico	1	73	0.59	1.31	0.0	43.7	0.0	9.6
Oregon	0	123						
Utah	0	26						
Washington	4	180	0.67	-0.25	100.0	54.7	0.0	7.2
Wyoming	6	32	0.20	0.96	50.0	56.8	0.0	22.9

NOTE: All values are the weighted projections to statewide totals; weights are the inverse of sampling probabilities.

compared by use of a t-statistic, and no test of significance exceeded the .05 critical value (or .01). Furthermore, the same procedure was employed for districts in each of five size intervals in each state. Seven of the test statistics exceeded their respective .05 critical values in size-different states, four in one direction and three in the other. The results, viewed in this manner, strongly support the conclusion that there is no difference in disproportion between districts under court order to desegregate and those not under such orders.

The percentage of districts in each category that exceed the state's average disproportion level also is shown in Table 10. In 25 of the 38 states the percentage of districts exceeding the state average is higher among court-ordered districts than the other districts; in the remaining 13 states the percentage is lower. The split is significantly different from half and half using a one-sided test, but only when $p < .05$. Viewed in this manner, there is some tendency for court-ordered districts to have higher disproportions. The final column of Table 10 lists the proportion of districts in each category that exceed an extreme disproportion level of one standard deviation above the state's average. In 10 of the 38 states, a greater percentage of court-ordered districts fall in this extreme range than the other districts; 7 of these are in the South or the border states.

There appears to be a slight trend for districts under court order to desegregate to have higher EMR disproportions than other districts, especially among the southern states. The difference is small in most cases. It is not possible to interpret these differences as arising from the desegregation order in any case since the EMR disproportion may have preceded the order in time and may even have prompted the court's intervention.

Other measures may be derived from the OCR survey data to reflect the minority-white imbalance in individual schools. Two indexes of racial imbalance were calculated for each district, Taeuber's "index of dissimilarity" (D) and a more refined index derived from an information theoretic basis (H).[16] Each attains a value of zero if the proportion of minorities in every school is equal to the proportion in the district as a whole, i.e., an "even" distribution of minorities, indicating the least amount of racial isolation. Values of D and H approach 1 as the distribution of minorities becomes increasingly uneven. Both D and H are equal to 1 if some schools in a district are comprised only of minority students and the rest only of whites, i.e., total segregation.

The correlations of these measures with the index of disproportion are

---

[16]These indexes are described and compared by Zoloth (1976).

given in Table 11. In general, the correlations are low. To the extent that EMR disproportion and racial imbalance are related, the association is negative. That is, districts with larger EMR disproportions are those in which the racial composition of the schools is more nearly balanced; those with racial imbalances tend to have more similar EMR rates for whites and minorities.

Table 11 displays a set of correlations that is largely negative across region and district size intervals, although not all are statistically significant. Those that are, with a single exception, are for districts in the intermediate size ranges (1,000–9,999 students). Otherwise, the correlations of racial imbalance with disproportionate EMR assignment are small and may represent a negligible association for small and large districts in the country as a whole. Community and school perceptions of racial balance may differ depending on the proportion of minority students in the local districts. However, the same pattern of relationships—no association among small districts, significant negative association among medium-sized districts—was found when the percentage of minority enrollments was statistically controlled. In general, there is some tendency for differences in minority and white EMR rates to occur in districts in which schools are more "racially balanced." The effect is not strong among larger districts—i.e., among those in which desegregation orders are the most common—and thus does not add support to the "resegregation" hypothesis.

TABLE 11   Correlations of Log-Odds Index With Measures of Racial Imbalance

Region	Fewer Than 1,000 Students		1,000 to 9,999 Students		10,000 or More Students		All	
	D	H	D	H	D	H	D	H
Northeast	−0.05	−0.08	−0.18*	−0.09	−0.11	−0.01	−0.09*	−0.03
Border	−0.09	−0.06	−0.26*	−0.21*	−0.41*	−0.20	−0.17*	−0.12*
South	−0.01	0.04	−0.17*	−0.08*	−0.12	−0.09	−0.10*	−0.04
Midwest	−0.05	−0.04	−0.16*	−0.10*	0.04	0.12	−0.11*	−0.05
West	0.00	0.10	0.04	0.11	0.06	0.05	0.01	0.09
All	−0.09*	−0.05	−0.20*	−0.07*	0.04	0.10	−0.13*	−0.02

NOTE: All correlations are the weighted projections to regional values; weights are the inverse of sampling probabilities.
*Statistically significant at $p < .01$ (two-sided test).

TABLE 12 Average Suspension Rates by District Size and Minority Enrollment

| | Percentage Minority | | | | | | | | | | | | |
| | 0 to 10 | | 10 to 30 | | 30 to 50 | | 50 to 70 | | 70 to 90 | | 90 to 100 | | All | |
District Size	Minority	All	Minority	All	Minority	All	Minority	All	Minority	All	Minority	All	Minority	All
Fewer than 1,000 students	2.59	1.96	3.45	2.28	3.65	2.92	3.20	3.03	3.61	3.65	2.03	2.10	2.87	2.19
1,000 to 2,999 students	3.13	2.78	6.19	4.22	4.96	3.83	5.44	4.78	4.48	4.40	2.55	2.55	3.84	3.19
3,000 to 9,999 students	4.06	3.69	6.84	4.75	7.59	5.45	6.50	5.69	5.24	5.08	3.30	3.27	5.13	4.24
10,000 to 29,999 students	3.93	3.56	6.87	4.61	9.09	6.82	7.28	6.24	6.13	5.81	3.60	3.62	5.99	4.64
30,000 or more students	4.25	2.76	8.10	4.90	8.18	6.34	9.28	7.91	5.52	5.25	2.08	2.02	7.34	5.45
All districts	3.25	2.81	5.83	3.96	5.89	4.44	5.60	4.94	4.71	4.60	2.59	2.61	4.11	3.33

NOTE: All percentages are the weighted projections to nationwide values; weights are the inverse of sampling probabilities.

STUDENT SUSPENSIONS AND EMR DISPROPORTION

The OCR questionnaire requires districts to report the number of students who were suspended for "at least one school day during the 1977–78 year." Both the percentage of all students suspended and the percentage of minority students who were suspended during the year were recorded for this analysis. Average suspension rates are given in Table 12 by district size and minority enrollment. On a nationwide basis, 3.3 percent of all students and 4.1 percent of minority students were suspended at least once in 1977–1978. Suspension rates increase monotonically with district size and peak at 5.4 percent of all students and 7.3 percent of minorities in the largest districts. The proportion of suspensions are lowest in all-white and in all-minority districts and highest in the 30–70 percent minority range. Large districts in this range suspend more than 9 percent of all minority students—more than twice the nationwide rate for minorities and almost three times that for all students.

The correlations of suspensions with EMR disproportion are given in Table 13. Among small school districts and the very largest, there is no association of suspensions with disproportion in EMR placements. Among districts with 1,000–29,999 students enrolled, however, there is a positive association of racial disproportion with suspension rates.[17] Furthermore, the association is stronger with minority suspension than with overall student suspensions. Thus, middle-sized districts tend to suspend greater

TABLE 13   Correlations of Suspension Rates With
Racial Disproportion in EMR Placement

District Size	Correlation With All Suspensions	Correlation With Minority Suspensions
Fewer than 1,000 students	0.04	0.03
1,000 to 2,999 students	0.06*	0.11*
3,000 to 9,999 students	0.12*	0.23*
10,000 to 29,999 students	0.12	0.34*
30,000 or more students	−0.05	0.13
All districts	0.08*	0.12*

NOTE: All correlations are the weighted projections to nationwide values; weights are the inverse of sampling probabilities.
*Statistically significant at $p < .01$ (two-sided test).

[17]The correlations of EMR disproportion by sex (M − F) with suspensions are generally very low and nonsignificant.

numbers of minority students and to assign them to EMR classes in greater numbers concomitantly.[18] Whether either of these practices is an antecedent of the other or whether both are functions of a plethora of other possible determinants is not revealed by the survey data.

TIME SPENT IN EMR CLASSES

The OCR questionnaire solicits information on the amount of time students spend in special education classes, categorized as "less than 10 hours per week, 10 hours or more per week but less than full-time, or full-time." There is some ambiguity in the item for EMR programs since it is not clear whether the intent is to count (1) hours outside the regular class, (2) all time during which the child is receiving some special attention, whether in the regular class or not, or (3) the total amount of time the child is considered retarded (which would usually be full-time). While different respondents may have interpreted the item differently, it is likely that the most common interpretation is the first—i.e., a report of the proportion of time EMR students spend outside the regular classroom—so that the response "less than 10 hours" describes children who are largely mainstreamed.

The average proportion of EMR students assigned for the three time intervals is summarized in Table 14. EMR programs usually involve more than 10 hours per week of class time; that is, they are not generally attended for one or two class periods but for most of the school day. In fact, 49.4 percent of all districts having EMR programs report no students enrolled in EMR for less than 10 hours per week, while 16.8 percent of districts place all EMR students in full-time special programs. The profiles of Table 14 indicate that typical districts split EMR students about equally between full-time and somewhat less than full-time programs; the latter may be, for example, all academic courses or all classes but one. Larger districts tend to have more full-time EMR placements.

The correlations between the proportion of full-time EMR students and differential placements for minorities and whites (Table 14) are negative in every size interval and attain their largest values for schools with 10,000–29,999 students. In general, there is a tendency for the highest racial disproportions to occur in districts with many part-time EMR placements. Among large districts, those with the greatest disproportions tend have less than 50 percent minority enrollment (see Table 8). In these set-

---

[18]The same pattern is obtained for each geographic region except the West, where EMR disproportion is not related to either suspension index.

TABLE 14   Distribution of Amount of Time Spent in EMR Classes

| District Size | Average Percentage of EMR Students | | | Correlation of Percentage Full-Time With Racial Disproportion |
	Less Than 10 Hours	More Than 10 Hours	Full-Time	
Fewer than 1,000 students	26.1	44.7	29.2	−0.08*
1,000 to 2,999 students	15.7	44.7	39.6	−0.07*
3,000 to 9,999 students	12.2	41.0	46.8	−0.10*
10,000 to 29,999 students	11.0	35.9	53.2	−0.24*
30,000 or more students	11.3	40.1	48.5	−0.21

NOTE: All percentages and correlations are the weighted projections to nationwide values; weights are the inverse of sampling probabilities.
*Statistically significant at $p < .01$ (two-sided test).

tings, for whatever combination of administrative factors and characteristics of the student population, less than full-time EMR placement for minorities may be deemed sufficient.

The survey data do not permit comparisons on a student-by-student basis. Nevertheless, to the extent that these variables are related on a districtwise basis, it is *not* the case that the placement of minorities in EMR classes is associated with greater amounts of time spent in those programs.

DISPROPORTION IN OTHER SPECIAL EDUCATION PROGRAMS

The average proportions of minority and white children assigned to four special programs other than EMR are listed by state in Table 15. Of the 5,486 districts in the sample with one or more special programs and with both minority and white students enrolled, 4,917 (90 percent) have children classified as EMR, 93 percent have children classified as having specific learning disabilities (SLD), and 85 percent have children classified as speech-impaired (SI). In contrast, only 2,651 districts (about 48 percent) have students who are trainable mentally retarded (TMR), and 2,628 have students classified as seriously emotionally disturbed (SED). The latter programs are less common than the others, although districts may contract with outside agencies for these infrequently needed services. The figures in Table 15 are the average placement rates for just that subset of districts in a state that report having one or more students enrolled in the specific program category.

TABLE 15 Average Special Education Assignments by State

State	Trainable Mentally Retarded			Seriously Emotionally Disturbed			Specific Learning Disabilities			Speech Impaired		
	N	Minority Percentage	White Percentage	N	Minority Percentage	White Percentage	N	Minority Percentage	White Percentage	N	Minority Percentage	White Percentage
Northeast												
Connecticut	84	0.28	0.40	116	0.61	0.63	155	4.27	3.83	146	2.19	2.73
Maine	41	0.0	0.52	88	4.19	0.73	105	2.50	3.39	101	1.56	2.07
Massachusetts	89	0.98	0.47	98	0.29	0.55	170	7.82	4.39	155	3.26	1.99
New Hampshire	30	0.0	0.31	37	0.0	0.29	68	3.12	2.56	58	0.50	1.41
New Jersey	150	1.55	0.51	278	0.92	0.59	413	3.45	2.77	315	5.56	3.60
New York	126	0.95	0.31	256	1.39	1.22	420	1.79	1.16	364	1.80	1.42
Pennsylvania	115	0.72	0.45	160	0.72	0.33	416	3.93	1.40	373	2.98	2.47
Rhode Island	19	0.52	0.26	22	0.04	0.20	36	4.49	3.23	32	3.12	1.61
Vermont	22	1.47	1.18	31	0.51	0.31	57	2.80	3.72	64	6.66	3.29
Border												
Delaware	2	1.10	0.66	12	1.92	1.39	17	5.82	3.86	13	1.43	1.72
District of Columbia	1	0.35	0.69	1	0.13	0.02	1	0.51	0.62	1	0.40	0.30
Kentucky	133	0.81	0.38	36	1.38	0.50	138	2.35	2.06	158	4.78	4.08
Maryland	22	0.75	0.40	23	0.32	0.22	24	5.98	3.68	24	2.49	2.44
Missouri	47	2.50	0.50	116	0.94	0.62	334	3.90	3.47	337	6.02	5.58
Oklahoma	110	0.66	0.79	35	0.37	0.24	311	5.47	4.85	261	3.70	4.68
West Virginia	33	0.32	0.28	20	0.15	0.17	30	2.43	2.23	30	1.54	2.10

South

Alabama	100	0.97	0.29	64	0.25	0.24	111	1.35	1.42	109	2.04	1.89
Arkansas	126	1.45	0.37	49	0.20	0.33	215	2.80	2.46	171	2.85	2.56
Florida	56	0.77	0.31	54	0.73	0.43	67	3.00	2.18	64	3.74	2.73
Georgia	116	0.79	0.38	137	0.70	0.51	178	2.01	2.10	162	2.79	2.31
Louisiana	64	0.54	0.23	48	0.20	0.27	64	1.32	1.57	65	4.05	2.97
Mississippi	109	0.70	0.69	16	0.09	0.12	110	1.25	1.41	118	3.05	2.34
North Carolina	136	0.69	0.40	87	0.26	0.17	147	2.46	2.01	139	2.37	2.23
South Carolina	71	0.65	0.34	64	0.67	0.77	81	2.23	1.91	89	4.54	3.27
Tennessee	119	0.71	0.31	69	0.27	0.16	133	7.54	3.64	134	3.30	3.18
Texas	499	0.68	0.28	354	0.74	0.50	785	8.31	3.76	677	3.86	2.82
Virginia	104	0.50	0.27	72	0.24	0.27	131	3.20	1.96	131	2.86	2.48

Midwest

Illinois	146	0.58	0.47	279	1.74	0.69	623	4.88	3.91	575	5.22	4.57
Indiana	129	0.70	0.44	81	0.11	0.15	245	2.04	0.79	263	13.15	3.31
Iowa	76	0.05	0.70	57	0.19	0.32	219	15.53	4.18	132	4.20	2.13
Kansas	64	0.69	0.40	82	0.37	0.32	216	18.08	2.28	197	3.42	3.10
Michigan	82	0.56	0.54	412	1.01	0.58	508	2.17	2.01	373	4.16	2.58

TABLE 15 (continued)

State	Trainable Mentally Retarded			Seriously Emotionally Disturbed			Specific Learning Disabilities			Speech Impaired		
	N	Minority Percentage	White Percentage	N	Minority Percentage	White Percentage	N	Minority Percentage	White Percentage	N	Minority Percentage	White Percentage
Minnesota	160	0.28	0.57	108	0.65	0.51	329	4.82	3.48	321	5.35	2.69
Nebraska	49	0.38	0.59	53	0.26	0.50	102	14.52	3.14	108	5.71	3.22
North Dakota	26	0.12	1.12	12	2.42	0.96	69	2.85	2.93	83	12.73	3.86
Ohio	29	0.46	0.39	88	0.73	0.28	611	2.21	1.96	525	3.10	2.58
South Dakota	42	0.13	0.35	22	0.09	0.37	60	1.51	2.09	82	5.81	4.89
Wisconsin	169	0.16	0.43	209	0.74	0.72	329	1.77	2.23	327	2.58	1.94
West												
Alaska	19	0.38	0.10	29	0.57	0.21	35	12.88	3.75	31	4.09	1.81
Arizona	85	0.34	0.31	99	0.48	0.74	135	4.15	3.59	116	2.24	2.40
California	115	0.34	0.49	190	0.35	0.39	665	3.01	2.93	557	3.88	3.09
Colorado	44	0.51	0.21	62	1.15	0.48	114	5.34	3.25	98	2.89	2.22
Hawaii	1	0.25	0.25	1	0.15	0.26	1	3.62	3.41	1	0.18	0.18
Idaho	52	0.15	0.26	61	0.34	0.27	79	5.04	3.55	64	1.65	2.13
Montana	49	0.70	0.52	34	0.11	0.21	94	4.43	2.13	71	2.62	2.86
Nevada	9	0.26	0.19	15	0.71	0.30	19	6.88	3.52	10	3.18	2.45
New Mexico	54	0.50	0.36	33	0.30	0.24	65	4.64	2.52	41	1.62	1.75
Oregon	61	0.27	0.27	68	0.45	0.53	139	5.13	3.87	124	3.65	2.60
Utah	22	0.26	0.26	26	2.29	1.87	26	7.72	3.30	26	2.14	1.70
Washington	106	0.99	0.47	131	0.60	0.60	196	2.28	2.35	110	1.15	1.71
Wyoming	24	0.04	0.22	21	0.15	0.44	47	4.75	3.66	41	3.01	2.47

NOTE: All results are the weighted projections to statewide values; weights are the inverse of sampling probabilities.

TRAINABLE MENTALLY RETARDED

The nationwide rate for TMR enrollments, according to Table 3, is 0.23 percent of all students in this classification, and 0.19 percent of white students. The proportion of minority students in TMR classes exceeds the proportion for whites in 34 states, but there is not a great deal of consistency in either the magnitude or direction of the differences. The few consistencies that are supported by the log-odds indexes for TMR placement occur in midwestern states (e.g., Iowa, Nebraska, North Dakota, and Wisconsin), where there are much lower placement rates for minorities than for whites, and in the West, where minority-white differences tend to be small.

SERIOUSLY EMOTIONALLY DISTURBED

Nationwide rates for children who are seriously emotionally disturbed are also relatively small. The percentage of all children classified as SED is 0.32 percent; for white students it is 0.29 percent; and for blacks—the only minority to diverge by much from either figure—it is 0.50 percent. The minority placement rate exceeds that for whites in 28 states and in the District of Columbia, almost always by small amounts, and the log-odds index shows little or no consistency in direction. In particular, there is no consistent trend for minorities to be assigned disproportionately to SED programs in the South; rather the rates are similar or even higher for white students in this region.

SPECIFIC LEARNING DISABILITIES

Classes for those labeled SLD have the greatest proportion of students on a national basis of all special education programs. The nationwide rate is 2.31 percent for all students and the same for white students and varies from 1.27 percent of Asian or Pacific Island students to 3.49 percent of American Indian or Alaskan native students. The national rate for blacks is very close to that for whites.

The average percentage of minorities in SLD programs exceeds that of whites in 40 states. The high proportion of minorities in Alaska typifies districts throughout the state regardless of size, while those in Iowa, Kansas, Nebraska, Nevada, Texas, and Utah reflect high SLD rates for minorities in the smallest districts. There is some tendency for districts in these states to have a low proportion of children in EMR classes and to make more extensive use of the SLD classification. For example, Alaska, Nevada, and Utah have statewide EMR proportions for all students that are substantially below the nationwide rate of 1.4 percent and SLD proportions that are well above the national rate of 2.3 percent.

The average disproportion in SLD classes, as given by the log-odds index, is not large, however; except for Alaska, the highest positive value is only +0.85. The large average rates for minorities in some states is inflated by some unusually high percentages in a few districts, while the average log-odds index is not affected to as great an extent. The standard deviation of the index, especially for small districts, is relatively large, reflecting high within-state diversity.

Tests of significance[19] were conducted on the average disproportion for each of three district size intervals in each of three regions of the country. The results are summarized in Table 16, which gives a general picture of the direction of difference between minorities and whites in SLD placements. In the northeastern and midwestern states, there is a significant trend for minorities to be placed in SLD classes to a lesser extent than whites, especially among small and medium-sized districts. In the South and among small districts in the West, significantly more minorities than whites are placed in SLD classes. In the border states and among all districts with more than 10,000 students enrolled, there is no evidence of average minority-white disproportion in either direction.

Thus, differences in minority and white SLD placements are generally small and inconsistent. Disproportion varies from district to district and from region to region and depends on specific demographic characteris-

TABLE 16   Direction of Minority-White Difference in Test for Disproportions in Specific Learning Disabilities

Region	District Size		
	1 to 999 Students	1,000 to 9,999 Students	10,000 or More Students
Northeast	Negative	Negative	—
Border	—	—	—
South	Positive	Positive	—
Midwest	Negative	Negative	—
West	Positive	—	—

NOTE: Only results significant at $p < .01$ are shown.

[19]These were t-tests for $H_0: \mu = 0$.

tics as well. In general, it can only be concluded that SLD disproportion—when it reflects greater percentages of minorities than whites—is
not as extreme as disproportion in EMR programs.[20]

SPEECH-IMPAIRED

The proportions of different racial groups in classes for SI students are homogeneous, including Asian or Pacific Island students, who are represented in other special programs to a lesser extent. The average assignment rates given in Table 15 are similar from state to state, except where
the figures are inflated by a high proportion of minority students in small
districts. The average log-odds indexes for 29 states are negative, indicating some (weak) trend for whites to be assigned to special speech classes in
greater proportion than minorities.

SUMMARY

The results for special education classifications other than EMR are more
variable than consistent. The data clearly demonstrate that disproportionate assignment of students in such programs depends on the region of the
country, the particular state, and district characteristics. It is not possible to conclude that there is no disproportion in one special program
category, while there is in another. Disproportion occurs everywhere to a
lesser or greater degree, in one direction or the other, in each special education classification in different ways and depends on many situational
characteristics.

The extensive correlational analyses conducted for placements in EMR
programs were not undertaken for other classifications and may reveal additional trends. It is clear from the state and regional patterns, however,
that disproportionate EMR placements for minorities are greater and
more consistent than differences in other programs. The data do not address the question of why this occurs—a question that can only be answered
through a more process-oriented investigation.

EMR DISPROPORTION IN SEPARATE RACIAL OR ETHNIC GROUPS

Table 17 lists the average percentage of students in EMR programs and
the average log-odds index for each minority group identified by the OCR

---

[20]Tests of the mean difference in specific learning disability and EMR disproportions revealed
a significant difference in every region of the country.

TABLE 17 Average EMR Percentages for Separate Racial/Ethnic Groups by State

State	Nonminority Percentage	American Indian/ Alaskan Native		Asian/Pacific Islands		Black		Hispanic	
		Percentage	Log-Odds	Percentage	Log-Odds	Percentage	Log-Odds	Percentage	Log-Odds
Northeast									
Connecticut	0.71					1.66	0.39	2.78	0.54
Maine	1.52								
Massachusetts	1.04					1.43	−0.18	1.02	−1.43
New Hampshire	0.90								
New Jersey	0.76			0.25	−1.74	2.48	1.08	1.58	−0.05
New York	1.17			0.26	−3.28	7.13	0.33	1.47	−0.23
Pennsylvania	1.60					3.31	0.33	1.80	−0.89
Rhode Island	0.66					1.78	0.01	11.55	1.47
Vermont	2.31								
Border									
Delaware	1.23					5.49	1.57	1.25	−0.43
District of Columbia	0.23					0.37	0.42	0.24	0.16
Kentucky	2.55					7.60	0.69		
Maryland	0.70			0.42	−1.21	2.83	1.46		
Missouri	2.41					7.86	1.15		
Oklahoma	2.15	2.48	−0.28			7.54	1.17	1.27	−0.65
West Virginia	2.11					1.83	−0.79		

South

Alabama	2.07				9.48	1.67		
Arkansas	2.23				7.71	1.26		
Florida	0.93				5.81	1.98	0.54	−0.77
Georgia	1.44				6.34	1.68		
Louisiana	0.93				4.09	1.52		
Mississippi	1.87	2.48	0.16		5.67	1.36		
North Carolina	1.72				7.42	1.59		
South Carolina	1.72				7.13	1.57		
Tennessee	1.99				6.63	1.11		
Texas	0.84				4.80	1.74	1.59	0.34
Virginia	1.14		0.64	−2.35	4.34	1.39		

Midwest

Illinois	1.47		0.60	−2.10	6.89	0.71	2.66	−0.07
Indiana	1.50				12.04	0.66	0.92	−1.62
Iowa	1.95				1.48	−0.36		
Kansas	1.60				4.69	0.36	2.50	−0.14
Michigan	1.07				3.68	0.62	1.13	−0.75

TABLE 17 (*continued*)

State	Nonminority Percentage	American Indian/Alaskan Native Percentage	Log-Odds	Asian/Pacific Islands Percentage	Log-Odds	Black Percentage	Log-Odds	Hispanic Percentage	Log-Odds
Minnesota	1.29	4.45	0.22			5.38	0.08		
Nebraska	1.91					3.18	−0.24	6.41	1.03
North Dakota	1.66	14.35	0.45						
Ohio	2.46					7.42	0.46	3.29	−0.99
South Dakota	0.80	3.08	0.50						
Wisconsin	1.40					1.34	−1.26	1.62	−0.37
West									
Alaska	0.59	2.52	2.34	2.93	0.61	1.78	0.23	0.04	2.28
Arizona	0.71	1.14	−0.00			3.35	1.08	1.16	0.04
California	0.61			0.22	−1.49	1.16	0.25	0.87	0.31
Colorado	0.80			0.07	1.91	2.61	0.78	1.52	0.18
Hawaii	0.49			0.91	0.61	0.53	0.11	1.60	1.23
Idaho	1.24	1.37	0.17					1.30	−0.71
Montana	0.89	1.14	0.22					1.44	0.16
Nevada	0.77	1.46	0.51	0.04	1.71	2.81	1.43	1.04	−0.53
New Mexico	0.83	0.65	−0.00			2.72	1.36	2.52	1.24
Oregon	0.71	0.50	−0.90	0.19	−1.51	0.42	−0.67	1.62	0.53
Utah	0.82	1.79	0.63					1.97	0.83
Washington	1.17	2.70	−0.30	0.64	−1.46	1.56	−0.05	1.52	−0.61
Wyoming	0.45	0.35	−0.76					1.45	1.20

NOTE: All percentages are the weighted projections to statewide values; weights are the inverse of sampling probabilities.

questionnaire, in every state in which the specific group comprises more than 1 percent of the school population. The averages are calculated for every district in the state that has both nonminorities and any students of the minority group in attendance. The nonminority rate, listed for comparison, is for all districts in the state (from Table 5).

BLACKS

Blacks comprise more than 1 percent of the student enrollment in 41 states and in the District of Columbia. Since they are also the largest minority group in 35 states and in the District of Columbia, the analysis of EMR placement rates for all minorities combined is most like that for blacks alone. However, some noteworthy differences arise when black placements are compared separately with those for whites. In three states, blacks have disproportion indexes that are lower than the all-minority results in important ways. In Alaska and Rhode Island, both having substantial positive all-minority indexes, the average disproportion for blacks alone is close to zero. In Wisconsin, with an all-minority average of 0.02, the log-odds index for blacks alone is -1.26; i.e., blacks are enrolled in EMR programs at a lower rate than are whites. In each of these states a higher disproportion for another large minority group raises the all-minority figure (Hispanics in Rhode Island and Wisconsin, and Alaskan natives in Alaska). In five states the disproportion for blacks alone is well above that for all minorities: Arkansas, Missouri, Nevada, Oklahoma, and Texas.

These exceptions, while showing changes from the all-minority results of Table 5, maintain the same pattern of noticeably higher EMR placement rates for blacks on a nationwide basis, especially in the South and in particular states in the border and western regions.

HISPANICS

Children of Hispanic origin—the second largest minority group—comprise more than 1 percent of the public school enrollment in 31 states; more than 5 percent of the enrollment in 12 states; and more than 10 percent of the enrollment in Arizona, California, Colorado, New Mexico, New York, and Texas. On a nationwide basis the proportion of Hispanic students in EMR classes is slightly below that for nonminorities and well below that of blacks. However, the average percentage of Hispanic students in EMR classes exceeds that of nonminority students in 26 of the 31 individual states.

The six states with the highest proportion of Hispanic students vary in the degree of EMR disproportion. In California and New York the EMR placement rates for Hispanics are close to those for nonminority whites in districts of all mixes. In Arizona, Colorado, and New Mexico, there are small or negative disproportions when the percent of Hispanic-origin students is low or moderate (up to about 50 percent); that is, the Hispanic EMR percentage is close to or below that of nonminority students. In each state, however, there are a number of districts in which Hispanics comprise 70 percent or more of the student body; there, EMR disproportion is high. In Texas the disproportion is relatively large in all districts with 10 percent or more Hispanic students and small among districts with smaller Hispanic enrollments.

To explore this varied pattern further, a subsample of districts was chosen in which Hispanic students comprised at least 5 percent of the district's enrollment and the number of Hispanic students was at least 50. This resulted in 854 districts being selected from the larger sample, of which 765 have EMR programs. The characteristics of these districts are summarized in Table 18.

Hispanic enrollments are found in the majority of districts in most states in the Southwest (and Texas), and the average proportion of Hispanic students within districts in these same states is generally higher than elsewhere. Hispanic enrollments in the Northeast tend to be concentrated in a few of the larger districts (i.e., with higher average enrollment), while in the West they are dispersed among many smaller districts. The "average bilingual percentage" is the average percentage of the districts' Hispanic population enrolled in bilingual education classes. On a nationwide basis the average district provides bilingual classes for about 12 percent of its Hispanic enrollment; however, the larger districts in the Northeast have consistently greater portions of Hispanic students in bilingual education.

The distribution of EMR disproportion is summarized in Table 19. The average disproportion for Hispanic students in these districts is positive for each of four size intervals and is especially high among small districts. However, it is striking that there are numerous large positive disproportions (i.e., many more Hispanics than nonminorities) in each size interval and also numerous large negative disproportions (i.e., more nonminorities than Hispanics). Unlike disproportion for all minorities combined or for blacks in particular, the small Hispanic-nonminority difference for the nation as a whole is an average of many sizable disproportions in both directions.

It has been hypothesized that disproportion in Hispanic EMR placement is smaller in districts with substantial black enrollments, as Hispanic students may come to be perceived as less prominent in terms of their minority status. To investigate this hypothesis and to examine the simple relationship of Hispanic enrollment to disproportion, districts were classified according to the percentage Hispanic enrollment (0–20, 20–40, 40–60, 60–80, 80–100), by percent black enrollment (0–25, 25–50, 50–75, and 75–100), and by geographic region. The mean disproportion index was tested for main effects and interactions in a three-way fixed-effects least-squares analysis of variance for unequal cell frequencies. Separate analyses were conducted for districts with fewer than 1,000 students, districts with 1,000–9,999 students, and districts with 10,000 or more students; the designs were incomplete, since not all combinations of Hispanic and black enrollments were present in the data and thus some interactions could not be tested in each analysis.

The mean disproportion scores representing districts in each minority composition category are presented in Table 20. For the smallest districts (N = 124) there is a strong trend for districts with a higher proportion of Hispanic students to have larger EMR disproportions; the differences among these means are statistically significant when $p < .01$. The same trend does not appear for medium-sized districts (N = 474) or for districts with 10,000 or more students (N = 167). Further, Hispanic enrollment does not interact significantly with geographic region, substantiating the fact that the mean difference is general to small districts, regardless of locale.

The mean EMR disproportion for Hispanic students decreases monotonically as the percentage of black enrollment increases among large districts but not among small or medium-sized districts. The difference for large districts is statistically significant when $p < .01$; furthermore, the difference does not interact significantly with Hispanic enrollment or with geographic region in any district size interval. Thus, there is a trend among large school districts—and only among large districts—for the relative proportion of Hispanic students in EMR classes to decline as the black enrollment increases; at the extreme, when the black enrollment exceeds 75 percent, substantially fewer Hispanic than nonminority students are classified as EMR. The original hypothesis is substantiated for large school districts, although the perceptions and mechanisms through which the effect is created are not addressed by the survey data.

Bilingual education classes are fairly common among schools with Hispanic populations, although they tend to be more prevalent in larger districts. Over half of small districts (fewer than 1,000 students) have no Hispanic students in bilingual programs. At the other extreme, among districts enrolling 10,000 or more students, about 78 percent have some formal bilingual education, and 18 percent have one fourth or more of

TABLE 18 Description of Hispanic District Subsample

State	Number of Districts	Estimated Percentage of State	Average Enrollment	Average Percentage Hispanic	Average Bilingual Percentage	Educable Mentally Retarded			Specific Learning Disability		
						Average Percentage		Average Log-Odds	Average Percentage		Average Log-Odds
						Hispanic	Anglo		Hispanic	Anglo	
Entire country	854		7,375	26.91	11.75	1.27	0.69	0.64	3.74	2.83	0.14
Northeast	75		21,592	15.11	21.12	2.00	1.21	0.55	1.40	1.99	-0.44
Connecticut	9	7.8	12,626	14.80	32.45	1.92	0.99	0.65	3.44	3.09	0.02
Massachusetts	6	2.7	26,745	13.81	32.23	1.78	1.34	0.28	1.61	2.92	-0.95
New Jersey	36	10.2	7,871	18.76	18.06	2.17	1.26	0.57	1.22	2.17	-0.56
New York	14	3.5	46,686	10.88	18.27	1.65	0.94	0.74	0.98	0.90	-0.10
Pennsylvania	8	1.6	37,086	9.83	20.07	2.77	1.95	0.28	0.66	1.43	-0.81
Rhode Island	2	5.2	10,710	8.25	34.55	0.43	1.17	-0.84	1.17	4.38	-1.29
Border	8		1,697	10.32	1.85	2.31	2.10	-0.15	1.52	1.60	-0.25
Missouri	1	0.7	4,577	5.05	0.87	1.73	2.09	-0.09	2.60	2.97	-0.07
Oklahoma	7	4.4	1,121	11.37	2.04	2.43	2.10	-0.17	1.30	1.33	-0.31
South	266		6,322	35.13	10.72	1.41	0.50	1.06	6.07	3.39	0.58
Florida	7	10.5	47,385	14.88	10.59	1.43	0.61	0.80	2.80	2.94	-0.13
Louisiana	2	3.0	8,557	10.62	0.00	1.33	0.97	0.35	2.88	3.30	-0.50
Texas	256	47.0	5,532	35.70	10.70	1.42	0.50	1.07	6.16	3.40	0.59
Virginia	1	0.8	16,964	5.65	37.96	0.10	0.13	0.20	0.83	0.51	0.55

Midwest	83		7,310	11.15	11.10	2.02	1.41	0.21	2.08	2.25	−0.28
Illinois	26	5.7	14,758	12.65	18.66	1.04	0.93	−0.01	3.62	4.03	−0.50
Indiana	4	1.9	11,803	14.51	3.86	1.18	2.21	−0.73	0.54	0.75	−0.13
Iowa	2	0.5	3,626	8.74	38.46	1.93	1.52	0.38	2.44	3.86	−0.34
Kansas	10	6.5	1,779	11.49	14.14	1.47	1.08	0.15	1.42	1.41	−0.41
Michigan	16	6.2	3,872	8.93	12.57	1.30	1.07	0.14	1.21	1.62	−0.29
Minnesota	1	0.3	34,181	5.11	13.22	2.58	2.83	−0.08	3.38	3.04	0.11
Nebraska	7	9.2	1,690	12.86	0.20	5.52	1.41	1.26	1.12	1.34	−0.10
Ohio	15	5.4	2,204	10.56	3.01	2.76	2.31	0.18	1.95	1.63	−0.06
Wisconsin	2	0.5	60,476	5.88	20.32	1.74	1.12	0.30	2.06	2.08	−0.12
West	422		6,246	27.78	11.43	0.94	0.55	0.52	3.27	2.80	0.08
Arizona	58	73.8	3,793	32.07	9.96	1.38	0.75	0.53	3.95	3.69	0.05
California	231	69.2	7,407	25.94	13.31	0.54	0.41	0.34	2.63	2.65	−0.11
Colorado	40	62.3	4,686	24.81	5.80	1.46	0.84	0.56	4.12	2.88	0.35
Hawaii	1	100.0	169,602	6.84	0.06	1.59	0.49	1.23	7.03	3.41	0.77
Idaho	8	16.4	3,609	10.65	17.41	1.50	1.10	0.51	3.58	2.41	0.23
Nevada	4	60.5	1,280	9.35	13.15	1.61	0.91	0.27	10.39	3.84	0.99
New Mexico	48	93.5	3,915	51.21	7.19	2.00	0.67	1.29	3.86	2.25	0.78
Oregon	6	6.0	1,916	18.07	18.83	0.52	0.55	−0.04	6.94	4.47	0.48
Utah	4	20.1	10,093	10.36	3.19	1.96	1.08	0.60	5.06	3.46	0.37
Washington	12	8.8	3,399	20.03	12.08	1.90	1.18	0.56	1.99	1.60	0.22
Wyoming	10	30.8	2,905	9.32	1.00	1.35	0.37	1.52	5.67	3.52	0.52

NOTE: Except for the number of districts, which is the actual number in the sample, all results are the weighted projections to statewide values; weights are the inverse of sampling probabilities.

TABLE 19   Distribution of EMR Disproportion for Hispanic Students

District Size	Number of Districts	Mean	Standard Deviation	Minimum		Maximum	
				Log-Odds	Q	Log-Odds	Q
Fewer than 1,000 students	124	1.08	1.71	−4.30	−.97	7.41	.99+
1,000 to 2,999 students	242	0.66	0.99	−2.13	−.79	7.67	.99+
3,000 to 9,999 students	232	· 0.47	0.85	−2.11	−.78	6.94	.99+
10,000 or more students	167	0.35	0.63	−3.35	−.93	2.17	.80
All districts	765	0.64	1.12	−4.30	−.97	7.67	.99+

NOTE: Except for the number of districts, which is the actual number in the sample, all results are the weighted projections to nationwide values; weights are the inverse of sampling probabilities.

their Hispanic student participating in bilingual instruction. At the same time the largest districts have the lowest EMR disproportion for Hispanic students (see Table 19).

To explore the relationship of bilingual education with EMR placements further, districts in each of four size intervals were classified by geographic region and by the extent of EMR disproportion for Hispanic students. Three levels of disproportion were formed. The high group is composed of those districts whose disproportion was greater than one standard deviation above the mean for all districts in the size interval; the low group is composed of those districts whose disproportion was less than one standard deviation below the mean; and the medium group contains those districts in between. Mean scores for the three groups were compared by fitting a two-way fixed-effects analysis-of-variance model to the data, with the percentage of students in bilingual education as the criterion measure. The results are summarized in Table 21.

Among districts in two size intervals the percentage of Hispanic students in bilingual programs is significantly related to disproportion, and a similar trend is seen in the smallest districts as well. In each case, districts with the highest disproportion levels have the smallest proportion of students in bilingual programs. It is possible that Hispanic students with poor English proficiency are misclassified as EMR when bilingual programs are not available.

It is apparent from the nationwide results (Table 3) that Hispanic students are placed in SLD programs to a somewhat greater extent than are

TABLE 20 Mean EMR Disproportion for Hispanic Students, by District Racial/Ethnic Composition

Size of District	Percentage of Hispanic Enrollment	Percentage of Black Enrollment				
		0 to 25	25 to 50	50 to 75	75 to 100	All
Fewer than 1,000 students	0 to 20	0.86		2.40		0.91
	20 to 40	1.01	0.55			0.99
	40 to 60	1.09				1.09
	60 to 80	1.07				1.07
	80 to 100	3.73				3.73
	All	1.08	0.55	2.40		
1,000 to 9,999 students	0 to 20	0.51	0.78	0.13	−0.55	0.51
	20 to 40	0.63	0.10			0.62
	40 to 60	0.81	−0.43			0.76
	60 to 80	0.59				0.59
	80 to 100	0.57				0.57
	All	0.58	0.62	0.13	−0.55	
10,000 or more students	0 to 20	0.43	−0.03	0.02	−1.17	0.32
	20 to 40	0.44	0.43	0.31		0.43
	40 to 60	0.30				0.30
	60 to 80	0.69				0.69
	80 to 100	0.23				0.23
	All	0.43	0.13	0.09	−1.17	

NOTE: Average log-odds index is the weighted projection to all districts in the particular size category. Empty cells indicate fewer than two districts in the sample with the particular racial/ethnic composition.

nonminorities. The state-by-state results (Table 18) show that while the Hispanic percentage in SLD is lower than the nonminority percentage in many states, the reverse is true in states with high concentrations of Hispanics (Texas and the southwestern states exclusive of California). The dynamics that create the SLD difference are not apparent from the OCR data. It does not appear that SLD placements substitute for EMR placements, since a few states have high average disproportions in both classifications simultaneously (New Mexico, Texas, and Wyoming).[21] In fact, the correlation of SLD with EMR disproportion among Hispanic students is

---

[21] It is important to recall that these data represent only the 1978–1979 school year. If pressure increases to reduce EMR enrollments, it is possible that programs for specific learning disabilities will become an alternative placement.

TABLE 21   Mean Percentage of Hispanic Students in
Bilingual Education

Size of District	Low Disproportion		Medium Disproportion		High Disproportion	
Fewer than 1,000 students	9.76	(11)	9.30	(101)	6.51	(12)
1,000 to 2,999 students	16.89*	(29)	9.97	(184)	7.52	(29)
3,000 to 9,999 students	13.19	(37)	11.84	(166)	14.33	(29)
10,000 or more students	23.87*	(18)	12.90	(123)	14.43	(26)

NOTE: All percentages are the weighted projections to nationwide
values; weights are the inverse of sampling probabilities. Actual sample
sizes are in parentheses.
*Significant differences among these three means at $p < .05$.

+.33 for all districts combined,[22] and close to this value for districts in
each of four size intervals. Examination of the SLD rates for Hispanics
and nonminorities (not shown) indicate that the correlation reflects different placement rates for Hispanic students, while that for nonminorities
is not related to EMR disproportion. The processes by which Hispanic
students are referred and assessed for placement in both special programs
need further investigation.

In summary, the apparently similar EMR placement rates for Hispanic
and nonminority students disguise enormous variation in practices among
school districts. There are a number of districts in which Hispanic students are assigned to EMR programs in large proportions. They are distinguished from other districts by having small enrollments that are often—but not always—largely Hispanic; furthermore, they have small
black enrollments, small or nonexistent bilingual programs, and high percentages of Hispanic students in SLD classes as well. Among large districts with the greatest pool of resources, low EMR disproportion and low
SLD disproportion occur where many Hispanic students participate in bilingual programs.

Further research on factors affecting the availability and utilization of
alternate programs for Hispanic students is certainly warranted. It would
be important to determine to what extent specific learning difficulties are

[22]Statistically significant at $p < .05$, using a two-sided test.

related to language or whether SLD programs, like EMR, may be used in some districts as a substitute for bilingual instruction. The criteria used for both EMR and SLD placements should be elucidated as well as the definition of these possibly amorphous categories and the actual instructional programming that is provided.

AMERICAN INDIANS OR ALASKAN NATIVES

American natives comprise over 1 percent of the public school enrollment in 15 states, largely in the West. Their placement in EMR classes exceeds the rate for whites in all but three of the states; in Alaska the average log-odds index exceeds the 80th percentile value of 1.6. The largest racial differences in Alaska are in districts with fewer than 1,000 students, but the disproportion in larger districts is substantial as well. Also, higher degrees of disproportion are concentrated in districts of all sizes with 70 percent or more Alaskan-native enrollment.

Other than in Alaska, the average log-odds index of disproportion is not sizable, and in several instances is zero or negative. In general, the difference in the placement of American Indians and Alaskan natives in EMR classes is not large or even consistently positive throughout the states. For this group in particular, however, the OCR survey may not tell the complete story, since numerous American Indians are enrolled in special schools and special programs that are not represented in the usual public school sample.

ASIAN OR PACIFIC ISLANDERS

Students who are of Asian or Pacific Island origins are assigned to EMR programs at rates considerably below those of whites in 10 of the 12 states in which they comprise more than 1 percent of the school enrollment. The average log-odds index is negative in 8 of the 12 states, with most values substantially so. Thus, in general, overrepresentation of Asian or Pacific Island students in EMR classes is not a problem; these groups might even be studied to determine why their placement rates are low.

Two states, however, have positive log-odds indexes of disproportion in excess of 1.6. In both Colorado and Nevada, larger disproportions occur in small school districts with low minority enrollment. Unfortunately, the OCR survey does not distinguish among Asian populations; it is possible that the students in these states are, for example, recent immigrants from Vietnam rather than Japanese or Korean children whose families have been established in the United States for longer periods of time. Newly arrived immigrant populations present a unique opportunity to monitor special education placement rates as they develop.

SOCIOECONOMIC STANDING AND SUSPENSIONS FOR SPECIFIC MINORITY GROUPS

General relationships between socioeconomic status and suspensions with disproportion in EMR placements for all minorities combined are given in preceding sections. Correlations for each minority separately are presented in Table 22.

Suspensions are not correlated with disproportionate EMR assignment for any individual racial or ethnic minority. The same correlations for all minorities combined (Table 13) are positive. While EMR disproportions are accentuated by students of one minority group, it may be students of a different minority classification who are suspended. Thus, only an association for all minorities together is observed.

There is a significant negative relationship between racial disproportion and socioeconomic status for each minority group except Asian or Pacific Islanders. The relationship is strongest for American Indian and Alaskan native students and least strong for students of Hispanic origin. However, the correlations for these groups, and blacks as well, are consistently negative. That is, disproportions even within a minority group tend to be smaller in districts serving populations with higher income levels. This relationship is worthy of further exploration to address such questions as whether individuals with higher income tend to live in suburban districts with lower overall EMR rates and also lower disproportion[23] and whether the same behavior and school performance are treated differently in middle- and lower-income districts. The answers to these questions may differ for particular minority groups and the attitudes and values associated with lower income for that population.

DISPROPORTION AND STATE EMR CRITERIA

To determine the extent to which state guidelines are associated with disproportion, information was obtained for 37 states on whether adaptive behavior assessments are required for EMR classification and the maximum IQ score a child may have and still be labeled EMR. The states were classified by region and by whether adaptive behavior assessments were

---

[23]The correlation of socioeconomic status with the proportion of all students in EMR programs for the total sample is $-.31$, suggesting support for this three-variable hypothesis.

TABLE 22   Correlations of Log-Odds Index With Suspensions and Socioeconomic Status for Separate Minority Groups

Racial/Ethnic Group	Number of Districts	Suspensions of All Students	Proportion Full-Price Lunches
American Indian/Alaskan Native	817	−0.03	−0.17*
Asian/Pacific Islander	936	−0.05	0.07
Black	3995	0.04	−0.15*
Hispanic	2681	0.00	−0.10*

NOTE: Correlations are the weighted projections to nationwide values; weights are the inverse of sampling probabilities.
*Statistically significant at $p < .01$ (two-sided test).

required, and mean differences were tested by fitting a two-way analysis-of-variance model to the data, with several different criterion measures. The results are summarized in Table 23.

There is no statistically significant difference between states that require and those that do not require adaptive behavior assessment for EMR placement on any of the measures listed, including average IQ cutoff score, average size of the states' EMR programs (in terms of percent-

TABLE 23   Comparison of States Requiring and Not Requiring Adaptive Behavior (AB) Assessment for EMR Placement

Variable	AB Required (20 States)			AB Not Required (17 States)		
	Mean	Standard Deviation	Correlation With IQ Cutoff	Mean	Standard Deviation	Correlation With IQ Cutoff
IQ cutoff score[a]	73.10	3.92		74.42	3.97	
Percentage of all students in EMR	1.61	0.94	0.11	1.43	0.69	0.0
EMR disproportion for race/ethnicity (log-odds)	0.44	0.93	−0.15	0.59	0.90	−0.59[b]
EMR disproportion by sex	0.45	0.15	−0.37	0.40	0.15	−0.31
Percentage of white enrollment	73.65	25.44	0.33	79.56	13.44	0.50[b]

[a] From Patrick and Reschly (1982).
[b] Significant at $p < .05$ (two-sided test).

age of students labeled EMR), disproportion either by sex or by race or ethnicity, or in terms of the average proportion of minority or nonminority students enrolled. Further, there is no interaction of region with the adaptive behavior factor, indicating no exception to this generalization in any part of the country; also, when further control was added by employing "percentage of minority enrollment" in the state as a covariate, no significant differences appeared. Thus, the imposition of a state requirement that childrens' adaptive behavior be assessed as a necessary condition for EMR placement does not have a statistically noticeable impact on any of the outcomes investigated. This is due at least in part to the relatively wide variations in practice including the use or nonuse of adaptive behavior ratings among districts within the states. It contrasts strongly with findings that adaptive behavior limits EMR programs within individual school districts (Fisher, 1977; Mercer, 1973).

Two of the measures have a significant correlation with the state IQ cutoff but only in those states not requiring adaptive behavior assessments. EMR disproportion by race or ethnicity is correlated negatively with statewide IQ cutoff scores. That is, on the average, the lower the IQ cutoff score—i.e., the more stringent the EMR criteria—the greater is the relative assignment of minority students to EMR classes. This is predictable for states in which adaptive behavior assessments are not made regularly, since EMR placements become more nearly a function of children's IQ scores. When adaptive behavior is included as an additional required assessment, however, the correlation with IQ cutoff score is reduced to nonsignificance.

The statewide IQ cutoff score is also correlated with the percentage of white enrollment in states not requiring adaptive behavior assessments. While this reflects a trend for states with greater proportions of white students to set higher cutoff scores for EMR classification, the motivation for this practice is not revealed from the survey data.

REFERENCES

Bishop, Y. M. M., Fienberg, S. E., and Holland, P. W.
　　1975 *Discrete Multivariate Analysis: Theory and Practice*. Cambridge, Mass.: MIT Press.
Fisher, A. T.
　　1977 Adaptive Behavior in Non-Biased Assessments. Revised version of paper presented at the meeting of the American Psychological Association. ERIC Document Reproduction Service no. ED 150 514.
Mercer, J. R.
　　1973 *Labeling the Mentally Retarded: Clinical and Social System Perspectives on Mental Retardation*. Berkeley, Calif.: University of California Press.

Patrick, J. L., and Reschly, D. J.
In   Relationship of state education criteria and demographic variables to school system
press prevalence of mental retardation. *American Journal of Mental Deficiency* 86.
U.S. Department of Health, Education, and Welfare
1978a *Fall 1976 Elementary and Secondary School Civil Rights Survey. Final File
        Documentation.* Office for Civil Rights. June. Washington, D.C.: U.S. Depart-
        ment of Health, Education, and Welfare.
1978b *1978 Elementary and Secondary Civil Rights Survey. Sample Selection.* Office for
        Civil Rights. February. Washington, D.C.: U.S. Department of Health, Educa-
        tion, and Welfare.
Zoloth, B. S.
1976   Alternative measures of school segregation. *Land Economics* 52:278–298.

APPENDIX

Examples of Smoothing Data for Small Districts

The 1978 OCR survey indicates 11 districts in Georgia with fewer than 100 minority students enrolled or fewer than 100 whites. When the numbers of students in these districts are summed, the proportions of students in EMR and in no special programs are as follows:

	Minority	White
EMR	0.0065	0.0131
No special program	0.1054	0.8751

In the following table the EMR odds for minorities is $0.0065/0.1054 = 0.0617$ and for whites $0.0131/0.8751 = 0.0150$. One specific district has the following numbers of students:

	Minority	White
EMR	1	11
No special program	31	922

The EMR odds for minorities is $1/31 = 0.0323$; one additional EMR student would bring the ratio to 0.0645, and no value between the two is possible. The odds for whites is $11/922 = 0.0119$, and the difference is $0.0323 = 0.0119 = 0.0204$. The smoothed frequencies for this district are as follows:

	Minority	White
EMR	1.0393	11.0119
No special program	31.5270	921.4218

From these values the EMR odds for minorities is 0.0330 (a small degree closer to the statewide value of 0.0617) and for whites 0.0120. The difference of 0.0330 − 0.0120 is 0.0210, which is close to the original value.

Another of the 16 districts with small enrollment has the following number of students:

	Minority	White
EMR	21	0
No special program	194	65

The EMR odds for minorities is $21/194 = 0.1082$, for whites $0/65 = 0$, and the difference is 0.1082. The zero value raises such questions as does zero of 65 students, for example, mean as much as zero of 100 or of 500 students? Would the number remain zero if the white enrollment were increased, as may happen from one school year to another, or is this value a stable zero? A partial answer may be provided by examining the larger statewide data set, in which the odds for whites is small but is nonzero (0.0150). Smoothing the district's frequencies yields the following results:

	Minority	White
EMR	20.9588	0.0079
No special program	193.6464	65.3870

The odds for minorities is 0.1082, for whites 0.0001, and the difference is 0.1081, which is close to the original value. While the original zero value did not allow calculation of the log-odds index, the adjusted values yield $\ln (0.1082) - \ln (0.0001) = 6.80$.

The smoothing procedure used in this analysis involves obtaining "pseudo Bayes estimates" of actual population frequencies in the manner described by Bishop et al. (1975: Section 12.1.1). This method has distinct advantages over the widely used practice of adding 0.5 to each cell count, especially when the total number of observations in one or both columns is small.